Innovation, Technology, and Knowledge Management

Series Editor

Elias G. Carayannis, George Washington University, Washington, DC, USA

For further volumes:
http://www.springer.com/series/8124

Andreas Altmann · Bernd Ebersberger
Editors

Universities in Change

Managing Higher Education Institutions in the Age of Globalization

Springer

Editors
Andreas Altmann
MCI Management Center Innsbruck—The Entrepreneurial School
Innsbruck
Austria

Bernd Ebersberger
MCI Management Center Innsbruck—The Entrepreneurial School
Innsbruck
Austria

ISBN 978-1-4614-4589-0 ISBN 978-1-4614-4590-6 (eBook)
DOI 10.1007/978-1-4614-4590-6
Springer New York Heidelberg Dordrecht London

Library of Congress Control Number: 2012946186

Printed on acid-free paper

Springer is part of Springer Science+Business Media (www.springer.com)

Series Foreword

The Springer book series *Innovation, Technology, and Knowledge Management* was launched in March 2008 as a forum and intellectual, scholarly "podium" for global/local, transdisciplinary, transsectoral, public–private, and leading/"bleeding" -edge ideas, theories, and perspectives on these topics.

The book series is accompanied by the Springer *Journal of the Knowledge Economy,* which was launched in 2009 with the same editorial leadership.

The series showcases provocative views that diverge from the current "conventional wisdom," that are properly grounded in theory and practice, and that consider the concepts of *robust competitiveness,*[1] *sustainable entrepreneurship,*[2] and *democratic capitalism,*[3] central to its philosophy and objectives. More specifically, the aim of this series is to highlight emerging research and practice at the dynamic intersection of these fields, where individuals, organizations, industries, regions, and nations are harnessing creativity and invention to achieve and sustain growth.

---

[1] We define *sustainable entrepreneurship* as the creation of viable, profitable, and scalable firms. Such firms engender the formation of self-replicating and mutually enhancing innovation networks and knowledge clusters (innovation ecosystems), leading toward robust competitiveness (Carayannis 2009).

[2] We understand *robust competitiveness* to be a state of economic being and becoming that avails systematic and defensible "unfair advantages" to the entities that are part of the economy. Such competitiveness is built on mutually complementary and reinforcing low-, medium-, and high-technology and public and private sector entities (government agencies, private firms, universities, and nongovernmental organizations) (Carayannis 2009).

[3] The concepts of *robust competitiveness* and *sustainable entrepreneurship* are pillars of a regime that we call "*democratic capitalism*" (as opposed to "popular or casino capitalism"), in which real opportunities for education and economic prosperity are available to all, especially—but not only—younger people. These are the direct derivative of a collection of top-down policies as well as bottom-up initiatives (including strong research and development policies and funding, but going beyond these to include the development of innovation networks and knowledge clusters across regions and sectors) (Carayannis and Kaloudis 2009).

Books that are part of the series explore the impact of innovation at the "macro" (economies, markets), "meso" (industries, firms), and "micro" levels (teams, individuals), drawing from such related disciplines as finance, organizational psychology, research and development, science policy, information systems, and strategy, with the underlying theme that for innovation to be useful it must involve the sharing and application of knowledge.

Some of the key anchoring concepts of the series are outlined in the figure below and the definitions that follow (all definitions are from Carayannis and Campbell 2009).

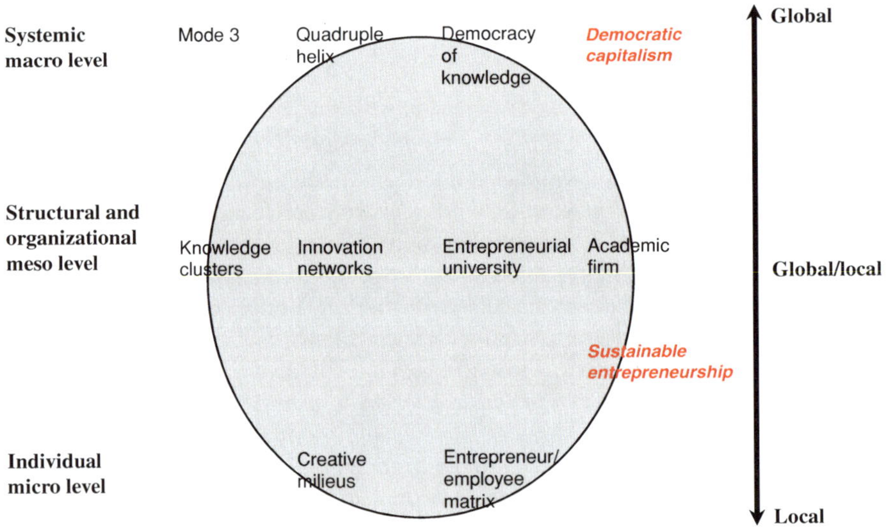

Conceptual profile of the series *Innovation, Technology, and Knowledge Management*

- The "Mode 3" Systems Approach for Knowledge Creation, Diffusion, and Use: "Mode 3" is a multilateral, multinodal, multimodal, and multilevel systems approach to the conceptualization, design, and management of real and virtual, "knowledge-stock" and "knowledge-flow," modalities that catalyze, accelerate, and support the creation, diffusion, sharing, absorption, and use of cospecialized knowledge assets. "Mode 3" is based on a system-theoretic perspective of socioeconomic, political, technological, and cultural trends and conditions that shape the coevolution of knowledge with the "knowledge-based and knowledge-driven, global/local economy and society."
- Quadruple Helix: Quadruple helix, in this context, means to add to the triple helix of government, university, and industry a "fourth helix" that we identify as the "media-based and culture-based public." This fourth helix associates with "media," "creative industries," "culture," "values," "life styles," "art," and perhaps also the notion of the "creative class."

- Innovation Networks: Innovation networks are real and virtual infrastructures and infratechnologies that serve to nurture creativity, trigger invention, and catalyze innovation in a public and/or private domain context (for instance, government–university–industry public–private research and technology development coopetitive partnerships).
- Knowledge Clusters: Knowledge clusters are agglomerations of cospecialized, mutually complementary, and reinforcing knowledge assets in the form of "knowledge stocks" and "knowledge flows" that exhibit self-organizing, learning-driven, dynamically adaptive competences, and trends in the context of an open systems perspective.
- Twenty-First Century Innovation Ecosystem: A twenty-first century innovation ecosystem is a multilevel, multimodal, multinodal, and multiagent system of systems. The constituent systems consist of innovation metanetworks (networks of innovation networks and knowledge clusters) and knowledge metaclusters (clusters of innovation networks and knowledge clusters) as building blocks and organized in a self-referential or chaotic fractal knowledge and innovation architecture,[4] which in turn constitute agglomerations of human, social, intellectual, and financial capital stocks and flows as well as cultural and technological artifacts and modalities, continually coevolving, cospecializing, and cooperating. These innovation networks and knowledge clusters also form, reform, and dissolve within diverse institutional, political, technological, and socioeconomic domains, including government, university, industry, and nongovernmental organizations, and involving information and communication technologies, biotechnologies, advanced materials, nanotechnologies, and next-generation energy technologies.

For whom is this book series published? The book series addresses a diversity of audiences in different settings:

1. *Academic communities*. Academic communities worldwide represent a core group of readers. This follows from the theoretical/conceptual interest of the book series to influence academic discourses in the fields of knowledge, also carried by the claim of a certain saturation of academia with the current concepts and the postulate of a window of opportunity for new or at least additional concepts. Thus, it represents a key challenge for the series to exercise a certain impact on discourses in academia. In principle, all academic communities that are interested in knowledge (knowledge and innovation) could be tackled by the book series. The interdisciplinary (transdisciplinary) nature of the book series underscores that the scope of the book series is not limited a priori to a specific basket of disciplines. From a radical viewpoint, one could create the hypothesis that there is no discipline where knowledge is of no importance.
2. *Decision makers—private/academic entrepreneurs and public* (*governmental, subgovernmental*) *actors*. Two different groups of decision makers are being addressed simultaneously: (1) private entrepreneurs (firms, commercial firms,

---

[4] Carayannis (2000).

academic firms) and academic entrepreneurs (universities), interested in optimizing knowledge management and in developing heterogeneously composed knowledge-based research networks; and (2) public (governmental, subgovernmental) actors that are interested in optimizing and further developing their policies and policy strategies that target knowledge and innovation. One purpose of public *knowledge and innovation policy* is to enhance the performance and competitiveness of advanced economies.

3. *Decision makers in general*. Decision makers are systematically being supplied with crucial information, for how to optimize knowledge-referring and knowledge-enhancing decision making. The nature of this "crucial information" is conceptual as well as empirical (case-study-based). Empirical information highlights practical examples and points toward practical solutions (perhaps remedies), conceptual information offers the advantage of further-driving and further-carrying tools of understanding. Different groups of addressed decision makers could be decision makers in private firms and multinational corporations, responsible for the knowledge portfolio of companies; knowledge and knowledge management consultants; globalization experts, focusing on the internationalization of research and development, science and technology, and innovation; experts in university/business research networks; and political scientists, economists, and business professionals.
4. *Interested global readership*. Finally, the Springer book series addresses a whole global readership, composed of members who are generally interested in knowledge and innovation. The global readership could partially coincide with the communities as described above ("academic communities," "decision makers"), but could also refer to other constituencies and groups.

Elias G. Carayannis

References

Carayannis EG (2009) Int J Innov Reg Dev 1(3):235–254
Carayannis EG, Kaloudis A (2009) Japan Econ Curr, pp 6–10
Carayannis EG, Campbell DFJ (2009) Int J Technol Manag 46:3–4
Carayannis EG (2000) Strategic management of technological learning. CRC Press, Boca Raton

Contents

Contributors

Dagmar Abfalter Department of Strategic Management, Marketing and Tourism, The University of Innsbruck, Universitätsstrasse 15, 6020 Innsbruck, Austria, e-mail: dagmar.abfalter@uibk.ac.at

Andreas Altmann MCI Management Center Innsbruck—The Entrepreneurial School, Universitätsstrasse 15, 6020 Innsbruck, Austria, e-mail: andreas.altmann @mci.edu

John M. Beehler Haile/US Bank College of Business, Northern Kentuky University, Nunn Drive, BEP Center, Highland Heights, KY 41099, USA, e-mail: beehlerj1@nku.edu

Thomas Brekke Vestfold University College, Boks 2243, 3103 Tønsberg, Norway, e-mail: Thomas.Brekke@hive.no

Elias G. Carayannis The George Washington University, 515 C Funger Hall 2201 G St NW, Washington, WA 20052, USA, e-mail: caraye@gwu.edu

Malcolm Cooper Graduate School of Asia Pacific Studies, Ritsumeikan Asia Pacific University, 1-1 Jumonjibaru, 874-8577 Beppu, Oita Prefecture, Japanc, e-mail: cooperm@apu.ac.jp

Jeremy S. Eades Graduate School of Asia Pacific Studies, Ritsumeikan Asia Pacific University, 1-1 Jumonjibaru, 874-8577 Beppu, Oita Prefecture, Japanc, e-mail: jse@apu.ac.jp

Bernd Ebersberger MCI Management Center Innsbruck—The Entrepreneurial School, Universitätsstrasse 15, 6020 Innsbruck, Austria, e-mail: bernd.ebersberger @mci.edu

Piero Formica International Entrepreneurship Academy, Innovation Value Institute, National University, Maynooth, CO Kildare, Ireland, e-mail: piero.formica@gmail.com

Manfried Gantner Department of Public Finance, The University of Innsbruck, Universitätsstrasse 15, 6020 Innsbruck, Austria, e-mail: manfried.gantner@uibk.ac.at

Allan Gibb University of Durham, Foundation for SME Development, Mill Hill Lane, DH1 3LB Durham, UK, e-mail: allan_gibb@hotmail.com

James R. Haltiner The College of William and Mary—Mason School of Business, 8795, Williamsburg, VA 23187-8795, USA, e-mail: James.Haltiner@mason.wm.edu

Gay Haskins Sa Business School Executive Education Centre University of Oxford, Egrove Park, OX1 5NY Oxford, UK, e-mail: Gay.Haskins@sbs.ox.ac.uk

Sverre J. Herstad Norwegian Institute for Studies in Innovation, Research and Education, Wergelandsveien 7, 0167 Oslo, Norway, e-mail: sverre.herstad@nifu.no

Carlos E. Juárez Center for U.S.-Mexican Studies, University of California, 9500 Gilman Drive, San Diego, CA 92093-0510, USA, e-mail: cjuarez@hpu.edu

Ekkehard Kappler Elisabethstraße 12, 6020 Innsbruck, Austria, e-mail: ekkehard.kappler@uibk.ac.at

Dietmar Kilian MCI Management Center Innsbruck—The Entrepreneurial School, Universitätsstrasse 15, 6020 Innsbruck, Austria, e-mail: dietmar.kilian@mci.edu

Wilhelm Krull VolkswagenStiftung, Kastanienallee 35, 30519 Hannover, Germany, e-mail: Krull@VolkswagenStiftung.de

Denise J. Luethge Haile/US Bank College of Business, Northern Kentuky University, Nunn Drive, BEP Center, Highland Heights, KY 41099, USA, e-mail: luethged1@nku.edu

Judith Marquardt HHL—Leipzig Graduate School of Management, Jahnallee 59, 04109 Leipzig, Germany, e-mail: gf@hhl.de

Kurt Matzler Department of Strategic Management, Marketing and Tourism, The University of Innsbruck, Universitätsstrasse 15, 6020 Innsbruck, Austria, e-mail: kurt.matzler@uibk.ac.at

Peter Mirski MCI Management Center Innsbruck—The Entrepreneurial School, Universitätsstrasse 15, 6020 Innsbruck, Austria, e-mail: peter.mirski@mci.edu

Joe Nellis Cranfield University School of Management, Bedford, Cranfield MK43 0AL, UK, e-mail: j.g.nellis@cranfield.ac.uk

Gabriel A. Pall The College of William and Mary—Mason School of Business, 8795, Williamsburg, VA 23187-8795, USA, e-mail: Gabe.Pall@mason.wm.edu

Alfred S. Posamentier The City College, Convent Avenue at 138th Street, New York, NY 10031, USA, e-mail: aposamentier@mercy.edu

Ian Robertson National Centre for Entrepreneurship in Education (NCEE), The Innovation Centre, Coventry University Technology Park, Puma Way, Coventry CV1 2TT, UK, e-mail: ian@enterpreneurialinstitution.com

Dirk W. Rudolph Centre for Financial Economics (CFE), Frankfurt School of Finance and Management, Sonnemannstraße 9-11, 60314 Frankfurt, Germany, e-mail: d.rudolph@frankfurt-school.de

David Slattery Cranfield University School of Management, Bedford, Cranfield MK43 0AL, UK, e-mail: david.slattery.phd.02@cranfield.ac.uk

Udo Steffens Centre for Financial Economics (CFE), Frankfurt School of Finance and Management, Sonnemannstraße 9-11, 60314 Frankfurt, Germany, e-mail: u.steffens@frankfurt-school.de

Hans Wiesmeth TU Dresden, Mommsenstraße 13, 1062 Dresden, Germany, e-mail: wiesmeth@hhl.de

Chapter 1
Universities in Change: As a Brief Introduction

Andreas Altmann and Bernd Ebersberger

Universities have always been changing. Ever since the inception of the first universities at the end of the twelfth century universities have responded to changing societal, economic, and political contexts. Cumulatively this process of change created a university system at the turn of the twenty first century, that is completely different from the system of centuries ago. This can be exemplified in three basic characteristics of the university system (Brockliss 2000). First, the size of the university sector has increased. For instance, the number of European universities has grown from 40 in the 1400s to 150 in the early twentieth century. In the mid-1980s there were 500 universities in Europe and this number has been growing continuously through higher education institutions obtaining university status, for instance in the UK . There the number of universities has increased by a factor of 2.5 since the early 1980s. Second, and not completely unrelated, the number of students has increased continuously. Brockliss (2000) identifies three growth periods, the thirteenth century, the sixteenth to the early seventeenth century, and the late 19th to the early twentieth century, which, however, does not compare at all to the growth experienced since the 1960s. While in the sixteenth century about 2.5 % of the male population enjoyed what now is a tertiary education (Brockliss 2000), it is currently in the Western Economies slightly less than 30 % of all adults (OECD 2010).

Third, the university's mission and context evolved from a traditional and medieval role as a storehouse of knowledge (Youtie and Shapira 2008) with a distinct teaching mission in the four sciences: theology, law, medicine, and philosophy. By

A. Altmann (✉) · B. Ebersberger
Internationale Hochschule GmbH, MCI Management Center Innsbruck—The Entrepreneurial School ®, Universitätsstrasse 15, 6020 Innsbruck, Austria
e-mail: andreas.altmann@mci.edu

B. Ebersberger
e-mail: bernd.ebersberger@mci.edu

A. Altmann and B. Ebersberger (eds.), *Universities in Change*, Innovation, Technology, and Knowledge Management, DOI: 10.1007/978-1-4614-4590-6_1,

and large the Humboldtian reforms contributed to the development of an organization where teaching and research were equally important. The university developed from a storehouse of knowledge to a locus of knowledge development (Youtie and Shapira 2008). In parallel with the new mission the portfolio of subjects changed, whereby the natural sciences, the humanities, and the arts developed rather independent curricula, methods, and approaches (Brockliss 2000). Further refinement of the universities' subject map contained the development of engineering sciences and social sciences.

This process went along with the universities assuming a more active role in society and economy and educating students in these technical disciplines, which met the needs of the growing industrial demand for skilled labor. Newly founded universities stressed their value to industry by applied research and teaching; see for instance the foundation of the MIT (Youtie and Shapira 2008) or for instance the Technical University of Munich (TUM 2011).

In addition to the two modes—storehouse of knowledge and locus of knowledge development—at the end of the twentieth century universities developed a third variant by adding a third dimension to their mission: The university is to support regional and local economic and social development (e.g., Etzkowitz et al. 2000; Etzkowitz 2003). This additional mandate is highly appreciated and supported by policy makers as it implicitly promises a new and expanding source of university financing (Slaughter and Leslie 1997). This new mode transcends the previous ways of university–industry interaction and results in a triple helix metaphor to describe the threefold interaction between universities, industries, and government (Etzkowitz and Leydesdorff 1999). Consequently, this new mode entails a university's strong position in the post industrial and knowledge-driven economy (Youtie and Shapira 2008).

Universities are seen as an integral part of the innovation system (Mowery and Sampat 2005), which includes a new and growing set of activities beyond the ivory tower (Rothaermel et al. 2007), which is not generally found to be rejected by faculty members (Van Dierdonck et al. 1990; Lee 1996). Basically, the third mission of universities paves the way for the concept of the entrepreneurial university. Gibb et al. (in this Volume, Chap. 2) give a broad analytical overview over the concept of entrepreneurial universities and the related discussion.

Universities can be entrepreneurial basically in two ways. The first way directly refers to the third mission increasingly found with a modern university. It relates to academic entrepreneurship, that is, it implies the commercialization of knowledge and research findings. In a sense, here, universities pursue the third mission by becoming knowledge entrepreneurs or knowledge hubs (Youtie and Shapira 2008) basically linking research—the second mission—and societal development—the third mission. The second way for a university to become entrepreneurial relates teaching as the first mission to the third mission, that is, supporting economic and social development. Generally, the entrepreneurial dimension is not only reduced to the coupling of research and commercialization. The entrepreneurial dimension of universities is represented here by the understanding that universities operate on a market for education (Gjerding et al. 2006), which usually rewards actors' entrepreneurial approaches (Guerrero and Urbano 2010).

For a university to become more entrepreneurial university management has to install appropriate incentive structures (Friedman and Silberman 2003). It has to ensure the provision of appropriate infrastructure (Gjerding et al. 2006). And it has to adopt a business inspired decentralized management style (Debackere and Veugelers 2005). In addition, a change in the (corporate) culture of the university is crucial (Jacob 2003; Gjerding et al. 2006). Yet, research suggests that the economic and business rationale, which is part of the internal organizational logic of an entrepreneurial university, cannot be shared by all parts of the faculty. Research suggests that parts of the faculty might maintain dysfunctional mental models toward business activities per se (Laukkanen 2003).

Too strong a dependence on entrepreneurial activities and too strong an influence of economic interests might cause the entrepreneurial universities to risk their autonomy (Slaughter and Leslie 1997). The concept of the entrepreneurial university as discussed in Gjerding et al. (2006), however, seems to accept the change of the societal and economic context, in which the universities operate. Yet, both views share a passion in favor of the autonomy of universities.

The above discussion entails three major areas, from where challenges for the management of universities originate and which have to be mastered by universities under a continuous process of change.

1.1 Embedding in the Social and Economic System

The third mission relates universities to their immediate environment, which they are to affect positively. The embedding of the university in an innovation system (Mowery and Sampat 2005) or in a entrepreneurial society (Audretsch 2007) leads to multiple and systemic interaction with various partners following different idiosyncratic rationales. As different systems, in which universities are embedded, are characterized by different institutional arrangements, different cultures of interaction, different development paths and dynamics, as well as different distributions of relevant other actors (e.g. Liu and White 2001; Asheim and Coenen 2005), entrepreneurial universities have to pursue various strategies and new organizational arrangements to support the generation and exploitation of knowledge and technology (Leydesdorff and Meyer 2003) jointly with governmental and industrial partners through teaching and commercialization. Hence, location does not only affect the performance of entrepreneurial universities (Friedman and Silberman 2003), but it also determines through the regional context, which external challenges the university has to master and which restrictions or constraints the university has to accommodate. In particular, the contributions in this volume focus how universities approach these challenges. They cover general temporal trends (Formica and Carayannis, in this Volume, Chap. 3), demographic trends and internationalization (Nellis and Slattery, Chap. 4

; Juarez, in this Volume, Chap. 5), political and regulatory constraints (Gantner, in this volume, Chap. 6), and dynamic change within the system and its repercussions (Krull, in this Volume, Chap. 7).

1.2 Strategic and Operative Issues

These issues arise in response to societal and economic changes and in response to changing demands. When responding to these changes the key challenge for university management in the era of entrepreneurial universities is to foster entrepreneurial activities of the academics in various ways without endangering the mission to diffuse knowledge through teaching and to develop knowledge through research on the basis of the basic and unique principle which sets universities apart: academic freedom of the individual academic and autonomy of the organization (e.g. Rothaermel et al. 2007).

If academic freedom is to be maintained university management does not have full control over the academics' activities; an overall boundary setting strategy, which is termed an 'umbrella strategy' by Mintzberg and Waters (1985) can serve as a general university internal framework to direct entrepreneurial and other activities within the organization and to guide university management when establishing an appropriate incentive framework (Grigg 1994). When it comes to tailoring incentive schemes for entrepreneurial activities the majority of research suggests that incentivizing academics generates positive effects (e.g. Friedman and Silberman 2003; Debackere and Veugelers 2005). Fundamentally, the members of a university have to become entrepreneurial in their interaction among themselves and with their environment for the university to be successful (Guerrero and Urbano 2010).

A coherent strategic orientation facilitates the success of entrepreneurial universities. Matzler and Abfalter (in this Volume, Chap. 8) take the entrepreneurial university by the very meaning for the word and show what universities can learn from the strategies of high performing firms. Wiesmeth and Marquardt (in this Volume, Chap. 9) discuss the positioning and the management of a private business school, which can be considered the successor of the oldest and most traditional business school in Germany. Steffens and Rudolph (in this Volume, Chap. 10) demonstrate how strategic management tools and techniques can be applied to foster the growth of business schools. Posamentier (in this Volume, Chap. 12) illustrates by anecdotal evidence the hardships of change. Cooper and Eades (in this Volume, Chap. 11) focus on research as the second mission of universities and how research capacity can be strengthened in a regional context. In turn Cooper (in this Volume, Chap. 13) refers to teaching as the first mission of universities and illustrates curriculum change processes in the light of global and local pressures on education in an institution that, before now, has operated within the close confines of a local Japanese context.

Covering the more operative end of the spectrum of activities university management of an entrepreneurial university, Pall and Haltiner (in this Volume, Chap. 14) as well as Mirski and Kilian (in this Volume, Chap. 15) show that the provision of infrastructure—the built environment in the case of Pall and Haltiner and the IT environment in the case of Mirski and Kilian—forms a crucial function of university management and that the provision of high quality infrastructure is key for the success of universities.

Measuring the success of higher education institutions is a necessary, yet not trivial task. Luethge and Beehler (in this Volume, Chap. 16) and Kappler (in this Volume, Chap. 17) discuss this issue from two opposing perspectives. The former focuses on the role and in particular on the benefits of accreditation in the context of business schools, whereas the latter takes a more critical stance and discusses measurement problems associated with evaluation and accreditation from a more general point of view.

1.3 Contributing to Economics and Social Development

The contribution to economic and social development of the universities, environment is the starting point of the discussion. Ebersberger et al. (in this Volume, Chap. 18) conceptually discuss this proposition from different theoretical perspectives. Although some parts of the literature about entrepreneurial university maintain a strong affinity to protection of IP and to the management of IPRs through specialized units, such as the technology transfer offices in order to limit spillovers and to facilitate commercialization of developed knowledge (see the summary in Rothaermel et al. 2007). However, Clark et al. (2007), for instance, do not explicitly mention the protection of knowledge, rather they directly relate to the third mission by referring to a well-structured technology transfer process into the region. Hence, entrepreneurial universities can pursue the third mission by managing the spillovers, and by allowing and facilitating spillovers (Ebersberger et al. , in this Volume, Chap. 19). Universities can contribute to regional economic development by the three channels highlighted by the three missions. Herstad and Brekke (in this Volume, Chap. 20) highlight a case of a regional university and its influence on regional economic and technological development.

Bibliography

Asheim BT, Coenen L (2005) Knowledge base and regional innovation systems: comparing nordic clusters. Res Policy 34(8):1173–1190. doi:10.1016/j.respol.2005.03.013

Audretsch DB (2007) The entrepreneurial society. Oxford University Press, Oxford

Brockliss L (2000) Gown and town: the university and the city in europe, 1200–2000. Minerva 38:147–170

Gjerding AN, Cameron SPB, Wilderom CPM, Taylor A, Scheunert K-J (2006) Twenty practices of an entrepreneurial university. High Educ Manage Policy 18(3):1–28
Debackere K, Veugelers R (2005) The role of academic technology transfer organizations in improving industry science links. Res Policy 34(3):321–342
Etzkowitz H (2003) Research groups as "quasi-firms": the invention of the entrepreneurial university. Res Policy 32(1):109–121. doi:10.1016/S0048-7333(02)00009-4
Etzkowitz H, Leydesdorff L (1999) The future location of research and technology transfer. J Technol Transfer 24(2):111–123
Etzkowitz Henry, Webster A, Gebhardt C, Terra Cantisano BR (2000) The future of the university and the university of the future: evolution of ivory tower to entrepreneurial paradigm. Res Policy 29(2):313–330. doi:10.1016/S0048-7333(99)00069-4
Friedman J, Silberman J (2003) University technology transfer: do incentives, management, and location matter? J Technol Transfer 28(1):17–30
Grigg T (1994) Adopting an entrepreneurial approach in universities. J Eng Tech Manage 11(3–4):273–298
Guerrero M, Urbano D (2010) The development of an entrepreneurial university. J Technol Transfer. doi:10.1007/s10961-010-9171-x
Jacob M (2003) Entrepreneurial transformations in the Swedish university system: the case of Chalmers university of technology. Res Policy 32(9):1555–1568
Laukkanen M (2003) Exploring academic entrepreneurship: drivers and tensions of university-based business. J Small Bus Enterp Dev 10(4):372–382
Lee YS (1996) "Technology transfer" and the research university: a search for the boundaries of university-industry collaboration. Res Policy 25(6):843–863
Liu X, White S (2001) Comparing innovation systems: a framework and application to chinachina's transitional context. Res Policy 30(7):1091–1114
Leydesdorff L, Meyer M (2003) The triple heliox of university—industry—government relations. Scientomatrics 58(2):191–203
Mintzberg H, Waters JA (1985) Of strategies, deliberate and emergent. Strateg Manag J 6(3):257–272
Mowery DC, Sampat BN (2005) Universities in national innovation systems. In: Fagerberg J, Mowery DC, Nelson RR (eds) The oxford handbook of innovation. Oxford Universtiy Press, Oxford, pp 209–239
OECD (2010) Education at a glance 2010. OECD Publishing, Paris
Rothaermel FT, Agung SD, Jiang L (2007) University entrepreneurship: a taxonomy of the literature. Ind Corp Change 16(4):691–791
Slaughter S, Leslie LL (1997) Academic capitalism: Politics, policies, and the entrepreneurial university. The Johns Hopkins University Press, Washington
TUM. (2011). Meilensteine der TU Geschichte. http://portal.mytum.de/tum/geschichte/index_html Accessed 22 Aug 2011
Van Dierdonck R, Debackere K, Engelen B (1990) University-industry relationships: how does the belgian academic community feel about it? Res Policy 19(6):551–566
Youtie J, Shapira P (2008) Building an innovation hub: a case study of the transformation of university roles in regional technological and economic development. Res Policy 37:1188–1204

Part I
The Entrepreneurial University

Chapter 2
Leading the Entrepreneurial University: Meeting the Entrepreneurial Development Needs of Higher Education Institutions

Allan Gibb, Gay Haskins and Ian Robertson

This paper focuses on the leadership challenge facing staff of universities across the world in moving their institutions to a more entrepreneurial mode (Bernasconi 2005; Keast 1995). It is based upon an extensive literature review, the results of which demonstrate clearly that the issues raised in this paper are widely shared internationally.[1] The paper has an action and innovation focus in that it constitutes part of the preparation for the development of the Entrepreneurial University Leadership Programme which was launched in 2010 at Oxford University's Said Business School for senior university leaders. This program now runs annually with the National Council for Entrepreneurship in Education (NCEE, formerly called the National Council for Graduate Entrepreneurship) and Universities UK as lead partners. This paper demonstrates the thinking and concepts behind the program and is used as key background material.

[1] The extensive referencing is designed to demonstrate that wide global context of the issues discussed. The authors thank Klara Capova of Durham University for her invaluable assistance in conducting an extensive bibliographical search.

A. Gibb (✉)
University of Durham, 10 Kimblesworth Grange, Durham, DH1 5SL, UK
e-mail: allan_gibb@hotmail.com

G. Haskins
Saïd Business School, University of Oxford, Egrove Park, Oxford, OX1 5NY, UK
e-mail: gay.haskins@sbs.ox.ac.uk

I. Robertson
National Centre for Entrepreneurship in Education (NCEE), The Innovation Centre, Coventry University Technology Park, Puma Way, Coventry CV1 2TT, UK
e-mail: ian@enterpreneurialinstitution.com

A. Altmann and B. Ebersberger (eds.), *Universities in Change*, Innovation, Technology, and Knowledge Management, DOI: 10.1007/978-1-4614-4590-6_2,

2.1 Introduction

There is now a considerable international literature addressing the notion of what has been termed 'the entrepreneurial university' (Wasser 1990; Clark 1998; Currie 2002; Barsony 2003; Jacob et al. 2003; Etzkowitz 2004; Gibb and Hannon 2006; Kirby 2006; Lazzeroni and Piccaluga 2003; Poh-Kam Wong et al. 2007; Guerrero-Cano 2008; Mohrman et al. 2008; Lehrera et al. 2009). The entrepreneurial university concept embraces universities of all types including those with a strong research tradition as well as newer organizations (Geiger 2006; Mohrman et al. 2008; Kauffman 2009). The literature, both academic and pragmatic policy oriented, ranges over a wide range of issues including:

- the basic philosophical 'idea' of a university and how this is changing over time (Coaldrake and Stedman 1999; Smith and Langslow 1999; Maskell and Robinson 2001; De Ziwa 2005) and the culture of the university (Daumard 2001; Davies 2001; Mendoza and Berger 2005);
- the commercialization of university know-how (Cook et al. 2008);
- the process of technology transfer and exchange (CVCP 1999; Leydesdorff and Meyer 2003; Sainsbury 2007; Mittelstädt and Cerri 2008; Zhou 2008);
- the associated closer engagement of the university with industry and indeed stakeholders of all kinds (Garlic 1998; Owen-Smith et al. 2002; Charles 2006; CIHE 2008);
- the movement towards a 'Triple Helix 'model of partnership among government, industry, and higher education (Etzkowitz and Leydesdorff 2000; Leydesdorff and Etzkowitz 2003; Thorn and Soo 2006);
- the employability and skills development agenda of graduates and their preparation for a global labor market (HEFCE 2003; European Commision 2005; ESECT 2005; Leitch 2006);
- the strategic response to the 'massification' of demand for higher education (Smith 1999; Shattock 2000);
- the internationalization of universities (Noir sur Blanc 1999; Kwiek 2000, 2001; Knight 2003; Altbach 2005; Altbach and Knight 2006; OECD 2004) and their strategies for dealing with global competition (both opportunities and threats);
- the changing nature of the knowledge society and the challenge this poses to the organization of knowledge within higher education (Barnett 2000; Viale and Etzkowitz 2005; Becher and Trowler 2007; Senges 2007);
- the pressures on universities to respond to social as well as economic local and regional development problems albeit in a global context (Charles 2003; AUQA 2005; Smith 2007; Arbo and Benneworth 2008);
- the central pressure upon higher education, from central government, to foster innovation and demonstrate relevance to national and international competitiveness agendas (Lambert 2003; Williams and Kitaev 2005; Mittelstädt and Cerri 2008);
- the autonomy and future funding of universities (Darling et al. 1989; Greenaway and Haynes 2003; Li-Chuan 2004; Moses 2005; Bridgman 2007; Armbruster 2008);

- and overall, in response to the above, reflections on the 'public value' of higher education institutions (Moore 1995; Weerts 2007).

The literature reveals the growing diversity of the university concept internationally (Thorn and Soo 2006), and within countries (Poh-Kam et al. 2007; Pan 2007). There are many different 'typologies' of universities, with different views of 'excellence' (van Vught 2008) and each with different strategic agendas, some with a strong industry, technology, and occupational focus (Pratt 2001; Jacob et al. 2003). This, in turn, leads to debates about the growing influence of vocationalism in higher education (Bridges and Jonathan 2003) and the linking of the higher education sector with other institutions in a country's education system particularly further education and community colleges (Hager and Hyland 2003). At a national level, however, traditions and power-influencing hierarchies and pressure groups (Bourdieu 1999) play a major role in both constraining and shaping the nature of higher education institutions and their capacity to adapt to change. Such influence is also reflected in the education policy frameworks of governments (EU 2006) which are increasingly directive (Slaughter and Leslie 1997; Hayrinen–Alestalo 1999; Henkel 2004). In general, (but not universally[2]) governments throughout the world still hold considerable sway over the sector because of its substantial dependency upon the public purse (Williams 2009).

All of the above pressures have served to shape change in organization and governance structures of universities (Higher Education in Europe 2004; Kohler and Huber 2006). They are also leading to changes in mission statements and strategies (Shattock 2000; Cherwitz 2002, 2005). These changes have been the focus of much of the debate concerning the entrepreneurial paradigm (Martin and Etzkowitz 2000; Leydesdorff and Etzkowitz 2001; Bok 2003; Becher and Trowler 2007). Leading writers on this theme have effectively made recommendations as to how to redesign institutions entrepreneurially (Clark 1998, 2004; Wissema 2008; Etzkowitz 2008), but without full exploration of the entrepreneurial organization concept. Considerable attention has also been focused upon the leadership challenges involved in the changing modes of governance, particularly in the UK, through the work of the Higher Education Leadership Foundation (CEL 2006, 2007), but with only limited focus upon the arguably highly relevant notion of the entrepreneurial leader. What appears to have been largely missing in the debate, therefore, has been deeper basic exploration of the two key relevant concepts of entrepreneurial organization and entrepreneurial leadership and their effective interface within the dynamic change environment facing the Higher Education sector. In this paper we will explore these concepts with reference to the 'debates' noted briefly above.

The remainder of the paper is organized as follows. Firstly, there is an exploration of the nature of the environment impacting on higher education, the varied institutional responses and how the entrepreneurial concept relates to this. Secondly, there is an analysis of the challenge to organization design as well as individual academic

---

[2] See, for example, the cross country analysis in IHEP (2009).

response, and how this relates to notions of the entrepreneurial organization. Thirdly, there is exploration of the leadership challenge and its particularly entrepreneurial flavor. Fourthly, there is a summary of what this means for the development of leaders and key managers in higher education institutions and how the Entrepreneurial University Leadership Programme was conceived and designed to meet their development needs.

2.2 The Entrepreneurial Environmental Challenges and University Responses

The entrepreneurial concept is centrally concerned with the means of coping with and creating uncertainty and complexity (Casson 1982, Chap. 5). Its traditional essence, (Schumpeter 1934), is that of creating and dealing with new and innovative combinations of 'factors of production' and 'ways of doing things'. The Schumpeterian notion of 'creative destruction', leading to innovation and renewal, manifests itself in uncertain and complex task environments for those within the system. Dynamic task environments with high levels of change therefore demand, and emerge through, entrepreneurial initiative. Conversely, static environments lend themselves to more predictable and routinized bureaucratic patterns of response.

The changing dynamic environment of higher institutions and their respondent evolution (Doutriaux and Barker 1996; Kohler and Huber 2006; Wissema 2008) is portrayed in Fig. 2.1. The figure attempts to characterize the evolving nature of the task environment facing universities on a simple/complex and certain/uncertain axis.[3] It highlights the way that the notion of 'Excellence' might be changing (Corbett 2006; Deem and Lucasa 2008; Huisman 2008; Wissema 2008). Within this frame, it seeks to summarize their response as evidenced by a growing body of the literature.

Certainty in the environment has been reduced by changes in funding. There has been a movement away from a system that was at one time nearly universal (with some private university exceptions, to be observed mainly in the US) of almost total central or regional public funding, to a situation where a growing proportion of finance has to be sought from nondirect public sources including fees, research grants, local development monies, alumni, industry and social enterprise, contract research, and philanthropy (Williams 2009). While government remains a key player in most countries, it has moved its disbursement stance into a more directive mode. Thus, the uncertainty resulting from having to seek a greater proportion of funding from other sources is matched by pressure to move

[3] Derived from Lawrence and Lorsch (1986), Covin and Slevin (1991) and Gibb (1985). Acknowledgement also to Professor Antti Paasio of the University of Turku Finland who provided the germ of the idea. While the arrows on the Simple/Complex and Certain/Uncertain matrix point in one direction it is possible for a university to move from any one segment to another.

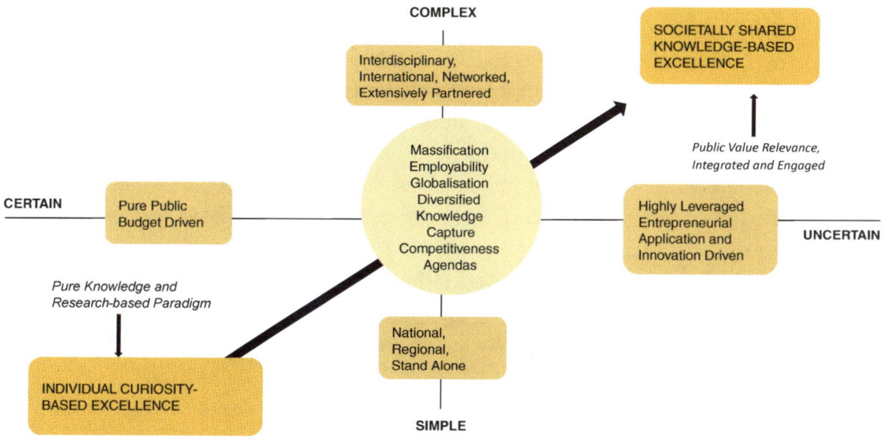

Fig. 2.1 The changing university paradigm

away from the simpler, more certain, 'autonomous' environment (guaranteed by the public purse) within which to pursue individualistic research and teaching. There is now an imperative to demonstrate more direct public value (see below). Some governments (for example Finland) are providing direct financial incentives to higher education institutions to leverage public funding.

The public pressures for change are underpinned by a number of factors which are also contributing substantially to uncertainties and complexities, as explored in the sections below.

2.2.1 The Massification of Higher Education

Of major importance is the move to what has been labeled the 'massification' of the education offer from the university sector (Rinne and Koivula 2009). The UK Government, for example, has committed itself to higher education being open to half the UK school leaving population. This is a trend evident in many other 'developed' countries (Rinne op cit.). It is difficult, if not impossible for this growth in 'demand' to be wholly funded by the state. The emphasis is, therefore, placed on other sources of funding, particularly fees-a controversial issue in many countries (Douglas 2008). This leads, in turn, to the creation of a more openly competitive market for students, requiring a more entrepreneurial response from institutions. It is also leading to a more critical and demanding student consumer group and many of them are now funding more of their own education through personal debt. There is already evidence of this in the UK[4]: this situation has been considerably exacerbated by the 2009 global crisis.

[4] Student protests across the UK. BBC News Wednesday November 5 (2008).

2.2.2 The Employability Agenda

The global downturn has also impacted substantially on the issue of the employability of graduates (ESECT 2005; Cranmer 2006). Universities are finding themselves in a competition focused upon the job take-up of their students. Students themselves face increasing regional and global competition in the labor market (Rajan et al. 1997; Westwood 2000). The employability issue, however, goes beyond that of simple graduate unemployment and employment prospects. There are calls by industry and indeed governments for graduate education to incorporate a greater skills focus across the whole curricula (OECD 2001; Papayannakis et al. 2008). More precisely, there is an articulation by employers of the need for graduates to be equipped with a range of 'enterprising skills' with foci upon creativity, capacity for innovation, networking, relationship management and risk taking (Moreland 2007). This 'need' has been extensively articulated by the European Commission in a number of studies calling for the development of the 'Entrepreneurial Mindset' in the student population (EU 2006). There is also some evidence that this view of the importance of entrepreneurial skills to future employment is shared by the student population (Coaldrake 2001) and that universities are not seen to be fully equipped to meet this need (Coaldrake 2001; Durham University CEL 2009). While, therefore, there is certainly a demand it is clear that it cannot easily be met within the existing institutional system (Cranmer 2006).

2.2.3 The Student Voice

Against the above backdrop, there has been a substantial growth of student societies in universities across the world many of them linked internationally in partnership.[5] They are becoming the vehicle for articulating the student need for entrepreneurship curriculum in the university. Many UK Universities, for example, now have student entrepreneurship societies some with very substantial membership and engaged in a wide range of activity. The Oxford University society, 'Oxford Entrepreneurs' (www.oxfordentrepreneurs.co.uk), has a membership of several thousand students. It has a full time (1 year sabbatical) president and runs a variety of activities, including competitions, networking and counseling events, start-up workshops, guest speaker presentations, placement programs, and links to venture capital. These societies become a mechanism for articulating student need to the university and demand for entrepreneurship programs across the whole curriculum (Edwards 2001). While they generally operate with a considerable degree of autonomy they can benefit substantially from dedicated staff and faculty support (Williamson et al. 2009).

[5] See, for example, the work of Students in Free Enterprise (www.sife.org), European Confederation of Junior Enterprises (JADE) (www.jadenet.org), and National Consortium of University Entrepreneurs (NACUE) (www.nacue.org).

2.2.4 Developing Entrepreneurial Skills

The articulation of employer need, coming from a range of private and public sources, has moved the focus of graduate entrepreneurship education beyond its hitherto major concentration upon equipping a limited number of graduates for self employment (Green and Saridakis 2008) into the area of the development of entrepreneurial skills for all (Jack and Anderson 1999; Klofsten 2000; Rae and Carswell 2000; Blenker et al. 2006; Miclea 2004; Kneale 2005). This matches a public policy rhetoric which goes beyond industry demand towards articulating the need to equip students at all levels in the education system with personal entrepreneurial capacities to deal with greater levels of uncertainty and complexity in both their work and personal life (Poon and Hee Ang 1995; Ravasi and Turati 2005; Gibb 2007). This includes the capacity to design organizations of all kinds, public, private, and NGO, to support effective entrepreneurial behavior (Barrie 2007). This focus has implications for the wider debate on the nature of university learning (Haggis 2006; Leisner 2006; Barrie 2007; Kinchin et al. 2008). This broad view of entrepreneurship places emphasis in a 'teaching' context upon the pedagogical and organizational processes necessary to the support of entrepreneurial competency and attributes across a range of different disciplinary and multi-disciplinary contexts (Volkmann 2004; Politis 2005). Entrepreneurship, therefore, becomes almost an intra-disciplinary concept intrinsic to the development of all students and university teaching staff (Coaldrake and Stedman 1999; Roman et al. 2008). This is far from the conventional business school model. The approach also, however, has implications for the organizational structures that will support the embedding of such an entrepreneurial concept within the institution (see below). Much of the recent thinking in this respect is influenced by the work of the US Kauffmann Foundation and its Cross-Campus Entrepreneurial Education Initiative (www.kauffman.org and Mendes et al. 2006). The broader employability and entrepreneurial skills agenda has also presented a major challenge for the work of university careers departments, many of them are now engaging with external agencies on the development of programs for enhancing a range of graduate entrepreneurial skills as well as capacity for self employment (www.ncee.og.uk). This shift in emphasis has major implications for the development of their own staff.

2.2.5 The Challenge of Globalization

Graduate employment futures, in the context of a global labor market, are characterized by frequent changes in job, occupation, and location, also potentially involving periods of involuntary self or contract employment (Rajan et al. 1997). This demands a capacity in graduates to think and act both locally and globally in an entrepreneurial way. Their ability to develop this capacity becomes a function of the nature of the university itself and its strategies to bridge the local–global interface. In this context, the policy thrust in Europe has been to firmly link entrepreneurship with competitiveness and education (EU 1998, 2005, 2006, 2007, 2008). There is much debate on this issue in the education literature (Carnoy 1999; Brush et al. 2003; Altbach 2005) with a distinction made between exploring the impact of globalization and the changes demanded or resulting from wide ranging global pressures (Kwiek 2000, 2001; Toakley 2004; Scase 2007) on the one hand, and internationalization or the processes by which a university seeks to respond to threats and opportunities on the other. In short, globalization is an external force and internationalization is a response to that force. Distinctions can, thereafter, be made among the motivations of universities to internationalize, the targets they set for themselves, the processes they pursue, and the desired outcomes.

Already, at the beginning of this century, across Europe, the vast majority of higher education establishments saw internationalization as of major importance (Noir sur Blanc 1999). The imperative in this respect has since become acute (UNESCO 2003; OECD 2004; International Association of Universities 2005). This reflects the fact that institutions increasingly perceive themselves as being in an internationally competitive market place, for staff, for students, for income generation, and for research (UNESCO 2003; Altbach and Knight 2006). Prestige, not finance, appears to be a major motivation: internationalization is seen to raise the national as well as the global profile (Altbach and Knight 2006). It can also be seen as part of a competitive strategy to improve quality of staff and students via overseas recruitment as well as a means of enhancing student experience and existing staff development (Green and Baer 2000). It can lead on to curriculum development and innovation as well as greater cultural sensitivity. Developing partnerships, both academic and industrial, also seems to be a powerful tool in this respect.

2.2.6 The Internationalization Strategies of Universities

Commitment to internationalization involves elements of entrepreneurial risk taking and strategic choice (Knight 2003). Figure 2.2 encapsulates the various target processes and activities involved in internationalization. Some of these activities and processes carry more risk than others. Establishing overseas campuses, for example, entails high risk. The major issue here is to what extent international activity adds to the global understanding of the institution, enhances student and staff learning, and enables it to truly understand, be sensitive to, and work with, different cultures (Green and Baer 2000). The centre-point of Fig. 2.2 is arguably the most important strategic outcome, that is the degree to which the institution adds value to its own learning as a result of the activities listed and the degree to which it rewards such learning. Overall, in outcome evaluation terms, there will be a need to measure the degree to which the activity brings both status and material rewards (income and other resources) that are sustainable. The former appears to be as important, if not more so, than the latter—although in the long run the two are intimately related.

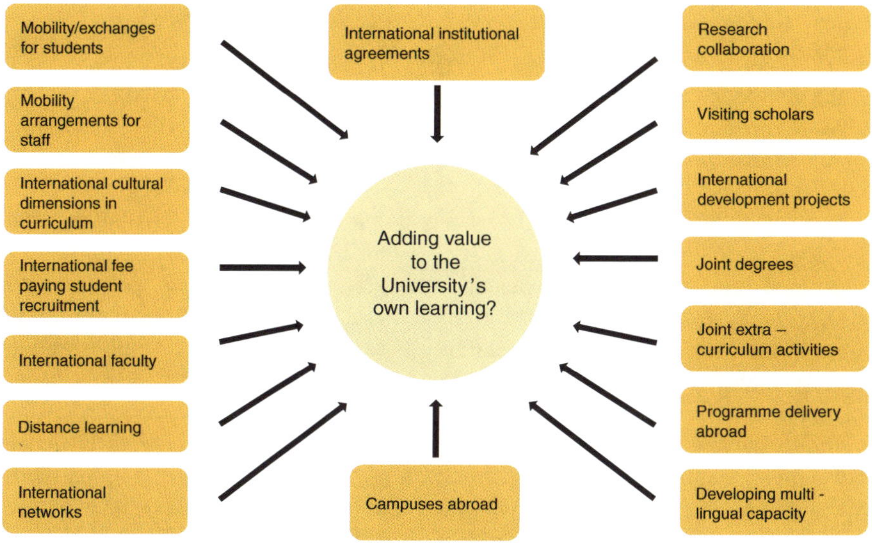

Fig. 2.2 Activities and processes involved in university internationalization

2.2.7 The Global Knowledge Configuration

A major influence upon the drive to internationalization is the rise of the global knowledge economy (Peters 2003) accessed substantially through the Internet (Senges 2007). The Web has effectively eaten into the local and national monopoly of knowledge that universities have traditionally enjoyed. It has also created new combinations and foci for knowledge (Delanty 2001) in that it has no respecter of traditional disciplines and more open to the organization of knowledge on a 'need to know' and issue basis. It challenges the monopoly that universities have hitherto had on the organization and delivery of 'explicit' knowledge (Habermas and Blazek 1987; Delanty 2003); and it challenges the power of elite groups who maintain and channel knowledge through major journals and publications. It considerably reduces the time it traditionally takes, through academic journals, to bring new knowledge into the public domain. Journals and their academic editors and boards are having to adapt to this competitive pressure exemplified by, increasingly, individual academics opening up their ideas and findings through their own websites and Facebook entries. The sharing of experiential and tacit knowledge via the Internet also exposes the 'know how' position of universities. Faced with this scenario, academe is confronted with the challenge of becoming more of a 'learning organisation' (Kristensen 1999) rather than solely a 'learned organisation.' Also, it is opening itself up to learning from a wider range of stakeholder sources, involving engagement in the 'community of practice' (Wenger 1998) as well as in more formal/informal processes of knowledge exchange.

2.2.8 Knowledge Transfer and Engagement Processes

In the developed economies, active university engagement in knowledge exchange has also been substantially driven by a public policy agenda which has placed higher education firmly in the forefront of enhancement of national innovation and competitiveness (Lee 1996; Agraval 2001; Shane 2004; Kweik 2005). Over the past decade, in particular this has been the lever for change in the way that universities disseminate knowledge (Lee 1996; Mendoza and Berger 2005). The traditional mode in respect of science (the main focus of public pressure) was independent creation of knowledge beyond direct control of government (although substantially funded by it). Research was driven by curiosity not economic interest, and disseminated by publication of the papers. This last mentioned was the main channel for placing new knowledge into the public domain. It was assumed that 'industry' would read, digest, and act when appropriate. Over the last half-century the limitations of this approach have been very exposed, in particular with reference to the time lags involved in publication, and the dependency upon the disposition of individuals who may move both location and field of interest and their associated interaction with industry.

An almost universal approach to dealing with this problem has been through knowledge transfer institutions and mechanisms, such as:

- the creation of science and technology parks, adjacent to, and sometimes owned by, universities;
- the development of the role of intermediaries such as industrial liaison offices;
- the opening of technology transfer and information offices (Chapple et al. 2004);
- the development of student and staff incubators (Ylinenpää 2001);
- the launching of new venture programs for staff and students;
- the development of clearer IP policies and arrangements for the licensing and patenting of university know-how (Baldini et al. 2006);
- the organization of spin off activity; and
- the creation of venture and loan funds.

There is evidence, however that this is not enough. A growing body of the literature (Hughes 2003; Link 2006; Dooley and Kirk 2007; Abreu et al. 2008) argues that the key to successful knowledge transfer is a process of continuous dialog building up social networks (Nicolaou and Birley 2003), success in which is a function of development of strong personal (as opposed to institutional) relationships over time leading to the creation of trust (a key element in entrepreneurial activity). It has even been argued that an over focus upon transactional mechanics such as licenses and patents may distract from the development of personal intimacy and trust (Dooley and Kirk 2007; Brown and Jenkins 2008).

The role of the individual academic in building the relationship is that of bringing a wider perspective to a client problem, being prepared to engage in the development out of research, and by this means help to bridge the gap between explicit and tacit knowledge which is often highly contextual. This relationship involves complete engagement with a process and is not just a simple case of commercial exploitation of a particular piece of university research (Agraval 2001). In this way, the concept of transfer partnerships takes on a deeper meaning than that embodied in some official policy recommendations (Sainsbury 2007). The building of relationships provides a number of benefits to the university including: potential additional funding for research; access to proprietary technology held by industry; and enhanced status and faster feedback loops on its own concepts and ideas (Geiger 2004, 2006; Dooley and Kirk 2007). It may also put pressure on the university to generate problem-focused multi disciplinary teams and centers (Campbell et al. 2002; National Academy of Science USA 2005).

2.2.9 Regional and Local Engagement

It is in the field of knowledge transfer and engagement that the regional role of universities has been most highlighted (Boucher et al. 2003; Charles 2003, 2006; IHEP 2007; Arbo and Benneworth 2008). There is an obvious potential link between a university's contribution to innovation and its contribution to a region's development (Smith 2007). This link is reflected in the growing focus of European government regional policies since the 1980s upon innovation and technology development and the exploitation of university knowledge (particularly with the support of the European Commission). Worldwide, the models of MIT (O'Shea et al. 2007), Silicon Valley and North Carolina in the US have become iconic along with the Cambridge Phenomena (Segal 1985) in the UK. There are, however, many other European examples on offer, for example, Linkoping in Sweden, Turku in Finland, and Twente in the Netherlands (Braun and Diensberg 2007). The label of the 'Entrepreneurial University' is, therefore, frequently associated with the notion of the university as a regional innovation hub (Sole-Parellada et al. 2001). It appears to be widely accepted in this context that successful innovation necessarily involves a highly interactive process of engagement among universities, industry, and government. This engagement process has been labeled the Triple Helix Model (Benner and Sandstrom 2000; Shinn 2002; Leyesdorff and Meyer 2003; Zhou 2008; Etzkowitz 2008).

The model portrays an interactive process of research funding through private and public partnerships focused upon the development out of research and learning, by all partners, from this process. This model is not solely a regional one, but has a strong regional orientation particularly when it engages with small and medium-sized firms. It assumes that entrepreneurs will work in the university and academic staff in the company, that the partnership may also link with other sources of funding and that there will be clear patterns of co-ordination (Etzkowitz 2008). Its full manifestation can be characterized as in Fig. 2.3. The model is also associated with the Mode 2 concept of a university discussed later below (Gibbons et al. 1994; Novotny 2003). While universities now frequently have 'professionally managed' offices for regional development and knowledge transfer issues, it

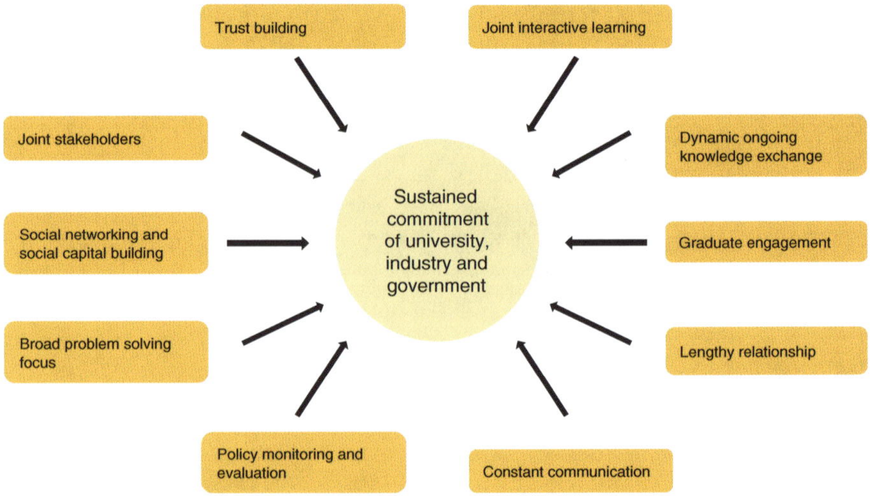

Fig. 2.3 The basis of the triple Helix Model—Higher education, government, and private sector partnership

has been argued above (Dooley and Kirk 2007) that even though they are a window to the outside world they may constitute a barrier to total academic staff commitment and ownership which is at the heart of Fig. 2.3.

While much of the discussion of the Triple Helix model is narrowly focused upon knowledge transfer, universities have increasingly been drawn into a playing a stronger regional social and economic development role in many other ways (Arbo and Benneworth 2008). While they are often important employees and indirect job generators in a region in their own right they can take on the mantle of being a leading network hub for focus upon regional development issues. They can act as animateurs for the development of sustainable networks of exchange on important issues. They can focus on supplying skilled young people to a region and are a mechanism for enhancing social mobility. Through their outreach education and training programs, they can seek to bring forward the future and act as a major learning source for regional stakeholders. They can, through their reputation and specialist expertise, play an important role in attracting investment to a region. Via research they throw independent light on key development issues and act as a means for independent evaluation. They are often an exporter, bringing in income to a region: but also, through their internationalization work, they can bring major contacts into the locality, and thus raise its visibility and capacity to build networks abroad. They also often act as an intermediary in articulating regional development issues to central government in areas of technology policy, education and skills development and competition policy. Overall, they may take a central place in the development of many aspects of a region's culture. There is clear evidence that across Europe universities are taking on more of the role of bridging local with global (Arbo and Benneworth 2008). Whether an individual university wishes to play a transformational role as a regional change agent is, however, an issue for its individual mission and strategy.

2.2.10 University Funding, Enterprise, Autonomy, and Academic Freedom

It was noted above that throughout the world there has been a gradual evolution in the way that universities are funded, as public budgets fail to take the strain of rapidly growing student numbers (Zumeta 2007; Williams 2009). In the UK, for example, base public funding provides only 40 % of university resource, the remainder expected to come from a variety of sources including hypothecated (targeted) public programs, European or local government funding, student fees (Greenaway and Haynes 2003), research finding, contract work, foundations, alumni donations, and catering and other services-altogether some £7bn of £18bn of the UK university income comes from non-state sources (Universities UK 2007).

There is no space in this paper to explore the intricacies of higher education funding, widely debated elsewhere (Cunningham and Cochi-Ficano 2000; Rolfe 2001; De Ziwa 2005; Douglas 2008; Williams 2009), but the issue is of relevance to the entrepreneurial concept in a number of ways. Most important is the degree to which funding impinges upon the autonomy of institutions (Darling et al. 1989; Li-Chuan 2004). Here, there has been, and continues to be, much debate. On the one hand, there are those who argue that public funding constrains academic freedom particularly as it becomes more directive and that diversified income sources ensure a higher degree of freedom (Li-Chuan 2004). Others argue that funding raised from elsewhere, particularly from the private sector, in many cases has strings attached to it (Leslie and Ramey 1998).

In reality the detail is more complex. Much depends upon the mix of funding; for example, monies from alumni, charitable donations, and research grants from independent bodies may be less likely to impinge upon autonomy than commercial contracts. More subtly, much also depends upon the impact of funding arrangements on choice of personnel (freedom to appoint staff and students), freedom to determine curriculum and the balance of research and teaching, the make-up of governing boards and the processes of accountability which impact upon freedom to develop (Li-Chuan 2004). A major issue in funding overall is the degree to which it impinges on the fulfillment of the university mission (Hearn 2003).

Funding strategies are therefore becoming more complex, with governments forcing the issue by giving matching incentives to fund-raising from private sources.[6] The search to 'buy autonomy' has created considerable interest in the

[6] For example, in Finland the government has introduced an incentive program to raising of finance by leveraging private with public funding.

cost benefit of 'fund raising' through development offices (Baade and Sundberg 1996) and has caused reflection upon the relatively poor performance of European universities in tracking, building relationships with and raising funds from, alumni compared with their American counterparts (Thomas 2004). In some countries, in response to the above scenario, the privatization of universities is very much on the public agenda (IHEP 2009).

Altogether, the financing issue is yet another central focus for entrepreneurial management, with considerable risk attached, not only of a simple resource nature.

2.2.11 Creating Public Value

The issues discussed above demonstrate the increasingly complex and uncertain task environment facing higher education. University responses to this have heightened the intellectual controversy concerning the central 'idea' of a university (Slaughter and Leslie 1997; Gilbert 2000; Graham 2002; Kirp 2003). At the heart of the debate is the notion that universities are being driven by a range of market forces into commercial organizations focused upon the 'sale' or 'capitalisation' of knowledge. The latter is defined as 'knowledge created for use as well as for disciplinary advance and linked with economic and social advance' (Etzkowitz 2004). Some writers go so far as to describe universities as 'knowledge factories' (Lazzeroni and Piccaluga 2003). Thus, the intellectual autonomy of the institution and curiosity-based research, in particular, is seen to be eroded in favor of 'value in use' (Albert 2003). This has been characterized as a move from a Mode 1 model where the university was an independent space for discovery, beyond control, with government, as key funder, the main guarantor, to a Mode 2 typology of an organization engaged in high levels of interaction with a range of stakeholders where sustainability is a function of a broader legitimization as seen through the eyes of the state, private partners, and indeed society as a whole (Gibbons et al. 1994; Dooley and Kirk 2007; Rinne and Koivula 2009). The University moves from being a niche organization towards a more open and comprehensive organization (Nowotny and Scott and Gibbons 2001). Funding in this Mode comes from an ever-widening range of sources. The university sees its offer as a public good embracing the concept of 'knowledge travel' as set out in Fig. 2.4 (Barnett 2000) and moving away from its dependency upon 'credentialism' (Rinne and Koivula 2009).

The Mode 2 characterization firmly places the university within the concept of being an instrument for creating 'public value' (Nowotny et al. 2003; Alperovotz et al. 2005). This concept developed by Mark Moore of Harvard University (Moore 1995) has commanded a great deal of attention world wide, and particularly from government in the UK (Kelly et al. 2007). It is seen as an alternative to the measurement of outcomes from public investment via cost benefit analysis. The three key essences of the model are: a strong initial planning focus upon the value of the proposed 'offer' to the community; the creation of legitimacy for courses of action by full engagement of the relevant community stakeholders; and

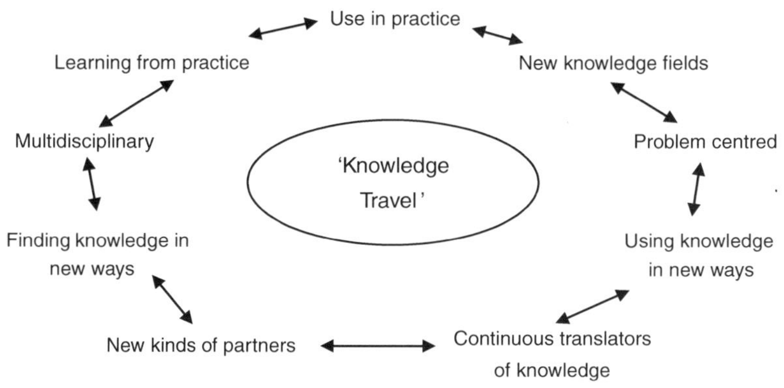

Fig. 2.4 The Mode 2 university and the new foci of 'Knowledge Travel'

ensuring that the plans and proposals are clearly within the capacity, goals, and values of the institution. Of key importance to the changing university scenario described earlier is the concept's emphasis upon gaining legitimacy by wide engagement of interested parties in the process of doing things.

2.3 The Entrepreneurial Organizational Challenge

2.3.1 The Entrepreneurial Organization Concept

Much emphasis has been placed by many of the referenced authors to the need for a university to be highly flexible in its response to the environment described above (Vaira 2004). The above paragraphs have briefly characterized some of the responses. The combination of different demands being made by government, still a major source of funding, via processes of quality measures rather than direct control, combined with the competitive market, and stakeholder demands described above, have presented considerable challenges to the university organization design around the world (OECD 2005, 2007; Olssen and Peters 2005; Pan 2007; Pilbeam 2008). Contingency organizational theory demands that institutions are designed around the specific nature of their task environment and thereafter flexibly adjust in response to change in the environment (Lawrence and Lorsch 1986; Covin and Slevin 1991; Namen and Slaven 1993). Many writers have focused upon this issue in the higher education context (Coaldrake 2001; Salmi 2001).

Burton Clark, perhaps the most influential writer in this field, argues (2004a) on the basis of a number of case studies (including two UK universities) for five key components of entrepreneurial university organization:

- a strong central steering core to embrace management groups and academics;
- an expanded development periphery involving a growth of units that reach out beyond the traditional areas in the university;

- diversity in the funding base, not only by use of government third stream funding but from a wide variety of sources;
- a stimulated academic heartland with academics committed to the entrepreneurial concept; and
- an integrated entrepreneurial culture defined in terms of common commitment to change.

While his arguments can clearly be seen to be in response to some of the pressures noted above, the depth of his research has been criticized (Deem 2001; Finlay 2004), Moreover, no strong conceptual argument (as opposed to an empirical conclusion) is put forward to link this with his call for institutions to be more focused upon innovation, taking risks, and dealing with uncertainty.

Etzkowitz, another leading writer on this issue, puts forward (2004) five propositions concerning the entrepreneurial university concept, namely that such institutions are focused upon: the capitalization of knowledge; managing interdependence with industry and government; are nevertheless independent of any particular sphere; are 'hybrid' in managing the tension between independence and interdependence; and embody reflexivity, involving continuous renewal of internal structures.

The observations of these writers and others can be plotted against a broader conceptual frame setting out key components of an organization moving to cope entrepreneurially with high levels of uncertainty and complexity. Such an organization is designed to maximize the use of effective entrepreneurial behavior appropriate to the task environment (Lawrence and Lorsch 1986; Covin and Slevin 1991). Figure 2.5 presents such a framework for evaluation of the broad entrepreneurial challenge to university organization design.

It is important to distinguish the entrepreneurial model from other organizational approaches and concepts introduced into academe over the past decade in particular the 'new managerialism' (Deem 1998, 2001), the 'corporate business model', 'professionalism' (Blackmore and Blackwell 2006; Kolsaker 2008) and 'marketisation' (Bok 2003). Entrepreneurial organization is not synonymous with any of these. The entrepreneurial concept stretches well beyond the business and new venture context. It is distinct from, but possibly overlapping with, components of the managerialist concept as it is to be associated with a certain style of leadership; but managerialism has become associated with many of the 'rules' of corporate bureaucracy, namely: highly formal planning processes and information systems; tight accountability and standard setting; audits; order; and demarcation.

'Professionalism' is clearly associated to some degree with this by the bringing into universities a new culture of professional managers (Sporn 1996) leading, some argue, to the possible marginalization of academics (Deema 2007). This contrasts with an entrepreneurial emphasis upon enhancing the capacity of the existing body of academe to lead change. Finally, the entrepreneurship concept is not at all wholly synonymous with 'marketisation' either in the pure commercial sense of setting up the university to 'sell' know-how nor in the sense of adopting business and other approaches to reaching customers although it may embody appropriate elements of both at times. Certainly, the concepts of 'branding' the

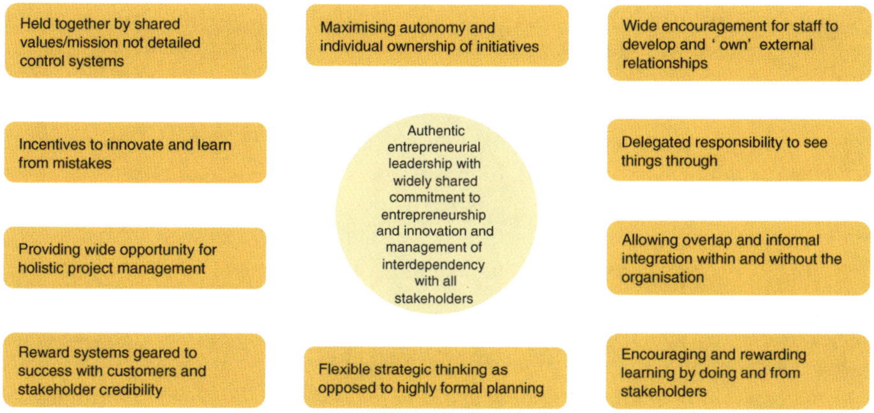

Fig. 2.5 The university as an entrepreneurial organization

university, image creation and reaching out to the public through various channels especially through the media are important.

2.3.2 The Organization Development Challenges

The frame above (Fig. 2.5) can be used to explore some of the organization development challenges noted above. Entrepreneurial organizations have a strong bottom-up development and initiative focus, empowering individuals at all levels of the organization to enjoy freedom for action. The dominant controlling and motivating parameter is not systems but shared mission, values and culture, and trust (Davies 2001; Daumard 2001). Thus, a major challenge and opportunity to universities is to build entrepreneurship upon the considerable freedom enjoyed by departments and individuals, traditionally embodied in the notion of a 'community of scholars' moving this more towards a 'community of practice' (Todorovic et al. 2005; Wenger 1998). In this respect there is a diverse number of issues. Universities can be characterized as pluralistic organizations with different departments having very different external orientations and indeed academic values. While a strong central steering group, as Clark has argued, may therefore be desirable in reinforcing the mission, the major challenge is that of placing ownership of innovation and change with academic departments, finding champions therein who, perhaps incrementally, can move innovation up the departmental agenda. This is not an easy task. There is evidence to suggest that departments are often heavily focused upon 'defending their patch' within the present organization system rather than upon innovating (Bryman 2007).

It has already been argued above that establishing intermediary professional units to 'manage' a range of externally focused activities, in the absence of departmental initiative, may emasculate the capacity and motivation for academics to take up challenges in their own distinct environment. In stimulating academic initiative, formal strategic planning and mission statements may be less important than encouragement of flexible strategic thinking, integrating action with strategy, when confronting opportunity, and threats (Courtney et al. 1999). Shattock argues that, in the present climate, strategic planning should be 'a framework only for opportunistic decision making' (Shattock 2000). Entrepreneurial innovation will also require flexibility in organization design to allow the growth of overlap and interdependency among different departments, projects, and even individuals in adjusting flexibly to the demands of society for new combinations of knowledge. This may lead to Schumpeterian 'creative destruction' (Schumpeter 1934), as those departments slow to adapt, fade or merge into new units. Overall, in this scenario, there will be a challenge to the reward system in the organization in moving it towards recognition of innovation, successful integration of knowledge, and relevance to the wider community.

While the above may challenge the university in the way that it measures excellence (Amaral and Magalhaes 2003; Schuetze 2007), incorporating the concept of 'public value' as described above, does not necessarily, as is sometimes argued (Mawditt 1998; Berglund 2008), threaten emphasis upon excellence in research, nor the essential 'idea' of a university. Etzkowitz, for example, argues that the current concern for the wider embedding of knowledge takes universities back to their original objectives. Others argue that the new 'DNA' of knowledge is 'polyvalent' and intellectual with the interdisciplinary, theoretical, and practical merging together (Viale et al. 2005). In a seminal paper for the US Kauffmann Foundation (2008), Michael Crow, the president of Arizona State University, a major US research university, argues the case for the 'New American Research University' with academic enterprise as the 'organising principle'. His targets for such an organization are:

- academic excellence focused upon, and backed up with, maximising social impact;
- competitiveness;
- agility;
- adaptability;
- inclusivity;
- focussing globally yet also locally;
- responsiveness to changing needs;
- and speedy decision-making capability.

His view of the university is as a 'force for societal transformation' with a culture of academic enterprise focused upon user-inspired relevance and transcending disciplinary-based limitations. The concept of the 'citizen scholar', also increasingly debated in the US (Cherwitz 2005) aligns with this where the focus is upon empowerment of the individual. These concepts have major organizational and physical design, as well as intellectual, implications.

2.3.3 Governance and the Entrepreneurial University

It is the view of the UK committee of university chairs (CUC) that stakeholders external to the university have a major role in holding it to account (CUC 2000, 2004, 2009). The main mechanism for this in most universities across the world is the council or board of governors (Dearing 1997; CUC 2000; Chan and Lo 2007). There has been much debate internationally on governance in universities (OECD 2003; Ka Ho Mok 2005; Kohler and Huber 2006; Bleiklie and Kogan 2007; Schonfield 2009; Mora and Vieira 2009). This has focused upon a number of issues of which the power of the council & board in approving and shaping a university's strategy is major. (Navarro et al. Navarro and Gallardo 2003; Shattock 2009: Chap. 4). The debate explores: the relationship between the chair of the council & board and the universities vice chancellor or principal; the size and composition of the board[7] and the balance of its representation; what should be its key performance indicators; and, perhaps most important, in the context of this paper, the board as an instrument for leading change (Lombardi et al. 2002).

In line with the ideas of Clark (2004a, b), there have been moves to streamline boards; and to strengthen their power and links with the VC or CEO and his or her management team. In the UK this was a main recommendation of the 1997 National Committee of Enquiry into Higher Education (Dearing 1997). This led to internal changes in many universities, with a strengthening of the power of an executive team at the expense of the traditional academic representative body, the senate. This has also been accompanied, in the UK and also more universally, by internal changes aimed at reducing bureaucracy and removing a heavy dependency upon committee structures which are said to impede innovation. There has also been a broad trend towards the appointment of professional administrators reporting to a small senior executive team. All of these changes are contested by some, on the grounds of weakening democracy in the institution and marginalizing the concept of a community of scholars (Graham 2002, 2003; Zhou 2008; Berglund 2008). They have, however, been counterbalanced in some cases by processes of greater devolution to academic departments.

In the context of this paper's focus upon entrepreneurship, the issue of governance can be assessed in several ways. First, by the degree to which streamlining the board enhances the university's engagement with external stakeholders across the whole institution, building the 'learning organisation' capacity as described above (Miller and Katz 2004). Second, whether, as a result, the university becomes more sensitive in its long-term strategies to wider societal needs. Third, whether there is an impact on decision-making structures throughout the organization, as discussed above, other than at the top. And, overall, whether it increases the capacity of the organization to innovate. There is currently little research that addresses these issues in the context of the effectiveness of governance arrangements.

---

[7] In the UK the Dearing report (1997) (Higher Education in the Learning Society) led to the streamlining of boards.

2.3.4 The Individual Academic Entrepreneur

Within every university, and perhaps within every department, there will be some academics who will be continuously looking outward, harvesting knowledge, and experience from a wider range of stakeholders than can be found within the 'halls of academe' (Bird and Allen 1989). There will also be some who in general 'buy into' the concept of the entrepreneurial university as outlined above, although they may have a widely different balance of views as to what this means in both concept and practice (Duberley et al. 2007; Mcinnis 2001; Meyer and Evans 2007). Moreover, academics find themselves in very different types of organization within the sector with different cultures and views of what constitutes 'excellence' (Finlay 2004). Etzkowitz, for example, has radically posited the notion of research groups as 'quasi firms' (2003). While there may have been an erosion of the power of academics in some universities the individual department and staff member still has considerable independence. In what has been described as the traditional liberal university model (Delanty 2001) the degree of interaction with the external environment was wholly an individual choice. As universities, in general, (some more than others) move to what Delanty describes as a reflexive model (based upon exchange and reciprocity between knowledge producers and users) there is more scope for rewarding the academic entrepreneur. In the scientific knowledge transfer context, described earlier in this chapter, this becomes important as it is the personal academic interface that is elevated above the impact of physical and administrative structures, as characterized by science and technology parks and technology transfer offices (Klofsten and Jones-Evans 2000; Franklin et al. 2001).

The evidence suggests that conflicting interests for academics do arise in the arena of practical engagement, with industry in particular, and that there are career uncertainties for those academics who actively engage (Duberley et al. 2007). But the same study demonstrates that scientists often view the prospect of commercialization of their work as a means to its full realization, and demonstration of their own potential. While the increased blurring of the distinction between pure and applied science seems to be more widely accepted, the key issues for academics seem to be more about resources, career concerns, processes, and rewards (non-financial as well as financial). Overall, the dynamics of the changes described earlier have major implications for the design of career structures in academe.

2.4 The Leadership Challenge

2.4.1 Summarizing the Basic Challenges

The previous sections of this chapter have painted a broad scenario of factors that seem to be moving many universities towards a more entrepreneurial mode and have also reviewed organization and individual development issues impinging on the institution's possible response. The US Department of Education sees this as a major test of leadership (2006). For those in a position to lead this change there are many tensions. Sir David Watson 2008 in a contribution to a 'Consultation' workshop organized by the UK Council for Industry and Higher Education and the Society for Research into Higher Education summed these up in a UK context as: Conservative v Radical; Competitive v Collegiate; Commercial v Charitable; Autonomous v Accountable; Traditional v Innovative; Local v International; and Public v Private. In the same publication Cubie, Chair of the CUC notes the dichotomies between the entrepreneurial culture and the audit and managerial culture (pp. 14–17). In reality the distinctions are much finer yet deeper. There are basic conceptual as well as ideological confusions about the nature of the entrepreneurial paradigm itself, which fundamentally affect individual academic attitudes (Ma 2000; Maunter 2005).

Despite recent changes, there remains in many organizations a tension between the academic collegiate view of a community of scholars (where disciplines are the 'invisible college') backed up by numerous committee activities and a powerful senate or academic council (in the traditional model of a university) and streamlined executive decision-making teams capable of more rapid response to change (Meyer and Evans 2007). Resources are increasingly scarce and fought over for maintenance rather than change (Clark 2004). The specialized administrative units focused upon outreach activities such as regional development, technology transfer. Knowledge exchange, alumni development and careers, noted above, may compete for resources and endeavor to build their own empires, limiting potential for synergy among them and limiting the capacity to give real ownership to academics. Reaching out internationally, and attracting new resource, demands large amounts of executive time. Thomas, for example, found that seeking external resource in the US could take up to 30 % of deans and heads of department time (Thomas 2004).

Managing a wider range of stakeholders. Multi-actors, multi-interfaces and multi-objectives constitute a major leadership challenge (Maak 2007; Bryman 2007). In the UK the restructuring of university councils and boards and their empowerment has added to this pressure. Despite these changes there is a strong sense of academic independence rooted in departments so that a distinctive leadership characteristic of departmental heads can be seen as their ability to 'defend the department' (Bryman 2007). In this context, the challenge can be seen to encourage innovative leadership throughout the organization (Mcinnis 2001; Greenhalgh 2008). There is, therefore, the issue of challenging certain aspects of the 'new managerialism' particularly those that control rather than stimulate risk and innovation. There is evidence that academics are uncomfortable with over-use of authority, finance led decisions, audit trails involving more paper work, and being cut off from decision making (Deem 2007).

2.4.2 The Entrepreneurial Leadership Concept

A key issue is the degree to which the entrepreneurial leader concept sits with the above challenge. The concept itself must also fit with the entrepreneurial organization framework set out earlier. From the literature (Schein 1992; Kilgour 1992;

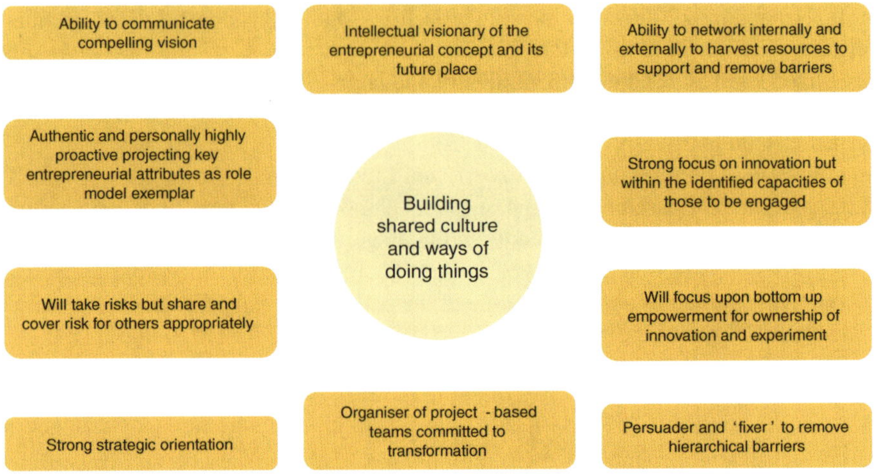

Fig. 2.6 The entrepreneurial leader

Kuratko and Hornsby 1999; Dulewicz 2000; Mcinnis 2001; Vecchio 2003; Gupta et al. 2004) a matching frame can be drawn as in Fig. 2.6 below, which contextualizes key characteristics against the challenges above and the frame in Fig. 2.5. The result has much in common with 'transformational leadership' (Bass 1990; Epitropaki 2001). Intellectual and visionary leadership is needed for two major reasons: first to remove ideological and 'concept of a university' barriers associated with the entrepreneurial paradigm; and second to carry this through in the particular context of the nature of the university itself and its existing culture, mission, and strategy. This is not to infer a concentration upon creating 'new' formal strategy statements (Shattock 2000); substituting strategy for leadership has been warned against (Watson 2008). Entrepreneurial change is achieved by doing, not by paper.

In the organizational climate described above, and perhaps in academe in general, leadership is a concept to be earned not formally designated. Managing the balance of relationships among formally engaged stakeholders (the board or council) and other external stakeholders and internal stakeholders is a complex process (Frooman 1999). Super complexity (CIHE and SRHE 2008) is within, as well as without, the organization. A key challenge will be to create entrepreneurial role models within departments and gradually to build a culture of rewarding innovation in every department rather than a culture of defence. This will demand capacity to identify potential change agents and build teams around them, encourage risk, and protect them. Shared purpose is thus built by example and reward.

In the UK it has been argued that leadership in the departmental context is low status with relatively few rewards for heads of programs or chairing departmental committees (Bryman 2007). Identifying potential departmental change agents will demand an ability to recognize different styles of leadership and different attitudes associated with potentially enterprising 'clever people' (Goffee and Jones 2007) with competency to build from them in different ways. As part of vision building there will need to be clear articulation of the concept of innovation and its applicability to all disciplines and departments.

The overall mission would be to infuse departments with entrepreneurial values. The key instrument for creating transformation will be finding resource to support innovation in departments, particularly so in the present climate. The leader in this respect will need to be the bridge between stakeholders and departments and between bottom up and top down initiatives (Kweik 2008): as such the persuader and fixer role will be dominant. Some resource may have to be found for new units some of which may reach across traditional discipline and departmental boundaries. But the key will be in building the entrepreneurial leadership capacity of academics (Blackmore and Blackwell 2006) incrementally from existing practice.

2.4.3 Building Appropriately upon Existing Capacity

In all universities there exists a range of activities that could be broadly described as part of entrepreneurial response to the environments described earlier. Given the diversity of vision, mission, resource, status, and tradition these will vary from one institution to another. A key to the practice of entrepreneurial strategy is an initial appraisal of the existing capacity of the organization upon which to build. Such an appraisal touches upon all of the areas of response to the environment covered above, including an analysis of the way that the existing academic mission of the university, its governance, funding (leverage), strategy, and organization structure fits with, or constrains, an entrepreneurial model and the capacity for change. Among the possible range of existing activity areas to be explored are:

- knowledge and technology transfer policies and activities (Dill 1995; Geuna and Muscio 2008);
- the effectiveness of any physical infrastructure that relates to this, for example, science & technology parks and the associated existence of incubators (Albert and Gaynor 2001) and venture funds;
- new venture programs; embedded entrepreneurship program or enterprising pedagogy activity within departments;
- careers department and student society activity in this respect;
- alumni policies and programs;
- entrepreneurial curriculum and pedagogy development within departments;
- the work of interdisciplinary centers;
- regional and local partnerships;
- focus upon social and community issues (Bloom 2006);
- international activities and relationships;
- links and partnerships with entrepreneurs and business in general including applied research and consultancy activity.

The results of such an appraisal should also reveal the degree of existing interface and potential synergy from different activities. For example, student activities may link with departmental project work, with external project work involving local entrepreneurs and may be used for wider promotional activity. Technology transfer activities can link with new venture education and training programs and engage the entrepreneur community as mentors. Career departments can work in partnership with academic departments. Such an appraisal can also be used to identify potential future entrepreneurial champions in the organization (Mendes et al. 2006).

2.5 Entrepreneurial Leadership Development and Program Design

The distinctive nature of the entrepreneurial leadership challenge arising from the changing paradigm of the university has been described above. Richard Lambert's review of Business-University collaboration in the UK, for example, found that the variety of stakeholders and different demands made upon universities made the leadership role the most complex in the field (Lambert 2003). Any program designed to meet this challenge has to be targeted upon senior personnel with sufficient visibility and status in the organization to take responsibility alongside senior management, or as part of the management team, for facilitating change (Blackmore and Blackwell 2006). Such a program, as befits the nature of an entrepreneurial venture, will need to be focused upon action and learning from action, bringing together all key aspects of the leadership challenge as described above.

The Entrepreneurial University Leadership Programme is therefore structured into a number of three to four day modules with space in between for action learning. The first module aims to build intellectual capacity to absorb the concept of the entrepreneurial university as it is being configured around the world and as it is being adopted and adapted by a diversity of different higher education institutions in different cultural and international policy contexts. A key component is the development of understanding of how in practice different institutions and their leaders are redesigning their organizations to cope with the different national and international pressures; also to understand how this is being supported or otherwise by policy makers and public and private organizations and their perceptions on the key issues. Overall, a key aim is to explore how a university's activity in this sphere creates public value.

The nature of the leadership challenge as described above is also considered, focussing upon personal, relational and institutional development. In particular, the focus is upon the issue of 'leading innovation from the bottom', creating leaders and empowering academics to take risks and build rewards around new ways of doing things. A key component is network and relationship management and building trust-based relationships with the local, regional, national, and international environment.

The next module focuses upon the best concept and practice in key activity areas described in Fig. 2.7, bringing together the best of the UK and international

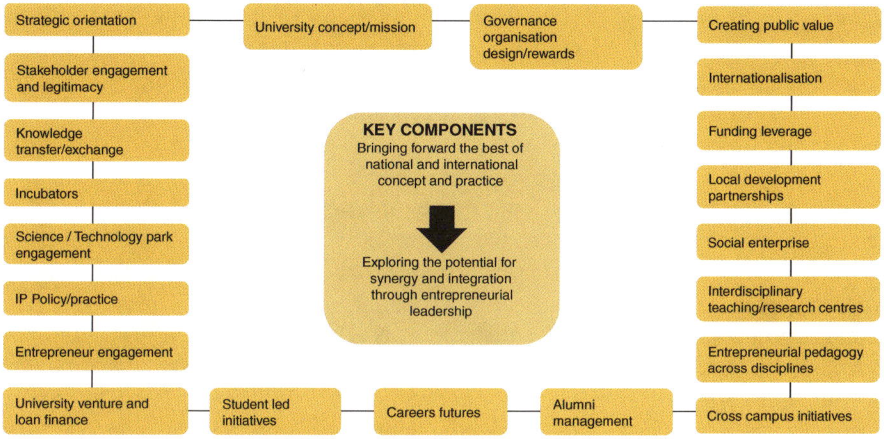

Fig. 2.7 Exploring best concept and practice

experience. This allows and workshops to discussions leaders to participate in a series of rotating workshops (a carousel) focused upon the important areas of development interest in their own institution. This can include optional tailored international visits to explore in more detail areas of particular interest.

The final module is focused upon individual action plans and strategies for the development of appropriate stakeholder and policy relationships. It provides an opportunity to raise and debate a number of outstanding issues arising from the program with a range of representatives from business, social enterprises, government, NGOs and student bodies. There is also a strong program focus throughout on 21st Century Challenges and their implications for the future of universities.

As noted above, the Entrepreneurial University Leadership Programme includes action learning. Between modules, participants explore relevant issues in their own institutions and work on a change project aimed at developing greater entrepreneurship (in the broadest sense of the word) either for the university as a whole or for their own department. The issues and challenges of implementing the planned changes are discussed in tutor groups and with external experts in the final module of the program.

2.6 Conclusion

The paper began with an acknowledgement that the focus was upon building a strong conceptual base for action, namely, the development of a program focused upon ‘Leading the Entrepreneurial University’. The pressures upon the higher education sector internationally and its responses have been summarized and the related organization development impacts have been set out, along with the resultant leadership challenges. Finally, there was a brief summary of the entrepreneurial university leadership program that has been developed and of the argument that there is considerable potential in the university sector to create synergy among the many activities currently observed in the responses of individual institutions to the various challenges. The scenario painted in the paper is arguably a global one, with many related references: but there has also been much reference to the UK in the light of the location of the program.

The paper set out to add value to the considerable debate by seeking to conceptualize the concepts of the entrepreneurial organization and entrepreneurial leadership as a basis for analysis. This is needed for a number of reasons. Firstly, to move the debate on the entrepreneurial university away from the narrow focus upon commercialization of intellectual property and the fears of ‘prostitution’ of the ‘idea’ of a university that results from this (Bok 2003; Kirp 2003). Entrepreneurship has been located as an individual and organizational behavioral and development response to uncertainty and complexity broadly relevant to citizens and organizations of all kinds, private, public, and autonomous. Secondly, to provide a stronger basis for bringing together all of the activities of a university that are reflective of its response to an environment of growing uncertainty and complexity. The entrepreneurial label is often attached to only certain aspects of an institution’s activity, for example knowledge transfer, regional engagement, student or staff new venturing, problem-centered learning, and so on.

Thirdly, to provide a stronger basis for an individual university to ‘situate’ itself within the concept. It was noted at the beginning of the paper that the university sector now embraces a wide variety of different ‘typologies’ of institutions with different missions and strategies. Moreover, they are undoubtedly ‘led’ in a variety of different ways. There are very different ‘power’ relationships between stakeholder councils/boards and academic ‘senates’ and different balances of power between the vice chancellor or principal, his/her team, intermediate professionals and the authority of the individual department and autonomy of the individual academic. Any individual on a program faced with the transfer of learning into action will need to adapt the approach taken appropriately to the distinctive existing structure, organizational and leadership characteristics, and values of the organization. The entrepreneurial organization and leadership concepts described above are not therefore recipes for change but frameworks upon which to reflect in guiding change appropriately.

The arguments, concepts and program design issues noted above also have, importantly, to be related to the overall objectives of the UK National Centre for Entrepreneurship in Education (NCEE) as the main driver of the programme. Its overall mission is to develop entrepreneurship across all disciplines in all UK universities (www.ncee.org.uk). It pursues this mission in a number of ways including: the creation of widespread student awareness; the building of understanding and motivation of key stakeholders, internal, and external to the university; the development of staff capacities via an international entrepreneurship educators program (IEEP); and the monitoring of practice and progress nationally and internationally to share with all stakeholders. The sustainable impact of these activities is strongly dependent upon associated elements of institutional change within Universities. It is upon this that the Entrepreneurship University Leadership programme is focused.

Bibliography

Agrawal A (2001) University-to-industry knowledge transfer: literature review and un-answered questions. Int J Manage Rev 3(4):285–302

Alaasarela E, Fallemies M, Halkosaari T, Huhta T, Jansson L, Jylha E, Lahtela M, Nivala K, Nokso-Koiovisto P, Telkki M (2002) Higher education as a pathway to entrepreneurship. Keski-Pohjanmann Ammatikorkeakoulu, Finland

Albert M (2003) Universities and the market economy: the differential impact on knowledge production in sociology and economics. High Educ 45:147–182

Albert P, Gaynor L (2001) Incubators—growing up, moving out. A review of the literature. Chair of High Tech Entrepreneurship, CERAM, December 2001

Alperovitz G, Howard T (2005) The next wave: building a university civic engagement service for the twenty-first century. J High Educ Outreach Engagem 10(2):141

Altbach PG, Knight J (2006) The Internationalization of higher education: motivations and realities. The NEA 2006 Almanac of Higher Education. NEA, Washington

Altbach PG (2005) Globalization and the university: Myths and realities in an unequal world. EPI, 2005. Global Higher Education Rankings. Affordability and Accessibility in Comparative Perspective. Washington, EPI, www.educationalpolicy.org

Amaral A, Magalhaes A (2003) The triple crisis of the University and its reinvention. High Educ Policy 16:239–253

Arbo P, Benneworth P (2008) Understanding the regional contribution of higher education institutions: a literature review. A research report prepared for the OECD Institutional Management in Higher Education Programme The contribution of higher education to regional development. OECD Paris

Armbruster C (2008) Research Universities: autonomy and self-reliance after the Entrepreneurial University. Policy Futures Educ 6(4):372–389

AUQA (2005) Proceedings of the Australian Universities quality forum engaging communities, Sydney, Australia, 6–8th July 2005 AUQA Occasional Publications Number 5. Melbourne. Australia. Universities Quality Agency

Baade RA, Sundberg JO (1996) What determines alumni generosity? Econ Educ Rev 15(1):75–81

Baar NA (1998) Higher education in Australia and Britain—what lessons? Australian Economic Review, 31(2):179–188. LSE Research Online, London

Baldini N et al (2006) Institutional changes and the commercialization of academic knowledge: A study of Italian universities' patenting activities between 1965 and 2002. Res Policy 35(2006):518–532

Barnett R (2000) University knowledge in an age of supercomplexity. High Educ 40:409–422

Barrie SC (2007) A conceptual framework for the teaching and learning of generic graduate attributes. Stud High Educ 32(4):439–458

Barsony J (2003) Towards the Entrepreneurial University. SEFI 2003 Conference—global engineer: education and training for mobility

Bass B, Riggio RE (2008) Transformational leadership. Taylor and Francis, London

Becher T, Trowler PR (2007) Academic tribes and territories. Intellectual enquiry and the culture of disciplines, Society for Research into Higher Education and Open University Press

Benner M, Sandstrom U (2000) Institutionalizing the triple helix: research funding and norms in the academic system. Research Policy 29(2000):291–301

Bergek A, Norrman C (2008) Incubator best practice: a framework. Technovation 28(2008):20–28

Berglund E (2008) I wanted to be an academic, Not 'A creative': notes on Universities and the new capitalism. Ephemera Theory Politics Organization 8(3):232–233

Bernasconi A (2005) University entrepreneurship in a developing country: the case of the P. Universidad Católica de Chile, 1985–2000. Higher Education 50(2):247–274 (Sep 2005)

Bird BJ, Allen DN (1989) Faculty entrepreneurship in research university environments. J High Educ 60(5):583–596 (Sep–Oct 1989)

Blackmore P, Blackwell P (2006) Strategic leadership in academic development. Stud High Educ 31(3):373–387
Bleiklie I, Kogan M (2007) Organization and governance of universities. High Educ Policy 2007(20):477–493
Blenker P et al. (2006) Entrepreneurship education—the new challenge facing the universities. Department of management. Aarhus School of Business Working Paper 2006–02. Aarhus School of Business, Aarhus
Bleiklie I, Kogan M (2007) Organisation and governance of universities. High Educ Policy 20:261–274
Bloom GM (2006) The social entrepreneurship collaboratory (SE Lab): a university incubator for a rising generation of leading social entrepreneurs. The Hauser Center for Non-profit Organizations and The John F. Kennedy School of Government Harvard University. Working Paper No. 31, Harvard 2006
Boucher G, Conway C, Van Der Meer E (2003) Tiers of engagement by universities in their region's development. Reg Stud 37(9):887–897
Bok D (2003) Universities in the market place. The commercialisation of higher education. Princeton University Press, USA
Bourdieu P (1999) Social conditions of the international circulation of ideas. In: Shusterman R (ed) Bourdieu. A critical reader, Blackwell Publishers, UK, pp 220–229
Braun G, Diensberg C (2007) Cultivating entrepreneurial regions—Cases and studies from the network project, baltic entrepreneurship partners. Rostock Contributions to Regional Science, Vol. 19. Rostock: Universität Rostock, Wirtschafts- und Sozial-wissen-schaftliche Fakultät
Bridges D, Jonathan R (2003) Education and the market, Chapter 7. In: Blake N, Smeyers P, Smith R, Standish P (eds) The Blackwell Guide to the Philosophy of Education, Blackwell Publishing Limited
Bridgman T (2007) Freedom and autonomy in the university enterprise. J Organ Change Manage 20(4):478–490
Browne T, Jenkins M (2008) Achieving academic engagement? The landscape for educational technology support in two UK institutions. Proceedings ascilite Melbourne 2008: Concise paper: Browne and Jenkins
Brush CG et al (2003) Doctoral education in the field of entrepreneurship. Entrepreneurship J Manage 29(3):309–331
Bryman A (2007) Effective leadership in higher education: a literature review. Stud High Educ 32(6):693–710
Casson M (1982) The entrepreneur. An economic theory. Martin Robertson and Co. Ltd, Oxford
Campbell WH et al (2002) Institutional and faculty roles and responsibilities in the emerging environment of University-Wide interdisciplinary research structures: report of the 2001–2002 research and graduate affairs committee. American Journal of Education, Vol. 66, Winter Supplement 2002
Carnoy M (1999) Globalization and educational reform: what planners need to know. Paris: UNESCO: International Institute for Educational Planning
CEL (2008) Research on diversity and governance in the FE sector recommendations and action plan
CEL (2007) Leadership kills for governance. 2008–2009 programme and support guide, CEL: http://www.centreforexcellence.org.uk
CEL (2006) World-class leadership for global excellence. CEL: http://www.centreforexcellence.org.uk
Chan KF, Lau T (2005) Assessing technology incubator programs in the science park the good, the bad and the ugly. Technovation 25(2005):1215–1228
Chan D, Lo W (2007) Running universities as enterprises: university governance changes in Hong Kong. Asia Pacific J Educ 27(3):305–322
Chapple W, Lockett A, Siegel D, Wright M (2004) Assessing the relative performance of UK university technology transfer offices: parametric and non-parametric evidence. Department of economics, rensselaer polytechnic institute. Working Papers in Economics, No. 0423. Source: http://www.rpi.edu/dept/economics/www/workingpapers

Charles DR (2006) Universities as key knowledge infrastructures in regional innovation systems. Innovation 19(1):117–130
Charles D (2003) Universities and territorial development: reshaping the regional role of UK universities. Local Economy 18(1):7–20
Charney A, Libecap GD (2000) Impact of entrepreneurial education. Insight. A Kauffman research series. Kauffman, Kansas 09005500
Chen S (2007) The features and trends of University development in Australia and China. High Educ Policy 20:223–242
Cherwitz AR (2005) Creating a culture of intellectual entrepreneurship, Academe 91, 5
Cherwitz AR (2002) Intellectual entrepreneurship. A vision for graduate education. Change, November/December
Council for Industry and Higher Education (CIHE) and the Society for Research into Higher Education (SRHE) (2008) Leadership in the Age of Supercomplexity, CIHE London
Clark BR (1998) Creating entrepreneurial universities, organisational pathways of transformation. Pergamon IAU Press, Oxford
Clark BR (2004a) Sustaining change in universities, society for research into higher education. Open University Press
Clark BR (2004b) Delineating the character of the entrepreneurial university. High Educ Policy 17:355–370
Coaldrake P (2001) Responding to changing student expectations. Expect High Educ Manage 13(2):75–93 OECD
Coaldrake P, Stedman L (1999) Academic work in the twenty-first century. Changing roles and policies. Higher Education Division, Department of Education, Training and Youth Affairs Occasional Paper Series. Australia, Higher Education Division, Department of Education, Training and Youth Affairs: 99H
Cook T, Dwek TR, Blumberg B, Hockaday T (2008) Commercialising university research: threats and opportunities-The Oxford Model. Capitalism and Society, Vol. 3, Issue 1 2008 Article 4
CVCP (1999) Technology transfer. The US experience, Report of a Mission of UK Vice Chancellors, Gatsby Trust London
Commission of the European Communities (2005) Mobilising the brainpower of Europe; enabling universities to make their full contribution to the Lisbon Strategy, Brussels
Courtney H, Kirkland J, Viguerie P (1999) Strategy under uncertainty, chapter 1 in Harvard business review Managing Uncertainty on'. Harvard Business School Press, Cambridge
Covin JG, Slevin DP (1991) A conceptual model of entrepreneurship as firm behaviour Entrepreneurship. Theory Pract 16:7–25
Corbett A (2006) Universities and the Europe of knowledge: ideas, institutions and policy Entrepreneurship in the European Union, Higher Education Policy, 1955–2005. Palgrave Ma, London
Crow MM (2008) Building an Entrepreneurial University, in The future of the research university. meeting the challenges of the global C 21st University. Paper to 2008 Kauffman-Planck summit on Entrepreneurship research and policy held June 8–11, in Bavaria, Germany. pp 31–41
Cranmer S (2006) Enhancing graduate employability: best intentions and mixed outcomes. Stud High Educ 31(2):169–184
CUC (2000) Review of University Governance 1997–2000. CUC: http://www.shef.ac.uk/cuc/pubs.html
CUC (1999) Progress report of the working party on the effectiveness of university governing bodies. CUC: http://www.shef.ac.uk/cuc/pubs.html
Cunningham BM, Cochi-Ficano CK (2000) The determinants of donative revenue flows from Alumni of higher education: an empirical inquiry. J Hum Resour 37(3):540–569 (Summer, 2002)
Currie J (2002) Australian universities as enterprise universities: transformed players on a global stage. In: Globalisation: what issues are at stake for universities? Université Laval, Québec Canada, 20 Sept

Darling AL, England MD, Lang DW, Lopers–Sweetman R (1989) Autonomy and control: a university funding formula as an instrument of public policy. Higher Education, 18, pp 559–583, Kluwer Netherlands

Daumard P (2001) Enterprise culture and university culture. High Educ Manage 13(2):67–75 OECD

Davies JL (2001) The emergence of entrepreneurial cultures in European Universities. High Educ Manage 13(2):25–45 OECD

De Ziwa D (2005) Using entrepreneurial activities as a means of survival: investigating the processes used by Australian Universities to diversify their revenue streams. High Educ 50(3):387–411

Dearing R (1997) Report of the National Committee of Inquiry into Higher Education, Higher Education in the Learning Society (The Dearing Report). July. HMSO, Norwich UK

Deem R (1998) 'New managerialism' and higher education: the management of performances and cultures in universities in the United Kingdom. Int Stud Sociol Educ 8(1):47–70

Deem R (2001) Globalisation, new managerialism, academic capitalism and entre-preneurialism in universities: is the local dimension important? Comp Educ 37(1):7–20

Deema R (2007) Managing contemporary UK universities-manager-academics and new managerialism, Academic Leadership. Empirical Research pp 1–14 (www.academicleadership.org/empirical_research/Managing_Contemporray_UK)

Deema R, Ka Ho Mokb, Lucasa L (2008) Transforming higher education in whose Image? Exploring the concept of the 'World-Class' University in Europe and Asia. High Educ Policy 21:83–97

Delanty G (2003) Ideologies of the knowledge society and the cultural contradictions of higher education. Policy Futures Educ 1(1)

Delanty G (2001) Challenging knowledge. The university in the knowledge society. SRHE and Open University Press Imprint, Buckingham

Dill DD (1995) University-industry entrepreneurship: the organization and management of American University technology transfer units. High Educ 29(4):369–384

Dooley L, Kirk D (2007) University-industry collaboration. Grafting the entrepreneurial paradigm onto academic structures. Eur J Innovation Manage 10(3):316–332

Douglas JA (2008) The big curve: trends in university fees and financing in the EU and US. CSHE centre for studies in higher education. Research & Occasional Paper Series: CSHE.19.08

Doutriaux J, Barker M (1996) University and industry in Canada. A changing relationship. Ind Higher Educ 10(1):88–103

Duberley J, Cohen L, Leeson E (2007) Entrepreneurial academics: developing scientific careers in changing University settings. High Educ Q 61(4):479–497

Dulewicz V (2000) Emotional intelligence. The key to successful corporate leadership. J Gen Manage 25:1–15

Durham University Centre for Entrepreneurial Learning Durham University Centre for Entrepreneurial Learning (2009) A study of graduate aspirations to and understanding of entrepreneurial behaviour. Durham UK

Edwards L (2001) Are E-Clubs the answer to entrepreneurial learning? WEI working Paper Series No. 17

Epitropaki O (2001) What is transformational leadership. Institute of Work Psychology, Sheffield England

ESECT (2005) Enhancing student employability, Higher Education Academy. Learning and Employability Series

Etzkowitz H, Leydesdorff L (2000) The dynamics of innovation: from National System and "Mode 2" to a Triple Helix of university-industry-government-relations. Res Policy 29(2000):109–123

Etzkowitz H (2003) Research groups as 'quasi-firms': the invention of the entrepreneurial university. Research Policy 32:109–121

Etzkowitz H (2004) The evolution of the entrepreneurial university. Int J Technol Globalisation 1(1):64–77

Etzkowitz H (2008) The Triple Helix. University– Industry—Government, Innovation in Action, Routledge, London
European Commission (1998) Promoting Entrepreneurship and Competitiveness, Brussels, September COM (1998) 550 final
European Commission (2005) The Competitiveness Challenge. Enterprise Europe, Jan–March
EU, Directorate-General for Enterprise (2004) Helping to create an entrepreneurial culture. A guide on good practices in promoting entrepreneurial attitudes and skills through education. Directorate-General for Enterprise and Industry. Brussels: EU, Unit B.1: Entrepreneurship (SC27 3/4)
EU (2006) Entrepreneurship Education in Europe. Fostering Entrepreneurial Mindsets through Education and Learning. Final Proceedings of the Oslo Conference 27–27 October, European Commission
EU Commission of the European Communities (2006) Implementing the community Lisbon programme: fostering entrepreneurial mindsets through education and learning. Brussels, EU, COM (2006) 33 final
EU Commission of the European Communities (2008) Towards more knowledge-based policy and practice in education and training. Brussels, EU, SEC (2007)
EU Commission of the European Communities (2008) Entrepreneurship in higher education, especially within non-business studies. Final Report of the Expert Group. Directorate-General for Enterprise and Industry. Brussels: EU, Unit B.1: Entrepreneurship
Finlay I (2004) Living in an entrepreneurial university. Res Post Compuls Educ 9(3):417–434
Franklin SJ, Wright M, Lockett A (2001) Academic and Surrogate Entrepreneurs in University Spin-out companies. J Technol Trans 26:127–141
Frooman J (1999) Stakeholder influence strategies. Acad Manage Rev 24(2):191–205
Geiger RL (2004) Knowledge and money: research Universities and the Paradox of the market place. Stanford University Press, US
Geiger RL (2006) The quest for; economic relevance by US research universities. High Educ Policy 19:411–431
Geuna A, Muscio A (2008) The governance of University knowledge transfer. SPRU Electronic Working Paper Series. Paper No. 173, September 2008
Gibb AA, Scott M (1985) Strategic awareness, personal commitment and the process and planning in the small business. J Manage Stud 22(6)
Gibb AA (2007) Entrepreneurship: unique solutions for unique environments. Is it possible to achieve this with the Existing Paradigm? Int J Entrepreneurship Educ 5:93–142. Senate Hall Academic Publishing
Gibb AA, Hannon P (2006) Towards the Entrepreneurial University? Int J Entrepreneurship Education 4:73–110
Gibbons M, Limoges C, Nowatny H, Schwartzman S, Scott P, Trow M (1994) The new production od knowledge. Sage Publications, London
Gilbert AD (2000) The Idea of a University beyond 2000. Policy Autumn 2000:31–36
Goffee R, Jones G (2007) Leading clever people. Harvard Business Review, Reprint R0703D
Graham G (2002) Universities. The Recovery of an Idea, Imprint Academic UK
Green M, Baer M (2000) What does globalisation mean for teaching and learning? CHET Transformation Debates July 21
Green FJ, Saridakis G (2008) The role of higher education skills and support in graduate self-employment. Stud High Educ 33(6):653–672
Greenaway D, Haynes M (2003) Funding higher education in the UK: the role of fees and loans. The Economic Journal 113:F150–F166 Blackwell Publishing UK
Greenhalgh R (2008) Perspectives on management and Leadership from HE and Industry, pp 17–21 in: Leadership in an Age of Supercomplexity, Edited by Keith Herrmann. CIHE and SRHE
Guerrero-Cano M (2008) The creation and development of Entrepreneurial Universities in Spain. An Institutional approach, Doctoral Thesis Universitat Automona Barcelona Spain
Gupta V, MacMillan IC, Surie G (2004) Entrepreneurial leader leadership; developing and measuring a cross- cultural construct. J Bus Ventur 19:241–260

Habermas J, Blazek JR (1987) The idea of the University: learning processes. New German Critique, No. 41, Special Issue on the Critiques of the Enlightenment (Spring–Summer, 1987), pp 3–22
Hager P, Hyland T (2003) Vocational Education and Training, Chapter 15. In: Blake N, Smeyers P, Smith R, Standish P (eds) The Blackwell Guide to the Philosophy of Education, Blackwell Publishing Limited
Haggis T (2006) Pedagogies for diversity: retaining critical challenges amidst fears of dumbing down. Stud High Educ 31(5):521–535
Hayrinen-Alestalo M (1999) The university under the pressure of Innovation policy—reflecting on European and Finnish experiences. Sci Stud 12(1):44–69
Hearn JC (2003) Diversifying campus revenue streams. Opportunities and risks, American Council of Education, Center for Policy Analysis; USA
Henkel M (2004) Current science policies and their implications for the formation and maintenance of academic identity. High Educ Policy 17:167–182
Herrmann K (ed) (2008) Leadership in an age of Supercomplexity. Council for Industry in Higher Education, UK
Higher Education in Europe (2004) Entrepreneurship in Europe Vol. XXIX no. 2 Carfax Publishing
Hughes A (2003) Knowledge Transfer, Entrepreneurship and Economic Growth, ESRC Centre for Business Research Working Paper 273, University Of Cambridge Small Business and Entrepreneurship
Huisman J (2008) World-Class Universities, Higher Education Policy, Vol. 21, (1–4) International Association of Universities 0952-8733/08 $30.00. ww.palgrave-journals.com/hep
IHEP (2007) Regional Universities and Civil Society Development. A Symposium and Study Tour. IHEP, Washington
IHEP (2009) Privatization in higher education: cross-country analysis of trends, policies, problems, and solutions. Issue Brief. IHEP, Washington
International Association of Universities (2005) Key results: 2005 IAU Global survey on internationalisation of higher education. www.unesco.org
Jack SL, Anderson AR (1999) Entrepreneurship education within the enterprise culture. Int J Entrepreneurial Behav Res 5(3):110–125
Jacob M, Lundqvist M, Hellsmark H (2003) Entrepreneurial transformations in the Swedish University system: the case of Chalmers University of Technology. Res Policy 32(2003):1555–1568
Johnson RN, Deem R (2003) Talking of students: tensions and contradictions for the manager-academic and the university in contemporary higher education. High Educ 46:289–314
Ka Ho Mok (2005) Fostering entrepreneurship: changing role of government and higher education governance in Hong Kong. Res Policy 34(2005):537–554
Kauffman Foundation (2008) The future of the Research University. Meeting the global challenges of the 21st Century. Conference papers from the Kauffmann-Max Planck Annual Summit Rethinking the Role of the University and Public Research for the Entrepreneurial Age, June 8–11 Bavaria Germany
Keast DA (1995) Entrepreneurship in universities: definitions, practices, and implications. High Educ Q 49(3):248–266
Kelly G, Mulgan G, Muers S (2007) Creating public value. An analytical framework for public service reform, Strategy Unit, Cabinet office, UK Government (www.strategy.gov.uk)
Kilgour FG (1992) Entrepreneurial Leadership. Library Trends 40(3):457–74 (Winter 1992)
Kinchin IM, Lygo-Baker S, Hay DB (2008) Universities as centres of non-learning. Stud High Educ 33(1):89–103
Kirp DL (2003) Shakespeare, Einstein and the bottom line. The marketing of higher education. Harvard University Press, Cambridge
Kirby D (2006) Creating entrepreneurial universities in the UK. Applying entrepreneurship theory in practice. J Technol Transfer 31:599–603

Klofsten M, Jones-Evans D (2000) Training entrepreneurship at universities: a Swedish case. J Eur Ind Training 24(6):337–344
Kneale P (2005) Imaginative curriculum guide. Enterprise in the higher education curriculum. Higher Education Academy, UK
Knight J (2003) Internationalization of higher education practices and priorities: 2003 IAU survey report. IAU: http://www.unesco.org/iau
Kohler J, Huber J (eds) (2006) Higher education governance between democratic culture, academic aspirations and market forces. Council of Europe Publishing, Strasbourg
Kolsaker A (2008) Academic professionalism in the managerialist era: a study of English universities. Stud High Educ 33(5):513–525
Kristensen B (1999) The entrepreneurial university as a learning university. High Educ Europe 24(1):35–46
Kuratko DF, Hornsby JS (1999) Corporate entrepreneurial leadership for the 21st Century. J Leadersh Organisational Stud 5(2):27–39
Kwiek M (2001) Globalization and higher education, higher education in Europe, Vol. XXVI(1)
Kwiek M (2000) The nation-state, globalization and the modern institution of the university. Theoria. J Soc Polit Theory 96:74–99
Kweik M (2005) Academic Entrepreneurship and private higher education in Europe (in a comparative perspective), Center for Public Policy. Policy Poznan University, Ul. Szamarzews-kiego 89, 60–569 Poznan, Poland. kwiekm@amu.edu.pl, www.cpp.amu.edu.pl
Kwiek M (2005) The university and the state in a global age: renegotiating the traditional social contract? Eur Educ Res J 4(4):324–341
Kweik M (2008) Academic entrepreneurship vs. changing governance and institutional management, structures at European Universities. Policy Futures Educ 6(6):757–770
Lambert R (2003) Lambert review of business-industry collaboration. HMSO Norwich, UK
Lawrence PR, Lorsch JW (1986) Organisation and environment: environment managing differentia-tion and integration, Harvard Business School Classics
Lazzeroni M, Piccaluga A (2003) Towards the entrepreneurial university. Local Economy 18(1):38–48
Lee YS (1996) Technology transfer and the research university: a search for the boundaries of university-industry collaboration. Res Policy 25(1996):843–863
Lehrera M, Nell P, Gärber L (2009) A national systems view of university entrepreneurialism: Inferences from comparison of the German and US experience. Res Policy 38:268–280
Leisner A (2006) Education or service? Remarks on teaching and learning in the entrepreneurial university. Educ Philos Theory 38(4)
Leitch S (2006) Prosperity for all in the global economy-world class skills. HMSO Norwich, UK
Leslie LL, Ramey G (1998) Donor behaviour and voluntary support for higher education institutions. J High Educ 59(2):115–132
Leydesdorff L, Etzkowitz H (2003) The Triple Helix as a model for innovation studies. (Conference Report). Sci Public Policy 25(3):195–203
Leydesdorff L, Meyer M (2003) The Triple Helix of university-industry-government relations. Scientometrics 58(2):191–203
Li-Chuan C (2004) The relationship between university autonomy and funding in England and Taiwan. High Educ 48(2):189–212
Link AN (2006) An empirical analysis of the propensity of academics to engage in informal university technology transfer. Department of Economics, Rensselaer Polytechnic Institute. Working Papers in Economics, No. 0610 Source Phan, P. H., Siegel, D. S. 2006, The Effectiveness of University Technology Transfer. Foundations and Trends in Entrepreneurship 2(2):77–144. http://www.rpi.edu/dept/economics/www/workingpapers
Lombardi JV (2002) University organization, governance, and competitiveness. An Annual Report from The Lombardi program on measuring university performance.
Ma R (2000) Enterprise education and its relationship to enterprising behaviours. A methodological and conceptual investigation. PhD Thesis Durham University UK

Maak T (2007) Responsible leadership, Stakeholder engagement, and the emergence of social capital. J Bus Ethics 74:329–343
Maskell D, Robinson I (2001) The new idea of a university. Imprint Academic, Thorverton
Mawditt R (1998) Lest we forget. High Educ Policy 11:323–330
Maunter G (2005) The entrepreneurial university. A discursive profile of a higher education profile. Crit Discourse Stud 2(2):95–120
Mcinnis C (2001) Promoting academic expertise and authority in an entrepreneurial culture. High Educ Manage 13(2):45–57. OECD
Mendes T, Estabrook L, Magelli P, Conlin K (2006) How academics really view entrepreneurship and Entrepreneurial behavior: A study of 2,000 faculty, 10,000 graduate students and 100 Academic administrators at the University of Illinois at Urbana-Champaign. University of Illinois, USA
Mendoza P, Berger JB (2005) Patenting productivity and intellectual property policies at research I Universities: an exploratory comparative study. Educ Policy Anal Arch 13(4)
Meyer LH, Evans IM (2007) Supporting academic staff: meeting new expectations in higher education without compromising traditional faculty values. High Educ Policy 20:121–144
Miclea M (2004) Learning to do as a pillar of education and its links to entrepreneurial studies in highereducation: European contexts and approaches. High Educ Eur 29(2):221–231
Miller, M. T. and Katz, M. (2004). Effective shared governance: academic governance as a win–win proposition. The NEA 2004 Almanac of Higher Education. NEA, Washington
Minshall T, Wicksteed B (2005) University spin-out companies: starting to fill the evidence gap. A report on a pilot research project commissioned by the Gatsby Charitable Foundation, St. John's Innovation Centre Ltd
Mittelstädt A, Cerri F (2008) Fostering Entrepreneurship for Innovation. OECD Science, Technology and Industry Working Papers, 2008/5. OECD publishing, 10.1787/227624785873
Mohrman K et al (2008) The Research University in transition: the emerging global model. High Educ Policy 2008(21):5–27
Moore MH (1995) Creating public value: strategic management in government. Harvard University Press, Cambridge
Mora J-G, Vieira M-J (2009) Governance, organisation change and Entrepreneurialism: is there a connection.In: Shattock M (ed) Entrepreneurialism in the Universities and the Knowledge Economy. Open University Press, pp 74–100
Moreland N (2007) Entrepreneurship and higher education: an employability perspective. The Higher Education Academy, UK
Moses I (2005) Institutional autonomy revisited. Autonomy justified and accounted. High Educ Policy 19:411–431
National Academy of Science USA (2005) Facilitating interdisciplinary research. National Academies Press, Washington
Namen JL, Slaven DP (1993) Entrepreneurship and the concept of fit: a model and empirical tests. Strateg Manag J 14:137–153
Navarro JR, Gallardo FO (2003) A model of strategic change: universities and dynamic capabilities. High Educ Policy 16:199–212
Neave G (1998) Growing pains: the Dearing Report from a European Perspective. High Educ Q 52(1):118–136
Nicolaou N, Birley S (2003) Social networks in organizational emergence: the university spinout phenomenon. Manage Sci 49(12):1702–1725
NIRAS Consultants (2008) Survey of entrepreneurship in higher education in Europe, FORA, ECON Pöyry
Noir sur Blanc (1999) Survey. Internationalisation of Universities. Development Strategies, Noir sur Blanc. Paris
Nowotny H, Scott P, Gibbons M (2001) Re-Thinking science. Knowledge and the public in the age of uncertainty. Polity Press, USA
Nowotny H, Scott P, Gibbons M (2003) Mode 2 revisited: the new production of knowledge. Minerva 41:179–194

OECD (2001) Journal of the Programme on Institutional Management in Higher Education Management. Special Issue: Education and Skills, Vol. 13, No. 2. Paris: OECD Publishing

OECD (2003) Changing patterns of governance in higher education. In: Education policy analysis. pp 59–78

OECD (2004) The Internationalisation of Higher Education. Policy Brief August OECD Publishing

OECD (2005) Higher Education Management and Policy. Special Issue: Entrepreneurship, Vol. 17, No. 3. Paris: OECD Publishing. In particular: entrepreneurial universities and the development of regional societies: a spatial view of the Europe of knowledge, pp 59–86

OECD (2007) Entrepreneurship Special Issue of Journal of Education Management and Policy, Vol. 17, No. 3-Special Issue. OECD Publishing

O'Shea RP et al (2007) Delineating the anatomy of an entrepreneurial university: the Massachusetts institute of technology experience. R&D Management 37:1

Olssen M, Peters MA (2005) Neoliberalism, higher education and the knowledge economy: from the free market to knowledge capitalism. J Educ Policy 20(3):313–345

Owen-Smith J et al. (2002) A comparison of US and European university-industry relations in the life sciences. Manage Sci 48(1):24–43

Pan S-Y (2007) Intertwining of academia and officialdom and university autonomy: experience from Tsinghua university in China. High Educ Policy 20:207–216

Papayannakis L, Kastelli I, Damigos D, Mavrotas G (2008) Fostering entrepreneurship education in engineering curricula in Greece. Experiences and challenges for a technical University. Eur J Eng Educ 33(2):199–210

Peters MA (2003) Classical political economy and the role of universities in the new knowledge economy. Globalisation Soc Educ 1(2):153–168

Pilbeam C (2008) Designing an entrepreneurial university in an institutional setting. High Educ Policy 21:393–404

Pirnay F et al (2003) Toward a typology of university spin-offs. Small Bus Econ 21:355–369

Poh-Kam W, Yuen-Ping H, Singh A (2007) Towards an entrepreneurial university, model to support knowledge -based economic development: the case of the national university of Singapore. World Dev 35(6):941–958

Politis D (2005) The process of entrepreneurial learning: a conceptual framework. Entrepreneurship in theory and practice, pp 399–424

Poon TFJ, Hee Ang T (1995) Enhancing entrepreneurial spirit: a resolve for university, graduates. Manage Res News 18(1/2):31–52

Pratt J (2001) Changing patterns of diversity in Europe. Lessons from an OECD study tour. High Educ Manage 13(2):93–105

Prabhu GM (1999) Social entrepreneurial leadership. Career Development International 4/3:140–145 MCB University Press

Rae D, Carswell M (2000) Towards a conceptual understanding of entrepreneurial learning. J Small Bus Enterp Dev 8(2)

Rajan A, van Eupen P, Jaspers A (1997) Britain's flexible labour market. What next? RS50, DfEE and CREATE, Tunbridge Wells

Ravasi D, Turati C (2005) Exploring entrepreneurial learning: a comparative study of technology development projects. J Bus Ventur 20(2005):137–164

Rinne R, Koivula J (2009) The dilemmas of the changing university, Chapter 10 in Shattock, op.cit

Rolfe H (2001) University strategy in an age of uncertainty: the effect of higher education funding on old and new universities. National Institute for Economic and Social Research Discussion paper 191 December

Roman S, Cuestas PJ, Fenollar P (2008) An examination of the interrelationships between self-esteem, others' expectations, family support, learning approaches and academic achievement. Stud High Educ 33(2):127–138

Roos G, Fernstrom F, Gupta O (2005) National innovation systems: Finland, Sweden and Australia Compared. Learnings for Australia, Report for the Australian Business Foundation. Intellectual Capital Service Ltd. 46 Gray's Inn Road, London. WC1X8LR. Email: intcap@intcap.com

Ropke J (1998) The Entrepreneurial University. Innovation, academic knowledge creation and regional development in a globalized economy, Department of Economics, Philipps-Universität Marburg, Germany. (e-mail: roepke@wiwi.uni-marburg.de)

Sa CM (2008) Interdisciplinary strategies in US research universities. Higher Education, Vol. 55, pp 537–552. Published online: 8 June 2007. Springer Science+ Business Media B.V. 2007

Sainsbury (Lord) of Turville (2007) The race to the top. A review of government's science and innovation policies. Norwich: Her Majesty's Stationery Office

Scase R (2007) Global remix. The fight for competitive advantage. Kogan Page, London

Schein EH (1992) Organisational culture and leadership. Jossey Bass Publishers, San Francisco

Schonfield A (2009) What is an effective and high performing governing body in UK higher education? LFHE: http://www.lfhe.ac.uk/publications

Schuetze HG (2007) Research universities and the spectre of academic capitalism. Minerva 45:435–443

Schumpeter JA (1934) Theory of economic development. Harvard Uni-versity Press, Development Cambridge Mass

Segal QW (1985) The Cambridge phenomena. Enterprise House Histon, Cambridge

Senges M (2007) Knowledge entrepreneurship in universities. Practice and strategy in the case of internet based innovation appropriation. Doctoral Thesis. Universitat Oberta de Catalunya Barcelona Spain

Shane S, Stuart T (2002) Organizational Endowments and the performance of University Start-Ups, Management Science, Vol. 48, No. 1, Special Issue on University Entrepreneurship and Technology Transfer (Jan 2002), pp 154–170

Shane S (2004) Encouraging university entrepreneurship? The effect of the Bayh-Dole Act on university patenting in the United States. J Bus Ventur 19(2004):127–151

Shattock M (2000) Strategic management in European universities in an age of increasing institutional self reliance. Tert Educ Manage 6:93–104

Shattock M (ed) (2009) Entrepreneurialism in universities and the knowledge economy. Diversification and organisational change in European higher education, society for research in higher education and the Open University Press, UK

Shinn T (2002) The Triple Helix and new production of knowledge: prepackaged thinking on science and technology. Soc Stud Sci 32:599

Slaughter S, Leslie LL (1997) Academic capitalism. Politics, policies and the Entre-preneurial University, John Hopkins University Press, London

Smith D (1999) The changing idea of a university' Chap. 8. In: Smith and Langslow (eds) The idea of a university, Higher Education Policy, Series 51, Jessica Kingsley Publishers London and Philadelphia

Smith HL (2007) Universities, innovation, and territorial development: a review of the evidence. Environ Plann C: Gov Policy 25:98–114

Sporn B (1996) Managing university culture: an analysis of the relationship between institutional culture and management approaches. High Educ 32(1):41–61

Tadmor Z (2004) The triad research university or a post 20th century research university model. Int J Educ Adv 17(2):167–182

Thomas E (2004) Increasing voluntary giving to Higher Education, Task Force Report to Government, UK Department for Education and Skills

Thorn K, Soo M (2006) Latin American universities and the third Mission. Trends, challenges and policy options, World Bank Policy Research Working Paper 4002, August

Toakley AR (2004) Globalisation. Sustainable development and universities. High Educ Policy 17:311–324

Todorovic WZ et al. (2005) Making university departments more entrepreneurial. The perspective from within. Entrepreneurship and Innovation, May 2005, pp 115–122

UNESCO (2003) Internationalisation of higher education: trends and developments since 1998. Meeting of higher education partners, background paper prepared by the international association of universities. UNESCO Paris,

UNESCO (2004) Higher education in a globalized society, UNESCO education position paper. UNESCO, Paris

UNESCO (2007) Main transformations, challenges and emerging patterns in higher education systems. UNESCO Forum on Higher Education, Research and Knowledge Occasional Paper Series Paper no. 16. UNESCO, Paris

Universities UK (2007) Spending Review 2007, Securing the Future, Policy Briefing Note

US Department of Education (2006) A test of leadership. Charting the Future of U. S. Higher Education, A Report of the Commission Appointed by Secretary of Education Margaret Spellings. Washington, Online: http://www.ed.gov/about/bdscomm/list/hiedfuture/index.html

Vaira M (2004) Globalization and higher education organizational change: a framework for analysis. High Educ 48:483–510

van Vught F (2008) Mission Diversity and Reputation in Higher Education. Higher Education Policy, 2008, 21, (151–174). International Association of Universities 0952-8733/08 $30.00. www.palgrave-journals.com/hep

Vecchio RP (2003) Entrepreneurship and leadership: common trends and common threads. Human Resour Manage Rev 13(2003):303–327

Viale R, Etzkowitz H (2005) Third academic revolution: Polyvalent knowledge; the "DNA" of the Triple Helix.

Volkmann C (2004) Entrepreneurial studies in higher education. High Educ Eur 29(2):177–185

Wasser H (1990) Changes in the European University: from traditional to Entrepreneurial. High Educ Q 44(2):110–122

Watson D (2008) Businesses or Business-like? Some thoughts on cultural convergence, pp 25–28 in Herrmann op cit

Weerts DJ (2007) Toward an engagement model of institutional advancement at public colleges and universities. Int J Educ Adv 7(2)

Wenger E (1998) Communities of practice: learning, meaning and identity. Cambridge University Press, Cambridge

Westwood A (2000) Winners and losers in the World of Work. Employment policy institute and academy of enterprise. London, pp 64

Williams G (2009) Finance and entrepreneurial activity in higher education in the knowledge society. Chapter 2. In: Shattock M (ed) Entrepreneurialism in universities and the knowledge economy, Open University Press. McGraw-Hill Education, pp 9–33

Williams G, Kitaev I (2005) Overview of national policy contexts for entrepreneurialism in higher education institutions. High Educ Manage Policy 17(3):125–141

Williamson T, Read E, Sarmiento T (2009) Enterprise societies—Are they necessary? Article provided by Mr. Williamson

Wissema JG (2008) Towards the third generation university: managing the university in transition. Edward Elgar

Ylinenpää H (2001) Science parks, clusters and regional development. Luleå University of Technology; Department of Business Administration and Social Sciences, Division of Industrial Organization & Small Business Academy. Luleå University of Technology: AR 2001: 48. Paper presented at 31st European Small Business Seminar in Dublin, Sept 12–14

Zhou Ch (2008) Emergence of the entrepreneurial university in evolution of the triple helix. J Technol Manage China 3(1):109–126

Zumeta W (2007) Financing higher education access in challenging times, The NEA 2007 almanac of higher education. NEA, Washington

Part II
Embedding in the Economic and Social System

Chapter 3
Reinventing Learning and Research in the Twenty-First Century via the Academic Firm and the Entrepreneurial University

Elias G. Carayannis and Piero Formica

"Mode 3" and "Quadruple-Helix" Architectures of Government, University,Industry and Society in the GloCal Knowledge Economy

3.1 Introduction and Definition of Terms and Concepts

> "The challenge for a lot of business schools is how to develop leaders and not managers", said James Tran, a candidate for an M.B.A. and a master's in public administration at Harvard. Many of the top schools are moving in that direction, he said, but "I don't think they have actually figured out how to do that in the most effective way".
>
> "Re-training Business Schools", NY Times, March 14, 2009.

Universities can be rightly considered the heart and soul of sustainable entrepreneurship leading to robust competitiveness as they act as generators of new and unique knowledge and as global trade shifts increasingly from the trade of commodities goods to the trade of knowledge-based tasks and services in terms of total value added.

In that sense, universities play a very important role in the knowledge economy that is now taking shape. As society changes, the role of universities inevitably changes as well. New capabilities are becoming essential. There is no given single model to be applied, but for universities to fulfill their potential, there must be room for dynamic and complex processes and competence development and leveraging pivoting on higher order learning (Carayannis 2000) as well as sustainable entrepreneurship

E. G. Carayannis (✉)
The George Washington University, 515 C Funger Hall 2201 G St NW,
WA 20052 Washington, D.C, USA
e-mail: caraye@gwu.edu

P. Formica
International Entrepreneurship Academy, Innovation Value Institute,
National University, Maynooth, CO Kildare, Ireland
e-mail: piero.formica@gmail.com

A. Altmann and B. Ebersberger (eds.), *Universities in Change*, Innovation, Technology, and Knowledge Management, DOI: 10.1007/978-1-4614-4590-6_3,

leading to robust competitiveness (Carayannis 2009) in a socio-economic and political framework of democratic capitalism (Carayannis and Kaloudis 2009).

We define sustainable entrepreneurship as the creation of viable, profitable, and scalable firms. Such firms engender the formation of self-replicating and mutually enhancing innovation networks and knowledge clusters (innovation ecosystems), leading toward robust competitiveness (Carayannis 2009).

We understand robust competitiveness to be a state of economic being and becoming that avails systematic and defensible 'unfair advantages' to the entities that are part of the economy. Such competitiveness is built on mutually complementary and reinforcing low-, medium-, and high-technology and public and private sector entities (government agencies, private firms, universities, and non-governmental organizations) (Carayannis 2009). Robust competitiveness results from an emerging twenty-first century Innovation Ecosystem (also called 'Mode 3' Innovation Ecosystem) (Carayannis and Campbell 2006, 2009).

The concepts of robust competitiveness and sustainable entrepreneurship are pillars of a regime that we call 'democratic capitalism' (as opposed to 'popular or casino capitalism'), in which real opportunities for education and economic prosperity are available to all, and especially—but not only—younger people. These are the direct derivative of a collection of top-down policies as well as bottom-up initiatives (including strong R&D policies and funding, but going beyond these to include the development of innovation networks and knowledge clusters across regions and sectors) (Carayannis and Kaloudis 2009).

3.2 The Academic Firm Versus The Entrepreneurial University: Implications for Policy and Practice

> 'It is so obvious that something big has failed', said Ángel Cabrera, dean of the Thunderbird School of Global Management in Glendale, Ariz. 'We can look the other way, brag about. We cannot say, Well, it wasn't our fault when there is such a systemic, widespread failure of leadership'.
>
> 'Re-training Business Schools', NY Times, March 14, 2009

The 'academic firm' should be understood as a concept or thought. Whether academic firm exists or diffuses and proliferates in the real world of business still represents an open question. Principles of the academic firm can address a whole firm and/or only a subunit of a firm. Similarly, as universities are confronted with different demands (teaching, research, and innovation), also firms may have to balance the following two paradigms either within the boundaries of the same company or within a cluster of firm arrangements: the 'commercial firm' (maximizing/optimizing profit) and the 'academic firm' (maximizing/optimizing knowledge and innovation). Also, firms represent a type of organization that must integrate a diversity of (partially competing) paradigms.

We propose the concept of the academic firm as a reaction and adaptation to the increasing importance of knowledge and innovation. Knowledge clusters and innovation networks of entrepreneurial universities and academic firms (academic and commercial firms) generate the synergies and 'creative milieus' for triggering and advancing performance in the knowledge-based knowledge economy and society. Important is the hybridization, which adds on to the diversity and pluralism ('Mode 3'), and does not imply a simple conversion of universities and firms, which in fact would be misleading (and wrong). The academic firm would demonstrate an extension of the world of academia to the world of business (e.g., 'academic culture and values', high-quality publishing, and life-long learning).

The entrepreneurial university also demonstrates a partial extension of business elements to the world of academia. Implications of the academic firm are that some concepts or strategies (such as publishing versus patenting) may be discussed in parallel for academia and business. 'Academic entrepreneurship' is being granted with an expanded meaning. Hybrid configurations of knowledge clusters and innovation networks may be approached from an organizational (university and firm) perspective or from the perspective of the individual (the individual entrepreneur). Academic entrepreneurship ties such features together, creating an academic knowledge entrepreneur.

The more money governments put into elite universities, the better those institutions will perform, with the associated benefits for the national R&D system, and the more likely it is that their academics' work will be published in highly reputed journals. This is a cherished tenet of most European public educational and research policies, which are currently under attack (Aghion 2006, 2008).

Yet, the strategy of concentrating public money on the 'citadel' of a few select academic institutions for the dual purpose of education and research (as is done, for example, in Germany, Sweden, and the UK) is highly questionable. What matters far more is the creation of a free and 'co-opetitive' environment which, through the interrelated forces of competition and cooperation, will spur all universities—not just the most prestigious—to innovative excellence across all aspects of their activities.

In the 'gloCalizing' (globalizing and localizing) knowledge economy and society, the ideas and knowledge marketplace is not divided into towns and regions but into affinity groups that derive from a high propensity to sociability and are structured by knowledge creation, diffusion, and use modalities (in other words, 'knowledge-ducts' along which flow 'knowledge nuggets' such as innovation networks and knowledge clusters—see Carayannis and Gonzalez 2003).

We therefore propose that universities, university-related institutions, and firms should join together in innovation networks and knowledge clusters (Carayannis and Campbell 2006; Curley and Formica (forthcoming)). The complementary and mutually reinforcing roles of academic firms and entrepreneurial universities are crucial for advanced knowledge-based economies and societies—and they should be at the heart of any strategy to reinvent learning and research in the twenty-first century. Despite the significant functional differences between universities and firms, there is the potential for productive overlap between entrepreneurial universities and academic firms, thanks to the fact that such organizations can engage more easily in university-business research networks. National governments should deploy public resources in accordance with three key strategies (Carayannis and Formica 2008):

- increasing the independence of universities,
- introducing more competition between universities, and
- channeling funds to departments that excel in multiple ways.

To stimulate competition between universities, national governments should liberate them from the rigid regime of tuition fees and student recruitment. Each university should have the right to specialize as it chooses, fixes its own fees for tuition, and selects its own students. Quality control and measurement are needed, but not in ways that stifle differentiation, innovation, and renewal. To achieve a state of successful competition, the life-long tenure of professors must also be ended. This would trigger a healthy process of horizontal and vertical mobility for scientists, researchers, and teachers (ibid).

New foundations are needed for an innovative learning environment that will epitomize the knowledge city of the twenty-first century renaissance. Here, academics will indeed become entrepreneurs of the mind, in the business of 'growing' people intellectually, culturally, and spiritually (Carayannis 2001).

3.3 Brain Circulation: Wandering Students Thrive in the 'Academic Firm' and 'Entrepreneurial University' Contexts

> Academics are Entrepreneurs of the Mind in the business of growing people intellectually, culturally, and spiritually.
>
> Elias G. Carayannis, Invited Lecture, World Bank/IFC, April 2001

Diversity makes the power of difference. It creates an intercultural context of mobility and integration rather than a multi-cultural context of emigration and separation. Open boundaries, education without borders, new connections, both physical and virtual journeys into other places and disciplines: all these are ingredients that foster new ideas.Thanks to mobility within the network, informal circles of exchange take shape that are sources of creativity and cross-fertilization of ideas.

Brain circulation can be defined as the international mobility of entrepreneurial scholars, teachers, and students, which gives birth to a collegiate society that incorporates a variety of influences, trades ideas, and makes easier the movement of the entrepreneurial knowledge nomads instead of forcing people to emigrate.

The 'brain circulation' concept has been recognized by a number of scholars and development agencies as a central one to catalyzing and accelerating sustainable development driven by science, technology, and innovation including a conference at the World Bank (April 30, 2009).

3.4 Multilayered Brain Circulation: The Role of STI Partnerships in Capacity Building

Dr. Kiyoshi Kurokawa, Former Science Adviser to the Japanese Cabinet and leading Japanese advocate on science and technology innovation, led discussions at the World Bank with experts from government, academia, and the private sector, on science, technology, and innovation (STI) capacity building for sustainable development and the potential role of the World Bank Group in brokering these strategic partnerships. STI partnerships have been established in order to reduce poverty, achieve the Millennium Development Goals, generate wealth, create better paying jobs, and foster sustainable development.

Innovative proposals for STI partnership programs include: A visiting professor program, referred to as a 'Professor Corps' where accomplished professors spend a significant amount of time in a developing country, focusing on building capacity for the indigenous scientific community; and a Venture Capitalist in Residence program or 'Venture Corps' where business innovators and entrepreneurs create an interface between the scientific and financing communities for the innovation of new products and services based on local scientific achievements.

The student mobility dimension evokes two societal breakthroughs that, respectively, the Phoenicians and medieval communities of scholars made by intuition rather than through a laborious linear logical process, which was the style of innovation embraced by the ancient Greeks.

The Phoenician travels and displacements spanned geographical barriers and shrunk the world of education. They generated interactive spaces for knowledge creation, knowledge dissemination, and knowledge sharing.

The circulation of professors and students, and the resulting exchange of ideas in a climate of freedom, gave birth in medieval Europe to centers of higher education as guilds of wandering scholars (clerici vagantes). The first was the Studium of Bologna around AD 1088.

Both the Phoenicians and medieval scholars showed how the culture of transnationality produces 'flexible citizenship (…) that induce(s) subjects to respond fluidly and opportunistically to changing political-economic conditions' (Karam 2001).

That form of mobility and the resulting intellectual exchanges foreshadowed those processes of cultural integration, knowledge creation, and result-oriented innovation actions that unfolded all through the Renaissance movement. Brain circulation triggered off nine inventions that were developed during the Renaissance: Clocks, Gunpowder and Artillery, Eye Glasses and Spectacles, Printing Presses, Flush Toilets, Microscopes, Telescopes, Submarines, and the Match. In turn, these inventions enticed the creation of economic value afterwards.

The university cities of the Middle Age used to harbor for a while students from other communities. Each of them played to his or her strengths, rather than ape the host university city. Along the route the clerici vagantes were pollinators of new ideas and projects that made the university cities wealthy.

Today's brain circulation is a very important driver of entrepreneurial growth. It refers to the flow of ideas, from clever young nationals who go abroad to study, then take a job abroad, and later bring back the fruits of that study and working experience to their home country. Some authors believe that this form of migration will increase in the future in some regions, especially if economic disparities between countries continue to diminish. Such a circular migration, for example, has been observed among Indians and Malaysians who had studied, respectively, in the United States and Australia. Notably, India, which has been deeply affected by the diaspora of brainpower that went in the direction of Silicon Valley, is experimenting with the new form of brain circulation that nourish tech entrepreneurship and fast moving start-ups in both nations.

During the 1990s, this was a vast phenomenon that mainly affected the emerging economies, with the United States having benefited heavily from this migration. By contrast, the mobility rather than the migration of high-powered intellectual assets stimulates the international transfer of ideas from the university to the marketplace and fosters international collaboration between academics and business people.

While the migration of high-powered intellectual assets enlarges the productivity gap, the international mobility of highly educated, talented young people helps to close that gap since it implies a two-way flow of entrepreneurship-led innovation between a sending country and a receiving country. This movement, in one way, holds off the phenomenon of brain waste that occurs when highly skilled workers migrate into forms of employment not requiring the application of the skills and experience applied in the former job. It also promotes the creation of 'nations of entrepreneurs' dedicated to transferring ideas from university to market, and fostering collaboration between academia and the business community.

A circuit of native missionaries like those in the Middle Age is a fertile ground for 'glocal' communities where the local dimension turns into a local and global dimension. One of the most striking examples of the formation of 'glocal' communities is the circuit of students that links Mumbai and Bangalore, Beijing and Shanghai with London, Boston, and California.

Twinning entrepreneurial projects cultivated at the university sites within the circuit open up the door to successful entrepreneurial-friendly environments that, in turn, foster new and emerging high-growth business communities.

Entrepreneurial universities design and manage global networks, onsite and online, which are created and developed by means of worldwide alliances with learning partners and business organisations that link student-centred learning to on-the-job activities. In such a co-operative environment participants can cultivate new business ideas and turn them into commercial realities.

Participants can move from one learning location to another and, in each location, the diversity and ethnic mix of both the student population and the faculty members play an important part in reducing the risk of a brain drain from developing countries and regions and enhancing the opportunity benefits resulting from the increased mobility or 'brain circulation' and manifested as strategic knowledge serendipity and strategic knowledge arbitrage events and processes (Carayannis 2008).

The network is an international platform for the mobility of the higher education communities of practice. These communities bring together in cross-functional teams academics and practitioners from around the world. The integration of thinkers from industrial and consultant backgrounds with their academic counterparts strengthens the quality of educational programmes. Each partner adds value to the network, but the real value of it is greater than the sum of the individual parts. What makes the difference is a synergistic collaborative process involving people with complementary competencies, which results in a symbiotic learning network.

Appropriate actions should be implemented through a combination of 'academic firms' and 'entrepreneurial universities'. This is a matter in regard to which responsibility has to be placed upon the shoulders of those who are responsible for changing the academic foundations on which human capital has been built during the machine age. The new foundations should set the stage for an innovative learning environment that epitomizes the clever polis or the knowledge city of the twenty-first century renaissance. Here knowledge and skills are encouraged, the love of learning and an inquiring mind are fostered, creativity and imagination are emphasized, and a digital-connected collective intelligence is designed to maximize the creative collaboration of small groups of entrepreneurial people addressing issues that interest and concern them all.

3.5 The International Entrepreneurship Dimension of Brain Circulation

> As in international entrepreneurship the world is our community, people mobility and intellectual exchanges are qualifying elements of the international dimension of entrepreneurship (Andersson et al. 2010).

International entrepreneurship spans cultural boundaries, emerging as a breakaway pattern of entrepreneurial activity with high expectations to grow. Instrumental in setting the trend for global born/stateless/cross-border/cross-cultural international start-ups has been a dramatic shift in the entrepreneurial environment from a local to a transnational focus.

Founders of international start-ups draw resources from and sell their goods in multiple countries from the very early stage of their development (Mc Dougall and Oviatt 2003). Among international start-ups there are those new ventures whose scope extends well beyond their globally dispersed mode to an organization without a clear national identity that thrives on the diversity of its cross-country founders. There needs to be a high level of trust between the stateless start-ups' founders—which allows them to be split between the different locations with the twofold role of developing high trust relationships between the cross-border parties and teams, and operating the globally dispersed units as if they were one (Halperin 2001).

Student mobility can serve the purpose of creating international start-ups and also an intercultural dimension. In fact, brain circulation is a vehicle for borderless thinking, cultural curiosity, and cross-cultural activities, which triggers a process conducive to the creation of start-ups whose operations are across borders. They are endowed with a mixed background that covers both cultural diversity and regional identity. In addition, those start-ups are adept at tapping into a global talent pool to form a hybrid management team and enticing knowledgeable founding entrepreneurs from the targeted markets, who complement each other on each other's home turf.

The challenge is how to get a small organization formed by students who decide to pool their resources almost from the start to think like a global organization. By playing the role of matchmakers and thereby building networks of contacts with students, the co-evolution of entrepreneurial universities and academic firms may have much to contribute to the creation of small entrepreneurial student teams that are cross-cultural and cross-country. The co-evolution can also serve the purpose of providing experimental labs, which helps to limit the exposure to risk and uncertainty in the course of actions once field experiments must be carry out in the marketplace (Curley and Formica 2008).

In experimental labs Knowledge-to-Business Achievement Teams (KBATs) of international students aiming at the creation of cross-border and across cultural boundaries firms make experiments in evaluating the performance and function of markets. The results give them a deeper understanding of the actual workings of real-world markets. Experiments also point out how vitally important are the "rules of the game", laws, regulations, customs, truth, and honesty in affecting both individual behavior and market outcomes.

Each KBAT constitutes a knowledge pool—a collective networked intelligence of knowledge-driven individuals with an entrepreneurial mindset, who can extend their knowledge to recognize business opportunities where others do not, to prove the power of their business concepts and to stretch out their capabilities by forging relationships with other KBAT members.

3.5.1 The Knowledge-to-Business Achievement Team

The following intangible assets contribute to build the platform for the KBAT:

Teambuilding to form a tight team:

- Each player covers a specific but not rigid role.
- Each player comes to terms with strengths and weaknesses of all the other players.
  - Creativity and curiosity for exploring key driving forces of the business environment.
  - Brainstorming to generate business ideas and to make business simulations.
- Observatory to get the maximum of information and knowledge of business opportunities.

- Co-opetition, a judicious mixture of competition and co-operation, to shape new business relationships and new forms of enterprises as well.
- Implementation and action to devote more energy to achieving gain than to avoiding loss.

In the KBAT context, connectivity and conductivity nurture a sense of community. By driving toward the access of everyone to everyone, everything to everything, and everything to everyone, connectivity creates circles of exchanges and facilitates journeys into other disciplines and business fields as well (see also the chapter 'Knowledge of Culture and Culture of Knowledge from Low-Tech to High-Tech' by Carayannis and Popescu in (Carayannis and Chanaron 2007)).

Bibliography

Andersson T, Curley M, Formica P (2010) Knowledge-driven entrepreneurship: the key to social and economic transformation. Springer, New York

Aghion P (2006) Primer on innovationinnovation and growth, Bruegel Policy Brief, October

Aghion P (2008) Higher aspirations: an agenda for reforming european universities. Bruegel blueprint, 5 July

Carayannis EG, Chanaron JJ (2007) Leading and managing creators, inventors and innovators: the art science and craft of fostering creativity, triggering invention and catalyzing innovationinnovation. Praeger Publishers, NY

Carayannis EG (2008) Knowledge-driven creative destruction: strategic knowledge serendipity and arbitrage as real options drivers triggered by co-opetition, co-evolutionco-evolution, and co-specialization. J Ind High Educ 22(6):343–353 December 2008

Carayannis EG (2009) Firm formation dynamics. *International Journal of Innovation and Regional Development* 1(3):

Carayannis EG, Kaloudis A (2009) A time to lead and a time to act: democratic capitalism and a new 'new deal' for the US and the world, Japan Economic Currents, January

Carayannis EG, Campbell DFJ (2009) Mode 3 and quadruple helix. Int J Technol Manage 46:3–4

Carayannis EG, Formica P (2008) Knowledge matters. MacMillan/Palgrave Press, NY

Carayannis EG, Formica P (2007) The concentration of resources and academic performance: reinventing learning and research. J Ind High Educ 21(2):121–123

Carayannis EG, Campbell DF (eds) (2006) Knowledge creation, diffusion and use in innovation networks and knowledge clusters: a comparative systems approach across the United States Europe and Asia. Praeger, CN

Carayannis EG, Gonzalez E (2003) Creativity and innovation = competitiveness? when, how, and why'. In: Shavinina LV (ed) The international handbook on innovationinnovation. Pergamon, Amsterdam, pp 587–606 especially at 593

Carayannis EG (2001) Academics as entrepreneurs of the mind, invited lecture, World Bank, IFC, April

Carayanns EG (2000) The strategic management of technological learning. CRC Press, Boca Raton

Curley M, Formica P (2008) Laboratory experiments as a tool in the empirical economic analysis of high-expectation entrepreneurship. J Ind High Educ 22(6):355–363

Curley M, Formica P (forthcoming) University ecosystems design creative spaces for start-up experimentation. J Ind High Educ

Formica P (2003) Industry and knowledge clusters: principles, practices, policy. Tartu University Press, Estonia

Formica P (2005) The argument for international entrepreneurship in the knowledge economy. In: Structural change in Europe—entrepreneurial spirit in cities and regions, Hagbarth Publications

Halperin A (2001) Globally dispersed startups—Executive summary of research Conducted at the Sloan School of Management at MIT

Karam JT (2001) Review of flexible citizenship: the cultural logics of transnationality by aiwha ong (Duke University Press, 1999). Anthropol Quart 74(1):45–46

McDougall PP, Oviatt BM (2003) Some fundamental issues in international entre-preneurship, Kelly School of Business, Indiana University, July, Mimeo

Chapter 4
Demographic Trends and the Internationalisation of Higher Education: Emerging Challenges and Prospects

Joe Nellis and David Slattery

Understanding demographic trends is key to the survival of universities over the next two decades
(Sir Muir Russell, vice-president of Universities UK, March 2008).

4.1 Introduction

Demography plays a major role in education, with key policies determined by the composition of populations. The pace and dynamics of population change are crucial to educational planning. The size of the school-age population determines the potential demand for higher education. Regional birth rates, migratory flows and geographic distribution of populations will directly impact educational costs, decisions on school types and academic recruitment (Mizikaci and Baumgartl 2007).

The purpose of this chapter is to survey the changing world demographic profile and to consider the implications for institutions of higher education. We examine the implications primarily from the perspective of the developed world.

This chapter is structured as follows. We first present the evidence of demographic change, comparing developed regions with developing regions and examining geographical differences. We also look at the variation within regions. We then put the observed demographic changes in the wider context of economic, social and political change taking place across the world. We move on to consider the perspective and objectives of institutions of higher education as preparation for

J. Nellis (✉) · D. Slattery
Cranfield University School of Management,
Bedford, Cranfield,
MK43 0AL, UK
e-mail: j.g.nellis@cranfield.ac.uk

D. Slattery
e-mail: david.slattery.phd.02@cranfield.ac.uk

A. Altmann and B. Ebersberger (eds.), *Universities in Change*, Innovation, Technology, and Knowledge Management, DOI: 10.1007/978-1-4614-4590-6_4,

an examination of the challenges and prospects for those institutions in the context of the changing world. Finally, we provide a summary of the key points and draw together the main conclusions.

Table 4.1 Population trends—average annual increment and growth rates (differences between developed and less developed regions)

	Population (millions)		Average annual increment (millions)		Annual growth rate (%)	
	2007	2050	2005–2010	2045–2050	2005–2010	2045–2050
More developed regions	1217	1236	3	−1	0.24	−0.10
Less developed regions	5398	7840	73	35	1.34	0.45

Source United Nations (2007)

4.2 The Changing World Demographic Picture

The United Nations (2007) reports that the rate of growth in the world's population is declining but there are substantial differences between countries and regions. In the developed world, population levels have almost reached a peak and will start to decline slowly from around 2030. In the developing world, however, most countries have fertility levels above replacement levels and populations are set to grow. Table 4.1 below illustrates the differences between developed and less developed regions. The developing world provides almost all the world's annual population increase in the decades ahead.

Table 4.2 below shows the geographical distribution which lies behind these general population trends. Population levels are already declining in Europe but are still rising elsewhere, particularly in Asia which will contribute most to the increase in numbers in the short to medium term. The highest growth rates are in Africa.

Population levels are affected by migration, particularly from the developing world to the developed world. In the period 2000–2005, immigration contributed about three quarters of the population growth of developed countries. If current trends continue, between 2010 and 2030 net immigration is likely to account for virtually all the population growth in the more developed regions.

The other significant phenomenon revealed by the United Nations data is the extent of population ageing—that is, the percentage of people over 60 is increasing while the percentage of children under 15 is falling. In the developed world, the percentage of older people (21 %) now exceeds the percentage of children (17 %). By 2050, the proportion of older persons in the developed world is expected to rise to 32 % while the proportion of children will fall to 16 %. The developing world is, however, still relatively young. Only 8 % of the population of developing countries is over 60 while 30 % are under 15, although these figures will start to come together in the coming decades.

Table 4.2 Population trends—average annual increment and growth rate—geographical distribution

	Population (millions)		Average annual increment (millions)		Annual growth rate (%)	
	2007	2050	2005–2010	2045–2050	2005–2010	2045–2050
Africa	945	1937	20	23	2.11	1.21
Asia	3996	5217	45	10	1.12	0.19
Europe	728	653	−1	−2	−0.07	−0.37
Latin America and Caribbean	576	783	7	2	1.29	0.22
North America	337	438	3	2	0.91	0.38
Oceania	34	48	0	0	1.15	0.45

Source United Nations (2007)

The World Bank (2007) reports that today, around 1.5 billion of the world's population are aged between 12 and 24, the largest cohort of young people ever. Around 1.3 billion of these cohorts are in the developing world. In the developed world, the number of people aged 12–24 is set to decline but in many parts of the developing world the numbers have yet to peak. Table 4.3 below shows the numbers for different regions of the developing world, together with the trends.

Over the developing world as a whole, the number of young people in this age range will remain fairly stable until 2035 and will then decline gradually. But the distribution across the continents will change significantly, with a very substantial

Table 4.3 Numbers of people aged 12–24 in 2007 (millions) and expected changes (developing countries only)

Region	People aged 12–24 in 2007	Expected trends	Estimate of people aged 12–24 in 2030
Europe and Central Asia	100	Declining now	80
Middle East and North Africa	100	Will peak in next 25 years	110
East Asia and Pacific	450	Set to decline	380
South Asia	400	Will peak in next 25 years	430
Latin America and Caribbean	140	Peaking now	140
Sub-Saharan Africa	200	Will peak in about 20 years	340

Source World Bank (2007)

increase in Sub-Saharan Africa.

Moreover, young people in the developing world are better educated than their parents as a result of initiatives to improve basic education, such as the World Conference on Education for All (EFA) in Jomtien in 1990 and the Dakar World

Forum on Education in 2000. The very success of EFA has been producing some of the largest cohorts of young school leavers ever recorded in some countries (King 2009). It is particularly notable that the developing world is now producing twice as many university educated professionals than the developed world (McKinsey 2008).

King (2009) expresses concern about whether EFA is sustainable. Countries may not have the economic and political environments to maintain current progress in the absence of external aid. The World Bank (2007) raises concerns about the quality of basic education. In standardised tests, students in developing countries still lag behind those in OECD countries. McKinsey (2008) raises questions about the validity of some educational qualifications from the developing world. But despite these issues, educational standards are improving substantially. This will undoubtedly lead to an increase in demand for higher education from the increasing numbers of young people living in the developing countries.

Further, young people now represent a significant proportion of the world's international migrants. The chance of obtaining an education in another country is one of the main motives for youth migration. In Niger, for example, many more young people go on to study in France than remain in tertiary education at home. The number of students abroad from Albania, Cameroon, Jamaica, Kenya and Malaysia exceeds 20 % of those in tertiary education at home (World Bank 2007). Universities UK (2008) reports that the number of students at UK higher educational institutions from outside the European Economic Area rose steadily from 98,000 in 1994/5 to 239,000 in 2006/7. The World Bank (2007) reports a similar trend within the OECD generally. The increasing demand for education in the developed world from students in developing countries is therefore already manifest.

Another significant factor in the demographic change across the developing world, identified by the World Bank, is the decline in the relative size of the 12–24 age group compared with the age group 25–60. Although the number of young people aged 12–24 in many parts of the developing world is growing, the number of those aged 25–60 is growing even more rapidly. This in turn leads to a reduction in the dependency ratio; the numbers of people aged 0–15 and 65+ compared with the population aged 15–64 (that is, those of normal working age). The World Bank sees this as a window of opportunity to improve economic growth by investment in young people. This is referred to again below.

4.3 Patterns of Demographic Change Within Regions of the World

The data in the tables above conceal some significant variations within regions. In the developing areas of Europe and Central Asia where the number of young people is set to fall overall, there are areas, such as Turkey and Tajikistan, where

Table 4.4 Educational enrolment rates in Sub-Saharan Africa

	Enrolment rates percent		
	Age 12–14	Age 15–17	Age 18–24
South Africa	96	90	43
Namibia	94	84	40
Kenya	92	77	22
Uganda	92	72	20
Cape Verde	91	63	21
Malawi	90	80	33
Swaziland	90	76	25
Lesotho	86	60	19
Ghana	85	67	22
Zambia	84	69	24
Cameroon	83	63	28
Tanzania	78	49	9
Rwanda	77	40	14
Sierra Leone	77	61	31
Sao Tome & Principe	76	48	14
Niger	69	43	25
Senegal	68	38	23
Benin	65	49	23
Nigeria	64	58	36
Cote d'Ivoire	61	39	17
Mozambique	58	37	10
Angola	55	45	18
Mauritania	53	39	20
Burundi	52	36	19
Guinea	36	29	13
Burkina Faso	32	20	9

Source World Bank (2007)

youth populations are set to rise (World Bank 2007). In Europe, some countries such as Germany, Denmark, Spain, France, the UK and Ireland have seen net immigration which has maintained population levels and will lead to a second generation of immigrants requiring tertiary education. Eastern European countries, however, have witnessed net emigration, which will lead to a reduction in demand for tertiary education (Mizikaci and Baumgartl 2007).

In East Asia and the Pacific region also, while the number of young people is set to decline, some countries such as Indonesia and Vietnam are peaking now, a few such as Malaysia and the Philippines will peak in the next 20 years while Cambodia will not peak in the foreseeable future. In Latin America and the Caribbean, Argentina, Brazil, Chile and Costa Rica have peaked or are peaking shortly. Others such as Nicaragua and Peru will peak in the next 20 years.

In Sub-Saharan Africa, the window of opportunity referred to by the World Bank is yet to open (see Table 4.4). In Uganda, for example, the dependency ratio will not start to fall until after 2015. Across the region as a whole, the average annual population growth rate is 2.3 % and the proportion of people under the age of 15 is 44 %. The population growth rate varies, however, within the region, from 0.5 % in South Africa to 3.4 % in Niger and 4.4 % in Eritrea. The proportion of people under 15 varies from 33 % in South Africa to 49 % in Niger. More importantly, from the point of view of tertiary education, the educational enrolment rates (the percentage of people attending school or university) varies very considerably across the region, as shown in Table 4.4.

South Africa and Namibia head the table in terms of enrolment rates for each age range. Kenya and Uganda follow closely for ages 12–14 and 15–17 but their enrolment rates for tertiary education are only half that of South Africa and Namibia. It is also interesting to compare Tanzania and Rwanda with Niger and Senegal. Tanzania and Rwanda have the higher rates of enrolment for ages 12–14 and 15–17 but much lower enrolments for tertiary education. Nigeria is well down the table for the younger age ranges but near the top in terms of tertiary education. There are therefore significant differences between countries in this region in terms of participation rates at various ages.

4.4 Globalisation, Economic Growth, Reducing Poverty and Sustainable Development

The changing demographic patterns across the world as outlined above need to be seen in the context of the phenomenon of globalisation and the development of the world economy. Also important are the economic and social objectives of governments and organisations such as the World Bank and UNESCO.

4.4.1 Globalisation and the Development of the World Economy

Much has been written about globalisation, about what it is, where it came from and where it is going. For the purpose of this chapter we take globalisation as given. Globalisation includes the increasing trade in goods and services across national boundaries. It involves the rapid movement of cash and capital around the world to support that international trade. It includes the increasing movement of people across national boundaries supported by improved transport infrastructures. This international trade and movement of people are in turn promoted by the rapid development of information and communications technology (ICT). Globalisation changes economic and political power balances between regions of the world, with major implications for economic and social welfare. Regions of the world are in competition with each other; some regions are benefiting in terms of economic growth, other regions have so far not been so successful. Social unrest and terrorism, poor health and disease are never far from the surface, particularly in those regions with poor records for both economic performance and political governance.

Globalisation has important direct and indirect implications for education. Education is itself a service which can now be traded across national boundaries. As identified above, an increasing number of students from the developing world are enrolling for higher education in the developed world. Educational institutions are also franchising their degrees and qualifications to institutions in the developing world to enable students to study in their home countries (Bennell and Pearce 2003). Such activities yield much needed revenue for the institutions and, for the countries concerned, this revenue constitutes valuable export earnings, with the potential to replace some of the exports lost for existing goods and services to other regions of the world. Data from Universities UK (2008) show that the income of higher educational institutions from non-EU domiciled students rose from £445 m in 1994/5 to £1,713 m in 2006/7. Data from the UK Office of National Statistics (2008) show that the value of the UK educational exports rose from £1.1 billion in 1987 to £3.8 billion in 2007.

More indirectly, education is influenced by the changing demand for skilled human resources from companies operating in national and international markets. McKinsey consultants talk of a "war for talent" between companies, the competition between companies to recruit people with the skills (technical and behavioural) needed in increasingly global markets. Companies face a demographic landscape dominated by the looming retirement of the 'baby boomer' generation in the developed world and by a dearth of young people entering the workforce in Western Europe. Question marks remain over the appropriateness of the talent in many emerging markets. Surveys of companies reveal concerns about poor English language skills, dubious educational qualifications and cultural issues such as a reluctance to take leadership roles in job applicants from the developing countries (McKinsey 2008).

4.4.2 The Economic and Social Objectives of Governments, the World Bank and UNESCO

Underpinning initiatives such as EFA is a belief that improving the quality and availability of education will result in reduced unemployment, improved health and engaged citizens. This in turn leads to economic growth and social cohesion. However, the relationship between education, the development of technical and vocational skills relevant for employment, economic growth, sustainable development and social stability are complex (King 2009; Little and Green 2009). Education may be seen as a public good, valuable in its own right, providing the individual with the skills for a healthy and fulfilling life. But to improve the individual's employment prospects, education must provide the skills, both technical and behavioural, which are required by employers.

King (2009) examines the relationship between EFA and technical and vocational skills development (TVSD). There is no automatic connection amongst school, skill and work. The question, therefore, is about the nature of enabling environments in which EFA and TVSD can lead to sustainable poverty reduction and economic growth. Arguably, EFA is unsustainable if it fails to lead to economic progress. The discourse within organisations such as UNESCO has therefore shifted to "Education for Sustainable Development" (ESD). As a result of the World Summit for Sustainable Development in Johannesburg in 2002, a decade of ESD was declared from 2005 to 2014 with UNESCO in the lead. ESD has four elements.

- Improving access to quality basic education.
- Reorienting existing education programmes.
- Developing public understanding and awareness.
- Providing training.

King (2009) critiques the UNESCO approach arguing that it lacks any analysis of how ESD can lead to economic growth and how developing countries can avoid long-term aid dependency. Little and Green (2009) examine the issue of sustainable development in the context of globalisation. They address the issue of the role of the nation state in a globalised world and they raise the question concerning whether failed states, corruption and mismanagement of economic resources are at the heart of much poverty.

To these issues may be added the risk of a "brain drain" from developing nations as migration increases and as competition for talent becomes more intense. Nations which cannot retain their better educated and skilled individuals will struggle to achieve economic growth even if they can conceptualise a route to it.

The World Bank (2007) sees the link between investment in young people and economic growth in the developing world in terms of the demographic window of opportunity created by the falls in the relative size of the youth population aged 12–24 compared with those aged 25–60 and the accompanying fall in the dependency ratio (referred to above). The argument is that many developing countries can anticipate over the next 30 years an increase in their working populations which can provide a platform for economic growth. Investment in young people now will therefore reap rich dividends in the years to come. The World Bank cites research which suggests that much of the higher growth achieved by East Asia over Latin America from 1965 to 1990 can be attributed to the faster growth of its working population and better policies for trade and human capital development (Bloom and Canning 2005). Sound investment in primary education alone contributed about one-third of the growth rate of the East Asian boom economies between 1960 and 1985 (World Bank 1993). But, as noted above, the window of opportunity for Sub-Saharan Africa is yet to open. This means that there is time to plan for it, but it also means, if the World Bank is right, that economic growth in this region may lag the rest of the developing world for many years to come.

Demographic change therefore takes place in the context of some complex economic, political and social issues. These changes and issues present major challenges for educational institutions engaging in the internationalisation of education provision. Before turning to those challenges we need to be clear about the objectives of institutions of higher education in the pursuit of an international strategy.

4.5 Internationalisation of Higher Education: The Perspective of Institutions

In 2003 the International Association of Universities (IAU), a UNESCO-based organisation, published a report entitled Internationalisation of Higher Education: Practices and Priorities. This report followed the issue of a questionnaire to institutions seeking information about the policies and perceptions of institutions towards the internationalisation of higher education. For this purpose, internationalisation was defined as a multi-faceted process which aims to integrate or introduce an international or intercultural dimension into the curriculum, into research and into the service functions of institutions (Knight and de Wit 1997). This process-oriented definition was intended to encompass concepts such as international education, international inter-university cooperation, international linkages, curricular change, cross-border education programmes and academic mobility.

The analysis of the responses to the survey (Knight 2003) showed that the mobility of students and teachers was considered to be the most important reason for making internationalisation a priority and was identified as the fastest growing aspect of an internationalisation strategy. Student, staff and teacher development, academic standards and quality assurance, and international research collaboration are ranked as the most important benefits of internationalisation. However, brain drain and the loss of cultural identity are seen as the greatest risks associated with internationalisation.

According to the IAU, there is a general consensus that the processes of internationalisation as well as globalisation are accelerating. The impact of this on educational institutions is influenced by a number of factors:

- The perceived importance of knowledge for the economic, social and cultural well-being of society worldwide.
- The development of ICT and its application to learning, teaching and research.
- New pressures on institutions to prepare graduates for life and work in an international context.
- The increased mobility of human resources.
- The reduction of public funding for higher education and the increasing pressure on institutions to diversify their funding sources.

The IAU (2003) sees international cooperation as an instrument for capacity building and for finding new ways to manage higher education. International cooperation can be seen, however, as a reconfirmation of the historical roots of the university and of its universal nature rather than as a new or unique phenomenon today. While the increasing interest in internationalisation in recent years is fuelled by globalisation, internationalisation is still driven in large part by academic purposes. The internationalisation strategies of universities are certainly driven in part by the far more competitive environment for students and as a means for raising additional finance. Institutions must also respond to the changing demands from students, employers, the public and other stakeholders. But assuring the quality of education and research requires the exchange of knowledge and expertise across national boundaries.

The IAU recognises, however, the ethical issues raised by internationalisation. It quotes research (Solomon et al. 2003) which suggests that about 20,000 professionals leave Africa annually and are replaced by expatriates, costing the continent $8 billion each year. Professionals emigrate to seek better working conditions or to flee persecution. Africa is not alone in experiencing this outflow. The situation is similar in many of the developing countries of Latin America, Asia and Eastern Europe. There is also a concern that cultural diversity will be undermined by an expansion of the strongest language and dominant culture.

The IAU recognises concerns amongst academics that the financial pressures for internationalisation may compromise academic standards. Increasing competition between institutions may reduce rather than increase cooperation. Economic pressures may compromise the fundamental values on which higher education rests, namely a commitment to the pursuit of knowledge and scientific excellence, access based upon merit, and the acceptance of social responsibilities that include a sense of solidarity with institutions in less developed nations.

Having set out the evidence of demographic change and having outlined the complex set of economic, social, political and ethical issues surrounding the internationalisation of higher education, we now summarise the key challenges and prospects for institutions of higher education. We also address the ways in which institutions can respond to these challenges and take advantage of the opportunities arising.

4.6 Challenges and Prospects for Institutions of Higher Education

4.6.1 The Direct Effects of Demographic Change

Undoubtedly, the most immediate impact of demographic change in the coming years will be upon institutions of higher education in the developed world from the reduction in the number of young people. Universities will be competing amongst each other for a reducing number of suitably qualified students. Governments may intervene to promote wider access to university education. But if this policy is promoted, questions will arise about whether young people who would not previously have entered university have the capacity and the motivation to pursue an academic education. This in turn raises questions about the future calibre of cohorts of graduates and about academic standards generally under a policy of wider access.

The alternative, if the higher educational sector in the developed world is to avoid reducing its capacity, is for institutions to attract an increasing number of students from the developing world. This alternative could be pursued in two ways. First, students could be encouraged to migrate to take up places in developed countries which are no longer filled by indigenous students. Second, institutions could increase their cooperation with institutions in the developing world to enable an increasing number of young people to study in their home country. This would be likely to involve greater mobility of academic staff to support this development.

The first of these strategies, attracting students from the developing world to study in the developed world, raises the ethical issues outlined above. This strategy could lead to increasing migration from countries which need to retain their talented and better educated young people for their own economic, social and political development. There would not be a problem if students did return to their own countries after a period of study but the risk is that they will be inclined to pursue their future careers in the developed world. This strategy also risks diluting cultural diversity as young people become influenced by the dominant languages and cultures of the developed world.

On the other hand it could be argued that, in an increasingly global economy and society, this migration will happen anyway. This phenomenon is not just an issue for higher education. It will arise from the development of global commerce and of international political institutions. Also, the developing world is now providing effective competition for trade in goods and services. The developed world needs to look after its own interests and replace existing exports of goods and services with new sources of earnings. Exploiting a competitive advantage in education provision is entirely justified and will ultimately lead to improved economic welfare worldwide.

The second strategy involving partnerships between institutions in the developed and developing world might be attractive to those institutions in the developed world which place ethical or sustainable development objectives higher on their own list of priorities. This would also match the aspirations of developing countries and so provide a natural synergy which could be beneficial to both developed and developing nations.

A further alternative is for developed countries to have different strategies for different regions of the developing world. Those countries such as China and India which are providing effective economic competition can be assumed to be capable of looking after their own interests. There is, therefore, no ethical issue for institutions in the developed world in pursuing whichever strategy suits their own interests. But for regions such as Sub-Saharan Africa, different considerations could apply. As noted above, this region is yet to enter the window of opportunity provided by a reducing dependency ratio. It is also well recognised as the region which has the greatest problems in terms of economic, social and political development. While educational standards and levels of participation are increasing, many countries still have a long way to go. The more sustainable approach for this region would be the partnership strategy.

The above analysis focuses on the interests of educational institutions in the developed world. The interests of institutions in the developing world could vary according to their respective stages of development. Those regions which are currently successful in the global competitive environment may wish to expand their own educational institutions or set up in partnership to import the expertise of the developed world. Less developed regions may be more dependent upon foreign aid for some years to come. Partnerships may be essential to reduce the risk of brain drain and to develop their own higher educational infrastructures.

Institutions of higher education in developed countries which seek to expand their activities internationally will need to decide which strategy to adopt. They will also need to decide in which regions and in which countries in those regions to target their activities. These decisions will inevitably be affected by current activities and by relationships already established, but to succeed and prosper in an increasingly competitive environment, institutions may need to target new areas. The data presented in this chapter provide a start for the analysis which needs to be conducted by institutions confronting their challenges and making their strategic decisions.

Whatever strategic decisions are made, institutions will face a number of other challenges from demographic change and from the inevitable increase in the internationalisation of higher education. We focus on three key areas: the educational model, faculty development and the implication of new information and communications technology.

4.6.2 The Educational Model

Altbach (1998) identifies the modern university as an international institution with strong national roots. The university was established in medieval Europe and attracted students from across the continent using Latin as the common language. The faculty system emerged from the University of Paris. The collegiate system arose in England. The research ideal emerged in late nineteenth century Germany. The modern American university adopts the English collegiate system and the German research ideal. Almost all the world's universities stem from the European models, driven by colonialism but sometimes by choice, as in the case of Japan; and by the increasing dominance of English as an international language. There were alternatives such as the Islamic model but the Western model has been dominant.

It may be argued, however, that while modern universities have common origins in terms of their educational models, there are differences between national systems. Some emphasise knowledge transfer, others analysis, argument and discourse; some focus strongly on technical skills, others place more value on behavioural skills. All universities are affected by the cultural context in which they operate. These differences have implications for students and for academic staff. Students educated in a system that values knowledge transfer will find difficulty in adapting to a system which values analysis and discussion. Students who specialise in technical skills may need to develop new interpersonal skills, and vice versa. Differences between national systems also affect students moving from one system to another in terms of the recognition of their prior studies and qualifications (Teichter 2004).

As international student mobility increases, and as diversity and cultural sensitivity become more valued, these issues will become increasingly important. Difficult questions arise about the model to be adopted by institutions, particularly those in the dominant developed regions, as they expand their international activities. The questions encompass the content of the curriculum, the style of teaching, the resources to be deployed and the nature of the examination process. Thompson (2001) argues that the appropriate style of learning, leading to the development of individual student characteristics believed to be associated with the generation of international mindedness, is essentially experiential in nature. His focus is on secondary school education but his argument could equally apply to tertiary education. He argues for an appropriately balanced curriculum, an exposure to cultural diversity through human resources and a balance in the selection of materials that promote the acquisition of knowledge, skills, concepts and attitudes.

These issues need to be seen in the context of the dominance of Western economic and political models, sometimes referred to as the 'Washington consensus'. Aid to developing countries is often linked to commitments from those countries towards economic and political reform along Western lines. The dominance of Western ideas has, however, come under increasing pressure from the resurgence of Islam, from the perceived failure of military intervention and more recently from the crisis in financial markets. Are Western ideas still the "best"?

Institutions of higher education in the developed world clearly need to examine their own ideas and methods. There can be no assumption that the current model and the theories in use are valid in an increasingly international context. Possible alternatives need to be considered to deliver the objectives and strategies adopted by the institution. The risk is cultural relativism, the assumption that all ideas are equally valid. While institutions must evaluate different options, they must also make value judgements.

4.6.3 Faculty Development

Whatever choices an institution of higher education makes in terms of its strategy for internationalisation and the education model adopted, there will be significant implications for faculty recruitment and development. Academic staff will need the appropriate competences and attitudes to succeed in an international and culturally diverse environment. Clearly, all staff will need to have an understanding of, and empathy with, different cultures and values. They will need interpersonal and other behavioural skills, including the ability to resolve any conflicts which may arise. Such conflicts are already creating challenges for organisations operating in multi-cultural environments. New legislation in many countries now requires organisations not to discriminate against people on the grounds of their gender, ethnic origin, sexual orientation or religious belief. But ethnic origin and religious belief are often associated and sometimes correlated with attitudes about sexual orientation or gender. Such issues require people working in multi-cultural environments to have new cognitive and behavioural skills together with an appropriate attitudinal approach.

A further issue is concerned with the question of language skills. English is increasingly becoming an international language but academic staff will need competence in the languages spoken in the regions in which they are operating. This is not just for day-to-day communication but valuing cultural diversity requires the recognition and use of different languages. This is a particular challenge in the English speaking world as the widespread use of English worldwide militates against the development of language skills among those who's first, and maybe only language, is English.

Academic staff, as teachers, will also need to be able to impart these skills and attitudes to their students. Educational institutions are under increasing pressure to prepare their students for life and work in an international context. This inevitably means a broadening of the curriculum but it also requires academic staff to behave at all times with their students in a way which is consistent with the behaviours and attitudes that the institutions seek to impart. It is incumbent on all organisations, commercial, governmental, voluntary or educational; to train and develop their employees in the skills and attitudes required to operate in an international context. But educational institutions have a leading role to play in developing young people in these skills and attitudes and institutions have a special imperative therefore to develop their faculty staff appropriately.

A closely related issue for institutions is their recruitment policy. An organisation which seeks to promote an understanding of cultural diversity needs to be itself culturally diverse. There is a clear advantage for an organisation to have a workforce that reflects the customer and client base it seeks to serve. Many organisations now monitor, for example, the gender and ethnic mix of their workforces and set themselves targets to increase numbers from under-represented groups. While in many countries it is illegal to discriminate on these matters in selecting people for positions to meet such targets, it is permitted to encourage applications from under-represented groups. Institutions of higher education will therefore need to devise the appropriate recruitment and selection policies to meet the needs of their organisational strategy and diversity policy.

4.6.4 New Information and Communications Technology

Collis and van der Wente (2002) present a survey of educational institutions which seeks to establish the emerging scenarios with respect to the use of ICT in higher education. They found that institutions did not expect revolutionary change as a result of new ICT. In general, institutions did not feel under pressure to change by external forces or developments. ICT had become part of the blend of on-campus delivery but the lecture was still seen as the core medium for teaching. Change was gradual and ICT was being adopted. Web-based systems were seen as valuable and led to more efficient practices. But overall, the survey suggested that institutions were taking a 'business as usual' approach.

This survey was conducted 10 years ago and since then the technology has further developed. The capacity, speed and mobility of ICT systems have increased dramatically, creating further opportunities for the transfer of information and the improvement of communication. More significantly, however, a new generation of young people is now coming into higher education with new skills and attitudes, having grown up in this technological environment. These young people will not be familiar with the era without home computers, the internet, gaming machines, mobile phones and iPods. They will have used these instruments from an early age. The skills necessary to exploit them will be much more deeply embedded than will be the case of people who were not familiar with these tools until adulthood. With the development of such phenomena such as Facebook and Twitter, a new medium for communication, networking and socialising has emerged. Young people will, therefore, expect their educational institutions to be familiar with and to exploit ICT fully.

In the context of the internationalisation of higher education, this presents new opportunities and challenges for institutions. ICT creates a new dimension to the strategic question of whether institutions seeking to expand internationally do so either by enrolling students migrating from their home countries or by setting up partnerships or branches in those countries. The greater familiarity of young people with ICT sharpens these questions. Is the lecture theatre still the most appropriate medium for the delivery of education? Can it now be replaced by the video link? At a time when concern over climate change and the contribution of air travel to climate change is increasing, is it appropriate to expect academic staff and students to become more mobile when there are more sustainable alternatives? Such questions present substantial challenges and risks for institutions of higher education now, and increasingly in the future.

4.7 Conclusion

In this chapter, we have set out the data showing the demographic change that is expected across the world and within different regions of the world in the coming decades. We have considered these changes in the context of globalisation and some complex economic, social and political issues. We have examined these issues from the perspective of institutions of higher education, particularly those in countries of the developed world which will have to respond to the reducing numbers of young people requiring tertiary education in those countries. At the same time, we have addressed the challenges these institutions face now and in the coming years and have identified some of the strategic decisions that institutions need to take in an increasingly internationalised world. We hope that this analysis will contribute to the debate on the implications of demographic change and the internationalisation of higher education.

Bibliography

Altbach PG (1998) Comparative higher education: knowledge. The University and Development, Greenwood
Bennell P, Pearce T (2003) The internationalisation of higher education: exporting education to developing and transitional economies. Int J Educ Dev 23:215–232
Bloom DE, Canning D (2005) Global demographic change: dimensions and economic significance, Havard Initiative for Global Health, Working paper number 1, www.hsph.havard.edu/pgda/working/working_paper1.pdf
Collis B, van der Wente M (2002) Models of technology and change in higher education, center for higher education policy studies, http://purl.org/utwente/44610, Dec 2002
IAU (2003) Internationalisation of higher education practices and priorities: 2003 IAU survey report. International Association of Universities, Paris
King K (2009) Education, skills, sustainability and growth: complex relations. Int J Educ Dev 29:175–181
Knight J, De Wit H (1997) Internationalisation of higher education in Asia Pacific countries. European Association for International Education, Amsterdam
Knight J (2003) Internationalisation of higher education practices and priorities: 2003 IAU survey report. International Association of Universities, Paris
Little AW, Green A (2009) Successful globalisation, education and sustainable development. Int J Educ Dev 29:166–174
McKinsey (2008) Making talent a strategic priority, the mckinsey quarterly, Jan 2008 www.mckinseyquarterly.com
Mizikaci F, Baumgartl B (2007) Demographic trends and risks for european higher education. Int High Educ 47:15 Spring
Office of National Statistics (2008) The pink book, page 50 and Table FJDD, www.statistics.gov.uk, London
Russell M (2008) The age of uncertainty, times higher education, 20 March 2008
United Nations Economic and Social Council (2007) World demographic trends, Report no. E/CN.9/2007/6, www.un.org, New York, 10 Jan 2007
Solomon T, Akerblom M, Thulstrup E (2003) Chemistry in the developing world. Analytical Chemistry, , pp 107–113
Teichter U (2004) The changing debate on the internationalisation of higher education. High Educ 48(1):5–26
Thompson J (2001) Towards a model for international education. In: Hayden M, Thompson F (eds) International education. Principles and Practice, Routledge
Universities UK (2008) Higher education in facts and figures, www.universitiesUK.ac.uk, London
World Bank (1993) World bank policy research report 1993: the east asian miracle: economic growth and public policy. Oxford University Press, New York
World Bank (2007) Development and the next generation, Report no. 35999, www.worldbank.org, Washington

Chapter 5
Global Learning in American Higher Education: Strategies for Developing Global Citizens in an Era of Complex Interdependence

Carlos E. Juárez

In the global economy of the early twenty-first century, 'knowledge societies'—those that constantly develop new ideas, technologies, methods, products, and services—are crucial for future prosperity. In order to meet these challenges, institutions of higher education are seeking new ways to further connect their faculty, students, and outside communities in a strategic way where ideas flow, new initiatives blossom, flexibility abounds, and global reputations expand (Wood 2006, p. 1). Universities are developing deep-rooted entrepreneurial cultures that are international in scope, which in turn can ensure that the creation, transfer, and use of knowledge is ongoing and evolving.

But how does a university, with so many stakeholders, entrenched interests, and bureaucratic bottlenecks and constraints, develop an effective strategy of internationalization? What are some of the key factors that can help facilitate a more entrepreneurial culture in higher education that can foster global learning, and in turn allow universities to compete more effectively in an increasingly interconnected world?

This chapter will first define some of the key terms to help clarify the nexus between globalization of the world economy and internationalization of higher education. It goes on to identify some of the skills sets and competencies needed to produce globally competent college graduates, and then highlights some of the weaknesses and strengths of internationalization efforts in American higher education. A case study of Hawai'i Pacific University (HPU), a private university located in the middle of the Pacific, will help to illustrate some of the challenges and opportunities of internationalization efforts at an American university. The concluding section will summarize the key elements of successful internationalization in

C. E. Juárez (✉)
Department of Social Sciences, Hawai'i Pacific University,
1188 Fort Street Mall Ste 305, Honolulu, HI 96813-2713, USA
e-mail: cjuarez@hpu.edu

A. Altmann and B. Ebersberger (eds.), *Universities in Change*, Innovation, Technology, and Knowledge Management, DOI: 10.1007/978-1-4614-4590-6_5,

higher education. These include effective leadership to set the tone and provide a vision, a range of innovative curriculum and extra-curricular activities, faculty policies and opportunities, and a key role for international students, who can help broaden perspectives and redefine a campus community and ethos.

5.1 Globalization and Higher Education

The deepening interdependence of the world economy—a process defined in many circles as globalization—is having a profound impact on higher education around the world. Globalization makes clear that the boundaries between countries are distinctly permeable. As Thomas Friedman argued in his classic study, The Lexus and the Olive Tree, globalization is not just a phenomenon and not just a passing trend. It is the international system that replaced the Cold War system. Globalization is the integration of capital, technology, and information across national borders, in a way that is creating a single global market, and to some degree, a global village.

Like trade, technology, and financial markets, education, too, has become a global enterprise, as students and institutions worldwide regularly find opportunities outside their home countries. In the USA, over the past three decades there has seen intense discussion about the skill set and competencies that are needed to address the challenges of an increasingly interdependent world. The following quotes reflect some of the discussion on the importance of internationalizing US higher education:

- "Nothing less is at issue than the nation's security. At a time when the resurgent forces of nationalism and of ethnic and linguistic consciousness so directly affect global realities, the United States requires far more reliable capacities to communicate with its allies, analyze the behavior of potential adversaries, and earn the trust and the sympathies of the uncommitted. Yet, there is a widening gap between these trends and the American competence to understand and deal successfully with other people in a world in flux." (Perkins et al. 1979, pp. 1–2)
- "Things have changed. We live in a society that has fewer and fewer boundaries. (…) The United States is becoming a permanent multicultural society in which the world is us, not some distant backdrop against which the American drama is played out. (…) How shall we prepare for this sea change (…)? Surely one of the answers is that in our democratic society, meeting the challenge of increased internationalization must be everyone's responsibility." (Lampert 1989, p. 1)
- "A pervasive lack of knowledge about foreign cultures and foreign languages threatens the security of the United States as well as its ability to compete in the global marketplace and produce and informed citizenry. The U.S. education system, has, in recent years, placed little value on speaking languages other than English or on understanding cultures other than one's own." (O'Connell and Norwood 2007, p. 1)

Some definitions are needed to clarify what is meant by 'internationalization' in the realm of higher education, and how the related term of 'globalization' might be understood to mean many different things. International or Global Education is defined as learning opportunities that are designed to help students understand other cultures and nations, communicate across borders, and acquire an understanding of the cultural, social, and political systems of other countries and regions, and the global forces that are shaping the world. As such, a survey, course, program, or activity would be considered international or global if it primarily features perspectives, issues, or events from specific countries or areas outside the United States. It can also refer to those that transcend national boundaries.

The term internationalization, by contrast, refers to institutional efforts to integrate an international, global, and/or intercultural dimension into the teaching, research, or service functions of an institution. As we will see ahead, successful internationalization efforts require support and focus from a broad range of areas: not only in areas of curriculum and extra-curricular affairs, which are essential, but also in such areas as leadership, faculty policies and opportunities, and students.

Globalization has increased the volume, velocity, and importance of cross-border flows of just about everything—from drugs, e-mails, greenhouse gases, manufactured goods, and people to television and radio signals, viruses (virtual and real), and weapons. The term globalization encompasses a range of social, political, and economic changes. Some disciplines including anthropology or sociology focus on cultural changes of growing interconnectedness, such as the expansion of brands like Nike and McDonalds, and the increasing ease of travel. Other disciplines such as economics track the exchange of finances, goods and services through expanding global markets. Still other disciplines such as political science examine the role of international political institutions like the United Nations and the increasing power of transnational corporations.

While one can try to dissect each of these topics to measure the changes of globalization, they are woven together in a complex manner, making it difficult to summarize positive or negative effects. On the one hand, globalization creates new markets and wealth, even as it causes widespread suffering, disorder, and unrest. But it is both a source of repression and a catalyst for global movements of social justice and emancipation. Clearly, a full spectrum of views about the pros and cons of globalization exist, some praising, some disparaging. However, many observers believe that the ability to harness the good from globalization and avoid the bad lies in the cultivation of knowledge (see, for example, Robertson 1992; Friedman 1999; Wood 2006).

5.2 Skill Sets and Competencies Needed for an Interdependent World

If knowledge societies are the key to success in a globalizing world, exactly what kind of knowledge is needed? As globalization connects people through different means and in rapid ways, the new global economy requires a set of skills and competencies that go beyond traditional training and education. The role of higher education is most apparent as universities and colleges are by and large the primary suppliers of globally competent individuals. What types of initiatives are successful higher education institutions doing to create an environment that nurtures promising individuals and helps to create such individuals? How are college and universities responding to the needs of students, faculty, and their communities such that each has the ability to prosper in an increasingly interconnected and globalized world? And do the leaders of such institutions possess a common body of thought, wisdom, or insights to help develop the skills and competencies needed for the twenty-first century?

In his study of 110 US institutions of higher education, drawn primarily from the Institute of International Education's (IIE) 2004 Open Doors Report, Wood (2006) found answers to many of these types of questions by discerning eight commonly shares perceptions of the "realities" of globalization and higher education. Each represents what leaders of US universities, in general, are thinking in terms of the internationalization of their institutions and communities. They include:

1. The internationalization of campus and community is both an opportunity and a challenge that must be dealt with today. University leaders understand and embrace this point and feel an urgency to deal with it. In effect, those in charge of programs, curricula, and initiatives are looking for solutions to the challenges of globalization.
2. Vision matters—an institution's buildings and infrastructure are only part of the success equation. A vision or philosophy transmitted from the highest levels of university leadership is essential, and should include enlightening and preparing, not just students, but the community as a whole.
3. Effective university leaders do not demand an embrace of the international arena at their institutions. What they do is establish broad policies and priorities related to innovate initiatives aimed at developing a global culture throughout their campus and community, and then let the creative entrepreneurs take over.
4. Exemplary international programs and initiatives succeed or fail based primarily on the dedication and capability of their faculty champions, or what might be termed their "creative entrepreneurs." This underscores the central and critical role of faculty to an institution's embrace of globalization. While many internationally-focused programs tended to have a clear vision of what they hoped to accomplish, along with solid backing from the president and other key leaders (as well as a dedicated and skilled support staff), it was a motivated, entrepreneurial faculty, more so than any other component, which drove international success.
5. Students are also central to the success of any university's attempt to internationalize its campus and community, and indeed, students are the primary reason why a university should embrace internationalization. This requires a concerted focus on both international students studying on campus and domestic students studying abroad.
6. Partnerships and alliances are critical components of international educational development and a global focus. This can include partnerships with local,

regional, national, or international communities, and can take many forms, such as links to local businesses, government agencies, non-profit organizations, private research organizations, and other educational institutions.

7. The organization behind a university's internationalization efforts appears to work best when it is both centralized and decentralized. Institutions with the most progressive and innovative approaches to their international programs, initiatives, and alliance had both centralized and decentralized dimensions: one on the one hand, a "one-stop" office for administering, advising, coordinating, implementing, and maintaining all international initiatives; on the other hand, most successful international programs were championed by a specific faculty (or individual) of a specific school, department, center, or other decentralized branch of the university.
8. Branding of the university in the international arena is a responsibility that all must understand and share. Most university leaders view their institutions as a brand, whose reputation (good or bad) is built primarily by the people that make up its entire of extended community, including creative faculty, loyal students, proud alumni, committed partners, and visionary administrators.

What emerges from Wood's study is a complex web of leadership and vision to facilitate the process, a crucial role for faculty as catalysts for change, strategic alliances with the outside communities, and ways of connecting students to innovative curriculum and co-curriculum programs.

5.3 Developing Global Citizens in the Middle of the Pacific: A Case Study of Global Learning at Hawai'i Pacific University

Many of the challenges and opportunities for internationalization in American higher education can be seen in a brief case study of Hawai'i Pacific University (HPU). HPU is the largest private university in the US state of Hawai'i, with an enrollment of approximately 8,500 students. Founded in 1965 as an independent, not-for-profit, coeducational, career-oriented secondary institution, HPU was in favorable position to carve out a niche as a more entrepreneurial private university, with a clear global focus in its student recruitment efforts and academic programs.

The university's mission and ethos are reflected in an established global learning community with a large international student body. The notion of "global citizenship" has been a vital part of the HPU conversation for many years. Commitment to sustaining an internationally diverse student community dates back to the early years of the school and a strategic priority to recruit students from around the world. When an Educational Effectiveness Planning Committee established in the late 1990s began its work, global citizenship was readily adopted and supported as one of the University's key strategic priorities. A mission statement followed that confirmed this priority:

> HPU is an international learning community set in the rich cultural context of Hawaii. Students from around the world join us for an American education built on a liberal arts foundation. Our innovative undergraduate and graduate programs anticipate the changing needs of the community and prepare our graduates to live, work, and learn as active members of a global society.

The primary learning outcome defined for global citizenship was that students would participate in learning experiences that would enable them to create individual personal definitions of global citizenship—no university definition was desired or drafted. Over the past decade, many learning opportunities have been created or strengthened that build on the international diversity of the community and advance students' learning about being global citizens who can effectively relate to the emerging global interconnectedness of people, countries, businesses and commerce, social change, and so on.

As a parallel to the notion of global citizenship, the concept of 'global learning' emerged to describe the content, skills and abilities, and outcomes that are relevant for college graduates going out into the world. Global learning is fostered in a wide range of HPU learning experiences, including degree programs and curriculum initiatives, student organizations, and a range of community-based participatory initiatives. The university enrolls a substantial international student population, at times ranging from 15–25 % of the total student population, and coming from over 100 countries, the result of aggressive marketing and recruitment. This helps to foster a global learning environment in what is already the most ethnically diverse state in the country.

A number of curriculum initiatives have been fostered by HPU's participation in 'Shared Futures,' a multi-project national initiative of the Association of American Colleges and Universities (AAC&U). By building a network of educators dedicated to global learning and social responsibility, Shared Futures facilitates curricular change and faculty development on campuses nationwide. An online social network allows collaboration on course design and pedagogy, shared strategies for curricular renewal and globalization of general education, and a fluid, decentralized exchange of resources that opens new opportunities for partnership and learning.

One example of a successful initiative that came out of HPU's participation in the Shared Futures project was a series of Global Learning First-Year Seminars, small courses offered to entering undergraduate students which help foster connections to the local community, and linking those connections to larger global issues. The seminars are offered in a wide range of discipline areas within the general education core curriculum, and form the basis for cross-campus sharing of global perspectives. This in turn helps to break down the traditional disciplinary 'silos' such that cross-functional insights and ideas can be nurtured and brought to fruition. Since all First-Year Seminar instructors meet regularly to plan and coordinate activities linking the program, a biology instructor can find common ground with an anthropology instructor, and an English composition instructor might share insights with a history instructor to connect topics.

The Global Learning First-Year Seminars are further connected through additional curricular initiatives like a 'Viewpoints' film series or a 'Common Book' program that links and weaves through a common topic through all of the courses. These types of innovative curriculum initiatives provide faculty with greater motivation and creativity as they get to design special topics courses, build bridges across discipline areas, and feel a sense of ownership over new courses and materials.

Another valuable way HPU has been able to foster global learning is through its students, both a large cohort of international students as well as a mix of 'local' Hawaii-based or mainland domestic students. The university supports these students through dozens of internationally oriented student clubs and organizations. The majority of these are designed to promote cultural interactions among all HPU students and the local community.

The university also makes effective use of its location in an ethnically diverse population, recruiting students from abroad and from the US mainland to experience a distinctive cultural experience beyond their home country or state. Moreover, apart from studying in Hawaii—which in and of itself helps students develop cultural competencies given a diverse local population—students are encouraged to participate in student exchange programs at partner institutions throughout Asia, Europe, and Latin America. Student mobility is a vital part of any successful internationalization effort as students need to adapt well to new environments, learn to work with people across borders, and attain foreign-language skills to better understand culture and societies outside of their own.

The university also hosts an annual 'Intercultural Day' that brings students, faculty, and the local community in a 'melting pot' of cultural activity. The event gives students invaluable leadership skills to help organize the program and showcase the many cultures that come together. It also helps the university brand itself in the local community as a global learning environment. Educating for global citizenship and fostering a global learning environment not only broadens student awareness of the world and its people. It also gives graduates a competitive advantage at a time when the first job after completing a degree could be far from a student's country of origin.

A final area that was worked very well at HPU are numerous opportunities to link students to the local community through field trips and service-learning experiences that take students outside of the classroom. The downtown campus, adjacent to a rich historical area of the city and neighboring Chinatown, is a laboratory of history and culture, and students, even local ones, gain a better understanding of the local community and its rich and diverse heritage. Field trips to a wide range of cultural sites and local organizations can go a long way to connect students to the community. Examples might include an anthropology course that takes students to a homeless shelter, a geography course that does a walking tour of the historic district, or a writing course that interviews clients in social service agencies. Students benefit from getting outside of their comfort zones, and gain empathy, and better understanding of social forces.

5.4 Lessons of Internationalization in American Higher Education

The case of HPU illustrates four key factors for successful internationalization in higher education. These include

1. strong institutional support, including a visionary leadership committed, and willing to support campus-wide global learning initiatives;
2. academic programs and extracurricular activities that help foster a global perspective;
3. faculty policies and opportunities, allowing space for a bottom–up approach to internationalization efforts; and
4. student initiatives such as clubs and organizations to help promote cultural awareness and connections to the local community.

The past few decades have seen steady progress toward greater internationalization of American higher education, a process that is being accelerated by globalization of the world economy. While clear changes have taken place, a recent comprehensive study by the American Council on Education (ACE) reveals a mixed picture for internationalization efforts in US universities. The findings vary considerably by institutional type and show some important gains but also many weaknesses. A minority of institutions (less than 40 %) mention internationalization in their mission statements, include it in their strategic plans, or have formally assessed their internationalization efforts (only 30 %). The majority of institutions provide some administrative support for international programs and activities, but most do not have a full-time person to oversee or coordinate international programs or issues. Curriculum requirements do not play a central role in internationalization as fewer than 37 % of all institutions require a course with an international or global perspective as part of the general education curriculum. Slightly less than half (45 %) have an undergraduate foreign-language requirement for all or some students; few have such a requirement for all students (Green et al. 2008).

One growing trend, though still relatively small, is the scheme of offering dual degree programs. The ACE study found that 16 % of all institutions offered joint degree programs, with doctorate-granting institutions being the most likely to do so. The growth of these innovative dual degree schemes shows how institutions of higher learning around the globe are eager to find ways to embed internationalization efforts into the curriculum. Dual degree program schemes are difficult to initiate on their own, and in recent years many have benefitted from financial support from a joint initiative of the European Union and US. Department of Education's Atlantis Programme, which provides funding to help establish and develop linkages across the Atlantic. While the actual number of dual degree recipients may be relatively small, dual degree programs can help foster deeper linkages with faculty exchange and collaboration, and otherwise expand the number of international students on campus beyond traditional study abroad programs.

Successful internationalization in higher education institutions requires a broad-based approach, and as we have seen, is the result of many factors. Leadership is essential both in defining a clear mission and strategy, and in providing institutional support. It begins not only at the top with presidents, chancellors, rectors, or provosts, but with key top academic administrators who can connect a vision with concrete programs and resources, and who can motivate and coordinate faculty and staff in support of institutional goals.

Curriculum and extra-curricular programs need to effectively embed global learning into the academic and campus life. This can take the form of specialized courses, seminars, speaker forums or symposia that address global issues. It should also include support for student groups and cultural organizations that enrich the campus life and empower students to share their interests and enthusiasm.

Successful internationalization also involves faculty policies and opportunities that will harness the energies and vitality of faculty and help to link internationalization efforts directly to students. This includes support for international travel for faculty and faculty exchange initiatives that bring visiting scholars from abroad and/or send faculty to lecture, do research, or lead study tours abroad. And it also includes supporting creative champions, or faculty entrepreneurs, who often provide the impetus or demand for internationalization as faculty are increasingly connecting to wider ranging and global knowledge communities. They also recognize the impact global issues have on pedagogy and in developing skill sets and competencies for future leaders.

And lastly, successful internationalization also depends on the vital role of international students, both as short-term study abroad or exchange students, or as a key part of the student body. International students help to enrich the learning environment by offering a range of perspectives in a classroom setting, and help to diversify what is typically a homogenous student body. International students will also help to spark interest among students to seek out study abroad opportunities, and they also help establish lifelong relationships with home country students as social media and communication technologies now help to facilitate an ability to stay connected after they return home.

5.5 Weaknesses in Internationalization

Despite movement on many fronts, the uneven progress toward internationalization in US colleges and universities is also made clear from a number of weaknesses in internationalization efforts. Overall, internationalization does not appear to permeate the fabric of most institutions. It is not yet sufficiently deep, nor as widespread as it should be to prepare students to meet the challenges they are likely to face a in a more globalized economy. Specifically, weakness can be found in the fact that many institutions do not see internationalization as integral to their identity and few institutions have an internationalization strategy.

In many institutions, there is a gap between institutional rhetoric as espoused in mission statements and recruiting materials and reality. Too few institutions expose all of their students to global learning be requiring internationally or globally focused courses. The problem is especially clear in areas of foreign-language learning and study abroad. The majority of American universities do not require foreign-language study for admissions and there has been a decline in the proportion of institutions requiring foreign-language study for graduation. And while institutions are increasing options for study abroad offerings, the reality is that only a very small proportion of US students study abroad: according to the Institute of International Education (IIE), approximately 9.5 % of US undergraduates in 2009/10.

A final key indicator is that many campuses to not have adequate senior-level staff support for internationalization efforts. An effective strategy of internationalization requires support at the highest levels of administration, with the strongest institutions providing clear support in the form of an identifiable, high-ranking administration official, often in the form of a vice-provost, vice president, or dean of international affairs. Such a position can coordinate efforts across the institution and provide resources and strategic vision to carry out policy changes and program and curriculum development.

5.6 Strengths of Internationalization

These weaknesses notwithstanding, there are signs of strengths in internationalization efforts at US colleges and universities. Institutions are working more to infuse internationalization into student life, to support faculty work in areas of internationalization, and to increase administrative support for global learning. A high-quality education should not see global learning and/or internationalization as an add-on, but rather as an integral part of course content and pedagogy, research, and service. It requires sustained attention and leadership to help prepare students for the multicultural and global society of today and tomorrow. One valuable way to achieve this is to build on student interests and demographics. Many US institutions are making progress to meet the challenges of preparing students to live and work as active members of a global society. This is reflected in greater institutional support on several levels, more infusion of internationalization into student life, and greater use of technology as a resource for global learning.

There is greater emphasis than ever before on investment in the international capacities of faculty. Between 2001 and 2006, the study by ACE found more institutions funded faculty to teach at institutions abroad, paid for travel to conferences abroad, and supported faculty study or research abroad. More institutions have also offered opportunities for faculty to strengthen their foreign-language skills, and more sponsored workshops on internationalizing the curriculum to promote global learning initiatives.

Institutions are also increasing administrative support for internationalization, with a similar shift between 2001 and 2006 from a single office supporting internationalization to multiple offices. This suggests that institutions are engaging in more global learning activities and are responding to the need to support them. Most institutions have at least a half-time staff member devoted to international student services, international student recruiting, English as a Second Language programs, and study abroad. While this is a positive trend, in the absence of a chief international officer, the proliferation of offices staffed by part-time professionals may at the same time be contributing to fragmentation of internationalization efforts on many campuses, as many of these various offices often have limited contact with each other.

An area where there is clear evidence of greater internationalization, as noted in the case study of HPU and the Shared Futures initiative of the AAC&U, is in infusing global learning initiatives into student life. This includes a rise in programs designed to increase student appreciation for different cultures as well as bringing together students from the US with their peers from other countries. In general, colleges and universities are sponsoring more international fairs, buddy programs, and international meeting places and residence halls, trends that further embed global awareness directly into student life.

A final area where there has been positive growth is in the use of technology as a resource for internationalization. While anyone who has experienced it will note that there is no substitute for the personal experience of going abroad, technology offers excellent opportunities for students and faculty to interact with their colleagues and peers from other countries. Video-conferencing as well as audio-conferencing, email and social media now enable students to interact with professors from abroad and to engage in collaborative projects with students sitting in classrooms far away. With the cost of using technology decreasing every year and the quality improving, institutions are in a better position to take advantage of the opportunities afforded by technology.

In conclusion, the overall picture for internationalization in American universities appears to be mixed. Institutions of higher learning are often slow to change, but that very slowness can often be of great benefit, ensuring that an institution is not simply caught up in the frenzy of an educational fad. Internationalization and global learning are not a fad. They are a reality that requires nurturing and support, and ways to get embedded into the curriculum and ethos of institutions of higher learning.

Bibliography

Friedman TL (1999) The lexus and the olive tree. Farrar, Straus & Giroux, New York

Green MF, Luu D, Burris B (2008) Mapping Internationalization on U. S. Campuses, 2008th edn. American Council on Education, Center for International Initiatives, Washington

Lambert R (1989) International studies and the undergraduate. American Council on Education, Washington

O'Connell ME, Norwood JL (eds) (2007) International education and foreign languages: keys to securing america's future. committee to review title VI and Fulbright-Hays international education programs. The National Academies Press, Washington
Perkins J et al (1979) Strength Through Wisdom: A Critique of U. S. Capability. A report to the president from the president's commission on foreign language and international studies. U. S. Government Printing Office, Washington, DC
Robertson R (1992) Globalization: social theory and global culture. Sage Publications, London
(2006) Shared Futures, Global learning & social responsibility. Association of American Colleges and Universities. www.aacu.org/SharedFutures, Washington, DC
Wood Van R (2006) Globalization and higher education: eight common perceptions from University leaders, IIE networker (institute of international education—Bi-annual journal for international education professionals), New York (Spring), pp 26–34

Chapter 6
Universities Between Politics and Economics: Autonomy, Performance Agreements and Global Budgets at Austrian Universities

Manfried Gantner

This article is targeted at university managers and people involved in the field of university (de)regulation. The focus is on autonomy for state-funded universities (hereinafter simply called 'universities') and their financial steering through performance agreements and global budgets, bearing in mind the fact that contract management and multi-year global budgets have been playing a key role as instruments of university funding and control for 10 years now. After so many years of testing and experience, the time has come to assess the current situation and the sustainability of these developments. In particular, this paper examines the long-term potential of economic thinking and the use of business management tools for and at universities in comparison with political rationality in this field.[1]

We find a wide playing field for autonomy, financial steering and performance agreements; depending on the rules, and on the tactics and strength of the teams, they develop a wide range of forms and hence of stimuli and effects. But behind it all—in addition to the parties' respective views with regard to the priorities of the development of the university involved—very real power structures exist. However great the scope for autonomy, there is no ignoring the power differentials that exist between the Ministry and the universities; the Ministry wears three hats: it has control over the financial resources, it is the referee at the supervisory level and it can normally induce changes of the laws. The universities, on the other hand,

[1] An assessment of such a complex subject as the development of financial autonomy in a changing legal framework and in practice is needed, and the universities deserve to have their—sometimes contradictory and sometimes mutually complementary—steering mechanisms made the object of scientific review and explicit evaluation. This paper was written in August 2009. There were no relevant changes of the framework until publication.

M. Gantner (✉)
Department of Public Finance, The University of Innsbruck, Universitätsstrasse 15, 6020, Innsbruck, Austria
e-mail: manfried.gantner@uibk.ac.at

A. Altmann and B. Ebersberger (eds.), *Universities in Change*, Innovation, Technology, and Knowledge Management, DOI: 10.1007/978-1-4614-4590-6_6,

have just one hat and are currently going cap in hand with it: they need resources. They can nevertheless derive a high degree of self-confidence from the fact that they are the actual providers on their markets. That is their strength.

In the course of time, the degree and specific features of autonomy in the individual case can be extended or reduced through convention and practice or by laws and decrees; in certain areas it can be a living organism, but the realities of the operating framework and circumstances may also reduce it to an empty shell. Financial steering can be practised in the form of multi-year global budgets; but practice can also degenerate into mere lip service as a result of annual or even more frequent interference in the specific case. Performance agreements may take the form of negotiations between equal partners or of a dictate on the part of the financiers. They can address the strengths and weaknesses and the profile of a university and its contribution in the overall university context, and they can focus on the specific wishes of the two parties.

The Austrian situation and the country's experience with the 2002 Universities Act (hereinafter called 'UG 2002') and with the 2009 University Law Amendment Act (hereinafter called 'URÄG (2009)') are perhaps exemplary insofar as questions of autonomy, steering, and funding on the basis of performance mandates or agreements in combination with medium-term global budgets are currently on the agenda in many countries with regard to tertiary education and its institutions.

The conflict between the goals of autonomy and state control in whole or in part is nothing new: at no point in the history of public universities have their political masters really absented themselves from the decision-making process relating to their objectives, operating conditions and resources nor—given the importance of the academic and scientific world—have they really been able to do so. It is not the case that the university of the past was under no economic constraints and did not have to take decisions in the face of finite resources.

In the last few years, however, a new and very pronounced conflict between political and economic rationality seems to have developed. On the one hand, this relates to the as yet unsolved question of the resources needed for a university to satisfy the objectives set: political rhetoric on the relevance of the universities for a country's future prosperity is in stark contrast with the realities of the allocation of resources. And on the other hand, it is only in the last 10 years that the legislator in Austria—and in many other countries—has given the universities much wider scope for autonomy and at the same time demanded economic thinking and imposed the use of business management tools. Has the economisation of university performance paid off? Is the pendulum now on its way back, once again restricting the scope for autonomy while leaving the new instruments in place?

In an attempt to answer the opening question and investigate the aspects touched upon above, this paper has been divided into a number of sections: fields of autonomy, economic rationality, medium-term global budgets, performance agreements, political rationality and conclusions. The theory is discussed with reference to the Austrian universities as presented in UG 2002 and URÄG (2009), which was enacted on 9 July 2009.

6.1 The New Fields of Autonomy at Austrian Universities: Goals and Results

UG 2002, which came into force on 1 January 2004, met with much praise at the time. Few members of the universities shared the general enthusiasm, however. They were occupied with their own specific problems: defending their status and vested rights in the light of the new organisational and development plans; the role of the new university management, with a participatory structure replaced by a "monocratic" model; the fight for an open system of university admissions and against the recently introduced student fees. But for the authors of the new law in the Ministry, for the Rectors and the Senate chairpersons who were involved at the time, for the general public in Austria and for competent opinion-leaders abroad, it was quite clearly a bold act of pioneering legislation.

The reason for the highly positive response at the highest university management levels, among policy-makers and the social partners, and also in the media was primarily the fact that—on the basis of contract management—UG 2002 offered the universities scope for autonomy in various significant areas, in exchange for a new allocation of responsibilities and extensive reporting requirements. The law transformed the universities from subsidiary agencies of the federal authority to legal persons in public law. The Ministry itself was able and (at the time!) willing to largely restrict its role to questions of legal supervision, strategic matters and the provision of funds on the basis of contract management and multi-year global budgets. "Autonomy is the fundamental principle of UG 2002" (Badelt 2007:1). The new autonomy related in particular to the following items[2]:

- Appointment of personnel, including professors, and collective bargaining rights for universities in general;
- The right of self-organisation in terms of organisational structure and workflow organisation;
- The internal allocation of funds, e.g. use of the multi-year global budgets granted on the basis of performance agreements drawn up with the Ministry, and of third-party funds acquired including the reimbursement of costs for the organisational units and university members involved;
- The university statutes, and
- The content of study programmes, and in-service and continuous education courses in addition to the autonomy already enjoyed in the field of research, and thus scope for the universities to set their own priorities and create their own profiles on the basis of development plans.

[2] Berka (2007):2, on the logic of the autonomous university: "Autonomy can never be an end in itself; the power of self-government is given to an institution to enable it to reach the set goals to the best possible extent."

This new and significant scope for university autonomy is defined in greater detail in UG 2002 and in a wealth of other laws, decrees and agreements (e.g. collective bargaining agreements, performance agreements).[3] In addition to the influence of the new URÄG (2009), autonomy can therefore be increased or reduced step by step through changes to other relevant laws and new agreements. Decrees issued by the Ministry are a popular means to this end. The facts of everyday university life derive not from the sales pitch and Sunday speeches but the realities created. As the saying goes, the practice is the best test of the theory.

Without wishing to go into greater depth with regard to the individual fields of autonomy,[4] one can list a large number of arguments in favour of greater autonomy in this phase of university development in Austria. They include the two major and related arguments: "Universities are no longer merely reactive" (Winckler 2007:5) and "Autonomy stimulates initiative". These are familiar arguments from the debate on (effective) competition or decentralisation in the context of the theory of federalism. For the universities they relate to such matters as local competence building for effective profiling and strategic focus setting, appointments to chairs, exploitation of potential deriving from cooperation and competition, activation of hidden productivity resources, and creative solutions for a wide range of positive developments, e.g. in teaching and research, at the organisational and management levels, and in the deployment of human, material and financial resources. Another attractive aspect is the fact that an increase in autonomy also strengthens implementation of the principle of subsidiarity for the more effective use of tangible and intangible resources at the local level. Admittedly, centralisation also has its advantages where the focus is on fair distribution, but that was explicitly not the remit in UG 2002.

It is not always immediately possible to make the advantages of the new autonomy apparent within the universities down to the individual organisational unit and for every individual employee; in such a period of radical change it is first of all necessary to develop the rules and instruments required for the whole university and collect the relevant experience. Often enough, it is not until a second stage of development that the advantages can also be exploited within the university. Whether the transition to autonomy is successful—and if so, how fast and to what extent—depends on many factors, hard and soft, some amenable to planning and some fortuitous, but the following are always relevant:

- Factual and mental preparation of the university members for the new situation;
- Their attitude to competition and their perception of international competition;

---

[3] For the relevant legal texts and ordinances, cf. "Universitätsrecht 2009".

[4] Autonomy at the level of personnel, for example, is defined in the relevant employment laws for civil servants, limited-term contract staff and salaried staffs, and also—for the latter—in a collective bargaining agreement that was not signed until 2009 after a long process of negotiation and review with regard to the available finance. In the case of their study programmes, the universities enjoy autonomy with regard to content, but autonomy does not extend to the question of university admission or the amount of student fees, nor did it include the length of the Bachelor programmes until URÄG (2009) came into force.

- The prevailing university culture;
- The specific actors at the level of senior management (University Council, Rectorate, Senate), and the employee and student representatives, and their personal conflict management skills;
- The pace of change;
- The self-imposed (to some extent at least) regulatory density (statutes, study programmes, agreements on objectives, personnel, finance, reporting);
- The real or perceived limitations at the local level in terms of personnel, finance and space, and last but not least
- The internal and external agreements entered into (e.g. in the framework of objectives and performance agreements).

In the following, the focus is on financial autonomy and the ways in which it is extended and restricted in UG 2002 and URÄG (2009). In this connection,it is necessary to address the fundamental differences in the rationalities and approaches of the economic and political worlds.

6.2 Economic Rationality at the Universities: Goals and Results

6.2.1 Economisation of Universities in UG 2002

Ten years ago, the economisation of the universities was the order of the day, and it was implemented by the relevant actors with great enthusiasm. The unquestioned logic derived from new public management (NPM), in which private sector management principles and instruments and related expectations are to be applied to the public sector—and in this case to the universities. Typical features of NPM:

- Output/results orientation instead of input orientation (e.g. what competences and what education do graduates acquire?);
- Customer and employee orientation;
- Effectiveness compared with efficiency (doing the right things compared with doing certain things right).

The resulting requirements:

- Identity of duties, authority and responsibility;
- Decentralised decision making (autonomy) combined with
- Contract management (objectives and performance agreement, multi-year global budget).

The latter concepts are to be interpreted as follows: in terms of NPM, the focus in contract management is on agreements between two partners at different levels of control (e.g. parliament–Ministry, Ministry–university, university–internal organisational unit). In order to achieve certain plans or objectives, they want—or ought—to communicate as equals. The loss of hierarchical power is replaced by the rights and obligations defined in the contract, i.e. rights of control on the one hand and the agreed entitlement to resources and duties of performance and reporting on the other, all with an overriding focus on transparency, incentives and orientation by results.

The term 'global budget' is used for the allocation of financial resources without any specific dedication, usually for a period of several years and for autonomous disbursement in return for accountability. Global budgets and performance agreements are interdependent, and the scenario is expected to deliver significant advantages.

Multi-year budget periods presuppose medium- and long-term planning and hence focus- and priority-setting. They prevent the short-term thinking that typically generates bouts of December spending fever in the public sector. They offer planning security and hence the requirements for satisfying the principles of efficiency, economy and expedience in decision making. The avoidance of earmarking enhances the long-term combination of the factors of production. Decentralisation improves the latitude for decision making, speeds up the decision-making process and increases the degree of responsibility at the local level, where there is greatest knowledge of the relevant details.

UG 2002 provides for a significant number of structures and instruments to permit implementation of these goals and requirements: what is perhaps the most important innovation for the universities takes the form of multi-year development plans for their own profile-building and focus-setting in the fields of research, teaching, continuous education and administration. Importance from the economic view must be attached to the autonomous statutes and the organisational plans to be established by the universities. Contract management is centred on multi-year performance agreements with the Ministry on the basis of a draft performance agreement prepared by the universities and secondary internal agreements on objectives drawn up with the organisational units involved in implementation of the development plan and performance agreement at the university involved. The detailed reporting requirements involve a comprehensive annual intellectual capital statement, annual statements of accounts including a statement of net worth, financial position and profit and loss account an activity report and a separate performance report (which forms part of the intellectual capital statement in URÄG (2009)), investment and financial controlling reports during the financial year and regular university statistics. The aim of these reporting requirements is to ensure continuous monitoring of progress made in the implementation of the performance agreement and the university's financial management. Implementation of the multi-year global budgets also presupposes the introduction of private-sector accounting tools including cost and results accounting. For this purpose, the accounts departments at most Austrian universities switched over to SAP. The universities met these requirements on schedule and to an excellent standard on the whole. URÄG (2009) has introduced one further innovation in the form of annual special funding requirements, which enable the Ministry to finance annual steering measures for certain universities. Within this system the Ministry can retain 2 % of total annual funds made available to the universities on the basis of the performance agreements and general pay increases for federal employees.

6.2.2 Corporate Governance: Universities are not Businesses

Universities are "not organisations just like any other" (Enquete 2008). They are constituted pursuant to UG 2002 as legal entities under public law. The focus at universities is on the production and communication of scientific knowledge and the training of young scientists. That is not to say, however, that research and teaching are unsuited to efficient, economical and expedient procedures. In this respect, universities are not profit-oriented and have multiple goals, principles and tasks in which quantification of performance is a non-trivial activity (e.g. in research), as the market cannot or should not be decisive. They also have a number of non-economic objectives (e.g. socio-political, regional–economy goals).

The universities' internal decision-making processes, i.e. corporate governance, also clearly differ from those in the private sector. Companies normally have an owner or owners, an operative management (management board) and a supervisory body (supervisory board), and not a mix of university management bodies with considerable duplication in their various functions comprising strategic, operative and supervisory tasks. That is something which URÄG (2009) has not really changed.

The same applies to the recruitment of personnel to senior positions, whether for members of the University Council, for Rectors or for new professors. In the case of a public company, it is normally the owners who appoint the supervisory board and the latter who choose the management board, but at Austrian universities things are slightly more complicated. One half of the University Council is appointed by the government and the other half by the Senate, with one additional member selected by the University Council itself. The Senate is also responsible—after consulting the Recruitment Commission provided for in URÄG (2009) (whose findings can be ignored as long as a reason is provided in writing)—for presenting the University Council with a shortlist of three suitable persons for the office of Rector, from which the Council may choose. Incumbent Rectors can be re-elected with a two-thirds majority of the University Council and the Senate. No-one can be appointed Rector without being previously shortlisted by the Senate. The members of the Senate are elected by the various groups of university members (and in view of the level of representation needed for the functions involved, a legal requirement for a minimum electoral turnout would be meaningful). When appointing new professors, the Senate elects the Appointments Committee and appoints the experts, while the Rector has to ensure correct handling of the (residual!) procedures and then negotiate the appointment on the basis of a shortlist of three drawn up by the Appointments Committee.

In practice the Senate is the most powerful body, because it elects part of the University Council and nominates the candidates for the office of Rector. Unlike the case of a public company, the situation at Austrian universities is that the employees (or their representatives) elect their "CEO" themselves and also nominate almost half the "supervisory board", a situation that is not without a certain influence on the Rector and the members of the University Council: those who wish to be re-elected will seek a good relationship with the Senate and not vice versa.

The resulting requirements, like the search for the smallest common denominator, a willingness to compromise, the pursuit of group interests, the defence of vested interests, the creation of a power base, the formulation of election promises, etc. are expressions of political rather than economic rationality. Without them, however, no power can survive and be effective in the longer term. As a result, effective reforms are not promoted, or only indirectly. From the economic point of view, this is the real obstacle to any serious reform policy at the universities (as in the political arena, too): those who are to introduce and implement the reforms are elected—or not, or no longer—by those who are affected by the reforms. Equally problematical are the asymmetries involved, for example in the distribution of the costs and benefits of reforms on the time axis and also in terms of their perception: reforms usually involve costs up front, and it normally takes some time before they become effective and the benefits can be reaped. These costs—mostly personified for the sake of simplicity by the actors involved—are subjected to vociferous attack by the representatives of the affected groups and sometimes by individual members of the university, usually with the help of external media. Here again, we see that universities are organisations sui generis. The resulting benefits are not normally associated with the actors involved; they achieve only diffuse recognition and tend to be taken for granted and tacitly consumed by the beneficiaries. Reforms usually require time and money, and that is what is often lacking in the political process when it comes to voting and elections.

With regard to the University Council and the Senate—and various other officials like the heads of the organisational units (e.g. Deans), the two employee representatives and the Equal Opportunities Committee representatives—the Rector and Vice-Rectors are the internal servants of many masters. In the light of the provisions of URÄG (2009) especially, their office is more like that of a Secretary General than a CEO. It is true that they still have very significant rights of initiative or agenda-setting, but with their various plans and proposals they are ultimately suppliers to the Senate, University Council et al., where the actual decisions are taken. The Rector and Vice-Rectors then take over again for the implementation phase—and are held responsible for the consequences, even though various other bodies (like the Senate with regard to the study programmes) have usually had their say on the subject in the meantime, either as a matter of principle or during the negotiating or drafting process.

The Vice-Rectors are elected by the University Council in a much simpler process. In UG 2002, it was the Rector who signed the contracts of employment and agreements on objectives with the Vice-Rectors, but with the coming into force of URÄG (2009) this has become the responsibility of the University Council. That is doubtless the normal procedure for a joint stock company, but in the case of the universities it will weaken the position of the Rector and significantly impact the decisions taken by the team of Rector and Vice-Rectors. Indeed URÄG (2009) has generally strengthened the position of the University Council, albeit without any corresponding adjustments in terms of qualifications and recruitment with the exception of an official quota for women: pursuant to URÄG (2009) the Rectorate must now obtain the approval of the University Council for the draft budget and also bring it to the attention of the Senate, which can be expected to trigger desires and objections there. This procedure enables the University Council to make meaningful comparisons between budgeted and actual figures, and between the preliminary draft and the final accounts. However, it also permits the University Council to become involved and exercise power at the operative level with regard to the volume and structure of the budget: should the University Council refuse to approve the draft budget, the Rectorate must now submit a new budget proposal without delay. Such a process could be repeated several times until the University Council considers all its wishes catered for in the draft budget.

Another specific feature of Austrian universities is that, with the exception of a small number of degree courses for which the government has defined minimum capacity requirements for the enrolment of students (currently medicine, dentistry, veterinary medicine and psychology), they have no influence over student numbers (i.e. demand for teaching)—regardless of their capacities in terms of personnel and facilities (i.e. space)—and yet are held responsible for the quality of the product. Nor are they normally free to price their services as they see fit. On the production side, their personnel mainly comprises civil servants with tenure and their buildings do not usually belong to them but are mainly owned by a federal real estate company ('Bundesimmobiliengesellschaft'), over which the client ministry has no control.

6.2.3 Assessment: Preventive Effect of the Economic Rationality Threat

Given the very tight time schedule provided for in UG 2002, the above instruments for self-steering, planning, controlling, organisation and accounting, and also for contract management and reporting, were implemented expeditiously. Further improvements in terms of professionalism were also achieved in many fields, e.g. human resources, course administration, third-party finance, quality assurance, facility management, procurement and public relations. The business management 'box of tools' is now well filled. Further progress is still needed here and there, for example in the form of realistic financing plans in support of the development plans, the development of robust cost/performance accounting and further quality assurance measures.

Given the sheer volume of requirements to be met for the various pilot projects and the prototypes for all the plans and reports, many of the Austrian universities spent the transitional years in more or less continuous crisis mode. That was highly challenging for all university managers, especially the Rectors and Vice-Rectors in their initiative-taking roles, and all administrative staffs.

A major additional burden of work was caused by implementation of the provision in UG 2002 for the withdrawal of the medical faculties from the Universities of Vienna, Graz and Innsbruck and their reconstitution as separate Universities of

Medicine, which had to be handled simultaneously—and more or less out of the national university budget—by the respective Offices of the Rectors. One of the original motives for the Ministry, namely to impose 'a ceiling on additional clinical costs' and transfer the financial burden from the federal authority and to the regional authorities of Vienna and Styria and the Tyrol, has not yet been completely achieved. The political excitement has died down, but a full evaluation including the economic. The Medical University of Vienna enjoys a special agreement with the federal level aspects is still outstanding.

Even though the resources spent on the decision-making processes and additional administrative work at the universities and the Ministry during the change-over probably total thousands of man-years (many of them at the expense of research and teaching), there is a general consensus that very considerable productivity gains were made in the first few years of the reform of the Austrian universities (BMWF 2008). The Ministry also benefitted from a number of useful lessons learnt:

- Relating to the unfamiliar feeling of letting go at the operative level in various new fields of university autonomy;
- In connection with the need for formal and above all timely coordination of the universities for the introduction of the new tools and instruments, and
- With the first performance agreements and the first multi-year global budgets.

The universities repeatedly asked the Ministry for greater transparency and timely coordination of the instruments to be employed. It is true that the Ministry cooperated fully with the Austrian Rectors Conference (since renamed Universities Austria) on the subject of the accounting system changes and creation of the intellectual capital statement and the formula budget. However, there was considerable room for improvement in terms of ex ante coordination on the part of the Ministry in other fields, for example:

- No clear instructions with regard to the content of the development plans during the drafting stage;
- Formal specifications only with no reference to content for the first performance agreements, as if there were no general requirements of a national science and research policy in Austria[5];
- Wide scope for interpretation of the items in the financial statement, which naturally reduces their soundness in terms of aggregate comparisons.

There were also higher level requirements not involving UG 2002, such as the need to coordinate the study programmes being created in the framework of the Bologna process. The absence of such coordination has resulted in clearly reduced student mobility in Austria and will probably necessitate revision of the curricula

---

[5] Cf. Footnote 32 to the 2007–2010 performance agreement. In the preparations for the 2010–2012 performance agreement, the Ministry went to the opposite extreme, providing the universities with highly detailed specifications for their drafts. As explained below, however, Austria still lacks an overall university policy concept in which such requirements could be embedded.

approved by the university Senates now operational. The doctoral programmes are the exception here.

There is no doubt that, given (still) better preparation, more coordination and greater realism with regard to the time horizons available and quality standards feasible, the material and immaterial resources consumed in the implementation of UG 2002 could have been substantially lower. Austria has 21 universities, and in many cases the same number of wheels were invented. As yet no full ex post cost/benefit analysis of the implementation of UG 2002 has been published.

To sum up, much greater progress was made in terms of transparency for the internal university processes involved in the implementation of UG 2002 than at the suprauniversity level. The universities were doubtlessly offered very considerable incentives to make sparing use of resources and significantly improve their economic performance. Planning security has not yet been achieved, however, because of the many question marks that still remain, for example with regard to study programmes, finance and buildings.

6.3 Multi-Year Global Budgets: Goals and Results

Research and teaching are university tasks with a multi-year time horizon, and university employment and rental contracts are normally open-ended or have a term of several years, too. Planning, decision making and funding should therefore (be able to) relate to a longer period of time as well.

With the earlier 1-year budgets and limited transferability of funds from one type of expenditure to another (e.g. personnel, tangible assets, capital spending), the tendency was to think in terms of rigid categories and spend the last cent by year-end. The reasons for the introduction of the multi-year global budget were to put an end to this inflexibility. One question is whether this bold step has paid off. The other is whether the universities still actually have financial autonomy and a multi-year global budget.

Let us start with a clarification of the terminology: pursuant to UG 2002 the universities receive a global budget set in advance for a 3-year period. It comprises a 'basic budget' determined on the basis of the performance agreement and an indicator- or performance-oriented 'formula-based budget' ('formula budget' for short). The basic budget accounts for about 80 % and the formula budget 20 % of the global budget. In addition, the universities are (normally) reimbursed annually (in some cases ex post) for the general salary increases awarded to the federal employees who were on their payrolls when UG 2002 came into effect.[6,7]

Of the total amount, comprising the basic and formula budgets plus reimbursement of calculated salary increases for federal personnel as defined above, the Ministry—pursuant to UG 2002—is entitled to withhold up to 1 % for special funding requirements over and above the performance agreement. In the first performance agreement period (2007–2009) only about half this amount was activated by the Ministry (Court of Audit 2009:21, text no. 23). The Ministry also informed the universities prior to negotiations that no university would 'loose out', i.e. would receive fewer funds than in the previous year, which is more an expression of egalitarianism than of a desire to stimulate competition.[8]

In view of the budgetary constraints confronting the Ministry, this introductory goodwill cannot be expected to last, all the more so as a university's global budget can be reduced in subsequent performance agreement periods (e.g. 2010–2012) in incremental annual steps of 2, 4 and finally 6 % compared with the amount agreed for the previous 3-year period. In addition, URÄG (2009) now permits the Ministry to withhold 2 % of the total amount 'for funding requirements over and above the performance agreement and for annual special funding requirements for the universities'.[9] This percentage translates into the not inconsiderable sum of €150 million per performance agreement period.[10] At a time when a ceiling has

[6] This regime is often underestimated: Any quantitative, structural or price changes which have been incurred in the meantime, i.e. since 31 December 2003, and relate to personnel that was not employed by the universities at the cut-off date must be financed by the universities themselves. The effect of this rule is becoming increasingly burdensome as the (semi-)autonomous universities are confronted with a growing workload (resulting from higher student numbers and improved staffing ratios as well as the implementation of UG 2002 and URÄG (2009)) and the need for better qualified administrative personnel. The fact that new professors now sign private-sector employment contracts with the universities instead of receiving civil servant status from the federal authority makes them much more expensive for the universities, also because of their pensions, which now have to be agreed with the universities, too.

[7] University funding in Austria can be broken down as follows (figures for total spending in 2007): 77 % global budget, 9 % other income and reimbursements, 7 % research and artistic work, 6 % student fees and 1 % artistic training (BMWF 2008:74). Part of the funding for research work and related reimbursements is ultimately paid by the federal authority, too, while student fees are subject to political decision-making. It can therefore be said that, on average, well over 90 % of the university budgets derives from the federal budget and legislative decisions at the federal level.

[8] Unlike the universities, the Ministry was aware of the outcome of the formula budget when financial resources were being allocated on the basis of the performance agreement and obviously ensured that this promise was kept.

[9] A maximum reduction of approx. 12 % per performance agreement period and university applies.

[10] What these special funding requirements are meant to be is not specified in the law. It merely includes one example, which offers great freedom of interpretation and hence scope for interference on the part of the Ministry: 'for certain projects for the creation or support of a national university space'. In the notes on Art. 12 paras. 3–5 and Art. 12 paras. 12 and 13 of

been imposed on total university funding, any increase in the allocation to one university can only mean a decrease for the others.

Universities have high overheads. With little scope for savings with regard to products and services (study programmes, ongoing research projects) and production factors (personnel with tenure in some cases, buildings, dedicated equipment), only minor reductions in university expenditures are possible in the short term. Given the notorious underfunding of the universities,[11] the amount of flexibly disposable funds for alternative expenditures is only a few percent points per year.[12] There are also legal limits to the generation of additional income (e.g. student fees) and often additional upstream expenditures that must be met before any revenue is forthcoming (e.g. research, training courses).

A reduction by just 1 % point is therefore bound to lead to a severely disproportionate curtailment of any freedom of action the universities may still have. At the beginning of the first performance agreement period, the Ministry[13] had additional funds to spend on the research infrastructure and socio-political objectives (e.g. anticipatory chairs and gender programmes) totalling about 1 % of the global budgets. Deployment of these funds had some positive results but also generated some of the effects described below.

At this point, it is worth considering whether we now have to say goodbye to the multi-year global budget and financial autonomy for the universities as provided for in UG 2002. The reason is to be found in such additional sources of funding and especially in the degree of annual interference caused by the forthcoming special funding requirements:

Such ad hoc programmes usually have only limited deadweight effects; they cause deviations from the priorities already set by the universities (without the additional funds). Although they do achieve the effects targeted by the Ministry, they also undermine the multi-year global budgets and thus autonomous implementation of the development plans. They are mostly packaged with a co-financing requirement for the universities and therefore tie down still more of the universities' flexibly disposable funds. The universities therefore see them as Trojan horses, which the Ministry is unwilling to forego as they permit influence to be exerted throughout the performance agreement period.

(Footnote 10 continued)
URÄG (2009), a number of uses are listed "for the targeted improvement of the current situation of the universities".

[11] Cf. examples of comparable universities outside of Austria and the repeated statements made on the subject and evidence provided by the Austrian Science Board and Universities Austria.

[12] Savings can be made, for example, by postponing appointments or procurement and capital spending items, and through the unexpected departure of personnel. Such options can hardly be expected to improve the quality of a university's offering and are in any case neutralised by additional expenditures relating, for example, to increasing student numbers, price increases and rising costs, additional research projects without adequate overhead financing, and new and additional requirements imposed by the Ministry (e.g. legislative changes, annual special funding requirements).

[13] Recent examples: "Research Infrastructure IV" and "Anticipatory Chairs 2007/08".

At the level of equipment, these funds are not normally employed for investment in the general modernisation of the infrastructure; they are used to finance very specific items of equipment and involve follow-up costs in the form of running costs which are not covered by the start-up funding for the purchase.

The same applies to the acquisition of research funding that does not cover the overheads involved (e.g. from the Austrian Science Fund) and subsequently ties down other university resources in the form of personnel, space and equipment. It also makes it increasingly difficult and less rewarding to identify and activate further potential savings.

The promised increase in university funds of about 10 % in total for the next performance agreement period (2010–2012) will in any case be necessary to help finance a large number of additional expenditures that cannot yet be quantified (e.g. parts of the new collective bargaining agreement, increases in salaries, rents and leasing costs, additional requirements imposed by URÄG (2009) and the Ministry's wishes relating to the special funding requirements that do not cover their own costs).

For a performance agreement as described in the following sections (requiring an amendment to the law), there should be three sources or sub-budgets as the basis for calculating the global budget. The second and third sub-budgets should be employed to promote competition between the universities, and the third sub-budget should be of a substantial magnitude.

6.3.1 Basic Budget

The basic budget presupposes coordination between the Ministry and the university concerned with regard to its teaching programmes and the financial resources required for the agreed student numbers. To ensure objectively correct allocation of resources to these basic university activities, the universities need to operate with standardised costs per study programme and student enrolled. In addition, it is necessary to quantify the additional financial resources required for each type of university for research or promotion of the arts (e.g. 50 % of the basic budget).

The standard teaching costs must be calculated with regard to student numbers and staffing ratios in line with international standards and on the basis of meaningful international comparisons. Universities which the standard cost method for teaching and research shows to be underfunded must receive additional resources, if necessary on a step by step basis over a number of years. In the case of a university that lies (well) above the standard budget there are—economically speaking—two possibilities: either the surplus amount corresponds to a study programme focus to be agreed with the Ministry, in which case the additional funds belong in the third budget (profile budget), or the additional expenditures must be reduced in the longer term except where they lie outside the sphere of influence of the university concerned (e.g. running costs for dysfunctional buildings). With regard to the as yet unknown parties affected and the difficulties of implementation, it is—politically speaking—obviously easier to let sleeping dogs lie.

6.3.2 Performance Budget

It would be advantageous to have a performance budget in the future, too, for allocation to those universities that are more successful than others in fulfilling certain predefined parameters. There should only be a negative performance budget for those universities that are well above the standard costs in their basic budgets (e.g. more than 10 %) and at the same time below average with regard to the performance parameters. This new performance budget should only account for 1 or 2 % points of the total amount and should partly be self-financing.

6.3.3 Profile Budget

For profile-building and focus-setting at the universities, there should also be a profile budget. The amount of this budget depends on whether the universities' political masters are willing to leave the rhetoric behind and actually spend more money on the universities over and above the basic budgets.[14]

This model offers three very distinct approaches to a multi-year global budget to be drawn up on the basis of performance negotiations. The same procedure can be followed for the annual special funding requirements.

Priority must be given to the basic budget. Only when this budget can be created as described above should work be initiated on the other two budgets. This would make it possible to finance all the objectives listed in the notes on URÄG (2009) as necessitating a special funding agreement: the interests of the Ministry (and thus of the universities) could be accommodated as follows[15]: 'measures for the creation or support of a national university space' could be financed in part out of the basic budget but mainly out of the profile budget. This would necessitate coordination of study programmes at individual locations and between universities and universities of applied science, and would also lead to further cooperation in the field of research.

The 'initiation of new scientific developments' could easily be accommodated in the profile budget. The 'promotion of cooperation between the universities' could

---

[14] The Austrian Science Board (2007):6, makes the point very clear: 'Only if the universities have a secure financial basis that permits them to properly fulfill their normal functions in research, teaching and the training of the next generation of scholars can it make sense to embark on a competitive process such as the performance agreements are meant to initiate.'

[15] Cf. special section of the notes on URÄG (2009), no. 8 (Art. 12 paras. 12 and 13).

also be achieved in this way. The 'promotion of interdisciplinary cooperation, especially with regard to study programmes and at the school–university interface' could be covered by the basic budget (coordination of study programmes) or—where very full coordination at individual locations is targeted—through the profile budget. 'Improvement of student/staff ratios' is also a function of the basic budget. 'Strengthening the promotion of women' is a function of the basic budget. Here again, standards need to be established. 'Creating additional classes for working students—part-time courses' is also an item for the basic budget.

A reserve must be created for unforeseeable events, i.e. accidents (e.g. a fire in a university), or developments which could not be anticipated when the performance agreement was drawn up. The reserve could be assigned as an additional funding requirement to the basic budget or the profile budget.

This model would also make both the performance agreement and the global budget (the annual special funding requirements) more transparent and logical and would above all strengthen the performance element.

6.4 Performance Agreements: Goals and Results

6.4.1 Subject, Process and Result of the Performance Agreement

Together with the global budget, the performance agreement is the second pillar of contract management. It takes the form of a contract in public law between the Ministry, acting on behalf of the federal authority, and the university. It above all describes the elements of performance to be achieved by the university within the performance agreement period on the one hand and the funding to be provided by the federal authority for that purpose on the other. In addition, the contract normally provides for sanctions in the case of inadequate performance. As with any other contract, the process begins with a dialogue phase, in which the parties' respective ideas and possibilities are communicated. If an agreement can be reached, the document is finalised. Performance can then be delivered by the university, while the Ministry verifies implementation. An arbitration procedure is provided for cases where no agreement is reached, and if the university is still dissatisfied it can take its case to the Austrian Administrative Court.

According to UG 2002, the performance agreement covers the following items: strategic goals, profile-building, university and human resources development, research and the development and communication of the arts, study programmes and continuous education, societal objectives, increased mobility and cooperation between the universities.

In URÄG (2009), the universities are confronted with a number of additional tasks relating in particular to their students:

- Defining the measures to be taken to reduce the number of students who fail to graduate;

- Improving the staff/student ratios and bringing them up to an international standard;
- Developing study programmes for working students, including part-time courses and blended learning programmes;
- Creating needs-based student capacities for certain study programmes (medicine, dentistry, veterinary science and psychology) on the basis of numbers to be defined in the medium term.

There can be no objection to this additional agenda as long as it is matched with additional funding. The first performance agreements were finalised pursuant to UG 2002 for the 3-year period 2007–2009.[16] At the universities, UG 2002 provides for the draft performance agreement to be drawn up by the Rectorate and approved by the University Council.[17] The performance agreement negotiation process and the detailed results are described in the University Report for 2008 (BMWF 2008:76–90). On the basis of a detailed specimen performance agreement and guidelines provided by the Ministry, the universities presented draft agreements listing their goals and plans in the above fields of activity. To facilitate subsequent monitoring, the goals had to be quantified on the basis of an indicator, while the plans could be presented in purely descriptive form. Then came a vetting phase, in which the Ministry checked the agreements for compatibility with the university development plans, followed by three rounds of negotiations with each university and finalisation of the agreements. The agreements were then implemented, with monitoring and follow-up provided by the Ministry.

The 22 performance agreements signed (including that with the Danube University of Krems) covered a total of 891 plans in all fields of university activity and 319 goals (BMWF 2008:81). In the framework of ongoing monitoring talks, the Ministry lists the percentage of plans and goals implemented on an annual basis.

6.4.2 *Assessment*

In the meantime, the results of the performance agreement for 2007–2009 have attracted some highly critical judgements (Austrian Science Board 2007; Gantner 2007; Hagleitner and Loisel 2008; Court of Audit 2009:3–24). The following is a summary of the main findings from the economic point of view. An assessment in terms of the political logic is to be found in Chap. 5.

---

[16] General provisions for the performance agreements are to be found in Art. 13 UG 2002 and URÄG (2009).

[17] Pursuant to URÄG (2009) the University Council approves not only the draft of the performance agreement but also that of the annual special funding requirement. The University Council also has the right to issue an opinion on the performance agreement before it is finalised by the Reactor but not on the special funding requirement.

Severe criticism came very quickly from the Austrian Science Board, which complained of a lack of commitment to forward-looking development. According to the Science Board, most of the universities' development plans were not worthy of the name: on the one hand they were not supported by relevant data with regard to the required resources and on the other hand they were vague,[18] especially in terms of priority-setting. The Ministry was criticised on the grounds that inadequate funds were employed, that the whole process resembled the old budget allocation model and that the universities had been let off the hook in advance with the assurance that there would only be winners.

It is true that the draft performance agreements are meant to be derived from the university development plans and that the agreements and their funding were designed as 'steps in the realisation of a binding university concept'. Due to 'clearly inadequate funding', however, that did not happen. Only in exceptional cases was the result of the negotiations the sum of the financial requirements for the university's agreed plans and goals, while the last round of negotiations was no more than a veritable process of haggling over additional resources'(Gantner 2007:11).

The dearth of information available in advance of the performance agreements also gave cause for complaint. Just as the goals and plans in the universities' draft performance agreements were to be derived from their respective development plans, the Ministry was expected to have produced an overall strategy for the country's tertiary education sector or at least for the universities. According to the Austrian Court of Audit, however, that was not the case: 'The Ministry had no overall strategy for steering the programmes offered by the various universities' (Court of Audit 2009:3).[19] Similarly: 'Before the start of the negotiations for the first performance agreement, the universities were largely lacking in information relating to any specific focus in the further development of the tertiary education sector and university research. They accordingly submitted repeated requests to the Ministry for priority-setting with regard to the range of activities expected of the universities' (Court of Audit 2009: Sect. 6.1). Not until the release of the 2008 University Report was it possible to identify the Ministry's internal priorities for the financial negotiations with the universities.[20]

With regard to sanctions for failure to achieve the set goals, the authors of the study produced by the St. Gallen Management Center said (Hagleitner and Loisel

[18] 'Far too often the impression cannot be avoided that the universities merely compiled the wishes of the various university units (e.g. departments and faculties).' What was intended as a sustainable focus-setting and profile-building exercise is revealed as a mixture of more-of-same and wishes for the future" (Austrian Science Board 2007:4).

[19] For examples and key data, see: Mittelstrass (2008); Austrian Science Board (2008a, b).

[20] According to the report, the Ministry's priorities for university funding were the innovative developments already launched, reorganization projects and the priorities listed in the development plans, improved staff-student ratios, implementation of the Bologna Declaration, support for young scientists, and an increase in the number of chairs awarded to women (BMWF 2008:79).

2008:11): ‘For many, the question of consequences for non-achievement is unclear:’ In a contract, provision must normally be made for impairment of performance, but that was not done in this case.

As far as the ‘clearly inadequate funding’ is concerned, the Ministry allocated about 3 % (€186 million) of total federal university financing to new and continuing focal fields. The remainder was assigned to general funding for the universities in the form of the basic and formula budgets. Largely as a result of earlier allocations for building projects, plus a reimbursement item for stand-by duties at the medical universities, however, this sum was greatly reduced even before the negotiations started (to €117 million), with the result that the Ministry had to offer the universities about 50 % of the ‘retention for special funding requirements’, i.e. the reserve for the following years, so as to obtain an agreement on the performance agreements, an amount that significantly limited scope for further interventions and assistance during the performance agreement period.

In the 2008 government programme and the Ministry’s presentation for URÄG (2009), the performance agreement was defined as a ‘discourse and funding tool’. The former has so far been true: ‘Never before have there been such intensive and targeted discussions between the Ministry and the universities on the content of university development’ (Austrian Science Board 2007:5). The first round of performance agreements, which had pilot project character with a focus on the learning effects, did not do justice to the funding aspect, however. Many of the Rectors questioned came to the verdict that ‘the content of the performance agreement had hardly any influence on the allocation of funds’ (Hagleitner and Loisel 2008:10). The Rectors themselves naturally preferred to have only a small volume of flexibly allocable federal funds for the performance agreements so as to avoid any unduly big surprises.

The Court of Audit also criticises the fact that, in the performance agreement process, hardly any significance has so far been attached to the cost of performance by the universities. ‘The question whether a university could also achieve the agreed performance at a lower cost or how high the costs are relative to those of comparable universities could not be answered on the basis of the available information’ (Court of Audit 2009:15, text no. 16.1). The degree of correlation between the development plans and their funding, and also between the draft performance agreements and the results of the funding negotiations has so far been low. This is a consequence of the fact that neither the development plans nor the goals and plans in the draft performance agreements had to be quantified in financial terms by the Ministry. In those cases, both parties benefitted from an improved negotiating position at the internal and external levels.

The above comment made by the Austrian Court of Audit raises the question of the comparability of the universities. In this context, one has to consider the structural and qualitative problems of the universities’ material resources. As far as the structural problem is concerned, it is not logical to measure general universities, technical universities, medical universities and art universities all by the same yardstick; they are too heterogeneous with regard to the needs of research and teaching, and also—given the differences in size—human resources, buildings, capital goods, etc. Even between comparable types of universities, major differences are to be found in terms of resources. That is the result of long years of lobbying with varying degrees of success by representatives of the individual universities, present realities such as student numbers, personnel structure, history (e.g. new versus old established universities), and the condition and functionality of the buildings.

With all these differences in structure and quality, the Austrian universities were made legally autonomous. For the performance agreements negotiated to date, the Ministry has based its approach on a simple working hypothesis: according to the Ministry, the 21 universities are fully comparable because they have been able in the past to offer their programmes in their respective fields and with the available resources, and the same can be expected in the future. This simplified assumption, however, does justice neither to the past nor to the future: on the one hand no attempt has been made to assess the extent to which quality problems and students' inability to complete their courses in the prescribed number of semesters are due to inadequate funding relative to the universities' functions; on the other hand expansion of their study programmes and the other future cost increases will have to be covered out of a budget for which only minor nominal annual increases are foreseen.

The funding shortfall is not easy to quantify for the individual universities, and qualitative aspects would have to be taken into consideration. Such a national financial survey is the responsibility of the coordinating ministry. It requires differentiation by subject with regard to student numbers as it is not possible to operate in terms of square metres per student where universities are using historical buildings or facilities that have become dysfunctional with changing requirements in research and teaching.

The performance agreements have so far paid too little consideration to the significant structural and qualitative differences between the various types of universities and their resource situation as the product of historical developments ("backlog"). Nor has any attempt been made to really address the question of the essential minimum ("basic resources of a university").

All in all, financing for the performance agreements reflects the old input-oriented and incrementalist approach that had been considered a thing of the past: no attempt is made to start with a clean slate; the status quo is treated as a given, with attention focussed primarily on add-ons and budgetary growth.

As stated above, only when basic funding is guaranteed does it make economic sense to discuss and finance new focus-setting plans and related profile-building. As a consequence of this problem such projects are often not costed correctly nor financed to the extent commissioned. On the contrary, the co-financing offered by the universities signals to the Ministry a corresponding degree of interest on their part. And any additional funding tends to be granted with no consideration for the resulting operating costs, and after the initial start-up there is often no guarantee of continued financing in future budget periods.

The results of the cost/performance calculations could point the way forward, but in their current state of development they are not yet robust enough and they are insufficiently coordinated for purposes of interuniversity comparisons. As there can hardly be any universities with a level of resources that is ‘too good’, it will certainly be necessary to upgrade those that are currently worst provided for in line with a mutually agreed standard, if their performance offerings are to continue to be consumed. The real difficulties in this context doubtless lie in the non-economic sphere.

Performance agreements involve the universities in a huge investigative effort of data capture and the Ministry in a very considerable burden of processing. In the first round of agreements, that included verification of the match between the performance agreements and the development plans for 22 universities and analysis of the above mentioned 1210 (!) goals and plans. In future, the Ministry will be additionally confronted with the financial statements, the intellectual capital statements and the university data that are also a regular reporting requirement of the universities, all of which is essential if interuniversity comparisons are to be made but which at the same time jeopardises them through information overkill. In this context, the Austrian Court of Audit also finds critical words: ‘The need for individual ratios must be examined critically in the light of the cost of data acquisition’ (Court of Audit 2009:14, text no. 12.2). Similarly: ‘It was found that in general only very few ratios from the intellectual capital statement surfaced as parameters in the performance agreements’ (Court of Audit 2009:14, text no. 13.1).

The Court of Audit also recommends that the number of university plans be limited, that the plans be prioritised and that the reports to be submitted to the Ministry by the universities be assessed in terms of the content required by the Ministry for its steering and information functions (Court of Audit 2009:23–25).

With regard to the performance agreement itself, there is a one-sided distribution of future risks to the detriment of the universities during the term of the agreement, and this has received too little public attention. The universities, for example, have to meet the additional expenditures arising from increasing student numbers and their distribution among study programmes that vary in terms of real costs—something they can rarely influence themselves—out of the fixed amount of the performance agreement. Regular difficulties also arise in terms of legislative risk. As in the case of URÄG (2009), additional costs deriving from changes to the legal requirements are reimbursed inadequately or not at all.

Nor do the Rectors know what the rate of inflation will be for the term of the performance agreements. And that is a major factor for developments in costs on the supply side (collective bargaining agreements, lease and rental payments). In addition, to the annual special funding requirements, which can be expected to involve co-financing on the part of the universities, the latter are particularly affected by increasing expenditures deriving from collective bargaining agreements for university employees, price increases for services and energy, cost-of-living adjustments for leased buildings, building adaptation works, as well as cost increases for general refurbishments and replacement buildings in the construction and fitting-out phases. Nor should the additional costs be forgotten that derive from the mandatory structural measures required to satisfy industrial safety regulations.

An assessment of the first performance agreement thus provides an unsatisfactory picture but also reveals a number of points of departure for improvements in the next round.

6.5 The Importance of Political Rationality for the Reform Process

6.5.1 Point of Departure and Developments

The analysis to date has delivered the following results:

1. The universities have implemented substantial private-sector instruments expeditiously and with great commitment. Further improvements are now called for. Such private-sector criteria as economy, efficiency and expediency, as well as transparency, positive incentives and planning tools are now part of the universities' standard repertoire. They have made full use of their freedom of action for profile-setting and focus-building, and of the instruments available for optimising their administrative processes. That is a major benefit of UG 2002.
2. Contract management has not yet passed the practical test. Experience to date with the performance agreements is varied. Ample use was made of the discussion function in the drafting process, during the negotiations and also during monitoring. Expectations of the steering and financing function, on the other hand, remained unfulfilled. This was because of the lack of strategic objectives based on a higher level political benchmark, continued protection from competitive pressures, and the inadequacy of the funds provided. The same applies to the internal agreements on objectives, which are not dealt with here. In this respect UG 2002 is a bitter disappointment.

In order to better understand the changes to date and the present situation, it is worth starting off by seeking answers to some questions. Why was new scope for autonomy generated in the framework of UG 2002? Why was this kind of (initially!) restrained steering and contract management introduced? Was the idea of autonomy for the universities and contract management on a level playing field in the interests of the senior civil servants and policy makers?

For many people, the debate surrounding UG 2002 was the continuation of a form of occupational therapy for the universities that had started 10 years earlier with the implementation of the 1993 University Organisation Act. For others, it was the final act in the long search for a performance-oriented framework and task-based funding. The range of verdicts was correspondingly wide: from ‘a jump in the deep end’ to ‘a bold step forward’.

On this long road to change, the stimuli came from above (the Ministry), from below (the universities) and from without (international developments, experts) (Titscher and Winckler 2000:700). It was felt at the time that the underpowered university management functions in UG 2002, the forms of self-government chosen there and the regulatory density were acting as inhibitors leading to internal blockages and delayed decision-making, while the stimulators in the form of the pressure of external competition and strategic objectives constituted an increase in performance potential. In the run-up to UG 2002, it went without saying that corporate governance needed to be improved and university performance put on an economic footing.

In this context, a new management theory for the public sector put in a timely appearance: NPM. It is seductive, as it contains familiar ingredients which all look highly attractive: contract management, global budgets, strategic steering, stimulus through competition and reduced regulatory control in the universities’ own interests.

Without being able to look into the heads of the leading policy-makers and senior civil servants of the time, it is plausible that they saw the withdrawal of the state and decentralisation combined with competition as a suitable mix for escaping the financial shortfall already impacting the universities and at the same time implementing essential processes of change that defied central implementation and were also politically delicate: let the universities pan for their own gold! The dominant view or expectation was that the difficult problems could be better solved at the local level, by and at the individual universities themselves. It was felt that self-interest and what at the time was a strengthened belief in the power of competition and the effects of private-sector elements of control would unleash the energies of the universities.

The universities were expected to act locally, at their own risk and in competition with others in various ways:

- Making a thorough search for potential savings,
- Setting a focus in research and teaching and building a specific profile,
- Implementing the Bologna architecture for their study programmes,
- Promoting internationalisation,
- Implementing modern, private-sector planning, accounting and reporting instruments,
- Preparing draft performance agreements,
- Introducing comprehensive quality assurance programmes,
- Introducing realistic costing,
- Creating separate universities for the medical faculties and conducting the difficult negotiations on the subject of additional clinical costs,
- Assuming the role of the employer,
- Jointly negotiating a collective bargaining agreement,

- Mutually communicating their needs for university buildings and general refurbishments,
- Implementing the provisions of the industrial safety laws, etc.

To relieve the Ministry of the pressures of annual budget negotiations, performance agreements and multi-year global budgets were introduced. The power of strategic control thus remained with the Ministry. It would not have been completely unrealistic in political terms, if the leading actors at the time had wanted to force the Ministry itself to let go in the future or had merely been playing for time with a new law to keep the universities busy.

The Rectors themselves wanted this freedom of action! In retrospect it could not be taken for granted that the universities would be capable of meeting the challenge of the tight schedule imposed by UG 2002 for the introduction of certain instruments and still achieve a high standard of results in implementing the new law, but it was expected. Many of the Rectors wanted UG 2002, which they had helped to create, to succeed. The rewards for the universities made it seem worthwhile.

In the meantime, the pendulum has swung back again. All concerned have learnt to deal with the law, to make themselves at home in their new legal house, where they continue to pursue their old interests. We have much old wine in new wineskins. The lower ranks in the universities and the Ministry had never been really convinced by the new strategy in any case. University and ministerial cultures deeply anchored in traditional thinking cannot be neutralised with new laws. And the financial resources did not flow as expected.

At all events, at the end of the process we now have URÄG (2009) with its improvements in terms of equal opportunities, a return to a degree of participation, a few changes to the study programmes, adjustments to corporate governance (strengthening of the University Council, weakening of the Rectors and the Office of the Rector, bigger Senate) and the annual special funding requirements. The latter, however, impact the 3-year performance agreements and multi-year global budgets to such an extent that the financial autonomy of the universities has been all but obliterated. Politically, the law has been promoted in terms of more autonomy and better quality.[21] Universities Austria, on the other hand, see in the new law "no further development of university autonomy, contrary to the publicly presented view" and no solutions to the still "unresolved fundamental questions of university funding and the problems of admissions and capacity" (Universities Austria). The list of unresolved fundamental questions and challenges confronting the political establishment becomes infinitely longer if one considers the demands made of the new Austrian government (Universities Austria) at the plenary session of Universities Austria or by the Austrian Science Board (Austrian Science Board 2008a, b). It is a pity that there is so much untapped expertise on the competitive capabilities and performance potential of Austria's universities.

[21] BMWF (2008) University Law Amendment Act, press release dated 8th June 2009, and preamble to URÄG (2009). The authors speak of "strengthening and further developing autonomy".

In the world of politics, however, majorities are needed to win ballots and make laws. In the case of a coalition government, majorities presuppose compromise between the parties in power. The universities' real needs have not yet been given the necessary priority. The backbone of a mission statement for university policy, a development strategy, a skeleton plan—whatever the terminology—could nevertheless be established in the Ministry at any time and made the basis for serious planning—for example, in the framework of performance agreements—were it not for the calls of political rationality.

6.5.2 *Political Rationality in the Field of the Universities*

At its core, political rationality is about the acquisition and preservation of power and influence over people and resources, and hence one's own position and progress and also income. The instruments involved include political parties as platforms for pooling interests, and also elections. The latter are necessary to come to and remain in or at least control power. Power and influence enable people to play a part in answering vital questions in society and the economy in line with their own ideology. That is not possible without being elected and re-elected or at least being in power. At the risk of exaggerating: what people think, say and do in the political world is targeted primarily at these facts of political life; the facts of the case are of secondary importance.

As stated in Sect. 6.2.2 and in keeping with human nature and our social structures, this political rationality exists at all levels of the universities, too, and it plays a role in practically all decisions. What the actors fail to gain "on the marketplace" (i.e. through performance in competition with others) they attempt—often with greater success—to obtain through political intervention. The following paragraphs contain examples of the mechanisms of political control in the context of the political (and bureaucratic) steering processes upstream of the universities. Readers with university experience will have no difficulty in finding relevant applications at the level of the individual university.

6.5.2.1 Some Closing (Anecdotal) Examples of Political Rationality

Power and influence: the annual special funding requirements provided for in URÄG (2009) constitute a licence for permanent interference by the Ministry—also at the operative level—in the management of the universities. In view of the universities' limited flexibly disposable income, they almost completely neutralise the multi-year global budget and reduce it to little more than an empty shell. At a superficial level, they also relieve the Ministry of the burden of carefully planning and implementing its strategic leadership role in the context of the multi-year performance agreements; new ideas or requirements can simply be made the subject of the annual special funding requirements. The tendency is clear: 'They (the universities, the Rectors) should have to come and ask us again.'

(Finding majorities): 'The amendment (i.e. URÄG (2009), M.G.) is really a compromise between the opposing demands of political parties and lobbies' (Universities Austria). Such compromises are naturally necessary with regard to practically all plans and decisions to be made within the universities, too. Because so many people can participate in the debate and decision-making process or simply drag their feet, while the Rector or the Rectorate remain responsible for the results, there is often a clear disparity between duties, authority and responsibility, and the decisions taken and solutions adopted are often not as appropriate as they should be. But they meet with the approval of the majority.

(Short-term thinking and focus on the present): the role of research and well trained young people for the long-term prosperity of the country is a constant in the hot air produced on the subject of universities and their role in research and teaching. But no one gets hot under the collar because the universities have been starved of funding for years. The blips on the political radar only indicate the next elections; the system is too myopic to really see the long-term economic implications for the country and its future prosperity. The decision to postpone painful decisions (e.g. coordination of study programmes, and teaching and research facilities in the various locations) and to ignore future costs (e.g. future loss of competitive strength) is a tried and tested solution in the current political process for maximising votes here and now.

(Focus on individual interests, clientelism): the parliamentary majority found for abolition of student fees and partial revocation of admission restrictions immediately before the Austrian national elections in autumn 2008 is a good example. In almost autistic style and on a largely independent orbit that has little to do with the implementation of UG 2002 or URÄG (2009) and the real problems of the universities, the students' representatives and—in mutual resonance—the Austrian media and all the political parties chose to focus on two holy cows: the abolition of student fees and the continued free admission to the universities.

(Spending other people's money): at the risk of labouring the point about student fees: their introduction contributed about €150 million a year to the federal budget. Now the taxpayers' money has to be used to help finance individual access to study programmes by students who have no crucial financial problems. The others in any case receive grants.

(Avoiding transparency with regard to costs and avoiding (political) costs in the present): in a world of scarce resources and prioritising constraints, it is unusual that no price tags should be required for the development plans or the draft performance agreements, and that costs, follow-up costs and the availability of the necessary finance do not seem to really play a role. That is a scenario for letters to Father Christmas containing the consolidated wishes of all university units, with no need to tread on anyone's toes. In the interest of zero cost transparency, no detailed comparisons with universities abroad relating to resources and their uses have been made or published. Nor has any attempt been made to define or make use of standard costs for a student place at university or the capacity costs of a university place.

(Ordering and letting others pay): in the supplement to URÄG (2009), the authors have this to say on the subject of the financial implications: 'No miscellaneous costs are to be covered out of the available budgets.' For the universities that can only be a dangerous threat. Policy makers are good at protecting themselves against the power of facts—as in the case of the Ministry's refusal to provide capacity-based funding for university places.

(Priority for the status quo): if one were to really compare the universities with regard to the structure of their offerings, and the quantity and quality of their resources, one would quickly arrive at the nitty–gritty of the necessary basic budget, the costs of university places at various locations and the funding backlog confronting some of the universities. Of course, sometimes it is better not to want to know.

(Spin doctoring): the 'international competitiveness' to be guaranteed and the 'international standards in work with the students' called for (URÄG Art. 13 para. 2e) will remain hollow phrases for as long as available resources remain below that standard, too. If 'needs-based student capacity development' in individual study programmes that also largely attract students from abroad is the responsibility of the universities according to URÄG (2009) (and will hopefully receive the necessary funding), it is a purely political decision not to apply the same principle to those study programmes that are mainly swamped by Austrian students.

(Open questions, partial information): penalties are not a subject of the performance agreements. That provides the Ministry with additional options: from 'forgetting about it' to the possibility of sanctions for recalcitrant universities in future negotiations. At the same time, the Ministry—in the absence of a yardstick in the form of a general concept for the universities or the tertiary sector and prior communication of its intentions—is free to select almost any internal funding focus for future performance agreements.

(New projects and add-ons (incrementalism) instead of a revision of the existing performance portfolios; experimenting mindset): supporting additional and new projects is obviously more fun than the difficult task of coordinating study programmes, including closures at certain locations etc. It is also quite normal political practice to launch a project (e.g. Bologna or development plans) and worry about the coordination or make improvements later. Experiments and 'provisional solutions' offer scope for political compromise and playing for time and constitute an elegant style of muddling through. After all, with the benefit of hindsight one can always change things again later.

(Divide and rule): such an article as this should not be written by an Austrian Rector; both the university and the Rector involved would have a really hard time in subsequent performance agreements or construction programme planning and also within the university itself. Financial resources are also a disciplinary tool—and generous use is made of that tool in the spirit of political rationality.

6.6 Conclusion

Political and economic rationality are interdependent. They need each other all the more in a field to which both social and economic importance are attached and which is also resource-intensive. The standpoints and proposed methods should be mutually complementary; these are not parallel worlds and they should not obstruct each other.

After several years of experience with UG 2002, the question is how the long-term potential of economic thinking and the application of private-sector instruments compares with that of political rationality in the world of the universities?

The use of economic instruments in the performance management process and steering of the universities has doubtless been a success. There is still room for improvement, but all in all the universities have done their homework. Their performance potential has clearly grown as a result. And yet life is being made increasingly difficult for the proponents of economic rationality:

- On the whole, no strategic performance specifications have been provided by the Ministry over and above the general legal provisions. No answers have been given to central political questions relating to the Austrian universities (e.g. admission rules and capacity-based funding; coordination between the various players in the tertiary education sector like universities, universities of applied science, private universities and teacher-training colleges; coordination of the programmes at the various locations; research overheads). Nor have hopes been fulfilled to date of an increase in funding in excess of the rate of inflation. The chronic underfunding of the universities is set to continue until 2012 at least. With a uniformist allocation of funds, the Austrian universities have so far been largely spared the pressures of national competition, and many sectors seem to have successfully isolated themselves from international competition.
- The duties of the funding partner in contract management, evaluating reports, and coordinating and counselling universities—they seem to be unpopular roles. The ministerial bureaucracy wants to be asked and be the master again. With the introduction of the annual special funding requirements in URÄG (2009), the performance agreements and multi-year global budgets have been made obsolete.
- Within the universities, too, things are not always taken quite so seriously: as soon as the various actors had learnt their parts within the play and identified their own powers of influence, such objectives as customer orientation and results-based thinking, efficiency and effectiveness, autonomy, strong leadership, low regulatory density, the time factor in decision-making, transparency, etc. were again relegated to a minor role. Self-interest, group thinking and clientelism took over again; the sense of entitlement is a stronger force than the spirit of competition.

At the university level, economic rationality is making its mark; but to date, political rationality is the winner on points.

Above all, it is clear that political and economic rationality are not on the same level. The economic instruments and approaches are primarily servants for the implementation of goals of university policy. It is true that the principles of economic activity are enshrined in the Austrian constitution, but their primary function is to create financial freedom of action and transparency with regard to decisions and performance. They can also indicate the general conditions required for successful operation in the long term, if they are used.

Due to the specificities of the political process, there are situations in which nothing can be achieved and an objective approach to the challenges involved is doomed to failure. Completely decent people are capable of knowing all about a matter and not knowing anything at the same time! Partial interests and ideologies are alive and kicking. What is important is respect for a minimum degree of objectivity that must be satisfied in the case of political decisions and processes, too. This applies in equal measure to financing and to the content and timing of basic decisions.

For those readers who have stayed the course, here is a—playful—solution: the difference is that politicians have a hard task and sometimes take the easy way out, while economists give themselves a hard time although things could often be made easy—because he who pays the piper calls the tune. But things are not as easy as that.

Bibliography

Austrian Science Board (2007) Stellungnahme zum Prozess und zum Ergebnis der Leistungsvereinbarungen. Vienna

Austrian Science Board (2008a) 10 Eckpunkte zur Österreichischen Universitäts- und Wissenschaftspolitik in der XXIV. Legislaturperiode, Vienna

Austrian Science Board (2008b) Perspektiven des österreichischen Hochschul- und Wissenschaftssystems. Zur Entwicklung eines hochschulpolitical Planungsrahmens für Österreich, Vienna

Badelt C (2007) Kooperationsmöglichkeiten und -bedarf im Profilbildungsprozess der Universitäten. In: Österreichische Forschungsgemeinschaft, Workshop: Fünf Jahre Universitätsautonomie. Das Universitätsgesetz 2002—Erfahrungen und notwendige Verbesserungen, Baden bei Wien, 7–8 Dec 2007. (www.oefg.at/text/veranstaltungen/UG2002/Beitrag_Badelt.pdf)

Berka W (2007) Reform der Reform? Zu den Zielsetzungen einer Novellierung des Universitätsgesetzes. In: Österreichische Forschungsgemeinschaft, Workshop: Fünf Jahre Universitätsautonomie. Das Universitätsgesetz 2002—Erfahrungen und notwendige Verbesserungen, Baden bei Wien, 7–8 Dec 2007. (www.oefg.at/text/veranstaltungen/UG2002/Beitrag_Berka.pdf)

Court of Audit (2009) Universitätscontrolling. In: Reihe Bund 2009/2, Vienna

Federal Ministry of Science and Research (BMWF) (2008) University Report, 2nd corrected edn, Vienna. (www.bmwf.gv.at/submenue/publikationen_und_materialien/wissenschaft/universitaetswesen/hochschul_und_universitätsberichte)

Gantner M (2007) Finanzierung durch Vereinbarung. Erfahrungen mit Leistungsvereinbarungen. In: Österreichische Forschungsgemeinschaft, Workshop: Fünf Jahre Universitätsautonomie. Das Universitätsgesetz 2002—Erfahrungen und notwendige Verbesserungen, Baden bei Wien, 7–8 Dec 2007. (www.oefg.at/text/veranstaltungen/UG2002/Beitrag_Gantner.pdf)

Hagleitner M, Loisel O (2008) (management zentrum st.gallen) Feedback zu den Leistungsvereinbarungen. Ergebnisse der Rektorenbefragung, Vienna

Mittelstrass J (2008) Wissenschaftsland Bayern 2020. In: Österreichische Forschungsgemeinschaft, Workshop: Profilbildung und Standortplanung der österreichischen Universitäten, Baden bei Wien. 12–13 Dec 2008

Parliamentary Enquete on the Further Development of the Universities Act (2008) Parlamentskorrespondenz/02, no. 318

Titscher S, Winckler G et al (eds) (2000) Universitäten im Wettbewerb, Munich and Mering

Universitätsrecht (2009) Kodex des österreichischen Rechts, 8th edn, Vienna. Correct at 1.3.2009

University Law Amendent Act (2009) (www.parlinkom.gv.at/PG/DE/XXIV/I/I_00225/pmh.shtml)

Winckler G (2007) Die Auswirkungen der Autonomie auf Forschung und Lehre an den österreichischen Universitäten. In: Österreichische Forschungsgemeinschaft, Workshop: Fünf Jahre Universitätsautonomie. Das Universitätsgesetz 2002—Erfahrungen und notwendige Verbesserungen, Baden bei Wien, 7–8 Dec 2007. (www.oefg.at/text/veranstaltungen/UG2002/Beitrag_Winckler.pdf)

Chapter 7
Who is Leading Whom, Where to, What for: And How? Governance and Empowerment in the University of the Twenty-First Century

Wilhelm Krull

7.1 Introduction

The question of the autonomy of the universities is now back on the agenda everywhere. A case in point is the recent manifesto on the subject of European university policy published in June 2010 (The manifesto "Empower European Universities" 2010). Clearly the subject of the university as an organisation, of university autonomy based on adequate governance structures, and above all the need to constantly redefine the balance between control and participation is not yet history. At the same time, one is tempted to point out that we have now spent some 20 years working with new management and decision-making structures, quality assurance and accreditation procedures, and strengths and weaknesses analyses, and that the time has therefore come—as I pointed out last year on the occasion of Leipzig University's sixth centenary celebrations (Krull et al. 2009, pp.207–220)—to finally address the challenges of content and especially the vital question of curricular reform.

On the same occasion, that is in Leipzig in mid-May 2009, Christoph Markschies as President of Berlin's Humboldt University suggested that we should neither succumb to the temptation of a "notorious doomsday pessimism" nor indulge in "institutionally calculated optimism" but that we should embrace a "decisive yes-but" approach or, to be more precise, embark on a "via media" and also take a look at the history of the universities (Markschies 2009, pp.89–116). That is precisely what I would like to do here—albeit not from the eleventh

This chapter is based on the Helmholtz Lecture delivered by the author at Berlin's Humboldt University on 21st January 2010.

W. Krull (✉)
VolkswagenStiftung, Kastanienallee 35, 30519 Hannover, Germany
e-mail: krull@VolkswagenStiftung.de

A. Altmann and B. Ebersberger (eds.), *Universities in Change*, Innovation, Technology, and Knowledge Management, DOI: 10.1007/978-1-4614-4590-6_7,

century to the present, nor even from 1810 until today (in spite of a few inevitable references to the genius loci), but primarily with regard to the last two decades in the history of the German university—with its galloping pace of change and far-reaching reforms, its many inadequacies, the still unresolved deficits and future action requirements. In short, I wish to take stock and open up avenues for new ideas and activities.

7.2 Challenges, Chances and Risks for the German University System

Given the problem-solving capacity that is doubtlessly present in the university system, one asks oneself why it is that the intelligent people that are typically to be found there should be operating within dysfunctional structures. Is it because of the often lamented legal or fiscal restraints? Is this due to a lack of moral courage? Or is it simply a result, as many would say, of a dearth of interest on the part of the individual members of the institution concerned in the latter's wellbeing (all the more so as their careers depend not so much on the institution as on recognition within the scientific community)? Whatever the explanation, the standard response—"Intelligence is no protection against foolishness"—can hardly be the whole answer.

Before we come to the German universities, I should like to present an example from the recent history of European research policy, which illustrates some of the above dilemmas: the governance structure of the European Research Council (ERC). From 2002 to 2004 I was a member of two expert groups charged with the task of defining the objectives and tasks of the ERC and developing a suitable organisational structure (European Science Foundation 2003). In the first commission, which was created by the European Science Foundation, I drew up an organisational chart with a clear proposal for a Max-Planck or DFG (German Research Foundation) type of structure (European Science Foundation 2003, p.17): Members nominated to the Senate by the big European scientific organisations and confirmed by the Commission would elect a Board, which would in turn have the authority to appoint technical committees and be responsible for running the central office. What was finally created, however, was no such autonomous organisation but a new programme within the 7th Framework Programme and a combination of a research-driven Scientific Council and an Executive Agency of the Commission, all headed by two different persons, namely a Secretary General to run the Scientific Council and a Director from the ranks of the civil servants at the Commission to manage the Executive Agency. The fact that such a structure was doomed to fail was clear to many from the start. That makes it all the more pleasing that the panel headed by Professor Freyberga clearly confirmed that assessment in an initial review of the ERC's activities. In the report published in July 2009 Professor Freyberga says:

> The review panel is deeply concerned that the present governance structure of the ERC is complex and a source of great frustration and ongoing low level conflict. A more coherent organisation is needed and the roles of the Secretary General and the Director of the Executive Agency should be amalgamated into one post and that a high level and recognized scientist with administrative experience be recruited for the post and made a member of the Civil Service of the Commission as necessary and eliminate the current and artificial division of authority and responsibilities between programme design and implementation (Vike-Freiberga 2009, p.4).

That is still a far cry from the autonomous, science-driven structure suggested in my proposal for the European Research Council, but the decision to combine the two offices is at least a step in the right direction. Now all the big science organisations must have the courage to keep pouring oil on the fire and insist on the science-based Research Council that was originally planned. Instead of a mere programme, which has not been immune to the usual inroads of Brussels bureaucracy either, an independent institution must be the goal in the medium term if we are to maintain and strengthen the trust of the European scientific community in the ERC as an effective science-driven body.

In many respects the ERC, with its transnational commitment to excellence, should be Europe's answer to the fast growing challenges of global competition in education and research to which the universities are increasingly exposed, because global networking and participation in such networks require not only platforms for competition, with their powerful steering mechanisms and forces for behavioural change, but also a much more focussed bundling of the local and regional actors than hitherto.

In many ways, of course, Europe's universities and research institutions compare favourably with the rest of the world: The European Union is by far the biggest scientific space on earth: The largest number of academics and also postgraduate students are trained there. European universities confer almost twice as many doctorates as the USA. Europe also produces the highest number of scientific publications. In this context Europe has been ahead of the USA since 1995 (although for the future we must also consider the fast growing contribution of the Asian-Pacific region, which is expected to overtake the USA and Europe some time between 2015 and 2020 to become the world's leading research area) (European Commission 2008).

If we look at Europe's share of the world's most frequently cited publications, however, and above all the numbers of benchmark science awards, including the Nobel prizes, etc., significant weaknesses emerge: Basically, too few fundamental scientific breakthroughs are made in Europe. In the last few decades a far greater number of Nobel prizes and similarly prestigious international science awards have gone to US scientists. Europe's ability to market basic innovations is also comparatively underdeveloped, a situation that has not changed significantly with the recently increased focus on linkage between research and industry or the Nobel prizes awarded to European scientists in 2007 and 2008.

Without wishing to go into the objectives and relevance of international university rankings, to a certain extent it can also be said that—for the natural sciences and engineering disciplines, at least—the 2009 Shanghai Academic Ranking of World Universities confirmed the global dominance of the Anglo-Saxon language and research area. With eight of the top 10, 36 of the top 50, and 55 of the top 100 universities ranked, the USA's leading position in the world of science remains unchallenged. In the Shanghai results and other rankings, the UK plays the role of the little but also very successful brother of the USA, with Oxford and Cambridge up amongst the best. German universities only make it to the top 100. On the other hand, if we look at the world's top 500 universities, the latest rankings actually put Germany ahead of the UK and, relative to the size of the population, roughly on a par with the USA. The fact that a considerable number of German universities are to be found among the top 500 in several rankings (out of an estimated total of 20,000 universities worldwide) but are nowhere up among the best reflects the approach to university policy adopted since the foundation of the Federal Republic of Germany, with its focus on broad-based and regionally distributed support for a large number of universities offering high quality standards and very good study programmes rather than funding for a few elite universities enjoying international visibility.

The speed of change in the international division of labour from a world of hands, tools and machines to one of heads, computers and laboratories is matched by the pace of development in the conditions to be met to run successful universities. If we are not to be left behind by the world's elite, Germany and Europe must provide first-class conditions for teaching, research and innovation. We have to develop a culture of creativity and trigger more innovation through the funds invested in research. The university as an institution is confronted more urgently than ever using the global race for the most creative minds. Their traditional self-image as a "central bank of knowledge" must be transformed into that of an autonomous, self-responsible facility devoted to knowledge and research management as well as to international quality standards. At the same time, we must revive the principles of "learning by researching" and "researching through inquiry". In this context, the publicly financed university and research system is being increasingly challenged by private initiatives. Multiple actor constellations call for new forms of governance and interaction, which in turn result in more intensive efforts for integration within the respective institution and location.

It will not be easy to confront these challenges; compared with other countries, German universities are clearly underfunded. On the whole, it can be said that the additional capacities created since 1974 have not been matched by similar increases in funding and staffing. From 1972 to 2004, the number of students grew by a factor of three compared with a factor of only 1.8 for the number of professors. In 2008, the student/professor ratio (on a full time basis) was 60.4 at German universities and 38.5 at the country's universities of applied science (Wissenschaftsrat 2008, pp.22–23).

Ultimately, the difference in funding between German universities and the world's elite universities is not a matter of percentages but of magnitudes. The difference between Germany's most generously financed Technical University (TU Munich) and ETH Zurich is one of a factor three, and between TU Munich and the Massachusetts Institute of Technology (MIT) factor ten. For years Germany's universities have found themselves in a downward economising spiral; as soon as the—often significant—savings had been made, the next round of cuts was announced. The decision to shorten secondary schooling by 1 year in Germany with a resulting doubling of the university intake in 2011/2012 is a further challenge imposed on the country's universities without taking adequate staffing measures to equip them to cope. In such circumstances, it cannot be said often enough that it is astonishing to see what Germany's universities nevertheless achieve and how high the quality of the output can be in terms of both graduates and research. On the whole, the quality of both teaching and research can still be considered very good.

Whilst the old problems primarily involve the university teaching situation, i.e. inadequate funding, catastrophic staff/student ratios and high dropout rates, the new challenges mainly relate to the Bologna process and the need to find convincing solutions in terms of curricula and content for implementation of the original objectives, and to make the universities still more attractive for young researchers from home and abroad. At this level, a forward-looking university policy must include not only solutions to the problem of large student year groups, but also ideas for the race for the most innovative minds and for the goal of lifelong learning. In addition to its teaching role, this means the university must itself develop into a learning organisation.

7.3 A Retrospect: Performance Through Self-Empowerment

The question of the functions of the rectors or presidents and reform of the management and decision-making structures of Germany's universities was first raised in the 1980s. At the end of the phase of university expansion, i.e. at the end of the 1970s or beginning of the 1980s, depending on the state involved, when the approach to steering the university system shifted from input-based to output-based, it became increasingly clear that the relationship between the state and the university and also the university's internal management and decision-making structures were in need of fundamental reform. In this context, the Volkswagen Foundation formulated the following diagnosis in 1987 already:

> In decisive aspects the universities are not independent; for important offices they elect amateurs in the positive sense of the word, who have no time to develop the necessary expertise for their offices and are dependent on well-meaning civil servants in the ministries and politicians in the parliaments who again lack experience in specific matters. This situation requires redress. (Board of Trustees of Stiftung Volkswagenwerk 1987).

In this context it was generally agreed that there was a need for support from private foundations. Finally, in 1988, a report on the management and decision-making structures of German universities was commissioned to Professor Karl Alewell, a business administration expert and former President of the University of

Giessen. Because of Professor Alewell's committed involvement in the process of German reunification, however, completion of the report was delayed until 1993 (Alewell 1993). On the basis of his review, assessment and recommendations, the Volkswagen Foundation finally invited contributions on the subject of "Performance through Empowerment" in 1994. The objective was not a university reform in the general and comprehensive sense of the word but more specifically a change in the realities of the universities, i.e. enabling them to review their structures, methods and processes and to develop proposals for a more meaningful definition and organisation of the individual fields of authority and responsibility, and to test new regimes and implement them on a sustainable basis. More specifically, the aim was to ensure that:

- responsibilities are no longer vaguely distributed but are clearly assigned on an identifiable basis,
- responsibility involves consequences for those who exercise it,
- decision-making powers and duties are assigned to people who face the consequences of their decisions,
- communications are intensified at all levels and between the various authorities, bodies, groups and individuals, and that
- university staff become aware that it is their university they are working for (Volkswagen-Stiftung 1998, p.6).

In the light of these goals, it was also clear that competition between the participating institutions should create opportunities for them to find their individual paths to improved performance rather than search for a universal structure to be imposed—possibly on the basis of university legislation—on all of them, whether they like it or not.

In spite of the many differences between the concepts submitted and procedures proposed, a series of problems emerged in all cases at the ten participating universities, e.g.:

- conflict between strategic top-down and participatory bottom-up approaches in the development of new management and decision-making structures,
- interaction and counteraction between the authorities and university self-government,
- coordination between organisational and human resources development,
- the threat to project continuity posed by rapid staff turnover,
- the problems of performance-based funding as an instrument of resource management (including self-blockades),
- additional workload and over-organisation deriving from the unintentional consequences of decentralisation, and finally
- redefinition of the relationship between universities and the state, and between university autonomy and ministerial supervision (Volkswagen-Stiftung 1998, pp.8–9).

Implementation of the reforms made enormous demands in terms of communication skills at the level of university management, particularly in matters requiring the acceptance, participation and powers of conviction of the university members. Often enough, the management teams themselves could not foresee the consequences of the changes they were introducing. In many cases, they placed their trust in the optimistic words of Göttingen's experimental physicist, philosopher and aphorist Georg Christoph Lichtenberg: "I cannot say whether things will get better if we change them; what I can say, however, is that they must change if they are to get well" (Lichtenberg 1825, P.293). In the course of the implementation process, however, it became clear that the measures introduced were essential for clear university profiling and priority wsetting, convincing quality assurance and optimum use of the individual universities' specific potential.

If we look back at the Volkswagen Foundation's programme today, it is clear—thanks above all to the successful outcome of the Excellence Initiative for many of the participating universities—that the measures taken at the time had positive effects on at least some of the universities, such as the Free University of Berlin, Göttingen University and Heidelberg University, and on the reform of the new University of Bremen.

However, the Volkswagen Foundation was not alone with its programme. The German Stifterverband pursued similar goals with two action programmes for University Reform and Faculty Reform. The Bertelsmann Foundation also delivered an input with the establishment of its Centre for University Development in 1994. On the other hand, a number of other foundations decided not to wait for the public universities to become capable of reform and established their own—relatively small—universities, like the Bucerius Law School in Hamburg, the Hertie School of Governance in Berlin, and International University of Bremen taken over in 2006 by the Jacobs Foundation. And it is no coincidence that most of the private institutions that satisfied university accreditation requirements were financed by foundations; significant third-party funding is essential in order to combine university structures with socially acceptable levels of student fees.

7.4 New Rules, More Freedom: Selected State Legislation

If universities are to fulfil their tasks in the production, processing and communication of knowledge—which also means training excellent young minds for leading functions in research, business and society in general—they must have the capabilities to cope with today's science- and technology-driven dynamic of change. Above all they must be able to

- respond to new challenges in continuous interaction with their environment and develop innovative fields of research,
- adapt their teaching and study programmes to future-oriented fields of knowledge,
- overcome rigid structures and develop interdisciplinary forms of knowledge-building and communication,

- provide a recognised standard of training for person to person knowledge transfer,
- network their teaching, study programmes and research and achieve top-class performance.

Around the turn of the millennium it became increasingly clear that reform was also required at the level of legislation. It had become essential for the universities to mobilise new forces on their part in order to implement the fundamental reforms needed to modernise, but at the same time the state had to help the universities, who were sailing hard on the wind of change, by eliminating legal obstacles. The first of the German Länder to do so was Lower Saxony with the 2002 amendment to its Universities Act (Oppermann 2002), followed 2 years later by Baden-Württemberg with its reformed University Law, although the latter was based on a company analogy rather than the foundation approach.

Since then many German states have moved in the same direction, like North Rhine-Westphalia with its University Freedom Act, but I should like to concentrate on Lower Saxony and Baden-Württemberg, especially against the background of my own experience as chairman of the Foundation Council of the Georg-August University of Göttingen and the University Council of Constance University (until February 2009). Although theoretically the universities had long been granted self-government in state university legislation, it was significantly curtailed in fact by the supervisory powers of the ministries. Important decisions, such as appointments to university chairs, were mostly taken by the latter; the universities were able to participate in the appointment of their top-level academic staffs, but the ministries had a statutory right to the final decision.

It was not until the new Lower Saxony Universities Act came into force at the beginning of the 2002/2003 academic year that responsibility was largely assigned to the universities themselves in that state. As a result, the universities have also been able to develop greater flexibility in terms of their management structures. The Lower Saxon authorities have since withdrawn from the operative business of the foundation universities. They limit their activities to legal supervision and also negotiate with the universities their strategic development and performance goals, which are defined in written agreements on objectives. For Thomas Oppermann, who was the Minister at the time, one of the objectives was also to achieve enhanced social integration for the foundation universities. He saw the foundation as "the most suitable legal form to eliminate the basic shortcoming of German universities, namely inadequate integration in society. German universities see only the poor state and ignore our rich society. The foundation is the institution of civil society. It enables the German universities' fixation on the state to be overcome and the university-state dualism to be replaced by the trinity of university, state and society" (Oppermann 2002, p.22).

The new Lower Saxony Universities Act also strengthened the position of the university management. Whereas the Senates had previously been able to build up significant powers of decision, the Presidential Committees now became responsible not only for signing the agreements on objectives but also for the creation, modification and dissolution of faculties, the introduction, amendment and termination of study programmes, and the approval of examination regulations. This permits the universities to react faster in teaching and research to the challenges imposed by the dynamic processes of change.

In their decisions, the Presidential Committees are counselled and supervised by the newly created Foundation Councils. The latter have seven members: five appointed by the Ministry in consultation with the Senate, one representing the Ministry of Science and one delegated by the Senate. With the exception of responsibility for the agreements on objectives, the Ministry has transferred its powers over the universities—including appointments to university chairs—to the Foundation Councils. That has involved a huge process of decentralisation at the level of the university, all the more so as the foundations are also in the role of employer and have control over university assets.

On the model of American universities, German foundation universities can build up capital on a long-term basis and employ the earnings to make a relevant contribution to funding for teaching and research. Fundraising and alumni programmes permit private finance to be acquired as an addition to basic assets, which further increases the foundation's revenues. Of course, German universities will nevertheless remain financially dependent on their respective state authorities in the foreseeable future, and the public law foundation and the university corporation are interconnected in a variety of ways. The Board of the foundation, for example, is also the Board of the corporation. The members of the Foundation Council are jointly appointed by the university and the ministry. One of the main tasks of the Foundation Council for its part is to appoint and dismiss the Presidents and Vice-Presidents on the basis of nominations put forward by the Senate. This is again a product of linkage between the foundation and the corporation. Legal and academic supervision of the universities is exercised by the Foundation Council. At the same time, the Lower Saxon authority is responsible for legal supervision of the foundation. The authority steers the activities of the foundation through its funding decisions together with the agreements on objectives for the further development of the university. To that extent it cannot be said that the universities have been completely "denationalised". Nevertheless, their freedom of action—especially in one matter that is decisive for the quality of the universities, namely appointments to chairs—has been significantly extended insofar as the influence of the state has been mediated in so many respects.

As mentioned above, for the amendment to the Baden-Württemberg Universities Act, Minister Frankenberg's approach is based on the analogy between universities and commercial enterprises. He explained his decision in an essay as follows: "The principle must be for the universities to act wherever possible with entrepreneurial freedom and responsibility, while the state handles coordination as required. The state and the universities are linked in a strategic partnership" (Frankenberg 2003, p.423). The central goal of the university reform in Baden-Württemberg was to increase university efficiency by implementing new management structures borrowed from the world of business. This involved the following main changes:

The Rector (Chairman of the Board) and the full time members of the university's Executive Board are elected by the Supervisory Board and confirmed by the Senate.

The Supervisory Board is composed primarily or even exclusively of external members, and its central supervisory role vis-à-vis the University Council significantly strengthened.

The authority to appoint new professors and decide their position on the salary scale was transferred from the ministry to the Executive Board.

Numerous ministerial reporting requirements and rights of approval were terminated.

As in the case of the Lower Saxony Universities Act, the new law in Baden-Württemberg also provided for a significant shift of power from the Senate to the Rector and the University Council. The reform met with considerable criticism on the grounds of the inadequacy of the commercial enterprise analogy and fears of excessive external influence on the part of the Supervisory Board. On the other hand, the resulting steering model corresponded in almost all respects to the process developed for the University of Constance and already implemented there on the strength of an experimental clause (Modell 1998). In the company model, too, there is much interlinking between the corporation and the supervisory bodies, especially with regard to the election of the Rector, and the structure and development plans. The Senate, the Rector and the university together have greater freedom of action, and at the same time more responsibility is assigned to the Rector and his/her team. The strategic power of decision is clearly vested in the Rector/Executive Board. It is limited by the need to convince the University Council as the supervisory body of the desirability of the measures proposed.

7.5 The Initative on Excellence as a Governance Competition

All three funding lines of the Excellence Initiative launched by the German federal and state authorities are primarily targeted at research performance and strategies. The application processes stimulated by the offer of additional financing and hope of enhanced prestige also facilitated a whole series of reform measures which otherwise would hardly have been possible and certainly not in such a short time. To that extent, the excellence race—especially with regard to the third funding line for institutional strategies—was above all a governance competition, too. The commission I chaired on "The cornerstones of a sustainable German research system: twelve recommendations" had already made the following recommendation for the independent university of the future:

> The universities must be given the freedom to participate and succeed in national and international competition in their respective fields of strength. This requires the appropriate decision-making, management and administrative structures for setting priorities in the competitive situation. The university of the future bases its actions on standards

deriving from science and research but also has an obligation towards society with regard to its activities and with regard to the return on funds invested in it (Krull 2005, p.12).

Many universities have since developed their institutional strategies in such a way that they do justice to the need to open the universities to other research and innovation actors, and facilitate internal processes for the allocation of start-up funds and the creation of new internal research units, e.g. Centres or Institutes of Advanced Study. When the experts—invited mainly from abroad—came to inspect the various universities, one major criterion in their assessment of the proposed institutional strategies was whether the universities had a clear understanding of their weaknesses and whether the proposed measures constituted an adequate response to them. In many of the successful concepts, the universities also reacted to the sixth recommendation of the "cornerstones", relating to universities and non-university research, with its central—and at the time highly controversial—postulate: "In the interest of their ability to compete at the international level, the universities must be strengthened through close cooperation or even structural integration with non-university research institutions" (Krull 2005, p.14).

This recommendation for the fall of institutional walls was applied most stringently in the Karlsruhe plan for a merger of the Technical University and the Forschungszentrum Karlsruhe to form the Karlsruhe Institute of Technology. This institutional strategy, which was accepted for funding in the first round of the Excellence Initiative already, is designed to combine two extremely different research cultures, namely that of a primarily tied research facility and that of an autonomous university. With an annual budget of about 700 million Euros, a total of 8,000 employees are now working under the single roof of this alliance between a university and research centre.

Similar goals, but with a different institutional structure, are being pursued by the Jülich-Aachen Research Alliance. What is particularly interesting in the case of Aachen's institutional strategy "RWTH 2020—Meeting Global Challenges" is that it also constitutes an attempt to make a real improvement to internal corporate governance, in particular through the introduction of a Strategy Board with the following mandate:

- implementation of an internal culture of competition,
- development of flexible funding for innovative ideas and projects,
- creation of incentives for the development and use of temporary structures,
- generation of synergies through consolidation of inadequately coordinated activities,
- strengthening cooperation beyond faculty limits through new institutional rules (RWTH Aachen University).

These new strategic departures are designed to promote interdisciplinary collaboration outside of the faculty with a minimum of bureaucracy.

At the University of Göttingen—following the feedback autonomy projects funded through the "Performance through Empowerment" programme and the creation of the foundation university at the beginning of 2003—the next step is also to introduce a new element of governance to permit the closest possible degree of cooperation with non-university actors in the interest of research and the future of Göttingen as a research location. The Göttingen Research Council (GRC) is the decisive platform for this purpose (Georg-August University of Göttingen).

Apart from that, Göttingen's institutional strategy also provides for other internal bodies, some with external participation, which are designed to improve the conditions for creative research, namely a university Research Committee which also includes external members, Courant Centres with three or four junior research groups each, and—last but not least—the Lichtenberg-Kolleg as a kind of Institute of Advanced Study with a focus on the humanities and social sciences.

There are no non-university research facilities in the Constance area. For this medium-size university (with approx. 180 faculty members and 10,000 students), it was therefore felt necessary to develop an independent strategy under the motto "Towards a Culture of Creativity" with the objective of helping the university, which was already considered one of Germany's leading research institutions, to make still further progress (University of Constance). A decisive step had already been taken in Constance at the end of the 1990s, when a commission comprising mainly external members and chaired by Professor Jürgen Mittelstrass was mandated to more or less reinvent the university. With a section model instead of faculties and the development of an integrated interdisciplinary concept for the creation of centres and a Centre of Advanced Study, the commission already laid the structural foundations for the development of an institutional strategy for the future. The key elements of the new structure for an enhanced culture of creativity were and are the creativity cells, which are designed to develop new scope for action, the Future College as a springboard for junior research groups and assistant professors in particular, and other concepts for infrastructural platforms to further improve the research situation at the university.

One thing these successful models have in common is the fact that university management acting in collaboration with key actors in the main fields of research has not only developed concepts but also created the structures needed to significantly enhance international visibility for the local and regional research capacities. At the same time, new structural elements—like the Constance Future College, the various Institutes of Advanced Study and the interdisciplinary and interfaculty centres—have initiated a new and exciting process of priority setting and career development. With the help of numerous inter- and transdisciplinary centres, clusters and other organisational structures, it has been possible to bundle top-level research at the various locations and offer new opportunities for career development based on the tenure track process for junior researchers (who still have to prove themselves, however, within the faculty-oriented university appointments system).

7.6 Where do we Stand: And Where do we Go from Here?

The Excellence Initiative has finally put paid to the widely nourished illusion of the equality and comparability of German universities. In the meantime, the German Research Foundation (DFG) and the German Council of Science and Humanities (WR) have presented an initial review, (Deutsche Forschungsgemeinschaft/Wissenschaftsrat 2008) in which the authors show that, through the Excellence Initiative, effective progress has been made in improving career prospects for young researchers and in encouraging researchers working abroad to return to Germany. In addition, German universities have increasingly succeeded in making appointments to chairs in the face of fierce competition from elite universities abroad and in encouraging professors to remain in Germany in spite of offers received from leading American universities. Another important aspect is the fact that the stronger links between universities and non-university research institutions called for in the Twelve Recommendations in "The cornerstones of a sustainable German research system" are now being vigorously introduced by the participating universities. That opens up wholly new joint career planning perspectives and opportunities for the shared involvement of university and non-university institutes in long-term research planning for the location involved. Given the fact that the system evaluations of the DFG and the Max-Planck-Gesellschaft (MPG) are only ten years old, (Forschungsförderung Deutschland 1999) this means we have achieved a level of confidence building and established a new architecture of collaboration for profile building for the respective locations and regions that was unheard of only a few years ago.

In view of the ever widening lacunae in the country's finances, it is clear that in addition to public funding, personal involvement is called for if we are not to fall even further behind in comparison with the rest of the world. In the OECD education spending statistics, Germany now comes a poor 25th (OECD 2009, pp.203–205). Of course, it is not just the political framework but the universities themselves that have to make a new start. In my view, foundations offer a more suitable platform for universities than a company-based structure or other legal form, in particular because of their focus on the common good in the given cause and their credibility in the acquisition of donations and endowments. Admittedly, we still have a long way to go before the truly autonomous university becomes reality. In order to achieve higher levels of performance in research, the universities must improve in terms of resource development, including access to new fields of finance, make more effective and efficient use of available funds, simplify and accelerate their procedures and administrative processes, strengthen communications at all levels, and above all ensure that all university members identify with their university. With regard to the governance structures, it is important to strike a new balance between the necessary degree of control and the equally essential involvement of all university members.

Ultimately all these reform measures can be evaluated by the degree to which creativity is achieved in research and research management alike. Really productive creativity is comprised of many components (Krull 2010), including the willingness to take risks, communication skills, fault tolerance and the ability to respond to the unexpected. And the questioning role of a critical colleague continues to be essential for the advancement of knowledge (unless we prefer to hope for epistemological miracles).

I should like to stress two aspects that can also serve as guidelines for the development of internal structures. I am referring to the relationship between the diversity of scientific disciplines and organisational units on the one hand, and the intensity of communication, i.e. the interdisciplinary exchange between members of the university involved, on the other. If it is too broad-based, diversity always runs the risk of slipping into heterogeneity. Conversely we find that, where the structure of the disciplines is too homogeneous, there is too little potential for stimulus from neighbouring fields (Hollingsworth 2001, pp.17–63). For that reason it is important to continually create new researcher-based opportunities for exchange and to modify the structures accordingly.

In other words, it is all about developing patience and trust in an institution so that flexibility and the willingness to take risks are just as assured as reliable career paths. Once taken, decisions must remain valid in the medium term at least, i.e. for 5–7 years. The actors in such contexts need this degree of certainty if they are really to explore new avenues in research. This is confirmed by such highly successful institutions as the Wellcome Trust and the MRC in the UK, and the Howard Hughes Medical Institute and Janelia Farm Campus in the USA.

With regard to the title of this paper, I should like to come back to three key concepts that are highly relevant in the context of autonomy, management and control: competition, governance and steering instruments. It is presumably now clear to what extent competition also has steering effects. That also applies on a smaller scale to the programmes for the reformation of management and decision-making structures initiated by the Volkswagen Foundation and the Stifterverband in the 1990s. It applies all the more to the Excellence Initiative. This has stimulated a series of long overdue reforms (e.g. postgraduate schools and structured doctoral programmes, and the opening of universities to non-university research), which had previously been a frequent subject of discussion but rarely a cause for action.

The second round of the Excellence Initiative is now approaching, offering new opportunities, for example for Berlin's Humboldt University. Admittedly the air at the top will be relatively thin for newcomers; funding can presumably only be extended to include another three or four institutional strategies and eight to ten postgraduate schools and excellence clusters (assuming that 10 to 20 % of current recipients will not be reselected). But these are still real opportunities for the advancement of the best, and the Excellence Initiative—as I have insisted from the very start—will be an open, living system and not a club for the establishment.

For the universities' internal organisational structures and decision-making processes, this naturally also means that a widespread redistribution of resources will be necessary. At the same time the recipients of funding to date will have to find a new internal balance of power; the "parallel structures" largely established by the universities' top performers and management actors—comprising new clusters, centres and Institutes of Advanced Study—must be given a platform for interaction with the faculties. Universities depend on the active involvement of all their members (including students); they are not enterprises that can be run by top-down management alone but institutions operated for the common good with the support of all their members. For that reason they require a continuous process of redefining the balance between participation and control. That also means they need an active management capable of driving things forward. An institution directed at the common good otherwise lacks the ability to remain vibrant.

The aspect of governance also includes the new supervisory bodies created in the last 10 to 15 years. Whatever the name—Board of Trustees, University Council or Foundation Council—a satisfactory solution to the question of role definition and the necessary learning process at the interface of supervisory body and the university's internal bodies has yet to be found, and use must be made of the opportunities for learning. In the meantime, as reflected in the lively debate in the relevant forums, there is a need to share experience and optimise the situation both in the national framework via the German Centre for Higher Education Development (CHE) and the Stifterverband and in an international context through the European Association of University Governing Boards. The many mishaps in the co-decision processes for the election of Presidents and Rectors have shown that too much arrogance can still be involved in the case of appointments to senior management positions in German universities involving cooperation between the Senate or Council on the one hand, and the Foundation Council or Curatorium on the other. There are too many loose ends here, but they can still be tied to form a knot.

A more serious steering problem at German universities is to be seen in the use of conflicting steering instruments. On the one hand, a consensus is reached on many items in agreements on objectives that are well documented in both qualitative and quantitative terms and seem to have the potential to help the universities move ahead, and at the same time steering instruments are employed—like indicator-based funding or finance allocation according to the cost of a university place or the number of graduates who complete their courses within the standard time—which are diametrically opposed to the agreement on objectives. This is where I see the most urgent need for corrective action. One cannot expect a university to develop into a top-class institution with international visibility (and correspondingly expensive faculty) while operating with state-wide funding categories based on average prices covering all types of university places. That is anathema to the higher level goal of excellence.

In Germany, we have long applied a policy of regionalisation to the university system, and it has generated good—albeit not outstanding—results. What has been on the agenda for a number of years now and will become much more important in the future is a process of further differentiation within the university spectrum. It will not be possible to develop all one hundred or so degree-conferring universities into top-class universities with an international presence. Many universities have already responded by rooting themselves more strongly at the regional level and finding a new identity under the label "Regional University". For traditional, high-performing universities like the University of Bonn, the Humboldt University in Berlin, the University of Kiel, the University of Tübingen or the University of Erlangen (to mention just a few), however, it will be necessary to make use of the Excellence Initiative to make effective progress on the path to international visibility.

Ultimately there can be no guarantee of success. In the sphere of university and research policy we have little choice but to accept Albert Camus' dictum: "We must conceive of Sisyphos as a lucky man." (Camus 1942, pp.50–51). Unlike the Sisyphus of Antiquity, however, at today's universities we need the courage and strength to keep pushing new stones up the mountain. Some of them will remain there!

Bibliography

Alewell K (1993) Autonomie mit Augenmass. Vorschläge für eine Stärkung der Eigenverantwortung der Universitäten, Göttingen

Camus A (1942) The myth of sisyphus, Paris

Deutsche Forschungsgemeinschaft/Wissenschaftsrat (2008) Bericht der gemeinsamen Kommission von Wissenschaftsrat und DFG zur Exzellenzinitiative, 1. Programmphase, Bonn 2008

Empower European Universities (2010) The manifesto, Brussels

European Commission (2008) A more research-intensive and integrated European research area. Science, Technology and Competitiveness, Key Figures Report 2008/2009, Brussels

European Science Foundation (2003) New structures for the support of high-quality research in Europe. An ESF position paper; and The Danish Minister for Education and Science, the European Research Council. A Cornerstone in the European Research Area. Report from an Expert Group

Forschungsförderung Deutschland (1999) Bericht der internationalen Kommission zur Systemevaluation der Deutschen Forschungsgemeinschaft und der Max-Planck-Gesellschaft, Hannover

Frankenberg P (2003) Strategische Partnerschaft, 17 Thesen zur Hochschulreform. In: Forschung & Lehre, Heft 8

Rogers Hollingsworth J (2001) Institutionalizing Excellence in Biomedical Research. The Case of the Rockefeller University. In: Stapelton DH (ed) Creating a Tradition of Biomedical Research. Contributions to the History of the Rockefeller University, New York

Krull W (2009) Hat das humboldtsche Bildungsideal noch eine Zukunft?. In: Wissen und Geist. Universitätskulturen. Symposium anlässlich des 600-jährigen Jubiläums der Universität Leipzig, 11–13. Mai 2009, Leipzig

Krull Wilhelm (2005) Eckpunkte eines zukunftsfähigen deutschen Wissenschaftssystems. Zwölf Empfehlungen, Hannover

Krull W (2010) Zukunft stiften—Kreativität fördern, Konstanzer Universitätsreden, Band 236, Constance

Lichtenberg GC, Sudelbücher, Heft K (1825) 293 (German original)

Markschies CV (2009) Woran krankt die deutsche Universität? oder: Warum es sich lohnt, Universitätsgeschichte zu schreiben. In: Wissen und Geist. Universitätskulturen. Symposium anlässlich des 600-jährigen Jubiläums der Universität Leipzig, 11–13 May 2009, Leipzig

Modell K (1998) Empfehlungen zur strukturellen Weiterentwicklung der Universität, Constance

OECD (2009) Education at a Glance 2009, OECD Indicators, Paris/Bonn

Oppermann Thomas (2002a) Vom Staatsbetrieb zur Stiftungshochschule. Moderne Hochschulen für Deutsch-land, Göttingen

Oppermann T (2002) Vom Staatsbetrieb zur Stiftung—Impulse für neue Hochschulen. In: ibid (ed) Vom Staatsbetrieb zur Stiftung. Moderne Hochschulen für Deutschland, Göttingen

Vike-Freiberga (2009) *Towards a World class frontier research organisation. review of the European Research Council's Structures and Mechanisms*, Brussels

Volkswagen-Stiftung (1998) *Leistungsfähigkeit durch Eigenverantwortung. Hochschulen auf dem Weg zu neuen Strukturen*, published by Volkswagen-Stiftung, Hannover

Wissenschaftsrat (2008) *Empfehlungen zur Qualitätsverbesserung von Lehre und Studium*, Cologne

Additional Materials

Georg-August University of Göttingen: www.uni-goettingen.de/de/56424.html

RWTH Aachen University: www.exzellenz.rwth-aachen.de

University of Constance: www.exzellenz.uni-konstanz.de/zukunftskonzept-modell-konstanz-towards-a-culture-of-creativity

Part III
Strategic and Operative Issues

Chapter 8
Learning From the Best: Implications From Successful Companies for Higher Education Management

Kurt Matzler and Dagmar Abfalter

8.1 Introduction

At the end of the first decade of the new millenium, the circumstances for both academic institutions and the marketplace could be easily described as adverse. A global financial crisis had increased pressure on the budgets of universities and on their actual as well as prospective students. Companies that had traditionally supported higher education were struggling with survival. In many cases, public money had been shortened or just distributed over an increasing number of recipients in the last years. In Austria and Germany, the university sector had also experienced a shift toward privatization of state universities and the foundation of private universities. By all means, competition for scarce resources in the academic environment—budgets, excellent staff, and students among others—had increased, forcing higher education institutions to become more market oriented. As in business, agility is demanded for universities if they want to win a competitive edge (Shattock 2000).

In their book on enduring success, Bailom et al. (2007) look at the pillars of success of high-performing companies and how they perform in areas such as innovativeness, market orientation, core competencies, leadership, and entrepreneurship culture. In their large-scale study of over 1,100 companies in 10 countries they reveal that success does not depend so much on market characteristics or industry attractiveness. A company's fate is largely self-determined—it depends on a few internal features that can be influenced by the top management.

K. Matzler (✉) · D. Abfalter
Department of Strategic Management, Marketing and Tourism, The University of Innsbruck, Universitätsstrasse 15, 6020 Innsbruck, Austria
e-mail: kurt.matzler@uibk.ac.at

D. Abfalter
e-mail: dagmar.abfalter@uibk.ac.at

A. Altmann and B. Ebersberger (eds.), *Universities in Change*, Innovation, Technology, and Knowledge Management, DOI: 10.1007/978-1-4614-4590-6_8,

Assuming that the same could be true for universities, this contribution strives at showing parallels between the academic and entrepreneurial sphere in order to derive viable solutions for the 'university of the future'.

8.2 Succeeding in Changed Conditions

As long as universities had a predictable future with public funding and resources oriented at student numbers, universities have been focused on planning. Now, with declining state funding and an increasing need for market orientation, there is a shift toward strategic management of universities. It has been suggested that in this changed environment the following characteristics are key for successful universities, 'requiring universities to take a holistic view of their activities, to coordinate institutional strengths so that they reinforce one another and to create machinery whereby academic, financial and physical planning strategy is decided on an integrated basis' (Shattock 2000):

- Competition. Competition between universities has highly increased through the reliance of funding on student numbers and especially international full-tuition paying students. Furthermore, there is competition for research-active staff and research funding from public and private sources. Membership to leagues and respective accreditations increasingly determine an institution's reputation.
- Opportunism. When resources are declining, the ability to seize opportunities becomes vital. This ability is highly dependent on an institution's management structure and decision-making processes, retaining crucial elements of collegial participation. In the world outside universities, 'time has become the competitive strategy of the firm' (Schoenberger 1997). Clear mission statements and goals provide a helpful framework within which opportunistic decisions may be taken.
- Income generation and cost reduction. The necessity of generating external income for institutions of higher education has become a matter of fact. An analysis of the costs of realizing income and the real benefits to the organization becomes crucial and demands a strong strategic input. Universities are expensive and the best universities appear to be the most expensive. They have to prioritize, cultivate niche markets, cut out weak departments, and build up strong units.
- Relevance. 'Relevance' and 'excellence' can be considered contradictory concepts. Still, universities need to demonstrate that they are not only ornamental but also useful to society. In need of public support they need to train students adequately and to address issues of public concern—such as regional unemployment, collaboration with industry, or commitment to the community—in order to justify public funding and support.
- Excellence. 'Universities traditionally claim excellence, whether or not they possess it' (Shattock 2000). A reputation for excellence secures a university's

financial security, provides opportunities for growth and development, and forms the basis for consensus on aims, missions, and values. Still, being excellent at some academic functions is no excuse for not being excellent in all facets of performance such as excellence of service provision or effective communication.
- Reputation. Excellence still is no guarantee for reputation. Reputation is built from public image, the perceptions of influential people, the media, and from the reactions of students and employees.

8.3 Serving Different Masters

A study undertaken by the TUM-Tech GmbH in Munich describes the university of the future as relying on individual's strategic, responsible, and individual actions when serving our complex society's diverse and concurring interests (TUM-Tech GmbH 2003). As such, institutions of higher education are positioned between the contradictory contexts of market regulation and autonomy requirements of ivory tower, workbench, and lighthouse (Faulstich and Graessner 2008).

The primary goal of a university is frequently defined as the advancement of science and/or society through research and teaching. For example, the mission of the University of Cambridge is "to contribute to society through the pursuit of education, learning, and research at the highest international levels of excellence" (University of Cambridge online). The mission of the California Institute of Technology is "to expand human knowledge and benefit society through research integrated with education" (California Institute of Technology online). A stronger focus on either research or teaching can have tremendous implications on the institution's strategic orientation, its organizational values, and preferred performance indicators. The primary orientations of universities may be as diverse as a product orientation, competitor orientation, or customer orientation. The focus of performance indicators can be on the revenue earned, the research output, or the number of graduates. As an antecedence or consequence, organizational values can be directed at social, market, financial, achievement, or research values (Fig. 8.1).

As a result, comparing the performance of community-based universities serving the regional stakeholders, achievement universities being oriented toward their competition or research universities striving for academic excellence, can prove to be a difficult exercise. Harvard College,[1] stating its mission as striving "to create knowledge, to open the minds of students to that knowledge, and to enable students to take best advantage of their educational opportunities" (Harvard College 1997), can be described as education-based and customer-oriented,

[1] Harvard University (comprising the undergraduate college, the graduate schools, other academic bodies, research centers, and affiliated institutions) does not have a formal mission statement.

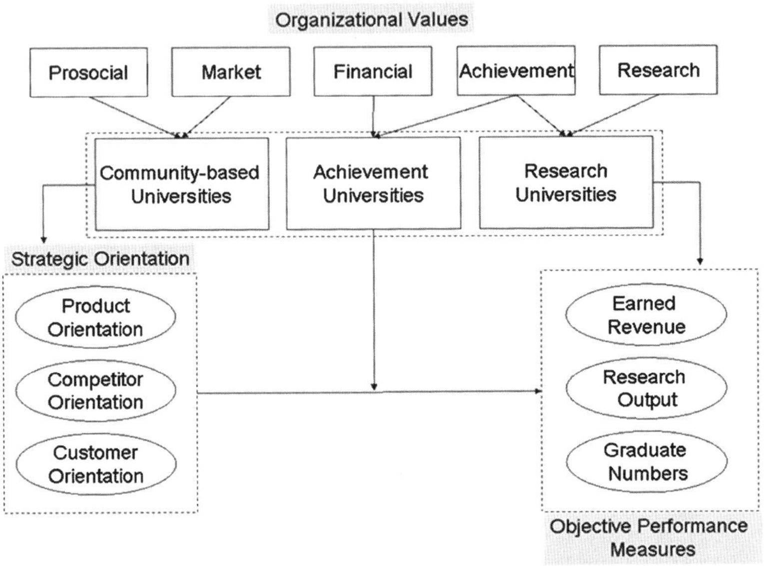

Fig. 8.1 Conceptual model of the interactions between organizational values, strategic orientation, and objective performance measures. (*Source* Adapted from Voss and Voss 2000)

whereas the London School of Economics' R&D division provides an example for research orientation: "A commitment to provide professional advice and support to the academic community, to assist colleagues to identify appropriate funding opportunities, and advise on the development of research grant proposals and research policy issues. We also provide support and advice on the management of the research projects and administration of the grant awarded." (London School of Economics online). The City University London is "providing students, the professions and business with the knowledge and skills essential to the success of London as a world city" (City University London online) and classifies as a community-based university. These examples also show how difficult it is to integrate competing values into a single institution-wide mission statement for universities.

8.4 University Performance

Albeit adverse circumstances, some universities appear to be more successful than ever. But what is success in a higher education context? This is the basic question to be answered when universities are forced to be accountable for their achievements: "Measuring for success and failure has to begin with identifying the 'right thing'. (This) is where the art of performance measurement begins" (Hodsoll 1998). In the 1980s, Alexander Astin (director of the Higher Education Research

Institute at UCLA) distinguished between education benefits, such as knowledge or skills, existential benefits referring to a stimulating and positive study experience, and fringe benefits, as later advantages from an institution's reputation or acquaintances picked up during the studies (Astin 1985). All these benefits are difficult if not impossible to operationalize for measurement. As a result, performance indicators, rankings, and other tools aimed at the comparability of higher education output have been developed. The following section deals with the difficult matter of performance measurement for higher education.

8.4.1 Performance Measurement for Higher Education

Companies are frequently evaluated on financial performance measures, mostly profit or return on investments (ROI).[2] For institutions of higher education, however, there is no single, ultimate criterion of effectiveness as they pursue multiple and often contradictory goals. Relevant criteria can also change over the life cycle of an organization, and so can the roles of influential constituencies (Cameron 1978). Performance indicators (PIs) have emerged as a method used internationally to manage and assess higher education (Gaither et al. 1994). The Higher Education Funding Council for England (HEFCE) has published sets of higher education PIs to cover

1. access and participation,
2. retention and progression,
3. research, and
4. employability (HEFCE 2007).

Cameron (1978, 1981) identified nine dimensions of organizational effectiveness for universities, clustering them into four groups: external adaptation (comprising the dimensions student career development, system openness, and community interaction), morale (including student educational satisfaction, faculty and administrator employment satisfaction, and organizational health), academic orientation (composed of student academic development, professional development and quality of faculty, and ability to acquire resources), and an extracurricular dimension (with the single factor student personal development).

Governments are progressively adopting strategies of information provision as a means of assuring academic quality and a foundation of their funding decisions. 'By specifying the performance indicators that will be publicly available and by subsidizing the development of measures of academic process and outputs, government can help improve the quality of information available to both student

[2] There is extensive literature and discussion on how to measure firm effectiveness in a more appropriate way considering complexity in a firm environment as well. This discussion, however, is not part of the present contribution.

consumers and universities. This in turn will help assure the more effective functioning of competitive academic markets.' (Dill and Soo 2005).

Some of the proposed performance indicators are the basis of university or higher education rankings that use information derived from subjectively perceived 'quality,' statistics and/or surveys of scholars, educators, students, or others in order to compare higher education institutions.

8.4.2 University Rankings

The worldwide expansion of access to higher education has created an increasing demand for information on academic quality, and thus led to the development of university ranking systems or league tables. 'Rankings serve as signals for attracting new faculty and retaining older ones in highly ranked institutions and also help attract the best graduate students. Such rankings are often used by university administrators to allocate scarce education funds to different departments according to their success in these rankings.' (Kalaitzidakis et al. 2003).

Although most rankings and leagues are done on a national scale, there seems to be increasing international consensus about how to measure academic quality adequately. For example, the Times Higher Education Supplement (THES) World University Rankings uses

1. peer review,
2. ranking by major graduate recruiters,
3. citations of published academic papers,
4. teaching staff : student ratios, and
5. international orientation as indicators.

The Shanghai Jiao Tong Academic Ranking of World Universities focuses strongly on research output, using

1. the number of Nobel Prizes and Field Medals won by alumni and faculty members,
2. the number of highly cited researchers,
3. the number of articles published by staff in academic journals, and
4. the academic performance with respect to the size of an institution as indicators.

As a result, a shift from focusing on teaching activities to (rewarded) research activities has been observed (Taylor 2001). Most rankings avoid subjective assessments of excellence and peer reviews and rely on rather objective quality and quantity of research output (Taylor and Braddock 2007).

University rankings are also heavily criticized. Publication and citation data often lack quality and rigor. 'The most serious problem of these rankings is that they are considered as 'quasievaluations' of the universities considered. This is not acceptable' (Van Raan 2005). Very often, indicators are criticized for not capturing the full qualitative and quantitative dimensions of research performance (Taylor 2001). Further problems include subjectivity of rating, the quality of the technical system, the (non-)matching of citing publications with cited publications, affiliation-related problems as well as a strong US bias in citation data, type of article, and language (Van Raan 2005). Also, there may be huge differences within various units of a higher education institution. Thus, Taylor and Braddock suggest an ideal ranking system giving scores for teaching and research output on a department-by-department basis (Taylor and Braddock 2007).

A ranking of economics departments throughout the world shows that the US retains its research dominance especially in the top 20 institutions; however, the European academic institutions are well represented in the remaining group of 180 that make up the top 200 universities in the world and so are universities from Asia and the Far East (Kalaitzidakis et al. 2003).

An objective evaluation of performance and effectiveness in higher education organizations has been shown to be difficult (if not impossible) and exposed to diverse criticisms. Still, distinguishing between successful and less-successful organizations can help to identify basic conditions, mechanisms, and processes that increase performance and effectiveness in higher education organizations.

8.5 What Top Companies Do Differently

Franz Bailom et al. (2007) identified high-performing companies as those companies disposing of a performance above-average on ROI, growth, and market position. In analogy, these companies could be compared for the intent of this contribution to institutions of higher education that perform well in university rankings stressing market and achievement indicators.

Both sectors, the business as well as the higher education sector, are characterized by similar market conditions. Hyper competition and isomorphism do not leave much room for differentiation. As a consequence, substantial potential for growth cannot be found in existing markets but in new—not yet discovered—areas. Good regional integration and functioning networks prove to be one of the most valued strategic assets. Successful universities have either established a unique selling proposition, such as distinctive study programs that are difficult to imitate as a result of unique networks and contacts, or perform well in the dimensions valued by university rankings. For example, the ETH Zurich has performed as a regionally anchored but internationally oriented university. The University of St. Gallen develops knowledge in close cooperation with best-practice corporations. The Mannheim Business School, leader of the German CHE ranking (ZEIT 2009), not only employs the best (according to the same ranking) management professor but also seven faculty members who are within the top 100 concerning their lifetime achievement, and eleven faculty members being within the 200 most active researchers since 2005. The University of Mannheim is the only German university being top achiever in all dimensions—research reputation, research funds, library endowment, student-to-teacher ratio, and student situation.

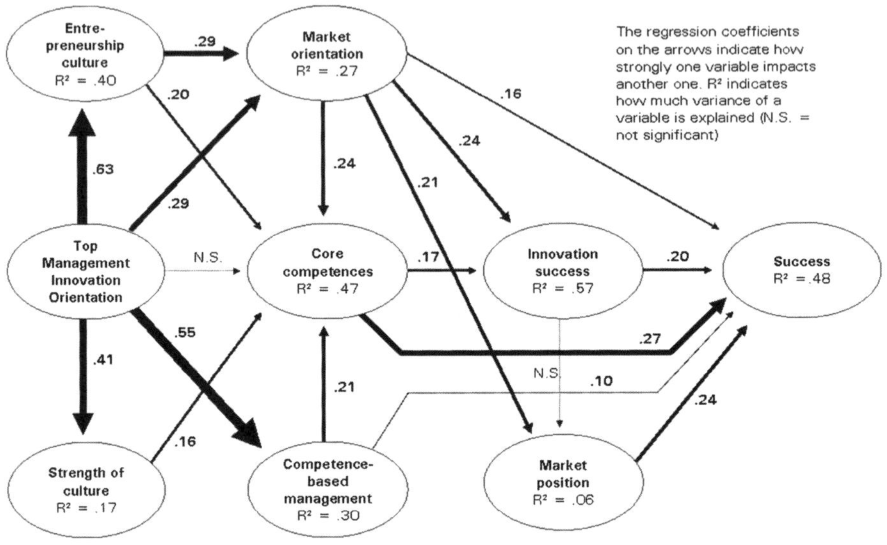

Fig. 8.2 Influence factors on Success of high-performing companies. (*Source* Bailom et al. 2007)

As in business, successful universities of the future will be characterized by fostering strengths, eliminating weaknesses, and niching the market. In the following, the main components of the IMP-Model (Fig. 8.2) of successful companies—market orientation, core competences, organizational culture, innovation, and the role of the top management—are explained in more detail and transferred to the sector of higher education.

8.5.1 Market Orientation

Market-oriented organizations are those which continuously generate knowledge about their markets and stakeholders, systematically distribute this knowledge within the organization, and make it accessible to key decision makers and which base their innovations and strategies on this market knowledge (Bailom et al. 2007).

Research and development is the central task and strategic asset for most universities and higher education institutions. Innovations, addressing and developing new ideas, materials, etc., are at the heart of university production. 'The long-term trend from simple to complex knowledge, arguably more important than the trend from elite to mass higher education, forces universities to position themselves between knowledge expansion and student expansion, with emphasis increasingly placed on the knowledge dimension. Innovative universities explore new ways of organizing knowledge and of more effectively exploiting the fields in which they are already engaged' (Clark 1996).

In universities as in business, there has been a shift from closed in-house innovation to work in research networks and open innovation processes. Being able to exploit these new sources of innovation is part of a higher education institution's competitiveness. Academic careers are characterized by high mobility and flexibility, which more and more requires the establishment and maintenance of networks that allow for exploitation of knowledge inside and outside of the organization. Conferences and research meetings are an important platform in academia where new ideas, concepts, and innovations are presented, discussed, and shared. In analogy to the lead user concept (von Hippel 1986), listening to and working with 'lead students' can be a way to create innovation in education and increase the graduates' employability. Being aware of and attracting top researchers (and lecturers) inside and outside the organization who can contribute to research and education excellence and establish co-operations becomes a vital task for top decision makers.

The academic market is an extreme example of a networked market, which may render the introduction and acceptance of (radical) innovations difficult as participants will only switch if they believe others to do so well. Therefore, it is important to understand the market as a system and to understand how the system works, what key problems of network partners need to be solved, and to continuously provide benefits to these partners in order to win support and cooperation that are important in order to seize network externalities and efficiently use power structures necessary for the critical mass of market participants that are necessary to implement innovations. Market research is essential for a market orientation but encounters new challenges:

- Very often innovations or developments do not meet the needs of the market (Christensen et al. 2005). In order to orient the organization toward customers' real problems and latent needs, market research can be of help, but innovators have to look ahead of actually expressed needs and wishes.
- As a consequence, it is important to get into contact with the right group of persons, i.e., innovators and early adopters rather than representative samples of the respective population. Innovators are adventurous and prepared to take risks, whereas early adopters—although more cautious—accept new ideas at an early stage and serve as opinion leaders (Rogers 1995).
- Generating useful information on the market is one part of the game, interpreting it in a way that allows for value-enhancing actions is another. Open and critical dialog with discussion platforms across functional and subject/content areas and involving the top decision makers is vital for an open discussion that can gain strategic relevance and influence the organization's fundamental position.
- When searching for the right persons for a university's top management, academic excellence is considered one of the basic job requirements. Still, leading a higher education institution has very much to do with leadership and stakeholder

management, finance, planning, and many other tasks requiring management expertise as well. As such, academic excellence is a necessity but not a sufficient requirement for a top management position. A considerable amount of time has to be devoted for interaction with the various stakeholders in order to establish their picture of customers and markets and become market experts themselves.
- Finally, top decision makers have to support the propensity to experiment and take risks when implementing the generated solutions. Mistakes are an important source of learning that cannot be exploited when employees are afraid to make them.

8.5.2 Core Competences

When searching for the roots of competitive advantage, two main strategic approaches have been developed: While the 'market-based view' considers an organization's success determined by the structure of the market, the 'resource-based view' centers on organization-specific factors.

Strategic resources that are valuable, rare, inimitable, and nonsubstitutable, be it tangible or intangible, are considered core competences (Prahalad and Hamel 1990; Barney 1991). This can be resources, skills, specific knowledge, or relationships. They are frequently based on unique historical conditions and sequences of events. For example, MIT's orientation toward entrepreneurship has been shaped by its founding as a 'land-grant university' or defense contracts issued in times of the cold war, as well as a long tradition developing ideas and commercializing research (O'Shea et al. 2007). Rival institutions cannot easily determine why and—more importantly—how these competences emerged and can hardly imitate them. Their social complexity based on personal relationships, trust, and a specific culture makes them even more unique and difficult to establish and copy. Another example is the University of St. Gallen in Switzerland, integrating a strong network with businesses and practitioners in research, education, and further education (University of St. Gallen online).

Core competencies are decisive for organizational success insofar as competence-based management requires a concentration on strengths and efficient use of resources and, furthermore, should provide the basis for innovations. Thus, a higher education institution should identify its particular strengths (and weaknesses) in order to determine core competences that can be the source of competitive advantage. Identifying and selecting attractive markets where these core competences can be exploited is the next step. Strategies based on the core competences have to be developed for these markets and—finally—implemented. Once core competences have been established and/or identified, they should be enhanced in order to seize new opportunities and further competences applicable to new markets should be developed.

8.5.3 Organizational Culture

The sources of value creation and competitive advantage have shifted from tangible assets to intangible assets such as the intellectual capital and relational resources. The 'knowledge-based view of the organization' considers knowledge the most important resource of an organization (Grant 1996). Knowledge workers carry their knowledge with them, taking it with them as they change workplaces. As expert organizations, institutions of higher education face specific challenges for employee retention: employment relations are frequently characterized by contingent and project work and academic careers are inherently flexible forcing academics to change their employing institutions in order to remain employable. Only those universities who succeed in creating value for their employees will be able to commit employees to the organization and to develop and exploit their knowledge potential. There are three sources of values, attitudes, and norms which shape a corporate culture (Schein 1992) and are at the basis of an entrepreneurship culture:

- the beliefs, values, and premises of the organization's founder,
- the employees' experiences in the course of an organization's development, and
- the beliefs, values, and premises that originate from new employees and senior executives.

Entrepreneurial cultures are organizations that think in opportunities and are willing to take risks, focusing on innovation and advancement, and being visionary and dynamic. In his study on five European universities Clark identified five pathways to become entrepreneurial universities (Clark 1998, 2003):

- Universities, which enhance their organizational capacity to respond more quickly and with greater flexibility to changing demands, dispose of a strengthened steering core. This is also characterized by a stronger line authority between rectors, deans, and department heads.
- An expanded developmental periphery describes organizational units across traditional academic departments engaged in outreach activities such as knowledge transfer, the development of industrial partnerships, fundraising, alumni, etc.
- A diversified funding base enhances the financial sources from non-government sources, such as industrial firms, royalty income or earned income from campus services, student fees, or alumni, and thus increases autonomy.
- The stimulated academic heartland refers to academic units that become entrepreneurial units, reaching out with new programs and relationships being stronger directed at third-level income.
- Finally, a blending of traditional academic cultures and values with a new entrepreneurial culture results in an integrated entrepreneurial culture.

Strong cultures are associated with homogeneity of effort, clear focus and higher performance (Cameron and Quinn 1999).

8.5.4 Innovation

Differentiation—be it on the product and services, process, or business model level—has become increasingly difficult. More than 70 % of the company executives interviewed (Bailom et al. 2007) see themselves too similar to their competitors to achieve differentiation. In the higher education sector, this is equally so, considering the increasing need for comparability, quality control, accreditation and agreed standards, as, e.g., established through the Bologna process in Europe. Also, within the last decades, the role of the student has changed, emphasizing his/her role as a customer and creating new demands and requirements.

Universities as institutions only slowly adopt change and innovation—their goal ambiguity and system complexity usually cause different constituencies to be involved in the process. For example, innovation in teaching not only affects students but also faculty and administrative staff. Educational institutions are both a source of supply and demand for innovations.

The idea of 'doing new things' also encounters barriers for institutions of higher education. Traditionally, 'academic institutions are basically conservative in educational purpose and in support structures for innovation programs' (Hefferlin 1969, p. 11). But in an era of decreasing public funding, universities have to respond to challenges resulting from globalization, commercialization, and the increasing availability and capacities of information technologies (Taylor 1998).

According to the model of Noriaki Kano (Kano 1984), customers are neutral when basic requirements are met but dissatisfied when not; they are satisfied to the extent their expected performance requirements are met, and can be delighted by some unexpected and/or unarticulated excitement requirements, without being dissatisfied when they are not met.

- Radical innovations represent an entirely new solution for a basic requirement. They usually result in a long-term competitive advantage for the issuing organization. The introduction of virtual universities and study programs has been such a radical innovation. The open computer conferencing forum at the Open University in the UK proved to generate more traffic than official discussion forums and became the main workspace. Fielding Graduate Institute in the US offered an educational opportunity for a group of geographically dispersed adult professionals with families, who were not able to follow a classical full-time study program. Many other universities have introduced distance-learning programs, and e-learning has become standard now. Also, the first student placement centers met the basic requirement of student employability without being expected.
- Differentiation innovations provide better solutions for explicit customer expectations than the competitor's products. Improved e-learning software and an elaborate exchange program are examples for differentiation programs.
- Incremental innovations solve small, unarticulated customer problems and by surprise delight the customers. Although they generally generate only short-term effect, they are able to create lasting goodwill towards the institution. This is

important for universities as alumni are powerful stakeholders, influencing a university's funding, and—of course—reputation. The improvement of teaching techniques such as 'active learning', 'student peer teaching', or 'writing across the curriculum' had the potential to delight students coming across these techniques for the first time.

8.5.5 The Role of Top Management

A university's top management plays a decisive role for its performance. Ultimately, it is not individual management methods or tools that form the basis for sustained success, but the top management team's attitudes, values, thought patterns, and approach. For good reason, the filling of top management positions is eagerly observed by the public, the media, competitors, and other stakeholders.

In short, top management has to fulfill two roles—a management function and a leadership function. Management and leadership are two different but interdependent concepts. On the one hand, management is 'creative problem solving' (Hinterhuber and Krauthammer 1998) and optimizes existing systems, procedures, processes, products, and services. Thus, management remains within a given paradigm or within a given system and ensures the basic environment and conditions needed for success. In a higher education setting, ensuring the availability of resources, improving administrative workflows or increasing the value of lectures to students are management tasks.

On the other hand, top management needs to create a strong corporate culture that allows for identification and meaning as well as innovation and that eases the employment of creative and unusual approaches. Strategic leadership theory argues that companies are reflections of top managers and of the teams they have built around them (Hambrick and Mason 1984). Being alert to opportunities and disposing of the imagination and vision to exploit them is at the basis of leadership. An interest in people and the creation of an environment of trust, innovation, and endeavor easing necessary changes in the status quo are also vital for good leadership. For this goal, leaders in higher education should be able to inspire researchers, lecturers, students 'to work enthusiastically toward goals identified as being for the common good' (Hunter 1998) and, as a result, achieve more than they thought they were able to (Hinterhuber and Krauthammer 1998).

Management or 'doing things right' is easier to learn than leadership, which is 'doing the right things', but university top executives need both—leadership and management. In turbulent times, however, i.e., when structural and budgetary reforms challenge the higher education sector, when new markets have to be invented and radical improvements in stakeholder satisfaction are needed, leadership is more important than management (Hinterhuber and Krauthammer 1998). You manage things but you lead people. In institutions of higher education, people are the core assets for achieving high performance.

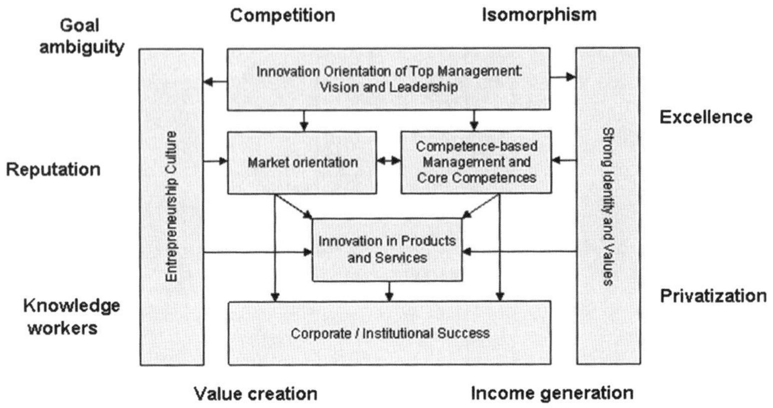

Fig. 8.3 Suggested model of influence factors on Success for higher education institutions. (*Source* Adapted from Bailom et al. 2007)

8.6 Conclusion

The innovation orientation of the top management and its leadership skills can be framed as the main drivers of success—for business companies as well as higher education institutions. They influence the character and strength of the corporate or organizational culture, its innovative ability, and the development of unique resources and skills, which constitute core competencies and serve as a basis for innovation and key strategic decisions. These success drivers only work if combined with each other, which again underlines the importance of appropriate attitudes, values, norms, and top management orientation. Therefore, an influence model in analogy to the IMP model (Bailom et al. 2007) (Fig. 8.3) as well as key questions higher education senior executives should ask to themselves about their institutions are suggested.

Today's competitive environment calls for an increase in the role of the top management of higher education institutions. Those leading teams that shape organizational success have to:

- create a strong corporate culture built on values, employees, and students can identify with and which are meaningful for them;
- create a culture of innovation that stimulates employees to strike new paths that recognizes and rewards creative solutions;
- create a culture of entrepreneurship that incites employees to strike new paths and be willing to take risk;
- set free resources that are dedicated to the development of unusual competences, skills, knowledge, and relationship networks, i.e., core competences;
- be able to understand markets and recognize or even anticipate developments in good time, i.e., have a market orientation;
- be aware of the organization and the environment it is operating in.

"There are no absolute predictors of what makes a university successful" (Shattock 2003), but a strategic orientation as learned from the lessons of Top CEOS can help universities to survive successfully in today's challenging environment. We would like to finish with the key questions, key decision makers in higher education institutions should ask to themselves (adapted from Bailom et al. 2007):

- Innovation orientation of the top management
  - Are we aware of the university's actual core tasks and have we really derived visionary objectives for the next 10 years from this (development plan)?
  - Do we at the top decision-making level have access to knowledge networks inside and outside the university and do we exploit these in order to get a firm idea of changes within the education market system, student, employee, and other stakeholder problems and technological developments?
  - Do our top senior executives constantly look for unusual and different approaches so as to be able to develop really innovative solutions to the company's core challenges?
  - Are we actually prepared to think entrepreneurially, in the sense that we invest in the development and strengthening of new core competencies?
  - Does the leadership work of our top decision makers put researchers, lecturers, and other employees in a position to appreciate the unusual qualities of the institution and to experience them on an emotional level?
  - Do the leaders in our institution possess sufficient skills to embed the spirit of change throughout the entire institution?
- Entrepreneurship culture
  - Is the university's culture characterized by entrepreneurship, dynamism, and the willingness to take risks, rather than standardization, formalization, and risk minimization?
  - Are a propensity to innovate, flexibility and a will to change the dominant forces that hold the university together and give it direction, rather than rules, procedures and plans?
- Strong identity and values
  - Are our employees proud to work for the university and for the realization of its objectives?
  - Do employees trust in the competence of management and their colleagues?
  - Do employees feel and sense that they are an important part of the overall process and that their individual contribution to the achievement of objectives is important?
  - Do the university's culture, the values it lives by, and its employees' daily interaction with one another promote a feeling of well-being for the individual?
  - Are errors tolerated, provided employees abide by the university's core values?

- Market orientation
  - Do employees at all levels within the university exploit the opportunity to generate future-related knowledge about markets, as well as customer/ stakeholder problems, to pass it on and to discuss it?
  - Do we have a network of experts, institutions, partner organizations, and lead users in order to be able to bring new knowledge into the institution?
  - Do we have discussion platforms within the university where the market knowledge that has been generated is discussed with the top decision makers?
  - Are we able to transfer this knowledge into forward-looking strategies, products, and processes, as well as new business models?
- Competence-based management
  - Do we in top management focus strategically on the enhancement and development of new core competences?
  - Do we have a suitable plan for enhancing and systematically developing new core competences?
  - Do we have a process aimed at finding new markets/opportunities for our existing core competences?
  - Do we specifically aim employee training at current or desired future competences?
- Core competences
  - Do we possess skills, technologies, resources, processes, know-how, etc., which are valuable in the market, since they deliver a particular benefit to the customers/stakeholders, are unique, cannot easily be imitated, and also cannot be substituted by other skills, technologies, etc.?
  - Are we able to systematically exploit these core competences for purposes of innovation and opening up new markets?
- Innovative ability
  - Do innovative products/services/research form a greater proportion of total turnover than that in competing universities?
  - When launching new products/services/research, do we pay particular attention to ensure that launches are based on innovative launch concepts?
  - Do constant process innovations enable us to achieve higher customer value and better cost structures?
  - Do we have an innovative business model that is very difficult to imitate?

The proposed model and key questions can be used as a guideline for strategic action in a higher education environment. Of course, the academic environment is highly complex and provides individual challenges and opportunities for different institutions. However, examples of successful institutions have shown that a focus on core competencies, a consistent orientation toward innovation and opportunities as well as a top management that provide the basis and culture for successful development can create sustainable performance in higher education, as it is the case in business.

Bibliography

Astin AW (1985) Achieving academic excellence. Jossey-Bass, San Francisco

Bailom F, Matzler K, Tschemernjak D (2007) Enduring success: what top companies do differently. Palgrave Macmillan, Basingstoke

Barney JB (1991) Firm resources and sustained competitive advantage. J Manage 17(1):99–120

Cameron K (1978) Measuring organizational effectiveness in institutions of higher education. Adm Sci Q 23(4):604–632

Cameron KS (1981) Domains of organizational effectiveness in colleges and universities. J Acad Manage 24(1):25–47

Cameron KS, Quinn RE (1999) Diagnosing and changing organizational culture. Based on the competing values framework. Addison-Wesley, Reading/Mass

Christensen CM, Cook S, Hall T (2005) Marketing malpractice. Harvard Bus Rev 83(12):74–83

Clark BR (1996) Substantive growth and innovative organization: new categories for higher education research. High Educ 32(4):417–430

Clark BR (1998) Creating entrepreneurial universities: organizational pathways of transformation. Issues in higher education. Elsevier Science, New York

Clark BR (2003) Sustaining change in universities: continuities in case studies and concepts. Tert Educ Manage 9(2):99–116

Dill DD, Soo M (2005) Academic quality, league tables, and public policy: a cross-national analysis of university ranking systems. High Educ 49:495–533

Faulstich P, Graessner G (2008) Aus dem Elfenbeinturm in die Exzellenz-Leuchttürme? Hochschule Weiterbildung 1:12–18

Gaither GH, Nedwek BP, Neal JE (1994) Measuring up: the promises and pitfalls of performance indicators in higher education. Graduate School of Education and Human Development, George Washington University, Washington

Grant RM (1996) Toward a knowledge-based theory of the firm. J Strateg Manage 17:109–122

Hambrick DC, Mason PA (1984) Upper echelons: the organization as a reflection of its top managers. Acad Manage Rev 9(2):193–209

Hefferlin JBL (1969) Dynamics of academic reform. Jossey-Bass, San Francisco

Hinterhuber HH, Krauthammer E (1998) The leadership wheel: the tasks entrepreneurs and senior executives cannot delegate. Strateg Change 7(3):149–162

Hodsoll F (1998) Measuring for success and failure in government and the arts. J Arts Manage Law Soc 28(3):230–239

Hunter JC (1998) The servant: a simple story about the true essence of leadership. Prima Publishing, Roseville

Kalaitzidakis P, Stengos T, Mamunes TP (2003) Rankings of academic journals and institutions in economics. J Eur Econ Assoc 1(6):1346–1366

Kano N (1984) Attractive quality and must be quality. Hinshitsu (Quality) 14(2):147–156 (in Japanese)

O'Shea RP, Allen TJ, Morse KP, O'Gorman C, Roche F (2007) Delineating the anatomy of an entrepreneurial university: the Massachusetts institute of technology experience. RD Manage 37(1):1–16

Prahalad CK, Hamel G (1990) The core competence of the corporation. Harv Bus Rev 68(3):79–81

Rogers EM (1995) Diffusion of innovations. Free Press, New York

Schein EH (1992) Organizational culture and leadership. Jossey-Bass, San Francisco

Schoenberger E (1997) The cultural crisis of the firm. Blackwells, Oxford

Shattock M (2000) Strategic management in European universities in an age of increasing institutional self reliance. Tert Educ Manage 6:93–104

Shattock M (2003) Managing successful universities, SRHE. Oxford University Press, Maidenhead

Taylor J (2001) The impact of performance indicators on the work of university academics: evidence from Australian universities. High Educ Q 55(1):42–61

Taylor P (1998) Institutional change in uncertain times: lone ranging is not enough. Stud High Educ 28(3):269–279

Taylor P, Braddock R (2007) International university ranking systems and the idea of university excellence. J High Educ Policy Manage 29(3):245–260

Van Raan AFJ (2005) Fatal attraction: conceptual and methodological problems in the ranking of universities by bibliometric methods. Scientometrics 62(1):133–143

von Hippel E (1986) Lead users: a source of novel product concepts. Manage Sci 32(7):791–805

Voss ZG, Voss GB (2000) Exploring the impact of organizational values and strategic orientation on performance in the nonprofit professional theatre industry. Int J Arts Manage 3(1):62–76

Additional Materials

California Insitute of Technology (online) At a glance. http://www.caltech.edu/at-a-glance/, 25 May 2009

City University London (online) Introducing city university London. http://www.city.ac.uk/aboutcity/introduction.html, 25 May 2009

Harvard College (1997) The mission of Harvard college. http://www.harvard.edu/siteguide/faqs/faq110.php, 25 May 2009

HEFCE (2007) Review of performance indicators: outcomes and decisions. http://www.hefce.ac.uk/pubs/hefce/2007/07_14/07_14.pdf

London School of Economics (online) Mission statement and target performance standards. http://ww.lse.ac.uk/collections/researchAndProjectDevelopmentDivision/missionStatement.htm, 25 May 2009

TUM-Tech GmbH (2003) Universität der Zukunft. Eine Vision—Handlungs- und Ordnungsprinzipien für Universitätsinstitutionen in Deutschland. http://www.tumtech.de/_resources/dynamic/hauptbereich/konzepte_und_expertisen/studie_universitaet_der_zukunft.pdf, (15 Jan 2009)

University of Cambridge (online) The university's mission and core values. http://www.admin.cam.ac.uk/univ/mission.html, (25 May 2009)

University of St. Gallen (online) Unique selling proposition. http://www.ifm.unisg.ch/org/ifm/dv.nsf/wwwPubInhalteGer/Unique+Selling+Proposition?opendocument, (25 May 2009)

ZEIT (2009) CHE Hochschulranking 2009/10. http://ranking.zeit.de/che10/CHE, (25 May 2009)

Chapter 9
Managing and Positioning of a Private Business School in Germany

Judith Marquardt and Hans Wiesmeth

9.1 Introduction to HHL: Leipzig Graduate School of Management

HHL—Leipzig Graduate School of Management (HHL), founded in 1992 after German reunification, is today one of the leading business schools in Germany. It is a private institution of higher learning, recognized by the Free State of Saxony, with the right to confer doctoral degrees ('Dr. rer. oec.' and 'Dr. habil.'). HHL continues the tradition of the renowned Handelshochschule Leipzig, which was established in 1898 as the first German business school, modeled on the French Grandes Écoles de Commerce. Professor Eugen Schmalenbach, the nestor of Betriebswirtschaftslehre, the more academic successor of the early versions of Business Administration, was one of its first students in 1898. Handelshochschule Leipzig, and with some right HHL, is thus often considered to be the cradle of Betriebswirtschaftslehre. This German version of Business Administration was crucial for the creation and development of some areas of today's academic business administration, which are taught in business schools all over the world.

HHL offers various study programs in general management with a strong focus on the development of key qualifications, 'soft skills', which are deemed necessary for today's business leaders, including strong social and intercultural competencies. A synthesis of theory and practice and, in this context, a close cooperation with national and international companies support HHL in its endeavor to cater to the needs of private enterprise.

J. Marquardt (✉)
ELBLAND Akademie Stiftung, Nassauweg 7, 01662 Meissen, Germany
e-mail: judith.marquardt@elblandkliniken.de

H. Wiesmeth
TU Dresden, 01062 Dresden, Germany
e-mail: hans.wiesmeth@tu-dresden.de

A. Altmann and B. Ebersberger (eds.), *Universities in Change*, Innovation, Technology, and Knowledge Management, DOI: 10.1007/978-1-4614-4590-6_9,

With approximately 300 students and 50 professors, research assistants, and guest lecturers, HHL is a comparatively small institution. However, it makes best use of the resulting excellent relationship between lecturers and students for the benefit of the latter. Almost 100 partnerships with first-class business schools worldwide together with a substantial number of foreign students render HHL truly international. To date it is one of only a handful of institutions of higher learning in business administration in Germany, which are accredited by the Association to Advance Collegiate Schools of Business (AACSB) International.

As a graduate school HHL offers master programs in general management with the degrees 'Master of Science (M.Sc.)' and 'Master of Business Administration (MBA)'. Due to HHL's international orientation with classes of students from 25 or more different countries, programs are conducted in English and last from 18 months (full-time) to 24 months (part-time). HHL's part-time programs are geared to professionals with significant work experience, who wish to accelerate their personal and career development, without giving up their current job.

Participants in the doctoral program are research associates supervised by the HHL chair holders, and also professionals investigating a research topic closely related to their work in the context of a doctoral dissertation. In contrast to the situation at most universities in Germany, HHL's doctoral program is already modeled to conform to the regulations of the Bologna Process, including courses at an advanced level, a summer school, and research colloquia. Credit points are awarded for the successful completion of each of the components of the program. Furthermore, the modularized structure allows for a considerable degree of flexibility with regard to participants' individual time constraints.

9.2 The Market for Higher Education in Germany

9.2.1 Public and Private Institutions of Higher Learning

The vast majority of institutions of higher learning in Germany are public, state-funded institutions (Universität, Fachhochschule). There are almost 400 public universities and private institutions of higher learning, whose degrees are recognized by public authorities. Of these approximately 70 are considered to be private or, to be more precise, non-public. The latter number varies according to the definition of 'private'. Moreover, both numbers are growing with more and more new institutions, both public and private, entering the market.

If we look at the student numbers we gain a somewhat different picture of the relevance of private tertiary institutions in Germany. Of the approximately 1.8 million students in Germany, only about 3 % attend a private or non-public institution. On the other hand, if we consider higher education exclusively in economics and business administration, about 20 % of all students study at non-public institutions, albeit only 2 % in those private institutions which have the right to confer a doctoral degree, and are thus considered to be research or academic institutions of higher learning.

With about 300 students, HHL thus has a substantial share of almost 9 % of the approximately 3,500 students in Germany, who study economics or business administration at a private research-oriented institution of higher learning. These numbers date from 2003, but with some probability today's numbers will not be too much different (http://www.alpheios.de/fileadmin/dateien/Private_Hochschulen_in_Deutschland.pdf).

9.2.2 Market Analysis: Programs and Services of Institutions of Higher Learning

The fact that there are no or only minimal tuition fees for a degree program at state-funded institutions is of course of utmost importance with respect to the positioning of a private business school. The immediate consequence is that programs in business administration offered at private business schools constitute, at first glance, a very expensive alternative to the corresponding programs of the state-funded public universities with tuition fees of at most 500 Euros per semester.[1]

However, study programs differ not only with respect to their degrees or tuition fees, but also with respect to the content and, even more importantly, the way this content is delivered. Moreover, services offered to the students in the form of round-the-clock access to the relevant infrastructure or advice regarding their career plans gain more and more importance with a growing customer orientation of the institutions. And it is exactly with respect to these issues that small private institutions have a clear advantage over the large public universities—if they know how to make use of it. Appropriate marketing strategies to effectively communicate these additional benefits, which are offered over and above the regular study program and which can be very valuable for a graduate's successful career start, are therefore indispensable. We will later return to this point.

Another aspect which is relevant for a thorough market analysis is the number of degree programs offered in business administration in Germany. This is of particular interest with respect to the MBA programs, which are 'mushrooming' in Germany with currently probably more than 100 institutions, both public and private, offering an increasing number of MBA programs. Again, these programs differ widely with respect to many characteristics, most important among them certainly the academic quality and reputation of the degree-granting institution. In addition to that, it is worth mentioning here that public universities often hesitate

[1] Some of the German states (Länder) meanwhile require public universities to charge a tuition fee of 500 Euros per semester. Moreover, public universities may also impose a fee on some non-consecutive master programs.

to offer evening or weekend programs for executive or further education. Besides a limited capacity regarding lecturers the remuneration for faculty at public universities is strictly regulated by the public sector in Germany. As a consequence, it is generally difficult for these institutions to deliver part-time programs outside of regular university hours.

Nevertheless, public institutions in higher education are gradually changing. An increasing number, among them University of Mannheim, Technical University of Dresden, and Technical University of Munich, just to name a few, have recently established private legal entities serving as platforms for developing and delivering part-time and executive programs in close cooperation with their home universities. These institutions are Mannheim Business School GmbH (http://www.mannheim-business-school.com), Dresden International University GmbH (http://www.dresden-international-university.com), and UnternehmerTUM GmbH (http://www.unternehmertum.de), respectively. By outsourcing further education in general and executive education in particular to their private subsidiaries, these public universities can thus avoid, at least to some extent, the intricacies and difficulties associated with the regulations for the public sector in Germany.

In addition to that, public institutions are now surprising the market with an increasing service orientation. They are starting to show they care about their alumni by establishing and cultivating alumni networks, they are offering career services for their graduating students, and they even seek closer contact with private companies, which was, until recently, beyond the horizon of many of the strictly academically oriented universities. All these observations are clear indications for changes in the perception of what public institutions of higher learning are, what they could be, and what they should become in the near future. The publicly funded providers of higher education are thus in a period of transition with direct and profound consequences for private institutions in general and private business schools in particular.

While there still seem to be enough possibilities open to private institutions to differentiate themselves, nevertheless, it is crucial to find and adopt the right strategy in this increasingly complex market with some national and also more and more international players setting high standards or at least aiming to do so. Again, we will return to this point later.

9.2.2.1 Market Analysis: The Bologna Process

The Bologna Declaration was adopted by the education ministers of 29 European countries at their meeting in Bologna in 1999. It is an attempt to reform the structures of the national higher education systems in a convergent way to develop a European Higher Education Area among the meanwhile almost 50 participating countries. The associated Bologna Process originates from the recognition that in spite of their differences, European higher education systems are facing common internal and external challenges related to the growth and diversification of higher education, the employability of graduates, the shortage of skills in key areas, and the expansion of private and transnational education. The Bologna Declaration intends in particular to facilitate coordinated reforms with respect to compatible systems of higher education (http://ec.europa.eu/education/policies/educ/bologna/bologna.pdf).

The Bologna Declaration was followed by the Prague Communiqué (2001), the Berlin Communiqué (2003), and the Bergen Communiqué (2005). The most recent meeting took place in London in 2007; the results were documented in the London Communiqué. The next Bologna Ministerial Conference will take place in Belgium in April 2009.

The London Communiqué attested, among other things, good progress at national and institutional levels toward the goal of a European Higher Education Area based on the three-cycle degree system. The number of students enrolled in courses in the first two cycles has increased significantly and there has been a reduction in structural barriers between cycles. Efforts should, however, concentrate in future on removing barriers to access and progression between cycles and on proper implementation of the European Credit Transfer System (ECTS) based on learning outcomes and student workload (http://www.dcsf.gov.uk/londonbologna).

The Bologna Process affects the German system of higher education more than most other participating countries because the traditional and internationally renowned German two-cycle degree system (diploma degree, doctoral degree) has to be replaced by the three-cycle degree system (bachelor degree, master degree, doctoral degree). This is a tremendous challenge, in particular for the public universities offering sometimes more than 100 different and diverse study programs. The fact that German authorities require bachelor and master programs to be accredited by special accreditation agencies adds to the complexity of these structural changes, which should be completed by 2010. Statistics for the academic year 2006/2007 show that 45 % of the approximately 11,500 study programs in Germany are already delivered as bachelor or master programs. More details are provided in the publications of the Standing Conference of the Ministers of Education and Cultural Affairs of the Länder in the Federal Republic of Germany (http://www.kmk.org).

What does this Bologna Process imply for a small private business school in Germany? There are two principle aspects: one offering an opportunity, the other providing a further challenge.

The great opportunity for private institutions, especially for smaller ones, is that they can typically react much faster regarding structural changes than a large public university. Thus, most private business schools already switched to the two-cycle degree system (if they have no doctoral programs) or to the three-cycle degree system (if they have the right to award doctoral degrees) a few years ago. They are therefore now profiting from a first-mover advantage if they developed innovative and attractive programs which continue to find the interest of students in the European Higher Education Area in general and in Germany in particular. The fact that the period of two years it usually took to get a Vordiplom (comprehensive intermediate exam in German diploma programs) is now replaced by the period of three years it usually takes to get a bachelor degree will cause only a temporary decline in the number of potential candidates for master programs, and thus constitutes only a minor challenge for the admission departments.

A much greater challenge results from the permanent shift in competition regarding the acquisition of students from the German level to the far more demanding European level. With respect to the former Diploma programs, competition among business schools for candidates took place essentially on a national level. The creation of the European Higher Education Area opened the German system of higher education for students from all over Europe, indeed from all over the world. The fact that the number of potential candidates has increased dramatically is at least partially offset by the fact that future students have the choice between significantly more study opportunities at excellent and internationally renowned business schools in Europe and abroad.

Thus, the Bologna Process requires German institutions of higher learning to be significantly more visible in other European countries than was previously the case. This is particularly true for top-ranked private institutions, which have to develop quickly into top-ranked European institutions. To achieve this goal, an institution must have a certain critical mass. The success of the necessary growth process is, however, first and foremost not only a question of financial means, but also a question of an appropriate strategy and, last but not least, of sufficient support from the various groups of stakeholders. This could become a challenging task as these issues are, at least to some extent, dependent on the excellent reputation of an institution. Consequently, small institutions will have to grow slowly in relation to the financial means which are at their disposal in order not to jeopardize the quality of their programs.

9.3 Positioning of a Private Business School: The Example of HHL

The competitive environment for universities in general and for private business schools in particular is changing dynamically, and "universities in transition" must undergo a strategic re-positioning in order to keep abreast of their international peers. This is especially true for private institutions.

In Germany, these changes are, to some extent, driven by the Bologna Process with the creation of the European Higher Education Area, which shifts competition between institutions of higher learning from a national level to a European level, and which encourages these institutions to offer a variety of new and innovative study programs within the worldwide recognized three-cycle degree system. In view of the demographic changes in most industrialized countries it also induces fundamental changes in the service orientation of many public universities in order to stay attractive or to become more attractive for future students. Moreover, the crisis on the financial markets followed by a gradually emerging economic downswing in the industrialized world poses an additional challenge—in particular for private institutions, which are more dependent on financial support from the private sector.

What does all this mean or imply for the positioning or, more precisely, for the re-positioning of a private business school? How can a private business school in Germany react appropriately to these rapidly changing competitive forces—both on the national and the European, if not international level? We will open this chapter with a careful analysis of the characteristics of the services provided by a private business school, which are necessary in order to survive and prosper in the current environment. We will take HHL—Leipzig Graduate School of Management as an example of a small private business school, which is exposed to these forces.

9.4 Positioning and Re-Positioning the Services

At HHL the slogan 'Your Path to Success' provides in combination with the mission to educate effective and responsible business leaders and HHL's presentation as 'Your Personal Business School' an excellent characterization of this business school's services. With Your Path to Success HHL succeeds in attracting the interest of potential candidates, who as students ask for more than just outstanding degree programs, who as professionals ask for more than just some arbitrary further education or executive program, or who as representatives of business companies seek to recruit well-educated and multi-talented graduates and ask for more than just some standard proposals for a strategic positioning of their company. And with the commitment which is expressed in Your Personal Business School HHL can successfully prove that it keeps its promises regarding an unusually high, individually tailored service orientation backed by academic quality.

9.4.1 Students as Life-Long Clients

Students at HHL obtain much more than a degree in an excellent and highly international study program with a strong focus on leadership qualifications. They are offered nothing less than the integration into a life-long academic and corporate network which provides them with support for their professional career—as long as they wish and to whatever extent they prefer.

All this starts with the first contact by potential students in the context of a formal or informal inquiry, participation in a workshop, or visit to HHL on the occasion of an Information Day. An administrative mentor takes care of the prospective students and answers all their questions. Graduating students or alumni act as academic mentors and provide guidance concerning HHL's academic structure and corporate philosophy.

The enrollment of the new students into the various study programs in early September marks a first important milestone. During the Welcome Event students of all programs are brought together to work on a particular practice-oriented task in small teams. From the very first day of their program they are thus offered opportunities to get to know each other; this is often the beginning of a life-long friendship. Again, the mentoring provided by older students and alumni helps the freshmen to become almost immediately familiar with life at HHL, with the 24/7 facilities, and the easy access to both academic and administrative staff. The concept of Your Personal Business School, enabled by the HHL's small size, starts to reveal its advantages for the students.

The Welcome Event is then followed by a variety of company presentations. These provide an insight into the world of business and a good opportunity to come into contact with potential employers, who appreciate the quality of the HHL graduates and who want to establish close ties with these young students as early as possible. Students can then deepen these initial contacts through internships at one or sometimes even two of these companies. Career Services at HHL is responsible for developing, cultivating, and intensifying HHL's relations to business and accompanies the students through their study period. The Career Services staff members provide valuable advice and help each student find his/her optimal entrance into the world of business. This extends beyond graduation day: HHL alumni can also approach Career Services and ask for support at any time if they have special needs in their professional life.

HHL's academic programs are characterized by a synthesis of theory and practice and are based on close cooperation with national and international companies. Field projects and professionally qualified lecturers from the private sector convey to students a hands-on understanding of what it means to be in a position of responsibility in a company, e.g., having to make decisions which may have potentially dramatic effects on the further development of the company despite having only incomplete information available. HHL's innovative, but resource-intense concept of co-teaching allows students to acquire a holistic view of the world of business. The relationships between marketing and finance, for example, which tend to become neglected due to an ever-increasing specialization, can thus be "rediscovered". And the various subjects of business administration can be directly embedded into a context of sustainability—underscoring HHL's mission to educate effective and responsible business leaders.

The Integrated Management approach, which provides the framework for the academic education at HHL, perceives business companies as dynamic systems with a need for continuous adjustments to the environment, but which themselves shape this environment through their decisions (Meffert 1997, pp. 4–21). This perception of the complex world of business "requires versatile thinkers who have benefitted from a broad education and research orientation avoiding over-specialization" (Meffert 1996) and calls for "an education which places emphasis on creative leadership behavior in conjunction with social competence" (Meffert 1996).

For these reasons, education at HHL and, interestingly, more than a century ago at the former Handelshochschule Leipzig has always focused on the whole person:

the development of analytical and problem-solving skills, and also the development of soft skills, of competencies, which are deemed indispensable for business leaders. Team work, intercultural experiences, student initiatives, and leadership presentations by renowned executives expose students to the challenges of real life, helping them to grow as a person. Needless to say that beyond analytical skills at least traces of these soft skills should characterize a student, who wants to study at HHL. It is therefore the pre-eminent task of the admissions committee to identify leadership potential in applicants to HHL's study programs.

The fact that human resources managers from the private sector are integrated into the admissions process helps to find and select appropriate students. This in turn is a crucial part of HHL's business model: when prominent employers understand HHL's policy for the selection and education of future executives, they are usually interested in coming to the business school for company presentations, hosting field projects, and inviting students for internships; furthermore, they tend to become more approachable regarding donations and financial support.

Interesting in the context of leadership competencies is also the composition of the classes with respect to the study background and the first academic degree of the students, and, in the case of part-time and doctoral students, also with respect to their professional activities. HHL's typically highly diverse student body with a substantial number of international students leads to cross-professional and cross-cultural encounters and to discussions from which all students benefit. As HHL's M.Sc. students are required to spend one term abroad at one of the almost 100 renowned partner institutions, many exchange students from all over the world help make HHL a truly international business school. Intercultural competencies are moreover stimulated by HHL's policy to send only one, in exceptional cases two students to a particular partner institution in a given period of time.

After their graduation, HHL students are encouraged to join the alumni network which provides further support for their professional career and which operates in close cooperation with Career Services. An Alumni Officer takes care of the special needs of the alumni, maintains their academic relations to HHL, and develops and strengthens their emotional ties to their Alma Mater. The mentoring program in which HHL alumni look after applicants to HHL's study programs and freshmen completes the cycle and helps to bring students and alumni together.

The question arises to what extent HHL's explicit service orientation provides a USP, a Unique Selling Proposition, with respect to public universities on the one hand and to other private business schools on the other. It seems to be obvious that the large public universities with sometimes tens of thousands of students can hardly compete with a small private institution in terms of career or alumni services or the special support offered to the students during their study program as outlined above. Also, a small business school can adjust more quickly the structure of the academic programs and the way they are delivered. The successful provision of these services is dependent on the concept of 'Your Path to Success' in combination with 'Your Personal Business School', which requires not only human resources but also a holistic approach to programs in business administration.

Things are more difficult with respect to a differentiation to other private business schools with educational concepts comparable in terms of quality to those of HHL. However, like other top-ranked business schools in Germany or Europe, HHL succeeds in convincing potential candidates to choose HHL for its leadership orientation, the quality of its services, and its academic reputation. Because a business school should be excellent with respect to all its programs and services, it is usually not advisable to develop a rather narrow USP. Of course, this might help to attract some students, but can also keep potential candidates from applying to this particular institution, because they are not willing to agree with such a special orientation which, moreover, could depend on developments outside the control of the business school. Some unexpected political or economic events can then badly damage this ‘USP’. For these reasons it seems to be preferable to rely upon the principle of being an ‘excellent’ business school—excellent with respect to each of the programs offered, with respect to academic research, and with respect to the services provided both to the students, and also to the public in general and to HHL’s stakeholders in particular.

The institutional accreditation of a business school by an internationally renowned organization such as AACSB International or EFMD should not be underestimated in this context. Both AACSB and EQUIS accreditations are recognized worldwide as a seal of approval given only to excellent institutions with excellent programs delivered by motivated and academically or professionally qualified faculty. HHL is currently one of only three German business schools or faculties, which are institutionally accredited by AACSB International. In addition, HHL’s study programs are accredited by ACQUIN, a prominent German agency approved by the Akkreditierungsrat. This national accreditation of the study programs is required according to the German regulations for the Bologna Process.

In summary, it is the philosophy of Your Path to Success in combination with Your Personal Business School which help HHL—Leipzig Graduate School of Management to position its study programs successfully in this dynamically changing environment.

9.4.2 Professionals as Clients

Executive education in business administration in Germany is most often provided by private institutions, as outlined above also by private institutions which operate closely with a public university in the background. One reason is that further education in the form of degree programs has only recently become part of the services public universities should offer, at least in principle.[2] Another reason is that

[2] E.g. the Law for Universities in the Free State of Saxony from December 10, 2008, obliges universities to offer further education (cp. http://www.smwk.sachsen.de/download/HG-Gesetz(2).pdf, §38). In earlier versions of this law universities were only asked to develop and offer study programs in further education.

many of these executive programs with or without a degree have to be delivered in the evenings or during the weekends. In combination with insufficient possibilities for appropriate remuneration, the motivation of the faculty of a public university to provide executive education in addition to the regular study programs, which require most of their attention, is most often rather limited.

This constitutes an excellent opportunity for a private business school. Not surprisingly then, almost all private business schools in Germany offer programs in further education. The range extends from full-time to part-time MBA programs and to executive programs with certificates but without a formal degree. HHL's study programs currently include a full-time and a part-time MBA program in general management with especially the part-time program attracting executives with considerable work experience.

HHL's subsidiary HHL Executive currently offers tailor-made programs for executives of renowned companies, which operate not only in Germany. Open enrollment programs with courses covering key topics in the area of general management are currently being introduced.

According to HHL's philosophy of Your Personal Business School, these executive programs are service orientated and, as made-to-measure advanced training programs and seminars, suit the requirements of the customers, be they companies or individuals. For these programs, HHL's small faculty is often complemented by external faculty consisting of former HHL professors or other experienced academically or professionally qualified lecturers. In addition to the regular faculty a "virtual" faculty is thus at HHL's disposal, and finding the right lecturer for a specific course is, in general, not a big deal.

Actually, this virtual faculty allows more flexibility with respect to assigning appropriate lecturers to a particular course. Moreover, guest faculty from other universities increases the visibility of HHL in the academic environment, and professionally qualified faculty emphasizes the practical orientation of HHL and its close cooperation with the private sector.

What then is HHL's advantage in comparison to other private providers of programs in executive education in management, which are continuously increasing in number? Of course, HHL Executive profits from HHL's reputation. Thus, the non-degree programs for executives are considered to be the programs of a renowned German business school. Moreover, due to its relatively small size, HHL can attract special clients, e.g., graduates of the humanities or from fine arts, and integrate them into its MBA programs without establishing a separate study program for these candidates. On the one hand this helps to increase the academic "diversity" in class, on the other hand, the MBA degree can certainly help to attract the interest of business companies in these graduates as potential employees. Bigger companies sometimes prefer graduates from the humanities for special tasks, e.g., in corporate communication or human resources development.

Again, the philosophy of Your Path in Success combined with Your Personal Business School allows a positioning of a private business school with respect to further education and executive programs. Private business schools seem to have a clear advantage over public universities although public institutions are currently intensifying their efforts to get more than a foot into the profitable markets of academic executive and further education.

9.4.3 Business Companies as Clients: The HHL Open School Initiative

The most effective forms of knowledge transfer from universities to the world of business involve human interaction and try to bring together people from companies and universities. However, the biggest challenge when it comes to encouraging business-university collaboration lies in stimulating the demand from companies, rather than in increasing the supply of products and services from universities—this is at least the result of various recent investigations in this important field (Lambert 2003).

With its Open School Initiative, for which it received a first prize in a national competition announced and funded by the Bundesministerium für Bildung und Forschung and the Stifterverband für die deutsche Wissenschaft, HHL tries to close this gap between academia and business. Eugen Schmalenbach's vision of a collaborative generation of knowledge between universities and companies is integrated with the latest developments in the area of Open Innovation to stimulate exchange processes and the transfer of knowledge, and to foster and accelerate innovation in companies. As Eugen Schmalenbach was one of the first students of the Handelshochschule Leipzig in 1898, the HHL Open School Initiative revisits an issue which had already gained considerable importance some 110 years ago.

Exchange processes between academia and business permeate all aspects of HHL. As mentioned above, they first of all characterize the study programs with the participation of professionals in the admission committees, with their real-life field projects, with their company presentations, with their student initiatives and the clear leadership orientation. A speciality in this context is HHL's program in International Entrepreneurship, which helps to position HHL as Your Entrepreneurial Business School in the business environment of the Free State of Saxony and of Germany. With this program, HHL provides support for small-and medium-sized companies, especially with respect to the problem of finding and establishing an appropriate successor as managing director of such a company. Moreover, HHL successfully educates and cultivates the entrepreneurial spirit and supports the start-ups launched by HHL graduates. Despite its small size, more than 70 start-ups have emerged from HHL since 1998, the year the first graduates left the re-founded HHL, creating more than 1500 jobs, many of them in Leipzig and in Central Germany. Quite a few of these young companies have received awards in business plan and start-up competitions. This network of successful start-ups helps to develop and foster HHL's competence as Your Entrepreneurial Business School.

The HHL Open School Initiative recognizes the gradual shift of innovation management from a model of 'Closed Innovation' to a model of 'Open Innovation'.

This development, sometimes characterized as 'Democratizing Innovation' (von Hippel 2005), pursues the goal of not only integrating academia, but also stakeholders, in particular customers, into the process of innovation management.

It is the vision of the Open School Initiative to establish HHL as an institution for this kind of collaborative generation of management knowledge. HHL addresses the core subjects in management (strategy, marketing, innovation, finance, and controlling) in a close and personal cooperation with business companies. Both sides benefit from this initiative: the companies receive valuable advice and access to the latest research results in management; HHL students have the opportunity to become familiar with real problems in the business world. This is, once again, a clear aspect of Your Personal Business School, characterizing HHL as a first mover with regard to implementing the goals of the Open School Initiative.

9.5 Managing a Private Business School

The dominant goal of the management of a small, private business school in Germany is to support this process of adaptation to a fundamentally changing environment for institutions of higher learning and to provide guidance to faculty and administrative staff.

9.5.1 Managing the Process of Adaptation

It is the responsibility of the management of a business school to 'steer' the institution through the 'troubled waters' which inevitably accompany this process of transition. The executive management, dean and chancellor, must come up with the right instruments at the right time and safeguard a 'balanced' growth in all parts of the business school according to the financial means available. Last, but not least, the stable financial development of the institution is a conditio sine qua non for the entire process.

This process requires a firm commitment to a strategy, which has to be the joint effort of the faculty and the heads of the administrative departments with further input and significant support from students, all employees and relevant stakeholders. The latter includes of course the shareholders, the members of the supervisory and the advisory board, and also the alumni, corporate partners, including start-ups, and the public administration, not only if financial support is needed or expected from these groups.

The process of transition itself is dependent on various framework conditions which are external to the business school. The regulations of the Bologna Process are a good example for this, requiring the transition from the traditional and esteemed two-cycle degree system to the three-cycle degree system, which was until recently not very well known in Germany. The willingness to switch to this new system was therefore limited, also because there was, at least for many academic subjects, no objective necessity, and no obvious need to adopt the new system.

The situation was a little different for business schools and faculties in business administration which have always been characterized by a large number of international students and very active programs for student exchanges. The completely different degree systems proved to be not very helpful for a further internationalization of the study programs. Therefore, business schools, in particular the private ones, were among the first institutions to adapt their programs to the new requirements. The executive managements of the private business schools in Germany recognized at an early stage the opportunity to improve the education of future business leaders who are going to face the challenges of an increasingly globalized world.

Nevertheless, there is the problem that in particular some large public universities switched only recently, one or two years ago, to the new system. The consequence is that graduate schools, such as HHL—Leipzig Graduate School of Management, have to deal with a comparatively small number of bachelor graduates in economics and business administration.[3] This fact is aggravated by the longer duration of the bachelor programs (typically three years) in comparison to the former Vordiplom (two years).

The marketing departments of the business schools had to propose and develop appropriate instruments to bridge these periods with a small number of potential candidates. In addition, it was necessary to "transfer" the reputation of the traditional diploma programs to the new master programs. For a private institution this is very important although it is not at all an easy task to accomplish. At HHL the concepts of Your Path to Success combined with Your Personal Business School proved helpful in addition to the active integration of stakeholder groups, in particular representatives of companies, into the development of the master programs. New programs, such as a part-time M.Sc. program, are in preparation and are oriented toward those bachelor graduates who started to work immediately after their graduation.

Furthermore, with its Open School Initiative HHL has succeeded in attracting the corporate interest in its degree and non-degree programs. The fact that this initiative is new with regard to its implementation on the one hand, but traditional with regard to its philosophy on the other, helped HHL to promote it with increasing returns. The visibility of HHL, still a small, private business school in the eastern part of Germany, has been significantly enhanced in Germany through the attention HHL is currently receiving in the media.

---

[3] In 2007 there were less than 6,800 bachelor graduates in the humanities (law sciences, economics and business administration, social sciences) in Germany. This is still a small number in comparison to approximately 94,000 graduations in these areas altogether with a vast majority of graduations in diploma programs. Cp. the reports of the HRK (Standing Committee of Rectors and Presidents) in Germany.

How can a small, private business school increase its visibility at a European level? One strategy, also applied by HHL, is to establish an intense cooperation with other prominent business schools in Europe. This cooperation may result in a joint degree program or in a joint executive program. In each case both HHL and the partner institution benefit from increased public attention on the European level in the short-run.

For a sustainable penetration of the European market, a business school has to be large enough to become a significant player in the European league of business schools. The accumulation of the financial means to fund the necessary growth process is a challenging task in times of a financial market crisis and an economic downswing.

9.5.2 Providing Guidance to Faculty and Staff

As in any other business company, the management of a business school is reliant on the support of its faculty and staff when it comes to adjusting the strategy in reaction to changes in the framework conditions. All stakeholder groups must be kept informed about necessary changes in the strategy. In the case of a business school with chairs in strategy and organization and in marketing management, it is advisable to let the experts lead discussions concerning modifications to the strategy. Given the degrees of freedom of faculty members,[4] this procedure makes it easier for faculty and staff to adopt and support the structural changes of a business school in transition.

9.6 Conclusion

The current competitive environment for business schools presents daunting challenges, but at the same time exciting opportunities. Adjustments in strategy and focus in response to new framework conditions are required of all players, and each institution of higher learning needs to re-position itself in the market on the basis of its strengths, self-imposed goals, and resources. While small private business schools face certain disadvantages compared with large business administration faculties in publicly funded universities, the example of HHL—Leipzig Graduate School of Management demonstrates that even a very small business school can position itself advantageously and with eminent success if it follows the right strategy, enjoys the support of its stakeholders, nurtures its partners, and implements an appropriate business model.

---

[4] In Germany, faculty enjoy the freedom of teaching and research which is guaranteed by the German Constitution (Grundgesetz).

Bibliography

von Hippel E (2005) Democratizing innovation. MIT Press, Cambridge
Lambert R (2003) Lambert review of business–university collaboration. HM Treasury, London
Meffert H (1997) Der Integrationsgedanke in der Betriebswirtschaftslehre—Leitbild für die Handelshochschule Leipzig (HHL). In: Meffert H , Gisholt O (eds) Managementperspektiven und Managementausbildung, Leipzig, pp 4–21
Meffert H (1996) Im Wandel führend (Directing Change), In: Klasse statt Masse—Managementkompetenz für Generalisten (Imagebroschüre der HHL)
http://ec.europa.eu/education/policies/educ/bologna/bologna.pdf
http://www.alpheios.de/fileadmin/dateien/Private_Hochschulen_in_Deutschland.pdf
http://www.dcsf.gov.uk/londonbologna
http://www.dresden-international-university.com
http://www.kmk.org
http://www.mannheim-business-school.com
http://www.unternehmertum.de

Chapter 10
Strategic Management for Growing Business Schools

Dirk W. Rudolph and Udo Steffens

10.1 Introduction

Strategic management as a field of study is part of the curricula at most business schools. Consequently, these schools should practice in-house what they preach for the business world. Yet, public university administrators might argue that the vast majority of universities and business schools are organized as not-for-profit organizations and, therefore, the use of strategic management techniques and tools is inapplicable for developing and growing these types of organizations. While it is true that the economics of the higher education industry differs substantially from the economics of, for example, the banking or the oil industry, these differences—once they are properly understood—do not preclude the use of strategic management techniques in universities and business schools. They can be and have been applied in many different types of non-profit and not-for-profit organizations

D. W. Rudolph (✉) · U. Steffens
Centre for Financial Economics (CFE), Frankfurt School of Finance and Management, Sonnemannstraße 9-11, 60314 Frankfurt, Germany
e-mail: d.rudolph@frankfurt-school.de

U. Steffens
e-mail: u.steffens@frankfurt-school.de

A. Altmann and B. Ebersberger (eds.), *Universities in Change*, Innovation, Technology, and Knowledge Management, DOI: 10.1007/978-1-4614-4590-6_10,

including, for example, hospitals [e.g., Yang et al. (2005), Khatri et al. (2006)], and even church organizations [e.g., Shah et al. (2004)].[1] Their applicability is not restricted to the large, publically traded for-profit firms. The strategic management literature has been paying attention to the growing segment of non-profit and not-for-profit organizations in our economies at least since Gruber and Mohr (1982) and Nutt (1984). A number of textbooks and guides, like Barry (1997), Bryce (2000), Bryson (1995), Courtney (2002), Dees (2002), Katsioloudes (2002), Kohm (2003), Oster and Sharon (1995) offer help and guidance for the non-profit and not-for-profit manager. Applications of strategic management to universities date back at least to Keller (1983) and Lockwood (1985). Despite these studies published about a quarter of a century ago, relatively little has been written on the use of strategic management in the context of higher education institutions in general and in business schools in particular.[2]

Part of the paucity of published work is due to the fact that a large number of universities, including their business administration and management departments, do not have what it takes to apply strategic management techniques: autonomy in decision making. Many public higher education institutions simply do not possess the autonomy in decision making required for designing, financing, implementing and controlling organizational strategies. However, a growing number of universities—private and public—are being granted an increasing degree of autonomy.

Besides the growing potential readership, there are two more reasons, why it is worthwhile to write about designing organizational strategies for business schools. First of all, new advances in analyzing the economics of higher education can lead to an improved understanding of the peculiarities of this sector. As is well known, possessing a sound comprehension of the economics of the industry to which the firm belongs is a prerequisite for those who are involved in strategy building. Second, there are some lessons to be learned from the strategic management of business schools for the strategic management of business firms. This rather surprising fact has been demonstrated by Mintzberg and Rose (2003), who examined the growth history of a successful private Canadian university, McGill University, over the course of its 150 years long evolution. In their conclusions, they pointed out the striking similarities between universities and innovative, creative, and

---

[1] Some legal systems do make a distinction between non-profit and not-for-profit organizations (like Germany), while others do not (like the US and the UK, where the two terms are used interchangeably). In Germany, non-profit organizations must not or do not want to make any profits (because of their mission statement or members contract). Not-for-profit organizations (like cooperatives) are allowed to generate a financial surplus. However, making profits is not the primary objective of these organizations. There are other objectives besides generating profits such as benefiting a special group of people or furthering a particular cause that the organization aspires to achieve.

[2] Exceptions to the scarcity of research on strategic management for universities and business schools include: Bailey and Dangerfield (2000), Hull and Lio (2006), Johnston and Marshall (1995), Julian and Ofori-Dankwa (2006), and Ringwood, et al. (2005).

knowledge-intensive firms.[3] The similarities further extend to the group of firms with multidimensional rather than one-dimensional organizational objectives such as entrepreneur-owned and family firms.

The objectives of our study directly follow from these introductory remarks. We want to offer insights from the strategic management literature and the economic analysis of the higher education industry that might help to improve the process of strategy making for business schools. To achieve our objectives, we will proceed in five steps. Since strategy building begins with defining a mission for the organization, we start in Sect. 10.2 with the process of defining a mission for the business school. Next, we will summarize and synthesize in Sect. 10.3 some insights from the literature on the economics of higher education and suggest differentiation strategies as feasible and potentially successful for business schools. Then, in Sect. 10.4, we will discuss one-dimensional and multi-dimensional goals of business schools and their relation to differentiation strategies. From this analysis, it directly follows that the existing structure of the business school industry works as an effective entry barrier. In Sect. 10.5, we give some practical suggestions on how to improve the transparency of the market for business degree programs and to lower the barriers to entry for newcomers. Barriers to entry are only one competitive threat to business schools. Other competitive forces impacting business schools are briefly examined in Sect. 10.6, where we pay particular attention to the bargaining power of suppliers of inputs and substitutes for an MBA. Envisioning potential strategies for a firm makes little sense without looking at the firm's market and its growth prospects. In the case of business schools, this market is a truly international one, both on the side of education providers and on the side of their students. Therefore, we examine some data in Sect. 10.7 that allows us to draw tentative conclusions about the potential of business schools' country and region-focused internationalization strategies. Sect. 10.8 concludes.

---

[3] They (2003, p. 289) write: "Can any of these conclusions inform strategic management in business? Universities seem so different from corporations, as has been noted in a few places. Yet delve into the knowledge work of corporations—the research laboratories, the design studios, and so on—and you find similarities, with corresponding implications for strategies there. Indeed, delve into the many rather loosely coupled corporations, such as 3 Ms and the Hewlett-Packards, and you find that a number of the conclusions here have application there: porous boundaries that let environmental forces in every way, accompanied by considered venturing, devolved strategists and fragmented strategies, an enormous amount of micro changes with relatively little quantum change, and so on. To the extent that this describes their strategic behaviour, so much that has been written about strategic management, with its focus on the planners, the chief executive as 'architect' of strategy, and the management of change as driven from the 'top', becomes questionable. Certainly all the hype about turnaround and revolution needs to be reconsidered in such contexts. Perhaps these companies change best from the inside out, at their own pace, rather from top down, frenetically."

10.2 Defining a Mission for the Business School

The strategy design process begins with defining a mission. And one of the first steps of defining the goals of the organization concerns the priority of the profit motive. Is the profit motive the organization's primary or exclusive objective? For publicly-traded companies, that is typically the case—they maximize shareholder value. Consequently, it seems to be natural that for business schools the primary measure of success should also be their profits. After all, how could they teach future managers to maximize profits if they fail to do it themselves?

Yet, profit maximizing firms are not the only type of business organizations where MBA graduates will work after graduation. The majority of firms in market economies all over the world and particularly outside of the UK and the US are cooperatives, state-owned firms, and entrepreneur-, family-, or employee-owned firms. For all of these types of firms the profit motive is often only a secondary goal; they pursue multidimensional objectives. So there is no pressing economic need that all business schools must mirror the shareholder maximization objective. Some of them might serve the future graduates of entrepreneur- or family-owned firms, for example. For these schools, there might be an incentive to adopt a similar set of objectives like the firms that their students eventually will join.

10.2.1 Business Schools as Not-for-Profit Organizations

The credence goods problem in higher education markets is one reason why some of the business schools might choose to be not-for-profit firms. Now, are there any economic reasons why all higher education providers including business schools should be organized as not-for-profit firms or is the concept of for-profit universities compatible with economic efficiency from a social welfare perspective? Analyzing the higher education industry with the tools of microeconomics reveals an economic problem that is the result of an extremely high degree of quality uncertainty and asymmetric information. Educators know much more about the true quality of their service and the quality of competing educational offers than their students will ever know. This type of market failure effectively turns the higher education industry into a credence goods industry.[4] Therefore, students cannot accurately assess the true quality of the educational service they received even after they finished the program. Rankings, accreditation, public reputation, and recommendations from friends and employers are means to mitigate the problem of quality uncertainty and asymmetric information in the higher education industry.

---

[4] Franck and Schönfelder (2000) point out the credence good character of educational services and the market failures resulting from the asymmetry of information between students and professors about the true quality of education delivered. There are, however, other conceivable ways that we will point out here to significantly mitigate this problem than the type of contractual arrangement discussed by these authors.

The high degree of quality uncertainty and asymmetric information gives rise to the risk of opportunistic behavior on the side of business schools. Winston (1999) points out that universities (and therefore business schools) could charge above average prices for below average educational quality and would not face a sufficiently high risk that their customers would become aware of this discrepancy. (Winston 1999, pp. 14–15) writes: 'By reducing incentives for the opportunistic behavior, nonprofits become the preferred suppliers in certain settings: they increase the probability—and the confidence of donors and buyers—that they're getting what they are paying for, tending to offset the contract failure inherent in such asymmetric markets.'

10.2.2 The Objectives-Based View: A Third Viewpoint for Strategic Management Scholars

The reader familiar with strategic management literature should note here a largely overlooked aspect of analyzing the sources of firm success. This literature is full of discussions between the proponents of two different schools of thought: the so-called market based view and the resource based view. The market based view argues that the competitive conditions and pressures in an industry largely determine the potential for the firm to be successful and to grow. In contrast, the proponents of the resource based view believe that only the peculiar competencies and strategic resources of the firm, which are hard to imitate, can provide the base for long-run sustainable competitive advantage. What has been largely overlooked by the management literature is the fact that the organizational objectives of the firm can also form the base for competitive advantages. For firms operating in credence goods industries, organizational goals which amount to a for-profit orientation pose a serious competitive disadvantage once potential customers become aware of the moral hazard problem. In such industries, only not-for-profit firms can receive the level of trust from their customers required for growing. So there might be room to establish a third viewpoint, which could be termed 'objectives based view'. Objectives matter for the success of firms. Firms in such industries are well advised to design strategies that pursue multidimensional objectives. In the higher education industry, institutions pursuing multidimensional objectives rather than focusing exclusively on the profit maximizing goal will enjoy a competitive edge vis-à-vis for-profit schools.

10.2.3 Unifying 1,000 Different Strategies

Such institutions have much more freedom in choosing their goals than for-profit organizations. Now, given this freedom, to what do they aspire? In the case of universities in general and business schools in particular, matters are complicated by the high degree of intellectual and organizational freedom professors enjoy.

Mintzberg and Rose (2003, p. 280) note: 'The mission of the university is research and teaching: to create and to disseminate knowledge. Yet these, especially research, are largely under the control of individual professors. A university of one thousand professors might be described as pursuing one thousand different research strategies, and many different teaching strategies.'

Yet, as Collins and Porras (1996) point out, mission statements can help to achieve congruence of goals between the organization and its employees. While the research strategies of individual professors working for the same business school might differ substantially, it should still be possible to find a common denominator, i.e., some elements that all or at least most individual missions have in common with the mission of the organization. Let us take an example from another creative industry that faces a similar problem: journalism. The more intellectually inclined newspapers and magazines also employ highly creative and intrinsically motivated intellectuals who pursue their individual missions, yet nobody would question that different newspapers take different and typically identifiable positions with respect to journalistic quality, selection of topics, and the political orientation of their commentary. Likewise, a professor working for the 'New School of Social Research' is part of an organization with a different type of mission than the University of Chicago, for example.

'In pluribus unum' is a living example that demonstrates how more than 300 million people with diverse ideas and missions can be united in a common purpose. And the European Union has proven with its more than 50 years of history that even its more challenging task of uniting diverse cultures and histories can be met successfully. Given the success of these entities, business school professors who monotonously insist on their individual freedoms should humbly recognize the need to subordinate at times their individual goals to the commonly shared organizational goals that unify them and allow them to be identified with successes of their organization that no individual professor could have achieved alone. It is certainly a difficult and complex task to find a common denominator for a universally acceptable mission statement of a business school, but it is not a 'Mission Impossible.'

10.2.4 What do Accreditation Institutions want to see in a Business School's Mission Statement?

Once the dean has identified goals and principles that are acceptable by the majority of faculty members despite their diverse research strategies and teaching styles and derived from these objectives the purpose for existence of the business school, she has to become more concrete and operational in communicating the mission to the stakeholders of the school. Such a mission statement also has to satisfy the demands of accreditation agencies. There are certain elements every mission statement should contain. (Palmer and Short, 2008, pp. 457, Table 10.1) mention that according to the AACSB standards and guidelines, the mission statement, for example:

Table 10.1 'Foreign trade' in the market for higher education within the EU (shares of students enrolled in higher education according to citizenship and destination countries; study year 2000/2001 in %)

		Total	BE	DK	DE	GR	ES	FR	IR	IT	LU	NL	AT	PT	FI	SE	UK
BE	Belgium	9.0	–	0	11	:	14	22	1	1	:	19	1	1	0	2	27
DK	Denmark	5.0	1	–	14	:	7	6	1	1	:	1	1	0	1	16	35
DE	Germany	38.7	1	1	–	:	11	14	1	2	:	8	16	1	1	5	35
GR	Greece	58.6	1	0	14	:	1	4		15	:	0	1	0	0	0	49
ES	Spain	21.3	6	0	27	:	–	18	1	1	:	4	2	2	0	3	34
FR	France	39.0	27	0	17	:	13	–	1	1	:	1	1	3	0	2	32
IR	Ireland	14.0	0	0	4	:	2	4	–	0	:	0	0	0	0	1	87
IT	Italy	34.2	9	0	22	:	15	11	0	–	:	1	21	0	0	2	18
LU	Luxembourg	5.6	25		29	:	0	25	0	0	:	0	5	1		0	13
NL	Netherlands	9.5	28	1	20	:	9	5	1	1	:	–	1	1	1	6	26
AT	Austria	9.7	0	0	68	:	7	4	1	1	:	1	–	0	0	3	13
PT	Portugal	9.5	7	0	19	:	15	30	1	0	:	1	0	–	0	1	24
FI	Finland	8.8	1	1	12	:	4	3	1	1	:	1	2	0	–	41	29
SE	Sweden	9.4	0	7	10	:	5	9	1	1	:	1	3	0	6	–	43
UK	United Kingdom	12.9	2	3	19	:	18	21	15	1	:	5	2	1	1	6	–
	Iceland	1.9	0	40	9	:	1	2	0	0	:	1	1	0	2	18	12
	Norway	9.5	0	15	10	:	3	4	2	0	:	1	1	0	1 0	13	41
	Bulgaria	10.8	1	0	47	:	2	17	0	2	:	1	13	0	0	1	3
	Cyprus	7.5	0	0	2	:	0	1	0	1	:	0	1		0	0	50
	Czech Republic	4.0	1	0	43	:	4	9	0	3	:	1	10		1	3	10
	Estonia	1.9	0	2	24	:	18	4	0	0	:	0	1		25	11	4
	Hungary	6.0	2	0	48	:	2	9	0	2	:	1	20	0	1	3	7
	Lithuania	2.8	0	2	34	:	1	4	0	1	:	0	1	0	2	6	3
	Latvia	1.4	1	1	44	:	1	5	0	1	:	1	2		2	10	8
	Malta	0.5	0		10	:	10	4	0	3	:	1	1				70
	Poland	16.7	2	1	61	:	3	12	0	3	:	1	6	0	0	5	4

(continued)

Table 10.1 (continued)

	Total	BE	DK	DE	GR	ES	FR	IR	IT	LU	NL	AT	PT	FI	SE	UK
Romania	10.9	2	1	22	:	3	26	0	6	:	1	4		1	2	4
Slovenia	1.6	1	0	34	:	1	2	0	11	:	0	35	0	0	2	8
Slovak Republic	8.3	1	0	12	:	1	3	0	1	:	0	13	0	0	0	2
Turkey	34.5	1	1	77	:	0	6	0	0	:	3	4	0	0	0	5
Albania	5.6	1	0	8	:	0	4	0	60	:	0	2	0	0	0	2
Federal Republic of Yugoslavia	3.1	0	0	19	:		2	0	2	:	0	3		0	1	1

Source European Commission 2003, p. 132, Table H 5

Remarks: Included in the data are students who work toward their higher education degree (ISCED 5) or toward their dissertation (ISCED 6). The figures for Germany refer to the group ISCED 5 only (http://www.uis.unesco.org/ev.php?ID=3813_201&ID2=DO_TOPIC) (ISCED = International Standard Classification of Education). The figure for Germany, Italy, the Netherlands and Austria does not include foreign and international schools

Interpretation: The rows of the matrix can be interpreted as follows: Out of the 38,700 students with German citizenship, who studied in countries of the European Union and the future member and candidate countries, 14 % studied in France and 35 % in the United Kingdom during the study year 2000/2001

- should cover the goals of the school,
- must include "(…) the viewpoints of 'various stakeholders'."
- specifies "(…) the student populations the school intends to serve."

In their study, Palmer and Short (2008) also addressed the question: What are actually the missions of business schools? They examined in an empirical study the content of mission statements of US. colleges of business. First of all, they found substantial diversity among the content of business school's mission statements. Surprisingly, only a little over one-third of the schools discussed key elements of the school's philosophy in their mission statements. And two-thirds of the business schools included in the sample did not make any reference in their mission statements with regard to growth, survival, and profitability of the institution. This is certainly an indication that a substantial share of schools do not pay too much attention to long-run organizational goals.

10.3 Some Insights from the Economic Analysis of Higher Education Organizations and Business Schools

Without a clear understanding of the economics of the particular industry to which a firm belongs, its strategy must necessarily fail. The economics of higher education is indeed anything but a straightforward application of standard microeconomic theory. And there are several good reasons—as Winston (1999) shows—why higher education organizations are not like business firms.

10.3.1 Business Schools Educate Managers and Entrepreneurs: Not Researchers

The economic analysis of the production process in higher education institutions that Winston (1999) provides fits well for the segment of economics departments. Economics students want to become researchers. For their later careers it is crucial to get admitted by those economics departments that are most competitive and are ranked among the top in the world. The quality of research conducted at these departments is the primary criterion for ambitious economics students to choose a graduate school. In contrast, business schools educate managers and entrepreneurs, not researchers. While the research results of economics, organizational and management science, psychology and law are the input of teaching content for the courses taught at these schools, the primary objective of business school courses is to apply already existing knowledge to the daily work in business organizations rather than to generate novel and innovative research results. In that sense, teaching at business schools has more—or should have more—in common with teaching languages than with training researchers.

This simple fact also becomes apparent when one compares textbooks for graduate courses in economics and management. The first group of books presents their content with a similar level of rigor like journal articles, whereas management textbooks have a lot in common with the type of presentation we find in the business press. Since much of the analytical core of management textbooks' content draws on fundamental insights and concepts that have been developed in economics long ago, it should come as no surprise that the suitability and popularity of these texts is more correlated with the quality of their pedagogy than with the originality and novelty of their content. Despite all the rhetoric about an ever-increasing speed of change in the business world, the basic problems and challenges of management that need to be addressed in graduate degree courses remain quite stable over time.

10.3.2 The Need for Diversity in Scholarship

These differences between research focused academic departments like economics and mathematics and application focused professional business schools have important consequences for the type of research that business schools need to emphasize. This is not to say that quality research was unimportant for business schools, but that the types of research needed to teach professionals on the one hand and researchers on the other hand are not identical. Ghoshal (2005, p. 82) pointed out the need for different kinds of scholarship and their proper place in business school research:

> In his book Scholarship Reconsidered, Ernest Boyer (1990) described four different kinds of scholarship: the scholarship of discovery (research), the scholarship of integration (synthesis), the scholarship of practice (application), and the scholarship of teaching (pedagogy). Historically, business schools have celebrated and accommodated as equals the practitioners of all four kinds of scholarship. Over the last 30 years, we have lost this taste for pluralism. What started off as an entirely justified effort for introducing the scholarship of discovery to the study of business has ended up in the excess of eliminating all other forms of scholarship from the world of business schools. Those with primary interests in synthesis, application, or pedagogy have been eliminated from our milieu or, at best, accommodated at the periphery and insulated from the academic high table that is now reserved only for the scientists.

Along these lines, Lorange (2008, p. 22) recently questioned the informational content of business school rankings about the quality of thought leadership that they are able to measure:

> Corporations and practicing managers tend to put heavy emphasis on how business schools are ranked in leading newspapers such as the Financial Times or the Wall Street Journal. They view the rankings as an important source in terms of assessing thought leadership. Most business school professors and staff, on the other hand, acknowledge that thought leadership is created primarily through research. While rankings tend to assume that schools are more or less alike, in reality of course, each school has a different profile and different strengths and weaknesses. To use rankings as an indicator for thought leadership is thus questionable.

We might add here the simple observation that thought leadership must be based on thinking that is critical (it must identify deficiencies of current practice), constructive (it must be applicable), and ahead of its time, otherwise it would not be leading. Then it directly follows that such thinking and research need not attract a high number of citations by other researchers who are not similarly ahead of their times but who rather choose to focus on those issues that for whatever reasons currently attract the largest number of academic articles.

10.3.3 The Case for a Differentiation Strategy

Once the plurality of quality dimensions in business research is recognized, the simplistic ordering of research output of scholars and business schools appears to be highly questionable. Moreover, this plurality gives business schools much more freedom in differentiating their programs if they resist the homogenizing pressures from the ranking exercises of the business press and the accreditation industry. There are many different dimensions of how degree programs in management and business administration can be differentiated from a "plain vanilla" MBA program, such as, for example[5]:

- focus on specific industries and their peculiarities,
- focus on not-for-profit and/or non-profit organizations,
- focus on stakeholder or shareholder view,
- focus on business failures and risk sources rather than the success stories that are typically portrayed in so-called business case studies,
- emphasis on particular management functions (e.g. accounting and controlling, finance, logistics, marketing, strategic management, procurement, logistics, exports, etc.), and
- differentiation through teaching styles (e.g. business simulation, role playing, service learning, etc.).

The world of businesses is much more heterogeneous than the standard for-profit, shareholder value-maximizing, publicly traded company featured in management textbooks wants to make students believe. The vast majority of all firms in our world are not publicly traded. They are not pure for-profit firms. They are headquartered in countries that lean more toward a stakeholder rather than a shareholder view. They have to struggle with industry-specific problems that are rarely mentioned in the generic type of business cases covered in management textbooks. And they are more concerned with potential risk sources that could

---

[5] Navarro's (2008) article entitled: "The MBA Core Curricula of Top-Ranked U. S. Business Schools: A Study in Failure?" documents how little content differentiation even the best business schools in the US. have achieved.

threaten their survival than with clues how to realize 25 % return on equity so that they become the darlings of the business press.[6]

Once business school deans realize that the simple case of firms covered in the standard management textbooks only applies to a minority of cases of business organizations in our world, they will become more confident that specialized degree programs can be designed that meet the educational needs of large numbers of managers and their firms. Consequently, a differentiation strategy is perfectly feasible for business schools. And because of the diverse business organizations that their graduating managers will join, there will be real value added to the education of young professionals if they can choose from a diverse set of degree programs rather than more or less standard MBA programs that differ from school to school by little more than the minimum required GMAT test score and the tuition fees.

The first step of crafting a differentiation strategy is to analyze the weaknesses of the competitors. Yet, gathering the type of information one needs for such a competitive analysis is a quite difficult task in most industries outside the higher education industry. The business press, industry journals, and published business case studies typically do not focus on the weaknesses but the strengths of firms. How else could they get any firm specific information and look behind the iron curtain of corporate information walls? In academia—by definition—one is tempted to say that such iron curtains are inacceptable and would violate academic standards. Criticism and open reflection about current practice in academia and its shortcomings are part of the work of academics. The higher education industry is the rare case where one can find published articles about the weaknesses of whole segments of this industry.

For the business school segment within the higher education industry numerous articles criticizing current practice show that academics fulfill their responsibility to reflect upon existing weaknesses. The most notable authors who triggered considerable debate are Mintzberg (2004), who essentially argues that the current practice of MBA programs is not effectively delivering the type of knowledge and skills to future managers that businesses need. Ghoshal (2005) attacks the very content that is being taught and its ideological roots. Adler and Harzing (2009) link the lack of substance of the type of questions that today's business school research addresses to the economic incentive structure for rewarding academics and their institutions for their research output through the quality hierarchy of journals, citation indices, and business school rankings.

---

[6] Lorange (2008, p. 13) also argued in his book that there is sufficient room for business schools to pursue differentiation strategies: "Indeed, in this book, I argue extensively for what might be seen as a viable alternative to the traditional US-Based organizational form. This is because I believe the traditional, axiomatic, discipline-based research to be less valid than it was before and that the interplay between best practice—the prescriptive knowledge coming from the best firms—and research—the propositional knowledge coming from professors—can give rise to an alternative model of academic value-creation. And this alternative model can perhaps challenge the classical, often US-based, business schools."

10.4 One-Dimensional and Multidimensional Organizational Goals and their Relation to Differentiation Strategies

A further characteristic feature of business schools is the fact that they are multi-product firms offering BAs, MBAs, and executive education. Following Winston (1999), we may characterize the production technology of business schools as a customer-input technology. In the sciences, mathematics, and economics, for example, the potential future contribution of students to their peers' learning success can be assessed beforehand and straightforwardly by standardized tests such as the GRE and the subject specific GRE Aptitude tests. The more intelligent the average enrolled student in a degree program is, the higher will be the quality of learning all of them will enjoy. This effect is simply so because students do not only learn from their professors but often times learn even more from their fellow students.

For business schools, however, matters are different. Their students do not want to become researchers. They want to become managers or entrepreneurs of for-profit and not-for-profit business organizations. Students with a low math score, for example, may still have high potential to become good managers and to contribute to the learning processes of their fellow students. Other abilities, talents, but also their experiences and goals must be criteria for selecting students from the group of applicants. Now, what are these criteria and who should set them?

10.4.1 Choosing Between One-Dimensional and Multidimensional Organizational Goals

Part of these criteria will be set by the business school. These criteria must follow directly from the mission statement of the school and the values that define the core of the organization. The identity of the business school reflected in these values should not be too far away from the identity of its students. For example, a more egalitarian oriented school with a strong emphasis on teaching the meaning of managers' responsibility for more than just maximizing shareholder value will look for similarly minded students. Other schools with a univariate rather than a multivariate measure of individual and organizational success will focus more on the ambition and ability to succeed in for-profit organizations. Both sets of values are legitimate for businesses as well as business schools. And given the large share of not-for-profit businesses in Europe and the intensifying discussion about employees seeking a well calibrated life-balance, both types of schools can be expected to find their market.

10.4.2 *Aligning the Marketing Strategy and the Assessment Criteria of the Business School*

A business school is well advised to share at least some of their goals with the business organizations it envisions as part of its stakeholder group.[7] Therefore, the set of criteria for the assessment of applying students should also incorporate some of the criteria firms use when assessing new applicants for their open positions. Thereby, the assessment process of the business school becomes a good predictor for the future ability to get a job at the group of firms that the school views as its stakeholders. The precision of this predictor is then reflected in the placement power of the school. The admission ratio as well as indicators of the placement power can effectively function as quality signals for applicant students, firms, and the public in general and, thereby reduce potential market failures resulting from the credence goods problem of the higher education industry. Optimizing the precision of this predictor requires that the strategic managers of business schools define the assessment criteria and design their marketing strategy simultaneously rather than sequentially. If the two strategies are not congruent, average placement ratios over time will be low, thus signaling a low economic value of the educational offering. Now, what are the control variables—so to speak—business schools can use to reach a close match between admitted students and the applicants stakeholder firms will hire in the future?

There are two ways to solve the problem: one is demand driven and the other one is supply driven. Demand driven solutions start with a look at the market and try to identify a group of firms that share similar business missions. Among the groups of firms with similar business missions, it is rational for the business school to target those groups that offer their students the highest salaries after graduation. Such schools attract a larger number of applicants. The small share of admitted students then allows them to be more selective in their admission process. Yet, firms offering the highest salaries typically have a one-dimensional goal: shareholder value maximization. In the pre-crisis times, the group of firms offering MBA graduates the highest salaries was the set of investment banks.[8] The other

---

[7] This is in line with the AACSB which "(…) require that colleges obtain input from stakeholders such as administrators, faculty members, students, and employers when developing the mission." See Palmer and Short (2008, p. 456).

[8] Pfeffer and Fong (2004), who work at Stanford University and the University of Washington, respectively deliver a critique of the current dominant organizational mission of US business schools and offer an alternative. They write: "(…) in return for the ability to obtain huge and growing enrolments and large donations, schools have presented themselves and their value proposition primarily, although certainly not exclusively, as a path to career security and financial riches" p. 1503. "In a related but somewhat different role, business schools might take the lead in making management a profession. This would entail articulating a set of professional values and responsibilities and developing standards of professional conduct and even sanctioning mechanisms for those who violate professional standards of organizational or business management. (…) Unfortunately, there is little evidence that business schools are enforcers of professional standards and norms of conduct. In a world in which economic success is frequently taken as the measure of value and merit, there are few sanctions coming from business schools for ethical malfeasance and there is not much evidence of what one might wish or expect in a self-policing profession" p. 1504.

solution approach is to first define a mission for the business school and then to search for a set of firms with similarly-minded business missions. While this approach reflects what most academics will view as a precondition for academic freedom, it is also a much more challenging task that requires a considerable degree of creativity.

10.4.3 One-Dimensional and Multidimensional Measures of Success and their Relation to Differentiation Strategies

The choice betweenone-dimensional and multidimensional organizational goals and success measures has important implications for the potential to pursue a differentiation strategy. A one-dimentional goal ultimately leads to what Winston (1999) describes as a hierarchy among schools. A hierarchy is a one-dimensional ordering and for such an ordering we need a univariate measure of success or quality. For business schools serving a group of firms with a more or less exclusive focus on shareholder value maximization, this univariate measure of quality typically will be the average salary of their graduates. Yet, business schools are not the only group of academic departments that might want to apply a univariate success measure. In mathematics, economics, and the sciences departments also use a univariate measure for the quality of applicants: their average GRE scores. The use of this measure hypothesizes that the degree of talent to become a future researcher could be tested by such standardized tests. Consequently, the average test score required to become admitted by a school as well as the ratio of the number of applying to admitted students then function as signals about the true quality of the school which is unobservable for applying students. For these types of academic fields as well as for business schools, the type of competition we observe is the type of rivalry described by Winston. Univariate quality measures allow journalists, for instance, to easily rank schools as we are used to rank the quality of, for example, soccer teams by the number of games won during a season. The resulting rankings establish hierarchies of soccer teams and schools.

The logic of the market in the industry of business schools, it seems, dictates the pursuit of a one-dimensional organizational goal for the business school, the measurement of quality according to a univariate measure, the establishment of a hierarchy among schools, and the resulting high barriers to entry for new business schools. The key to this market logic is the seemingly low degree of transparency of the quality of service provided by educational offerings and the need to mitigate this lack of transparency through business school rankings which are designed by business magazine journalists. The highest ranked business schools can live with this industry structure quite well for simple reasons. They serve as highly effective barriers to entry. For equally obvious reasons, the newcomers to the industry of business schools cannot.

10.4.4 The Existing Structure of the Business School Industry as an Effective Entry Barrier

The enormous barriers to entry in the business school industry are not only a problem for the strategic managers of business schools. These barriers are also highly undesirable from the viewpoint of society and of the economy because they impede dynamic competition among business schools. The engine that drives dynamic competition is innovation. In the industry of business schools, innovation must also include novel sets of goals and values for training future managers, the development of innovative curricula, and the use of new teaching methods and approaches. Such innovations naturally increase the diversity of educational offerings and eliminate the informative value of one-dimensional quality measures offered by business magazines.

Besides impeding dynamic competition, this type of archaic industry structure only attempts to improve the transparency of the education market for the top—the first league. However, because of the limits to the scalability of educational institutions, elite business schools can serve only a very small group of future managers. Yet, education in a civil society can never be a subject matter for the few. Improving the transparency of the true quality of the different educational offerings and empowering prospective students to judge the characteristics of schools must not be restricted to the highest caste of the business society. High quality business education must be accessible to a broad base of managers. Otherwise, much of the growth potential of an economy will remain underutilized. It is an economic commonplace that caste systems severely impede economic growth because they prevent that the human resources of a country are fully utilized.

10.5 Improving the Transparency of the Market to Reduce Entry Barriers

At first sight it seems that business school deans cannot change the structure of their industry; that they have to accept it as given. However, new business schools entering the market will be pursuing a differentiation strategy more often than the incumbent elite schools. They are the ones that will be gaining the most from innovations that lift the veil that conceals quality differences among different providers in the business school industry. The incumbent schools can rely on the rankings, yet the newcomers have to wait for many years before they will be appearing on these hierarchical lists, and most of them never will. Consequently, for them there will be gains from thinking about and searching for innovative approaches and solutions to improve the transparency of the market for business school programs. Entering business schools should not wait for incumbent elite business schools to take the lead in developing such innovations. For the incumbent schools such innovations will pose a threat rather than an opportunity.

What type of innovations could increase the transparency of educational offerings? First of all, a business school that follows a differentiation strategy must explicitly communicate its mission and its underlying educational objectives to prospective students and its stakeholders. If it differs from the average MBA school, it should not hesitate to frankly tell the public where it differs and why. By explaining the need for different goals and approaches, the school can already demonstrate its competency and credibly define the quality standards it aspires to meet. Second, the school should link its educational goals to the organizational and individual goals of firms and potential students, respectively, and thereby try to appeal to similarly-minded organizations and individuals. Third, schools with a differentiation strategy must answer the question: How can the achievement of each of their goals be measured and benchmarked objectively? It is not sufficient to assess each of these goals for the school's own achievements. Reducing the quality uncertainty also requires the assessment of the competitors' achievements for each of these goals.

Fourth, the group of business schools with a differentiation strategy should form an alliance that offers future students a web-based interactive tool which allows them to design their own personal quality ranking of business schools. The student would input her own personal weighting scheme for the different criteria that are relevant for assessing the quality of business schools. Based on this vector of normalized weights, the tool would then instantly generate the individualized ranking of business schools. Such individualized rankings would be much more informative for students than the published rankings of business magazine rankings which do not make the weighting of criteria transparent and only reflect the weighting scheme of one person: a journalist working for a magazine that reflects the business goals of FORBES 500 firms (Vidaver-Cohen 2007; Morgeson and Nahrgang, 2008).

10.5.1 Using E-learning to Improve the Transparency of the Market

Finally, the internet and e-learning tools offer an enormous potential to improve the transparency of educational offerings of business schools. While millions of individuals put their private videos for everybody to see on YouTube, few business schools open their brick walls to prospective students and allow them to sit, via the internet, in their classrooms for receiving free educational samples. Education is an information good and for these types of goods the internet offers many advantages for both marketing and delivery. E-learning tools and techniques can make the content and teaching methods much more transparent than ever before and, thereby, considerably reduce the uncertainty about the educational quality students will be receiving at the business school.

Two new marketing trends, called 'tryvertising' and 'trysumer' show that customers increasingly demand free samples of the offering before they are willing to buy.[9] Choosing a university or college degree program is one of the most important choices we have to make in our lives, much more important than a subscription for a magazine or the purchase of a car. Yet, universities and colleges still do not offer 'free issues' or a 'test drive'. Before the emergence of the Internet and e-learning, it was simply impossible to offer such free samples. Today, potential foreign students could receive them regardless how far away from the school they live. In other words, free e-learning samples can not only be a key tool for making differentiation strategies feasible and successful, but they can also be important for internationalization strategies.

10.5.2 Weighting Schemes of Business School Rankings are no Substitute for Market Research

Business schools that are about to enter the market should devote a substantial amount of time and resources to investigate the criteria that business school students—not business magazine journalists—apply when selecting their school. While the average number of publications in A-level journals per year of the faculty members might be an extremely important quality indicator for those students who want to learn how to produce a similar research output, it is quite doubtful that the majority of students at business schools will pay much attention to this indicator. For them, other criteria might be much more important such as:

1. The living expenses and quality of life at the location of the business school;
2. The average commuting distances and costs;
3. Local opportunities for internships;
4. The academic excellence of all four types of scholarship mentioned by Ghoshal and not just the scholarship of discovery, but also the scholarship of integration (synthesis), the scholarship of practice (application), and the scholarship of teaching (pedagogy);
5. The share of course content that is relevant and directly applicable in future occupations;
6. The quality of service in terms of student orientation (e.g. low drop-out rates, support for students during their learning process, etc.);
7. The accuracy of matchmaking between the admission policies for incoming students and the quality demands of future employers;
8. The placement power of the school in the job market;
9. The network the school can offer.

Market research using customer surveys should attempt to gather information about the weight students attach to these criteria when choosing a business school.

[9] See http://trendwatching.com/trends/TRYVERTISING.htm first published April 2005, and http://trendwatching.com/trends/trysumers.htm first published March 2007.

When deans of business schools try to assess the competitive position of their schools, they must gather information about these quality dimensions of their competitors and benchmark the performance of their own school with their peer group.

10.6 A Brief Examination of Competitive Forces in the Business School Industry

Another essential step of crafting a business strategy is to conduct a competitive analysis of the industry to which the firm belongs. Such an analysis systematically considers all the relevant factors in the firm's market environment which do or could have an impact on its profitability and growth. The standard starting point of competitive analyses of the industries is Porter's (1980) famous "Five Forces" framework. As the name already suggests, his framework covers five different factors that do impact the profitability of any firm:

1. Intensity of Rivalry among Competitors;
2. Entry;
3. Bargaining Power of Customers;
4. Bargaining Power of Suppliers;
5. Substitutes;

Let us begin with the first three market forces. First of all, competition in the higher education industry is dynamic competition about the quality of educational offerings. Unfortunately, the lack of transparency of the true quality of degree programs severely impedes competition and hinders innovation in the higher education industry in general and in the business school industry in particular. The traditional means of this industry to improve transparency—rankings and accreditation—can only prevent the worst cases of quality fraud (the so-called "degree-mills"), but they are a far cry from delivering future students what they need to make optimal choices given their individual preferences. Second, this type of market failure and the deficient ranking mechanism of the business school industry effectively erect barriers to entry for innovative business schools that pursue differentiation strategies, and, thereby reduce the intensity of dynamic competition. Third, Porter's market force of customers' bargaining power has little relevance in the context of the business school industry because students typically have no bargaining power. Another group, however, does have considerable market power.

10.6.1 Bargaining Power of Suppliers of Inputs

The most important input for universities and business schools are their faculty members. With e-learning technologies and internet accessible databases for literature, faculty members are less dependent on buildings and libraries than universities are dependent on faculty members. But even before the advent of the internet, the position of faculty members in universities and business schools was always very strong. In fact, universities and business schools might be viewed as employee "owned" firms, in the sense that they decide almost autonomously the quality, quantity, and content of their supply.[10] We already discussed the strong position of faculty members in setting the goals of the school and in defining—at least implicitly—its mission. This strong position is the result of several factors: the scarcity of academic talent, the tenure system, and the constitutional right (in many OECD countries) which grants faculty members the freedom of academic research and teaching.

Because of the scarcity of academic talent and the relative transparency of cost and revenue structures in business schools, faculty members can and do extract a large share of the economic rent the school generates. Especially, elite schools are particularly dependent on their "star faculty." Business schools that do not aspire to become a member of the top-10 but position themselves considerably below that group might have an edge with extracting economic rents because they are less vulnerable to the bargaining pressures of their faculty. Their members are much easier to replace than the celebrities among the elite business schools.

10.6.2 Substitutes

Finally, let us consider the market force that arises through substitute services. The first question we need to answer is: What are possible substitutes for an MBA? Two such substitutes can be identified: Other academic degrees and self-study. A degree from a business school is not the only type of education students can choose to speed up their occupational advancement in business organizations. Industry-specific expertise and superior knowledge in the scientific field which generates the innovations of the production process were often a precondition to reach senior management positions. For example, in the pharmaceutical industry, most senior managers have studied chemistry or pharmaceutics. Today, businesses, regardless of their industry affiliation, have come to understand that senior managers must possess a high level of knowledge in the fields of business, management, and economics. Advanced degrees in these fields have become educational substitutes

[10] Pusser and Turner (2002: 6–7) write: "Glaeser (2001) argues that in the face of weak governance structures, colleges and universities have evolved to resemble "worker cooperatives," representing the preferences of faculty with particular emphasis on the institution of tenure and the rise of the importance of research as a faculty activity. Yet, while this model may have characterized the nature of governance in higher education through the late 1970s, when Jencks and Reisman wrote the Academic Revolution, the revenue shortfalls of the last three decades brought about yet another transformation in academic organization. To varying degrees across colleges of different types, the locus of control has shifted from faculty to professional administrators (Slaughter and Leslie, 1997)."

for other academic fields in many industries and in others they have become complements. Another group of substitutes for a generic MBA-degree are industry-focused business degrees. Such degrees are the result of one group of differentiation strategies. Lindsey (2005) discusses some of the pros and cons of such a differentiation strategy for business schools.

10.6.2.1 Self-Study as a Substitute for MBA Programs

The second type of substitutes is the educational advances people can reach through self-study. Anybody who teaches at a business school must be highly proficient in self-study. Moreover, the idea of 'life-long learning' puts people's ability to self-study at center stage. However, those who have acquired sufficient self-study skills during their academic education in another non-business related field have other options than to enroll in an MBA program they can just teach themselves. Never before had self-study become so time saving and accessible 'anywhere, anytime'—to use a marketing slogan invented during the e-learning hype. Google-Scholar, Google-Books, Amazon, and Wikipedia provide tools for the self-learner that allow them to acquire relevant business knowledge when they need it rather than many years in advance.

10.6.2.2 Different Emphasis on Self-study Skills in the US and Germany

The very marked difference in emphasis on acquiring self-study skills between the US and Germany might also be one contributing factor, why MBA programs are a hard sell in Germany. For those readers of the present article who can compare from first hand experience the differences in organizing studies for students in the US and in Germany, one crucial difference will be quite clear. In the United States, universities at the undergraduate as well as at the graduate level organize student life in general and the process of study in particular in a much more detailed and efficient manner. Students receive guidance and support throughout their studies. In contrast, at German public universities, students receive comparatively little help or guidance for organizing their studies. Also, individual courses in Germany are far less aligned with the content of other courses than one can typically find in American degree programs. In each department in Germany, there are many different professors and each of them defines her or his own 'program.' For beginning students in Germany, the transition from high school to the university comes with a shock. In high school, only to a relatively small degree are students allowed to make their own decisions when organizing their own studies. Then, at the university, they are all of a sudden forced to find their own way through the opaque terrain of their academic field that they are not yet familiar with.

The negative side of this lack of organized help at many German public universities are high drop-out rates and an inefficiently organized and excessively time consuming study processes. Now, are there only disadvantages coming from the German 'lack of system'? Those students who finally graduate from a German public university have acquired one of the most important competencies of a university education: they must have become highly proficient and effective self-learners. If they were not, they could have never finished their studies. For example, someone who survived the graduate degree program in economics at the University of Bonn will have very little difficulty to teach herself the content of business administration and management. Such students have learned how to study and for them such content is only moderately challenging.

10.6.2.3 Are Students' Self-Study Skills a Threat or an Opportunity?

Self-study might be indeed a competitive threat to incumbent providers of MBA programs. Yet, highly proficient self-study learners can also offer promising opportunities for business schools. A higher level of self-study skills reduces the time involvement of teachers per student. Thereby, educational offerings become more scalable. Also, poor self-study skills reduce the effectiveness of e-learning much more than the traditional mode of teaching and learning. These two effects of self-study proficiency make clear that self-study skills are both a substitute and a complement for educational offerings.

Most business schools have alumni networks. And through these networks the school also markets its continuing education offerings to executives. If the school's alumni can be expected to possess a rather high level of self-study skills, the school needs to invest a much smaller amount of time in designing novel executive courses. Consequently, the content of these executive courses can be much more timely, thus increasing the economic value of the human capital acquired through these courses. Deans are well advised not to view the self-study skills of their students as a competitive threat. Quite the contrary; they should actively promote and nurture these skills. After all, a network of alumni with a high level of self-study skills will be a strategic resource for a school of the first order.

10.7 The Potential of Business Schools' Country and Region Focused Internationalization Strategies

For nations and firms, exports are crucial for growth. However, business schools are small organizations, and small firms have a disadvantage in exporting their products and services vis-à-vis large corporations. Because of their quite limited marketing budgets, small firms typically have to focus their export activities at the beginning of their expansion process on just one country, a small group of countries, or a region. The same applies to business schools, which immediately raise questions for business school deans such as: Is our home country a competitive location in the higher education market? And on which country or

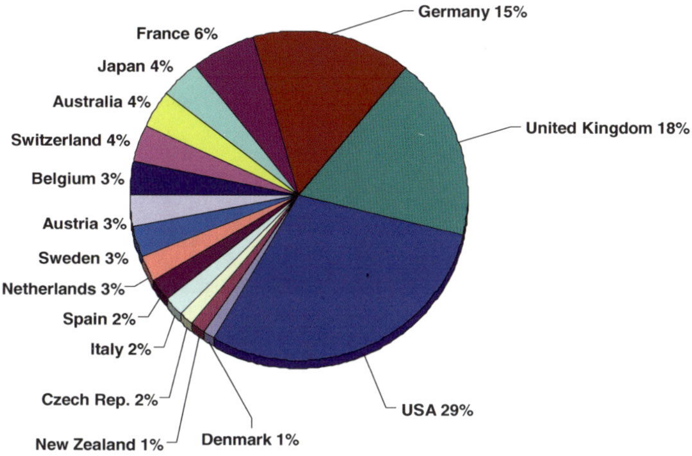

Fig. 10.1 Shares of OECD countries in the market for foreign students. *Source* Education at a Glance 2007, OECD Indicators, Table C 3.3

countries should we focus our marketing activities? This last chapter of our article will present some quantitative data which allow us to give some tentative answers to these questions.

Policy makers as well as university deans need to know more about the competitiveness of their home country in the market for international students. Eurostat and the OECD are gathering a wealth of data about foreign students and we draw here on these sources. Figure 10.1 shows the market shares of OECD countries in the market for foreign students (the numbers, however, are based on a total comprising OECD countries only). As expected, the USA appears as the leading country in the market for foreign students. Its share is about 60 % larger than the one of the second most important country, the United Kingdom.

However, market shares are the wrong indicator to rank the competitiveness of countries in the market for foreign students because they are heavily influenced by the size of the education sector at home. Consequently, it is not surprising that a country with more than 300 million inhabitants has a market share that is more than two and a half times as large as the market share of Germany, a country with a population of less than a third of that of the USA. To take account of these country size effects the OECD developed an index which is more informative about the real competitiveness of a country. Figure 10.2 shows this indicator for various OECD countries. This index compares the share of foreign students among all students in a particular country with the average of that share across all OECD countries. Values of the index above one signal a high degree of competitiveness, whereas index values smaller than one show below average competitiveness. Surprisingly, much of the ranking of the market share index is reversed. The USA appears as a country with below average competitiveness in the world market for foreign students. France, Germany, and the Untied Kingdom rank much higher, but smaller countries like Australia, Switzerland, and Austria hold the top positions.

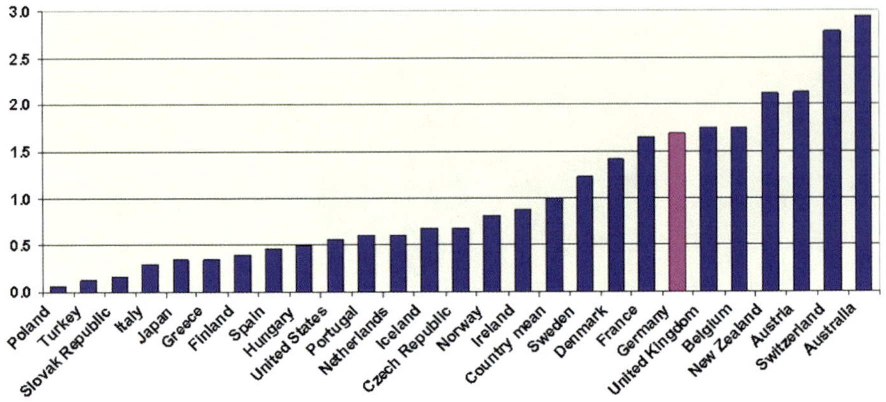

Fig. 10.2 Index of intensity of foreign students' intake relative to OECD reference area (2003). *Source* Education at a Glance 2005, p. 267, OECD (2005) Indicators, Table C 3.1

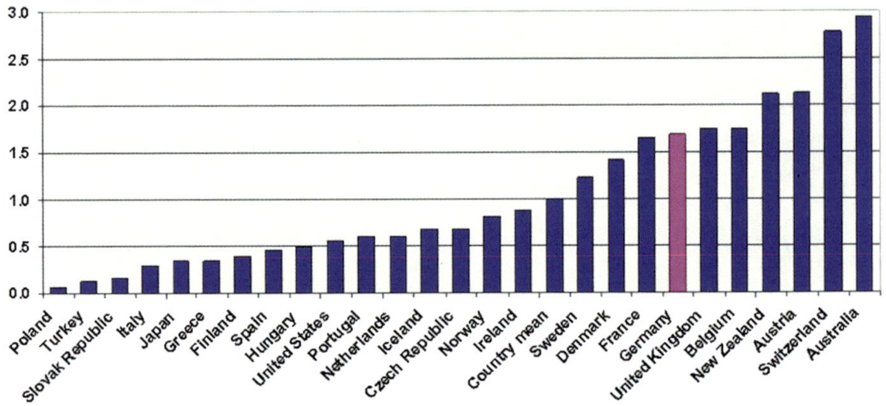

Fig. 10.3 Change of the domestic share of foreign student enrolments (1998–2003) in OECD countries. *Source* Education at a Glance 2005, p. 267, OECD (2005) Indicators, Table C 3.1

Another indicator that is important for the assessment of the growth prospects for business schools is the change of the domestic share of foreign student enrollments in that country as compared to other OECD countries. Figure 10.3 shows these shares. The two leading countries with market shares, the USA and the United Kingdom, are far behind other OECD countries with respect to growth rates. They may have reached a saturated stage. Germany is in the middle but behind France, Australia, and New Zealand for example.

For crafting a country- or region-focused internationalization strategy, it is important to know which countries view the home country as an attractive place to study and send a relatively high share of their foreign students there. By now, Eurostat compiles data which allows us to see the countries in Europe that European students choose when studying abroad. From these data it appears that

Table 10.2 'Foreign trade' in the market for higher education within the EU (shares of students enrolled in higher education according to citizenship and destination countries; study year 2005 in %)

Countries of Origin	Countries of Destination Germany	USA
OECD Countries		
Austria	52.5	7.8
Czech Republic	34.7	13.4
Hungary	36.4	12.3
Italy	19.9	8.8
Luxembourg	31.0	0.6
Poland	49.0	9.2
Spain	21.8	14.1
Switzerland	22.6	14.8
Turkey	48.9	25.0
Total from OECD Countries	14.0	27.3
Partner Countries		
Brazil	9.0	38.3
Chile	6.8	38.0
China	6.7	22.8
Estonia	17.8	6.8
India	3.1	60.4
Israel	9.6	27.3
Russian Federation	28.3	12.3
Slovenia	23.0	11.8

Source Education at a Glance 2007, OECD (2007) Indicators, Table C 3.3 (selected countries)

Germany is the preferred country by foreign students in: Turkey, where 77 % of all Turkish students that study abroad do so in Germany, followed by Austria (68 %), Poland (61 %), Bulgaria (47 %), Czech Republic (43 %), Latvia (44 %), Lithuania (34 %), Slovenia (34 %), Luxembourg (29 %), Italy (22 %), and the Federal Republic of Yugoslavia (19 %). These numbers are quite useful when crafting a marketing strategy. Table 10.1 gives the detailed picture of foreign trade relations in the European market for foreign students for the year 2000/2001 and the interested reader can find updates of this data on the OECD website.

For 12 European countries, the UK is the most popular destination country for students studying abroad. Despite the language barrier, Germany runs a close second with 11 countries, followed by France with three countries. The next Table 10.2 shows where foreign students from some selected OECD and non-OECD countries go to. Germany is the number one destination for students from Central and Eastern Europe, but also for Italy, Austria, and Switzerland.

What is interesting to note here from a German perspective is that 6.7 % of the Chinese students that study abroad do this in Germany, as compared to 22.8 % who do so in the US. Since the US is about 3.7 times as populous as Germany, the share would have to be 24.8 % if those Chinese students that study abroad would view both countries as equally attractive. In other words, with respect to the group of Chinese students who chose to study abroad, Germany was more competitive in 2005 than the US. The competitive edge is even more pronounced with students from Israel. Given the share that Germany attracts from this student group and given the differences in population sizes, the US would have to draw 35.5 %, yet attracts only 27.3 % of the Israeli students.

Certainly, these are aggregate numbers combining foreign students from all academic fields and not just business administration, economics, finance, and related fields. However, these figures show that the perceived dominance of the US in attracting foreign students from all over the world is no longer there. Other countries have emerged that are equally, if not more competitive, than American schools. Despite the poor showing of German business schools in international rankings, these data about international student mobility nurture at least some hope that there is considerable potential should business schools outside of the US pursue their internationalization strategies.

10.8 Conclusion

Palmer and Short (2008) provide evidence indicating that a substantial share of business schools in their sample do not pay much attention to achieving long-run organizational goals. Yet as we showed in our paper, advances of the microeconomic analysis of the higher education industry and credence good industries as well as the tools of strategic management can help business school deans in designing strategies for growing their organizations. Now, let us briefly summarize the main insights that can be gained from our paper:

1. From the microeconomic analysis of credence good industries it directly follows that business schools will enjoy a competitive advantage if they are not-for-profit organizations. Such organizations do not have the same type of incentives as for-profit business schools to take advantage of the asymmetry of information about the true quality of the educational offering. Therefore, they enjoy a competitive advantage vis-à-vis their for-profit competitors.
2. Business schools teach professionals, not researchers. Consequently, the quality of the scholarship of their faculty is multi- and not one-dimensional and business schools should pay attention not only to the quality of scholarship of discovery (research), but also to the quality of the scholarship of integration (synthesis), the scholarship of practice (application), and the scholarship of teaching (pedagogy).
3. This plurality of scholarships that is relevant for professional schools including business schools opens a multidimensional space for differentiation strategies to position the school.
4. Furthermore, there is a large body of literature that criticizes the current practice of business school education. Instead of falling prey to the homogenizing pressures from newspaper rankings and accreditation processes, the

shortcomings identified there should be the beginning for designing innovative differentiation strategies.

5. New business schools pursuing differentiation strategies should form an alliance that offers students a web-based interactive tool which allows them to design their own personal quality ranking of business schools.
6. Business schools that are about to enter the market should devote a substantial amount of time and resources to investigate the criteria that business school students—not business magazine journalists—apply when selecting their school.
7. In order to increase the transparency of the market for business degree programs and to reduce the quality uncertainty of their offerings, business schools should use e-learning tools for offering free educational samples. Thereby, they could effectively lower the barriers to entry for new business schools that currently severely impede their growth.
8. Deans are advised not to view the self-study skills of their students as a competitive threat. Quite the contrary; they should actively promote and nurture these skills. After all, a network of alumni with a high level of self-study skills will be a strategic resource for the school of the first order.
9. For designing internationalization strategies, business schools outside the US should recognize that the perceived dominance of this country in international trade in the market for higher education when measured by their market shares does not give an accurate picture of its competitiveness. Other, more informative indicators show that countries like Australia, Switzerland, Austria, and New Zealand clearly are more competitive in these markets than the US.
10. When allocating the quite limited marketing budgets for executing business schools' internationalization strategies, their deans should focus on those countries that send relatively large shares of their students who study abroad to the country where the school resides. OECD and Eurostat data by now make the differential competitiveness of receiving countries with respect to the sending countries transparent.

In summarizing, we may answer the question quite simply whether or not new business schools can, by applying the tools of strategic management and economic analysis, become successful and grow despite the tough competition from highly ranked incumbent schools. The short answer is: "Yes, they can!"

Bibliography

Adler NJ, Harzing A-W (2009) When knowledge wins: transcending the sense and nonsense of academic rankings. Acad Manage Learn Educ 8(1):72–95

Bailey JJ, Dangerfield B (2000) Applying the distinction between market-oriented and customer-led strategic perspectives to business school strategy. J Educ Bus 75(3):183

Barry BW (1997) Strategic planning workbook for nonprofit organizations. Amherst H. Wilder Foundation, Saint Paul

Boyer EL (1990) Scholarship reconsidered priorities of the professoriate. San Francisco, Jossey Bass
Bryce HJ (2000) Financial and strategic management for nonprofit organizations: a comprehensive reference to legal, financial, management, and operations rules and guidelines for nonprofits. Jossey-Bass Publishers, San Francisco
Bryson JM (1995) Strategic planning for public and nonprofit organizations: a guide to strengthening and sustaining organizational achievement. CA, Jossey-Bass Publishers, San Francisco
Collins JC, Porras JI (1996) Building your company's vision. Harvard Bus Rev 74:65–77
Courtney R (2002) Strategic management for voluntary nonprofit organizations. Routledge, London
Dees JG (2002) Strategic tools for social entrepreneurs: enhancing the performance of your enterprising nonprofit. Wiley, New York
Franck EP, Schönfelder B (2000) On the role of competition in higher education—uses and abuses of the economic methapor. Schmalenbach Bus Rev 52:214–237 July
Ghoshal S (2005) Bad management theories are destroying good management practices. Acad Manage Learn Educ 4(1):75–91
Gruber RE, Mohr M (1982) Strategic management for multiprogram nonprofit organizations. California Manage Rev 24(3):15–22
Hull CE, Lio BH (2006) Innovation in non-profit and for-profit organizations: visionary, strategic, and financial considerations. J Change Manage 6(1):53–65
Johnston J, Marshall N (1995) Strategic management in australian universities. Public Prod Qual Strateg Manage 1:197–211
Julian SD, Ofori-Dankwa JC (2006) Is accreditation good for the strategic decision making of traditional business schools? Acad Manage Learn Educ 5(2):225–233
Katsioloudes MI (2002) Global strategic planning: cultural perspectives for profit and nonprofit organizations. Butterworth-Heinemann, Boston
Keller G (1983) Academic strategy: the management revolution in American higher education. John Hopkins, Baltimore
Khatri N, Wells J, McKune J, Brewer M (2006) Strategic human resource management issues in hospitals: a study of a university and a community hospital. Hosp Top 84(4):9–20
Kohm A (2003) Strategic restructuring for nonprofit organizations: mergers, integrations, and alliances. Praeger Publishers, New York
Lockwood G (1985) Planning. In: Lockwood G, Davies J (eds) Universities: the management challenge. SRHE & NFER-Nelson, Berkshire
Lorange P (2008) Thought leadership meets business. Cambridge University Press, Cambridge
Mintzberg H (2004) Managers not MBAs—a hard look at the soft practice of managing and management development. Berrett-Koehler Publishers, Inc., San Francisco
Mintzberg H, Rose J (2003) Strategic management upside down: tracking strategies at Mcgill University from 1829 to 1980. Can J Adm Sci 20(4):270–290
Morgeson FP, Nahrgang JD (2008) Same as it ever was: recognizing stability in the business week rankings. Acad Manage Learn Educ 7(1):26–41
Navarro P (2008) The MBA core curricula of top-ranked u. s. business schools: a study in failure? Acad Manage Learn Educ 7(1):108–123
Nutt PC (1984) A strategic planning network for nonprofit organizations. Strateg Manage J 5(1):57–75
OECD (2005) Education at a glance—OECD indicators 2005, Paris
OECD (2007) Education at a glance—OECD indicators 2006, Paris
Oster, Sharon M (1995) Strategic management for nonprofit organizations: theory and cases. Oxford University Press, New York
Palmer T, Short J (2008) Mission statements in u. s. colleges of business: an empirical examination of their content with linkages to configurations and performance. Acad Manage Learn Educ 7(4):454–470

Pfeffer J, Fong CT (2004) The business school 'business': some lessons from the us experience. J Manage Stud 41(8):1502–1520

Porter ME (1980) Competitive strategy. The Free Press, New York

Ringwood J, Devitt F, Doherty S, Farrell R, Lawlor B, McLoone S, McLoone S, Rogers A, Villing R, Ward T (2005) A resource management tool for implementing strategic direction in an academic department. J High Educ Policy Manage 27(2):273–283

Shah AJ, David FR, Surawski III, Zigmont J (2004) Does strategic planning help churches?: an exploratory study. Coast Bus J 2(1):28–35

Vidaver-Cohen D (2007) Reputation beyond the rankings: a conceptual framework for business school research. Corp Reputation Rev 10(4):278–304

Winston GC (1999) Subsidies, hierarchy and peers: the awkward economics of higher education. J Econ Perspect 13(1):13–36 Winter

Yang C–C, Cheng L-Y, Yang C-W (2005) A study of implementing balanced scorecard (BSC) in non-profit organizations: a case study of private hospital. Hum Syst Manage 24:285–300

Chapter 11
Training Researchers in the Asia-Pacific: A Regional Response to Global Leadership in Research

Jeremy S. Eades and Malcolm Cooper

11.1 Introduction

The growth of the audit culture in the world academic research system as typified by the United Kingdom Research Assessment Exercise (RAE) has led to an extreme preoccupation with research league tables, and their associated branding, marketing and managerial strategies. The most examined of all research league tables is the UK RAE, which has been held every 5–6 years since 1985 (Taylor 1995; McNay 1997; Elton 2000; Bence and Oppenheim 2004). This was introduced during the Conservative Thatcher regime in the UK, when questions were being asked about 'value for money' in relation to higher education investment by the government, and the old system of 5-year plans and expanding budgets for the sector were being challenged. A substantial proportion of the higher education budget (about 15 %) was set aside for distribution on the basis of the assessed quality of research, in relation to indicators such as quality of published output, quantity of research funding, and output of PhD graduates. Departments were ranked on a five-point scale (later extended to 7, from 1 to 5* via 2, 3b, 3a, 4 and 5) and the higher the ranking, the greater the funding that universities received. While to nobody's surprise, the top spots ever since have been occupied by Oxford, Cambridge, and the top London institutions, i.e., Imperial College, University College, and the London School of Economics (wherever these exercises have been introduced the main beneficiaries have been the longer established and politically important universities), there have been some surprises lower down

J. S. Eades (✉) · M. Cooper
Ritsumeikan Asia Pacific University, Graduate School of Asia Pacific Studies,
1-1 Jumonjibaru, Beppu City, Oita Prefecture 874-8577, Japan
e-mail: jse@apu.ac.jp

M. Cooper
e-mail: cooperm@apu.ac.jp

A. Altmann and B. Ebersberger (eds.), *Universities in Change*, Innovation, Technology, and Knowledge Management, DOI: 10.1007/978-1-4614-4590-6_11,

in the ranking, with the strong showing of comparatively new institutions and older established provincial universities. The competition between universities became increasingly intense, with universities hiring in international superstars with big publications and research grants to boost their fortunes in advance of the 'census days' by which staff members had to be in post to count in the assessment.

Nevertheless, universities are seen to be leading providers of training for future researchers and the generators of much of the new knowledge, which is essential to a nation's long-term economic growth and social cohesion. However, given that a few top universities are recruiting the best students, earning most of the research money, and generating most of the PhDs under the current system, there is a concentration of resources in a few elite institutions on a world-wide basis. This chapter explores the Asia-Pacific's response to this concentration, which remains heavily biased toward the USA and Europe. And we do it through an examination of recent changes in the flows of research students within the Asia-Pacific region and to the outside. We also examine what lessons the UK experience of RAEs have for the increasingly competitive universities of the Asia-Pacific region, and what strategies does it suggest for new and/or upwardly mobile Asia-Pacific universities?

11.2 University Rankings and the Asia-Pacific Region

As mentioned above, the increased emphasis on the audit culture means that university managements are increasingly obsessed by university rankings, and ranking tables based on all kinds of criteria abound, both nationally and internationally. One of the most interesting of the ranking web sites is that developed by Jiaotong University in Shanghai, PRC. This is based on indices calculated from a number of criteria: ranging from the number of Nobel prizes to the number of citations of alumni and researchers in international journals; in other words heavily research output oriented. The Jiaotong list ranks the top 500 universities in the world, and provides separate rankings for Europe, the USA, and the Asia-Pacific regions. Results are starting to accumulate over time, and the site allows comparisons extending back to 2003.

The first glance at the list would appear to confirm the predominance of American and European Universities. In 2006, Harvard was at the top with a notional score of 100 and the other universities were ranked in descending order from there. Cambridge ranked second, but with a much lower score of 72.6. It was closely followed by Stanford (72.5), University of California Berkeley (72.1), MIT (69.7), California Institute of Technology (66), Columbia (61.8), Princeton (58.6), Chicago (58.6), Oxford (57.6), Yale (55.9), and Cornell (54.1). In other words, the top 12 universities were all Anglophone, with 10 in the United States (US) and 2 in the UK. The first universities to break this pattern were Tokyo (ranked 19), and Kyoto (ranked 22), the highest ranked of the Asia-Pacific Universities. Overall, 37 of the top 50 schools were in the US, 2 in Japan (Tokyo, Kyoto), 2 in Canada (Toronto,

University of British Columbia), and 1 each in Switzerland (Zurich Institute of Technology), the Netherlands (Utrecht), Sweden (Karolinska Institute of Technology), and France (Paris 06) (Table 11.1). After the first 100 institutions, the list results typically become increasingly bunched (the distribution is highly skewed), and the index does not differentiate between numbers 202–252, 253–202, 203–300, 301–400, and 401–500.

If the US scored heavily in the top 50, the picture is not so clear-cut if we look further down the table. Taking the top 100 or 500 universities as a whole, and dividing the percentage of the universities in any one country by the percentage of the world population in that country, the league table changes radically (Table 11.2). The table has been arranged with the countries with the highest representation in the top 500 institutions, relative to the size of their populations, at the top. An index of 100 % suggests that a country is pulling its weight in world terms (the Czech Republic at 100 % and South Africa at 114 % are the nearest), though the top countries are considerably higher. The highest ranked countries now become Sweden (2,200—i.e. over-represented by some 22 times), Switzerland (1,600), Austria and Israel (1,400), Australia (1,070), and New Zealand, Hong Kong, Finland, and Denmark (all on 1,000). What these countries (or territory, in the case of Hong Kong) have in common is that they are relatively small in terms of population (Australia being the largest), relatively affluent, and they are English speaking. The larger countries then follow, with the UK (9,500), and Canada (8,800). On this reckoning, the US is only 14th (726), while Japan ranks 20th with 320, roughly in the same league as France (470), Singapore (400), and Spain (260).

The results are perhaps hardly surprising. The figures seem to suggest that though the best schools in the US (plus Oxbridge in the UK) are pre-eminent from a global point of view, the more welfare state minded and egalitarian countries of Northern Europe (plus a few offshoots like Australia, Israel, and New Zealand) may have a more consistent standard of higher education provision. China, India, and Russia just make it into the top 500, but seem set to move up the rankings in future, if their economic growth continues. China has recently overtaken Japan as the second largest investor in research after the United States. Apart from the regional heavyweights (South Africa, Egypt, Chile, Argentina, Brazil, and Mexico), the states of Latin America, Africa and Central Asia are conspicuous by their absence. Perhaps more surprisingly so is Southeast Asia; with the obvious exception of Singapore.

Despite this degree of English-speaking hegemony, Japanese universities still dominate in the Asia-Pacific region, given the size of the country's population and the large number of institutions. Not surprisingly, the former Imperial Universities predominate within Japan according to the Jiaotong list. In order of ranking the top Japanese universities are Tokyo (ranked 20), Kyoto (23), Osaka (61), Tohoku (76), Tokyo Institute of Technology (89), Nagoya (98), Hokkaido (107), Kyushu (108) and Tsukuba (116). Hiroshima, Keio (the first of the private universities), and Kobe follow along in the 200s, Chiba, Kanazawa, Nihon, Niigata, Okayama, Tokyo Medical, Waseda and Yamaguchi in the 300s, and Ehime, Gifu, Gunma, Kagoshima, Kumamoto, Nagasaki, Nara IT, Osaka Prefectural, and Tokyo

Table 11.1 Top 50 universities in the jiaotong world ranking of universities 2006

World rank	Institution*	Country	Total score
1	Harvard University	USA	100.0
2	Stanford University	USA	77.2
3	University Cambridge	UK	76.2
4	University California—Berkeley	USA	74.2
5	Massachusetts Inst Tech (MIT)	USA	72.4
6	California Inst Tech	USA	69.0
7	Princeton University	USA	63.6
8	University Oxford	UK	61.4
9	Columbia University	USA	61.2
10	University Chicago	USA	60.5
11	Yale University	USA	58.6
12	Cornell University	USA	55.5
13	University California—San Diego	USA	53.8
14	Tokyo University	Japan	51.9
15	University Pennsylvania	USA	51.8
16	University California—Los Angeles	USA	51.6
17	University California—San Francisco	USA	50.8
18	University Wisconsin—Madison	USA	50.0
19	University Michigan—Ann Arbor	USA	49.3
20	University Washington—Seattle	USA	49.1
21	Kyoto University	Japan	48.3
22	Johns Hopkins University	USA	47.5
23	Imperial Coll London	UK	46.4
24	University Toronto	Canada	44.6
25	University Coll London	UK	44.3
25	University Illinois—Urbana Champaign	USA	43.3
27	Swiss Fed Inst Tech—Zurich	Switzerland	43.2
28	Washington University—St. Louis	USA	43.1
29	Rockefeller University	USA	40.2
30	Northwestern University	USA	39.5
31	Duke University	USA	38.9
32	New York University	USA	38.7
33	University Minnesota—Twin Cities	USA	38.3
34	University Colorado—Boulder	USA	37.8
35	University California—Santa Barbara	USA	37.0
36	University British Columbia	Canada	36.3
36	University Texas Southwestern Med Center	USA	36.3
38	Vanderbilt University	USA	35.1
39	University Utrecht	Netherlands	34.9
40	University Texas—Austin	USA	34.8
41	University Paris 06	France	33.9
42	University California—Davis	USA	33.6
43	Pennsylvania State University—University Park	USA	33.5
44	Rutgers State University—New Brunswick	USA	33.4
45	Tech University Munich	Germany	33.3

(continued)

Table 11.1 (continued)

World rank	Institution*	Country	Total score
46	Karolinska Institute Stockholm	Sweden	33.0
47	University Edinburgh	UK	32.9
48	University Paris 11	France	32.5
48	University Southern California	USA	32.5
48	University Pittsburgh—Pittsburgh	USA	32.5

Source Jiaotong World Ranking of Universities 2006

Metropolitan in the 400s. Of these 29 Japanese universities, only 3 (Keio, Nihon, Waseda) are private universities, and only 2 are 'public' (i.e. run by prefectures or cities, namely Osaka Prefectural, and Tokyo Metropolitan). The other 24 are former national universities, led by the former imperial universities (Tokyo, Kyoto, Osaka, Nagoya, Kyushu (in Fukuoka), Tohoku (in Sendai), and Hokkaido (in Sapporo)), together with Tokyo Institute of Technology. The private universities in Japan which make up the overwhelming majority of Japanese institutions of higher education are thus strikingly under-represented. Over a quarter of the former national universities make it into the ranking, compared with less than 1 % of the private universities. Despite their high rank in some of the Japanese domestic league tables (see for instance the Asahi Shimbun Daigaku Rankingu), other leading private universities such as Doshisha and Ritsumeikan in Kyoto do not make the cut in the Jiaotong list.

It is also increasingly recognized in Japan that links with Asia, and especially the rising economies of India, South Korea, and China are particularly important. A report by Demos, a policy think tank in the UK, noted that China had now moved ahead of Japan in terms of its investment in research, and spelled out the implications of such changes:'Britain has a choice. Either we become a marginal science and innovation player in world terms, just as we have in the car industry, or we can take our lead from the City of London and become a global hub for research initiatives. That means choosing our areas of specialization, collaborating with others, and placing ourselves at the center of knowledge and innovation networks'. Between 1999 and 2005, there was a massive increase in the number of UK students from China (a 735 % rise) and from Korea (a 79 % rise). However, not all the students were happy with the education they received. Indian students in particular tended to complain at their treatment. Relatively few of them attended the more prestigious universities, and some in lower ranking institutions complained that they were treated as 'cash cows' and subjected to 'mass produced degree courses'. International links therefore should be a means of raising research profiles, and not just a source of revenue through the recruitment of students.

Table 11.2 National representation in top 100/500 universities, by percent of world population

Country	Percent of top 100 (A)	Percent of top 500 (B)	Percent of world population (C)	Percent ratio A/C	Percent ratio B/C
Sweden	4.00	2.20	0.10	4000.00	2200.00
Switzerland	3.00	1.60	0.10	3000.00	1600.00
Austria	0.00	1.40	0.10	0.00	1400.00
Israel	1.00	1.40	0.10	1000.00	1400.00
Australia	2.00	3.20	0.30	666.67	1066.67
New Zealand	0.00	1.00	0.10	0.00	1000.00
Hong Kong	0.00	1.00	0.10	0.00	1000.00
Denmark	1.00	1.00	0.10	1000.00	1000.00
Finland	1.00	1.00	0.10	1000.00	1000.00
UK	10.90	8.60	0.90	1211.11	955.56
Canada	4.00	4.40	0.50	800.00	880.00
Netherlands	2.00	2.40	0.30	666.67	800.00
Norway	1.00	0.80	0.10	1000.00	800.00
USA	53.50	33.40	4.60	1163.04	726.09
Belgium	0.00	1.40	0.20	0.00	700.00
Germany	5.00	8.00	1.30	384.62	615.38
Ireland	0.00	0.60	0.10	0.00	600.00
Italy	1.00	4.60	0.90	111.11	511.11
France	4.00	4.20	0.90	444.44	466.67
Singapore	0.00	0.40	0.10	0.00	400.00
Japan	5.90	6.40	2.00	295.00	320.00
Spain	0.00	1.80	0.70	0.00	257.14
China-Taiwan	0.00	1.00	0.40	0.00	250.00
South Korea	0.00	1.80	0.80	0.00	225.00
Greece	0.00	0.40	0.20	0.00	200.00
Hungary	0.00	0.40	0.20	0.00	200.00
South Africa	0.00	0.80	0.70	0.00	114.29
Czech	0.00	0.20	0.20	0.00	100.00
Poland	0.00	0.40	0.60	0.00	66.67
Chile	0.00	0.20	0.30	0.00	66.67
Argentina	0.00	0.20	0.60	0.00	33.33
Brazil	0.00	0.80	2.90	0.00	27.59
Egypt	0.00	0.20	1.10	0.00	18.18
Russia	1.00	0.40	2.30	43.48	17.39
Mexico	0.00	0.20	1.60	0.00	12.50
China	0.00	1.80	20.40	0.00	8.82
India	0.00	0.40	17.00	0.00	2.35

Source Jiaotong World Ranking of Universities and the authors

11.2.1 University Research Rankings in Japan

Because its economic restructuring occurred rather later than that of the UK, Japan's embrace of the research audit culture also came rather later than the 1980s (Goodman 2003). Nevertheless, by the late 1990s, a series of government reports on higher education (and an interest in ministry circles in the UK experience) suggested that serious reform might well be on the cards. By this time, commentary on Japanese higher education from outside was scathingly critical (e.g. Cutts 1997; Hall 1998; McVeigh 2002). During the 1990s, the number of 4-year universities expanded, along with the percentage of high school leavers continuing to university, despite a decline in the number of 18-year olds in the population, which fell 3 % in between 1992 and 2004. More recent developments have included the appearance of vocational universities, a new generation of international universities with multinational students and staff members, and the Center of Excellence (COE) Programs, designed to fund new international exchanges and research collaboration, to raise research in Japan to an 'international' standard (Eades 2005). There have also been awards for teaching best practice, and a UK-RAE style research evaluation exercise is also being planned. But perhaps the most important of the reforms took place in 2004, a 'big bang' (Eades et al. 2005) in which the national and public universities were turned into educational foundations, thus putting them on a similar legal footing to the private universities, and creating an apparently level playing field for all institutions.

It is clear from the vantage point of 2009 that under the new dispensation not only are the average abilities of the groups of students going to the research and non-research universities becoming increasingly polarized, but so is research output and research funding. The case of the COE program is interesting in this regard (Eades 2005); the first proposal from the Ministry was for 30 institutions to be chosen and for most of the money to be invested in them. After a vigorous protest from other universities that wanted to be included as well, the eventual competition was much more open. Subject committees were formed, applications were called for, proposals were reviewed by the subject committees, and after a round of interviews a final shortlist was selected and ranked. The final selection was carried out by the Japanese Society for the Promotion of Science, a part of the Education Ministry, which simply worked down the list allocating the budget for each subject until it ran out. The net result at the end of the exercise, which lasted from 2002 to 2004, was that the top 20–30 institutions, mostly national universities, did in fact get most of the money. A few large prestigious private universities (Keio, Waseda, Ritsumeikan) also made it into the list, though with only a fraction of the awards of the top national universities, as did one or two of the local public institutions, but the general distribution was similar to that of the Jiaotong list—the prestigious national universities predominated and the private universities were barely in the frame.

Fig. 11.1 Two-stage process *Source* The authors

11.3 The Mobility of Research Students

Given this situation it can be seen that the mobility of research students will be a critical factor in the raising or lowering of rankings and in the health of the higher education sector as a whole. In this regard, some interesting patterns are beginning to emerge. This section therefore looks at two of the primary indicators of effective research capacity development in a nation or region—those of research student mobility and interuniversity research links—in the East Asia Region focussed on Japan, China, and the Republic of Korea. Recent government policy directives in this region resulting from the trends discussed above indicate that there is a need to encourage institutions to be more flexible and responsive in developing a strategic portfolio of research activities and research training programs in order to secure national benefits arising from the endeavors and achievements of individual researchers and teams in an international context.

The evolution of the framework for research student mobility and international research links in the East Asian Region must however be seen in the context of that region's emergence as an economic powerhouse in the world economy. As a result of growing interdependence within this region, comprising China, Korea, and Japan (with as yet fairly tenuous links to East Russia, India, and Mongolia), an independent economic system is forming that does not rely on the rest of the world for its rationale or strength. This development can be seen in the emerging trade patterns within East Asia, among other indicators (Watanabe 2004).

In an interesting paper, Kuroda (2007), asked the obvious question: can the trend of economic integration at the trade and production level that is occurring in East Asia be confirmed in the sphere of student mobility and research links? In other words, is de facto economic integration being transformed into a framework for full institutional integration including higher education? While the data on student mobility in East Asia is at best partial and the history of research linkages is in the main those created with third parties from outside of the region (most often based on historical linkages between institutions and/or governments in Europe and the US), it is possible to trace emerging intraregional patterns in recent times.

The traditional higher degree pattern in most parts of the world has been that Masters and Honors level research students carry out local and low-level supplementary research in the major paradigms of the time or place, and this is examined 'in house'. Also In this system, the PhD is personal and subject related but might include a foreign location and/or mentor.

In a major shift in emphasis, a new pattern is emerging in Asia-Pacific countries. In this pattern, the Masters by Course Work remains a personal development tool (post graduate), but may also be used by government/business as a form of capacity building for their employees (with government, business or ODA sponsorship). Here also the PhD is changing, with the basic traditional PhD declining in importance and being replaced by PhDs in fixed topic research as part of team (locationally footloose students, paid directed research) and explicitly designed for country or regional needs. Post-doctoral research is now also becoming footloose, and is often directed research or paid team research. Business, universities, and governments have of course invested in higher degree students at various times and at various levels in the past through scholarships and the like; what seems to be occurring now is a much more intense and directed form of such investment. In essence, this is a two-stage process (Fig. 11.1).

In this situation, the reputation of a university and/or its research centers for applied research is critical; 'pure' research is less well thought of, and increasingly less well funded. Externally based research training is also less well thought of—in a situation of rapid Asian growth, each of the countries involved is moving away from sponsoring its research students, and perhaps eventually all students, studying in European, American, or Australasian institutions.

11.4 Recent Patterns of Research Links and International Student Mobility in East Asia

East Asia as an economic powerhouse and major contributor to the internationalizing of linkages involving student mobility and research is quite a recent phenomenon. Before the late 1980s, only Japan was in a position to contribute much to international student mobility and research in the region, and those Japanese students and research universities that chose to internationalize their education or research experiences looked mainly to Europe and North America (Umakoshi 1997). Since then Korea and more recently China have become major contributors in both areas, and the East Asian Region as an entity in its own right has become much more important to the flow of students and research ideas in its part of the world.

11.4.1 East Asia Student Mobility Patterns

Taking 1987 as the base point (before the Asian Financial Crisis), Table 11.3 shows that the number of foreign students studying in the Universities of the East

Table 11.3 Student mobility in East Asia compared to the US, UK, and France

Inbound—selected country	1987	2002	Rate of increase
USA	3,43,870	5,86,316	1.70
France	1,33,848	2,21,567	1.65
UK	45,416	2,55,233	4.62
Japan	10,697	95,550	7.93
China	3,250	85,829	25.41
Republic of Korea	900	4,956	4.51
Total for East Asia	14,847	1,77,290	10.94

Source 2007

Table 11.4 Student mobility in East Asia compared to the US, UK and France

Outbound—selected country	1987	2002	Rate of increase
France	12,500	53,152	3.25
USA	19,707	40,750	1.07
UK	14,513	30,201	1.08
China	42,491	2,74,144	5.46
Japan	15,335	62,938	3.10
Republic of Korea	22,468	83,242	2.71
Total for East Asia	80,294	4,20,324	4.23

Source Kuroda 2007

Asia Region had increased markedly by 2002 (the latest year for which figures for *all* regional countries are available; Kuroda 2007). While the US, France, and the UK, which had traditionally taken large numbers of foreign students, recorded increases (the UK by nearly 500 %), those moving to and within East Asia (led by China) increased by 1,100 %. Table 11.4 confirms that this pattern of considerable change is also found in the outbound flows of students from the countries of East Asia, China especially.

These data show that there has been a sharp increase in student mobility within the region, in the form of student exchanges between individual institutions and countries, based on government sponsorship. In more recent times, these have included a fair number of postgraduate research students, mainly at the Masters level, moving from China and Korea to Japan.

Coupled with this is the current very significant investment in research capability by China, Korea, and Japan (and other countries close by). Each country is investing huge amounts in research capability and in student mobility, but this is intended to make the region self-sufficient in both higher degrees and research and development, not to provide students for institutions outside the region. While research and development in specific fields of endeavor may still require that East Asian students and research centers look for opportunities and partners from outside the region, this appears less and less attractive to the funding bodies involved as time goes on.

Table 11.5 Number of international students in Japan

Source country	2001	2002	2003	2004	2005
China	44,014	58,533	70,814	77,713	80,592
Taiwan	4,252	4,266	4,235	4,096	4,134
Korea	14,725	15,846	15,871	15,533	15,606
Malaysia	1,803	1,885	2,002	2,010	2,114
USA	1,141	1,217	1,310	1,456	1,646
Thailand	1,411	1,504	1,641	1,665	1,734
Indonesia	1,388	1,441	1,479	1,451	1,488
Philippines	490	483	508	525	544
Brazil	343	347	353	330	338
Bangladesh	805	823	974	1,126	1,331
Others	8,441	9,205	10,321	3,331	3,461
Total	78,812	95,550	109,508	117,302	121,812

Source Unesco Statistical Yearbooks, various

11.4.1.1 Japan

A complication in this analysis, but one that actually reinforces these changes in research student mobility and research links in the East Asian Region is that of the demographic change now affecting Japan and other countries in the region (Cooper and Eades 2007). During the twentieth century most of the advanced industrial societies moved toward increased life expectancy and decreased fertility—more old people and fewer children—and Japan led this process. By the late twentieth century, the birthrate in Japan and most of the other industrialized countries had fallen so low that any population growth still happening was due to immigration and people living longer. While the very high life expectancy in Japan has offset the effects of declining fertility on the total population size of the country for some time, the impact of this ran out during the first decade of the twenty-first century with the population peaking at 127 million, since when it has started to plummet. By 2050, it could be back to World War II levels, or around 70–80 million if no new offsetting trend occurs. The impact of this population decline with respect to the higher education sector is twofold. First, the number of young Japanese seeking higher education has declined rapidly in the past few years—so much so that on a yearly basis it is now less than the total number of places available at domestic universities—and, second, there is an increasing desire to fill the surplus places with Japanese students who would otherwise go offshore for such education, and/or with foreign students. So, while the mobility of undergraduate students is not at issue in the present discussion, these trends will also have an impact on the flow of research students from Japan because this demographic situation is forcing internationalization on Japanese universities (the alternative, that of foreign universities setting up in Japan has largely failed, for reasons that will not be discussed here). We may therefore expect that in the future there will be a much greater concerted effort to keep both types of student 'at home' in the region and ultimately in individual countries.

How this is already impacting on Japan as shown in Table 11.5, where the number of foreign students in Japan is rising rapidly partly due to the need fill these surplus places, but partly also due to the push for Asianization outlined above.

11.5 Models of Research Student Mobility and Research Linkage Development

As Kuroda (2007) notes, the original model of student mobility was one of universalism, or unbounded study, where universities were seen as communities of universal knowledge not bounded by state borders or business requirements. Thus, universities could be and were open to all regardless of cultural origin and political background, and faculty members and students could be international as much as local (the 'Cosmopolitan University' model—Kerr 1990).However, as time went by, the nation state came to the fore as a funding agent, and universities lost some of their independence. Universities were gradually transformed into 'National' universities (e.g., the University of Tokyo, or the Australian National University; Kerr 1990); a model diametrically opposed to the Cosmopolitan model, even though it is doubtful if faculty and students recognized much difference.

Research student mobility developed within this period of change. To the extent to which the Cosmopolitan model prevailed in any given situation, the nationality of students and faculty, seen as a community of world-wide scholars, did not matter and the existence of foreign research and other students was proof of the universality of higher education. Under the National University model, the dispatch of students abroad and the recruitment of foreign faculty (usually in limited numbers because of funding or legal constraints) were also seen as important. However, this was because of the needs of the nation (e.g., 'nation building'), and did not include the receiving of students from abroad or the cultivation of an international outlook on the part of domestic students. Research student mobility was nevertheless important.

11.5.1 The Third model: The Cosmopolitan Nation State University

It is possible to distinguish a third model—that of the 'Cosmopolitan Nation State University' and of its research links—as being useful for the development of a country's science and engineering research and development (Ebuchi 1997). As a result, a strong sense of the need for internationalization combined with national control of research student support and research linkage development is becoming the preferred approach in Asia, especially East Asia, in line with this model. Its counterparts in Europe can be seen in the ERASMUS programme and the Bologna process.

This model has become more important in the Asia-Pacific because the current preference for the formation of a 'knowledge economy' centering around universities is clearly a part of the national strategies of Asian Countries, and they are actively engaged in moves to secure excellent students from any source as well as to promote research linkages based on domestic needs. Organizations set up to achieve these aims have been promoted by ASEAN, Australia (the University Mobility in Asia and the Pacific or UMAP programme, established in 1993) and others. As with the European ERASMUS and similar American initiatives, these moves should be seen as much a human resource strategy as an exercise in cosmopolitan intellectualism in today's world market. From the point of view of the nation states involved, in order to achieve Asia-Pacific regional integration, international research, other student mobility within the region, and the creation of intraregional research links should be considered and promoted from the perspective of strengthening competitiveness in human resources *vis-à-vis* the other regions of the world. And, as we have seen earlier in this chapter this is precisely what is now happening.

11.5.2 Connecting Research Links and International Student Mobility to Community Development in East Asia

The most salient trend in higher education on a world-wide basis in the early twenty-first century is the rapid process of its marketization (Kuroda 2007). The current trend toward transforming national universities into either incorporated administrative bodies or privatizing them is undoubtedly contributing to this, but so are business and government HRD, research, and development needs. The diversification of higher education funding, closer industry–university–government partnerships, and networks of universities are all aimed at the acquisition of research (and other) students in the international market, or retaining/developing their services on a regional basis. In the World Trade Organization context, and consequently within the framework of many of the new Free Trade Agreements, higher education has become a marketable commodity on an international basis. And, in line with the discussions and behaviors seen in relation to other important commodities, there are varying degrees of protectionism and liberalism throughout the sector and the World.

This is true of the Asia-Pacific as much as of elsewhere in the world. In particular, the rapidly growing demand for higher education and research and development in China cannot be fully absorbed domestically and must therefore be satisfied elsewhere. What is apparent though is that satisfaction of this demand is increasingly being sought in Asia itself, or at the very least in countries where higher education and research are being transformed into a service commodity market in close proximity to that region. Malaysia, Singapore, and the Philippines, as well as Korea and Japan, are becoming the preferred sources of supply as their own higher education and research sectors become as sophisticated as those in Europe and the Americas. Thus, a regional market in higher education and research is rapidly forming in East Asia, bolstered by South East Asian suppliers.

This can be illustrated by reference to the research plan for the period 2006–2010 of our own university, Ritsumeikan Asia Pacific University (APU). This business plan provides a preamble to its substantive content which is encapsulated by the following statements:

11.6 A Framework for Research and Research Training at APU

Universities are the nation's leading providers of training for future research workforce and generate much of the new knowledge which is essential to the Asia-Pacific's long-term economic growth and social cohesion. In order to achieve this, APU established the following research framework policies for 2006–2010:

1. To serve as a hub for research in Asia-Pacific Studies by responding to issues of the Asia-Pacific region and contributing to the development of Asia-Pacific Studies as a core field of study in global terms;
2. To establish and/or contribute to the academic networks of research institutions, organizations, and individuals in the region and in various countries of the region;
3. To promote a research policy that enhances the social contribution of research. First, emphasize various types of international and regional exchanges; second, share research findings; third, contribute to regional capacity building through research;
4. To emphasize research supported by public and private funds. APU should obtain funding from as many external sources as possible, in particular for international research appropriate to the eventual creation of a COE in Asia-Pacific Studies;
5. To Contribute to the improvement of the content of education and to educational systems in the Asia-Pacific Region at an international level.

11.7 Conclusion

We can see from this example and the very many others like it that international student mobility and international research linkages will continue to grow—but there will be significant limits (boundaries) to that growth. In particular, demand patterns are now much different than before: countries, industry, and indeed universities themselves have an increasingly different outlook on research student mobility and international research links. While it is a truism that there are more competitors fishing in the same pools on a world-wide basis—for students, for researchers, for staff, for revenue from higher education, for research outputs and linkages, etc.—we should expect that a form of protectionism will increasingly come to the fore. In other words, the demand for and supply of higher degree and research students in regions like the Asia-Pacific will become increasingly concentrated within those regions, for reasons that have more to do with the playing out of regional trade, investment, and market forces than of the promotion of cosmopolitan styles of education.

As the Asia-Pacific Region becomes an 'Asia Pacific Community', international research student mobility and the formation of intraregional research links will be just as much part of the discussions on tactics and strategy as will political and economic issues such as trade and security. Other regions of the world should expect a decline in the numbers of research students from the Asia-Pacific and of research links with the Asia-Pacific as this process works itself through. The model of higher education and research that the Asia-Pacific is adopting at present is thus the 'Cosmopolitan Nation State University' and its research links will reflect this as the region broadens and deepens its economic and intellectual capacity.

In this chapter, we have argued that higher education has become increasingly competitive, and that one symptom of this is the increasing obsession with national and international rankings. The UK has taken the lead in the development of the audit culture, and many of the UK initiatives have been noted or adapted by the Ministry of Education in Japan, in attempting to raise teaching and research in Japanese universities to 'international standard'. These models may be of use in analyzing the situation in the Asia-Pacific as well, and especially the changing university landscape in Japan. On the one hand, Japan aspires to be the higher education hub of East Asia, and indeed its most prestigious universities are dominant in the region, particularly in the sciences. However, the Japanese higher education sector is numerically dominated by private universities, few of which feature in international rankings. This raises the question of how they can raise their international profiles, and this is where the mobility of research students and methods to attract them will become an increasingly important battleground.

One alternative has already been tried in Japan. In recent years, there have been several bold attempts to set up institutions to attract students on the international market, including the International University of Japan, Akita International University, and initiatives from both Waseda and Ritsumeikan (Ritsumeikan APU). The scale of these experiments varies, from the very small (IUJ and AIU) to the substantial (APU). They vary in their approach to language, and in the markets they are trying to attract, as well as in the strategies they are using. APU appears to be going clearly down the vocational-teaching route, expanding student numbers, while at the same time trying to maintain an academic-research base, particularly in the graduate school. How far this strategy will work in the long run is an open question, given that the major universities competing in the international market are generally academic-research based in the first instance. Meanwhile IUJ and Waseda seem to be going more down the academic-research route, with a more limited curriculum, a smaller infrastructure, and smaller numbers of students. Seeing how these programs fare in the next few years should make for an interesting comparison, one which will tell us much about whether Japanese universities can gain a foothold in the global mass market for research students, or whether their futures lie more in cutting edge research in a few high prestige institutions, leaving most universities in the country to compete for an increasingly precarious domestic research student market resulting from long-term demographic decline (Kinmonth 2005).

Bibliography

Asahi Shimbun (Annual) Daigaku Rankingu [University Ranking]. Asahi Shimbun, Tokyo

Bence V, Oppenheim C (2004) The role of academic journal publications in the UK research assessment exercise. Learned Publishing 17(1):53–68

Cooper MJ, Eades JS (2007) Landscape as theme park: demographic change, tourism, urbanization and the fate of communities in 21st century Japan. Tourism Res Int 11(1):9–18

Cutts RL (1997) An empire of schools. Japan's universities and the molding of a national power elite. ME Sharpe, Armonk

Eades JS (2005) The Japanese 21st century center of excellence program: internationalism in action? In: Eades JS, Goodman R, Hada Y (eds) The 'big bang' in Japanese higher education. Trans Pacific Press, Melbourne, pp 295–323

Eades JS, Goodman R, Hada Y (eds) (2005) The 'big bang' in Japanese higher education. Trans Pacific Press, Melbourne

Ebuchi K (1997) Study on the internationalization of universities. Tamagawa Daigaku Shuppanbu, Tokyo

Elton L (2000) The UK research assessment exercise: unintended consequences. High Educ Q 54(3):274–283

Goodman R (2005) Whither the Japanese university? An introduction. In: Eades JS, Goodman R, Hada Y (eds) The 'big bang' in Japanese higher education. Trans Pacific Press, Melbourne, pp 1-31

Hall IP (1998) Cartels of the mind: Japan's intellectual closed shop. Norton, New York

Kerr C (1990) The internationalization of learning and the nationalization of the purposes of higher education: two laws of motion in conflict? Eur J Educ 25(1):5–22

Kuroda K (2007) International student mobility for the formation of an east asian community, creation of new contemporary Asian studies paper 37, Graduate School of Asia Pacific Studies, Waseda University, Tokyo

Kinmonth E (2005) From selection to seduction: the impact of demographic decline on private higher education. In: Eades JS, Goodman R, Hada Y (eds) The 'big bang' in Japanese higher education. Trans Pacific Press, Melbourne, pp 106–135

McNay I (1997) The impact of the 1992 research assessment exercise in English universities. High Educ Rev 29(2):34–43

McVeigh B (2002) Japanese higher education as myth. MS Sharpe, Armonk

Taylor J (1995) A statistical analysis of the 1992 research assessment exercise. J R Stat Soc 158(2):241–261 Series A (Statistics in Society)

Umakoshi T (1997) Internationalization of Japanese higher education in the 1980s and early 1990s. High Educ 34(2):259–273

Watanabe T (2004) The path toward East Asia market integration. Keisoshobo, Tokyo

Chapter 12
The Rejuvenation of a Professional School in the United States

Alfred S. Posamentier

12.1 Setting the Framework: The City University of New York

University reform is always a challenging undertaking. It is hoped that through this anecdotal adventure, the reader will take away some useful pointers to be used when faced with the need to revitalize a school steeped in a too-familiar culture. This paper traces the history of the City College of New York (CCNY), the founding of the School of Education within the college and the evolution of the School of Education into its current form. Interestingly enough, City College itself predates by more than 100 years the rest of the City University of New York (CUNY) that was established in 1961 as a governing institution to encompass a combination of senior colleges (including City College) and community colleges, and has become the largest urban public university in the United States. CUNY is governed by a Board of Trustees who establish, in concert with the Chancellor of the City University and representatives from its various constituencies, the precepts, and standards that determine the guidelines for admission policies and academic and fiscal operations. Although there may be times of disagreement between the Board of Trustees and the semi-autonomous colleges, these matters are settled within the framework of goodwill and common goals.

A. S. Posamentier (✉)
School of Education, Mercy College,
555 Broadway Dobbs Ferry, NY 10522, USA
e-mail: aposamentier@mercy.edu

A. Altmann and B. Ebersberger (eds.), *Universities in Change*, Innovation, Technology, and Knowledge Management, DOI: 10.1007/978-1-4614-4590-6_12,

12.1.1 The City College of New York

Founded in 1847, City College is the oldest public urban university in the United States, originally designed to provide higher education opportunities for those who could not afford to attend private universities. From its inception until 1975, it was a tuition-free institution and attracted many of the brightest students in New York City. Among its graduates are nine Nobel laureates and a plethora of scientists, actors, politicians, educators, and other societal leaders. In short, the College was dedicated to educating the brightest students regardless of their financial wealth or social status. Because of its fame, age, and historical significance in the life of New York City, City College is regarded as the flagship of CUNY.

Although admission to City College for most of its history was considered an acknowledgement of outstanding scholarship, in 1970, in response to the social pressure of the times, CUNY established an "open admissions" policy that permitted many students who were unprepared for college work to enter its senior colleges, requiring that resources, heretofore available for scholarship, be reallocated for remediation. Consequently, many alumni of City College were disaffected and students who would have been the natural constituents of the college turned elsewhere, leading to a decline in academic standing and public perceptions of the institution. A stricter admissions policy reinstating higher entrance requirements and standards for retention was introduced by the Board of Trustees in 1978, beginning the retransformation process for City College, which once again is attracting and retaining a superior student body. The history of the School of Education, a teacher training school within City College, closely parallels the rise, fall—and rise again—of City College as the premier public college in New York City. In 1998, with the historical low point of the School of Education, we began the process of its transformation the School of Education in order for it to become again a vibrant and successful teacher training institution. This paper describes that journey.

12.1.2 The School of Education

The City College School of Education was established in 1921, and was the first such school at a public institution in the metropolitan region. For decades, it produced the leading educators for the City of New York and its suburbs. The number of departments in the School of Education has fluctuated from as many as five to the current three departments: the Department of Secondary Education, the Department of Childhood Education, and the Department of Leadership and Special Education. Today, the School of Education—with 40 faculty members in addition to many support staff—is just one division of many at the City College, which is often seen as a university within a university. The other divisions at the College are the School of Engineering, the School of Architecture, the School of

Medicine, the Division of the Humanities and the Arts, the Division of Science, and the Division of Social Science. The latter three comprise the College of Liberal Arts and Science.

12.2 Understanding the Problem: The New York State Board of Regents and Accreditation of Teachers

To fully understand the educational scene in New York City one has to consider the larger scope of education in the United States. First of all, as guaranteed by the United States Constitution, education at every level is the prerogative and responsibility of the individual states. Therefore, each state government determines the standards for education within that state. In New York State there is a body called the Board of Regents, which is responsible for regulating all professions (except lawyers who regulate themselves) including education. Thus, the Board of Regents, established in 1784 and comprised 16 members, each elected by the legislature for a 5-year term, through its Education Department, is responsible for certifying teachers and consequently assures the effectiveness of schools of education. The Board of Regents is the commission that approves and certifies all institutions of education in the State of New York, including universities and in some cases its divisions. Any college or university within New York State is in peril of losing its accreditation status if it does not meet the academic standards outlined by the Board. In 1998 this loss of degree-granting status was a real possibility for the City College School of Education.

In the mid-1990s, the New York State teacher certification examination scores by City College School of Education graduates were on a steady decline. Subtle warnings from the State Board of Regents Education Department seemed to go unheeded. A subsequent edict by this body stated that in order for schools of education to remain viable, 80 % of its graduates had to have a passing score on state teacher examinations. This was clearly not the case at the City College where less than 40 % of the School of Education graduates passed these comprehensive tests. The Board of Regents Education Department consequently monitored the activities of the School of Education through frequent visits that did not bring about much change, but rather demoralized the faculty. Simply put, a continuation of this sort of performance meant that the School of Education, the oldest public school of education in the region with a heretofore stellar history—graduating a huge number of teachers, principals, superintendents, chancellors, and luminaries such as Stanley H. Kaplan, the founder of the immense network of private support schools throughout the United States—was in jeopardy of its existence. In June, 1999 the dean of the school was removed, and I was asked to assume this position. I had been on the faculty since 1970 and had served as a department head (6 years) and as associate dean (10 years). My charge was clearly to bring the School of Education out of these doldrums and onto the road to recovery.

12.3 Assessing the Issues at the School of Education

Prior to my appointment as dean, the School of Education found itself in a most peculiar position at the college. In reaction to the State's displeasure with the School of Education's performance, the college president made a dramatic move and, for the first time since the school's inception, placed the school within the College of Liberal Arts and Sciences (this is the unit which includes the Division of Science, the Division of Humanities and the Arts and the Division of Social Science). Hardly anyone at the college understood the reasoning behind this structural change. One might assume that it was done to show that "change" was made to effect the desired modifications. In short, the college president removed the School of Education's autonomy. Naturally, this further demoralized an already demoralized faculty; any changes in curriculum and personnel had to be approved by the College of Liberal Arts and Sciences, which had never been the case previously. For a university, these aspects (i.e., what is to be taught and who is to teach it) are perhaps the most important governance prerogatives. The task of moving the School of Education from this restricted position was certainly a daunting one.

In a real way, I had the opportunity to use an impending disaster to effect positive change. At a much later date, Rahm Emanuel, President Barack Obama's Chief of Staff noted, "You never want a serious crisis to go to waste." (Wall Street Journal, November 8, 2009). In 1999, the School of Education had its crisis and we had a chance to create a dramatic reversal of fortune.

I first surveyed each component of the school that required change and revitalization, ultimately focusing on four vital factors: faculty, curriculum, physical space, and technology. Change in admissions standards by the City University would bring us a better student body—but students would come only if the school warranted their respect. A former Chancellor of the New York City Public Schools (Anthony Alvarado) once stated that "students vote with their feet" and the School of Education had to again attract student boots if it was to retain budget capability and regain individual school status.

12.4 Changing the Culture of the School of Education

As stated by Smith (1994), "A university culture is based on the belief that college and university faculty members share a common view of the world and scholarship and have similar understandings of the nature and purposes of higher education and the role of faculty." I believed we had to restore that confidence and shared belief. The first task that needed to be addressed was how to resuscitate pride in the faculty. The media, other universities, and the educational community at large had lost respect for the School of Education, and this change of perception had to be addressed immediately. How do you show faculty that society can still look favorably upon them?

12.4.1 The Dean's Advisory Council

In an effort to stem this negative image and to immediately provide a positive tone, I set out to establish a Dean's Advisory Council, consisting of a collection of highly respected individuals from many varied positions of our society, which—beyond the expected advisory advantages of such a group—would demonstrate to the faculty and others that there is confidence in the institution. It is a common practice for universities to have advisory boards; however, it is less common for individual schools (i.e. divisions of universities) to have such a board. No such council at the School of Education existed previously. An earlier attempt, by a predecessor dean, to develop a School of Education advisory council with outside members had elicited great conflict among the faculty who could not agree about its membership—everyone had their particular favorites and agreement was just not attainable—and a stalemate resulted. To circumvent such political conflicts, I chose to establish a Dean's Advisory Council, allowing the dean alone to make the selection of its membership. While, oftentimes such board members are selected on the basis of the individual financial support that they can provide, my interest was not financial. Rather, it was to select a prestigious membership to demonstrate that important members of society still had confidence in this important school of education. All the individuals who I approached to join this Dean's Advisory Council immediately accepted the appointment. The Council included: the Chancellor of the New York City Public Schools, the president of the teachers union, the president of the supervisors union, two Nobel laureates, the president of an educational publishing company, the president of a major engineering firm, a deputy mayor, two members of the Board of Regents, several school teachers, principals and superintendents from the New York City public schools, a local religious leader from the neighboring community, and some senior faculty members. The Advisory Council had met every semester during my tenure and provided invaluable advice and guidance with regard to the direction of the School of Education. More importantly, the Dean's Advisory Council began to reverse the negative feeling among the faculty about its own school, becoming the first of many steps toward rejuvenating the School of Education.

12.4.2 Utilizing Physical Space to Impact Faculty Collaboration

As indicated by Damrosch (1995), faculty belief in shared purpose and their collaboration in scholarship and team-building are essential if successful transformation of college culture is to be realized. I attempted to reach these objectives through a series of initiatives. Naturally, faculty seminars and other professional activities could stimulate such cooperation; however, the physical setting can play a role as well. In prior decades, offices had been assigned to new faculty on a space-available basis. This meant that faculty in the same discipline were not necessarily near one another and consequently had to make an effort—or simply not—to meet colleagues with similar academic interests. There was a serious dearth of cooperation among the faculty. Closer cooperation could result in increased grant support for research and outreach programs, which would further help to improve the external image of the School of Education. Faculty esprit de corps would then also improve. I felt this cooperation among faculty had to be addressed immediately. Therefore, I had approximately 25 faculty members move offices. One should not think that this is a simple matter, since faculty members treasure their office space and do not wish to change anything in this regard. Moving sometimes requires consolidation of files. For many faculty members, discarding old files—particularly those that had not been looked at in well over a decade—is a very painful matter. Yet, I undertook this effort with the conviction that it would foster departmental and program collaboration, and the result was that faculty members in the same discipline were now neighbors. This improved academic cooperation so that joint grant proposals were developed by faculty who previously went about their research individually, co-authorships evolved, and other fruitful camaraderies could be seen. All this produced a much more favorable image of the School of Education for the outside world. One specific example of these closer faculty ties has been the organization of subject-specific conferences and seminars which did not exist previously.

12.4.3 Changes in Teacher Certification Procedures: Motivation for New Curriculum Development

Improvement of the professional climate in the School of Education came at a propitious time, coinciding with the decision of the New York State Board of Regents Education Department to make a dramatic move in teacher certification procedures. Heretofore, certification of teachers and administrators was done at the New York State Education Department in New York State's capital, Albany. The new proposal was to have the state's schools of education take over this responsibility. That is, the Board of Regents would issue teachers and administrator certification to any student who successfully completed a certification program at a state-approved school of education. This meant that each of the 115 schools of education in New York State would have to have their curriculum approved by the Education Department. Furthermore, the Education Department issued a set of standards that had to be met by each of the schools of education in order to merit this approval. For City College, this came at a very important juncture, since one of the factors that had to be addressed to improve the school was the curriculum. Faculty, aware of the critical nature of the problem, responded by undertaking a major curriculum reform—sorely needed, in any case, at this school. In a very cooperative mode and over several months, the faculty developed an entirely new curriculum for prospective and in-service teachers and supervisors. This effort resulted in full approval by the Board of Regents' Education Department. The City College School of Education now ranked as a certifying agent for teachers and supervisors in New York State. Gradually, we were on our way to a renaissance of the School of Education.

12.4.4 Faculty Culture: Creating the Climate for Change

As would be expected, senior faculty resisted change while younger faculty—of which there were relatively few at this time—were enlightened and eager to try new things. Therefore, to move the School of Education ahead clearly required getting new, young, and inspired faculty. However, the economic times in 2001 did not allow for hiring additional faculty, only replacements for retirements. Since the 1980s, federal law has prohibited a mandatory retirement age; in short, faculty may work as long as they wish. Bearing in mind that there is hardly a more comfortable occupation than being an academic at a university, where typically one does what one wants to do, when one wants to do it, and how one wants to do it, I saw counseling nonproductive senior faculty—those who did not publish and made little or no effort to enhance their teaching—to comfortably retire, as my next challenge.

I had to consider this new task on a case-by-case basis. I certainly could not force anyone to retire, nor was it wise for me to directly suggest retirement to most of these faculty members, for they would see that as an affront and perhaps likely do the opposite. I, therefore, suggested retirement only to those faculty members who were senior enough not to take a financial loss and who, at the same time, were not benefiting the college nor their special field of interest with any significant contributions. For each of my targeted faculty, I had to use a special strategy. For example, when one of these faculty members had an inordinate amount of storage space, I gently (and truthfully) suggested that the college could no longer afford to provide this person extra space, which prompted some dissatisfaction, which I dealt with in an amiable fashion. A more egalitarian assignment of classes and privileges was also used to encourage the retirement of non-productive senior faculty.

Typically, faculty members like to minimize their teaching hours—a strange phenomenon for educators. Having faculty live up to their teaching obligations and scheduling courses spread out across the entire week to discourage faculty from merely being at the college for one and two days a week—a perfectly legitimate request—also encouraged a number of unproductive senior faculty members to retire, while at the same time providing students with broader program options. Some senior faculty members were accustomed to getting everything they wanted—oftentimes privileges not available to junior faculty members. Curtailing this tradition also contributed to the sought-after retirements. Before long quite a few faculty members who had deferred retirement, finally chose to exercise their right to retire. These retirements allowed us to hire enthusiastic young faculty, which in a short time began to change the character of the faculty, creating a more diverse faculty in age, ethnicity, and background.

In fact, a number of formerly unproductive senior faculty members became rejuvenated and became valuable members of the faculty. Furthermore, as new faculty members began to join the School of Education some of the more senior productive faculty members volunteered to spearhead an effort that I had initiated, namely, to publish an international education journal I felt that by producing an international education journal, when none existed anywhere in the university and hardly any in the region, we would have another way to motivate faculty, engage them across disciplines, and simultaneously improve the school's image beyond the university. With the cooperation and partnership of a commercial publisher, The New Educator journal was born. To date, this quarterly journal, with its peer reviewed articles written by some of the top experts in the field of education, has brought international prestige to the School of Education. Today, the faculty consists of a majority of junior faculty who eagerly work up the tenure track, providing fruitful work to the school and their profession.

A further incentive to see their career path in the framework of a legacy was achieved by bringing back long-retired faculty to support faculty work. A retired-faculty fund was established to provide support for various faculty initiatives. There has been much goodwill and motivation that resulted from the encouragement from these long-term retirees—benefits that sometimes even overshadowed the financial benefits they provided.

12.4.5 The Student Body

An important component in the school's turnaround has thus far not been addressed: namely, the students. Through the 1990s there was a lax attitude on the part of the faculty in admitting students to the School of Education. Often, students not meeting the prescribed admissions criteria were nevertheless accepted to the school. This, despite all else, put the School of Education at a definite disadvantage. Extensive discussions among the faculty ensued and consensus was reached that the admissions criteria had to be raised. The renewed admissions criteria included an entry grade-point average of B+, a successful interview and completion of an essay. Letters of recommendation were also required for the admission process.

At the same time, various support programs were put in place for those students already enrolled in the School of Education. These included computer laboratories, which would provide extra support for students' coursework, and also prepare them for the teacher certification examinations. This remedial effort did not in any way compromise standards—quite the contrary—it strengthened standards and helped students meet them and then go on to earn a degree. Remember, now that the State of New York had granted the City College School of Education the power to certify teachers upon completion of their approved academic program, higher standards had to be maintained. Today, the admission requirements for the School of Education are higher than some other units at the college, and in order to receive a degree, a student must have at least a B+ average.

With all of these changes in place, in 2002 we finally reached (and maintained) a point at which 100 % of our students achieved passing scores on the teacher certification examinations. Naturally, this made news throughout the City of New York and it gave us the legitimacy we sought to once again have our independence within the college. This meant appealing to the College of Liberal Arts and Science faculty to have them allow us to extricate ourselves from that body. With a somewhat larger faculty, of whom the majority were untenured (indicating their youth) and with a high performing student body, the only thing that remained for us to accomplish before we could extricate ourselves from the College of Liberal Arts and Science, was to establish a new set of bylaws that the faculty senate—a body that represents the entire college faculty (today numbering almost 600 members)—would approve. When all this was completed, my personal appeal to the faculty senate was successful and today the School of Education is once again an independent body within the City College.

12.4.6 Achieving National Accreditation: 2003

Part of the state's requirements for the School of Education to qualify as their certification agent was to achieve national accreditation. Consequently, immediately after revising the curriculum to meet the State of New York's new standards for schools of education, we began the laborious process of seeking accreditation from the National Council for Accreditation of Teacher Education (NCATE), the non-profit agency responsible for accrediting the majority of teacher education institutions in the United States. This process took several years, involving many faculty meetings and substantial individual faculty reports. One should not think that the meetings—and there were many—were not contentious. Data had to be collected to demonstrate teaching effectiveness, research output, and various curricula issues. In addition, substantially detailed reports from each of the subject subspecialties had to be submitted to achieve accreditation. Naturally, with a newfound motivation, the faculty rose to the challenge and produced a stellar program which, after a week-long site visit by a team of NCATE evaluators, achieved national accreditation with the highest ranking in 2003.

12.4.7 Technology Support

As we were building both faculty and student morale, it was important to make the physical space of the School of Education as attractive as possible. Over the past several years, specialized classrooms were enhanced. All of our designated classrooms were outfitted with smart boards along with other appropriate technology. We sought and received the external financial support for a number of our special programs and further embellished our facilities. We then had perhaps one of the technologically best divisions at the college. These sorts of things do not go unnoticed by the faculty and served to motivate them further to enhance their instruction and their commitment to our students.

12.4.8 International Innovations

A successful school of education cannot rest on its laurels, so we continued to innovate where appropriate. For 16 years we have been offering a master of arts degree in various cities in Austria (Feldkirch, Innsbruck, and Vienna), which for a time was the only offshore graduate program offered by the CUNY—the largest urban university in the United States. Furthermore, we continually evaluated our instructional program and revisions are made on an as-needed basis. This has led us also to develop new master's degree programs. Most of our programmatic changes result from faculty input and student reaction to the programs. In addition, current trends are carefully scrutinized for their applicability to our students' needs and also impact our curricular decisions.

12.5 Conclusion

Today, the School of Education continues to flourish with its energetic faculty pursuing a solid academic program for students, and offering the larger community professional development according to the needs of the city. They are in regular contact with the education leaders of the New York City School system and therefore are well prepared to meet their needs, even if articulated late in the process. This strong communication link is the result of many years of cooperative work with the school system. They currently conduct a number of innovative grant-supported programs to enhance, for example, mathematics instruction at the elementary and secondary levels, to strengthen science education in New York City, and to improve literacy and bilingual education in the schools.

The renaissance of the City College School of Education began to take shape shortly after my appointment as a joint initiative of the faculty and me, resulting in a steady upwards climb. It is important to realize that, unlike what can be done in the industrial world, to bring about change in the university is a very different challenge, since historically—the faculty feels that they are the change agents and that most decisions come from them. University administrators are best served if they can allow the faculty to experience this perception. So, when one speaks of turning around a university division, program, or faculty, change must be motivated by the will of the faculty and must reflect their own achievement. Perhaps, it is the role of a university leader to assess the faculty wishes and then channel these toward the productive end: a renewal of positive climate and culture.

It should not go unnoticed that this successful turnaround of a previously failing school of education was also rewarded with numerous grants from both the public and private sector to conduct special programs beyond the normal course work of the school. Without constantly seeking to improve even an already well-tuned operation, one stands a chance of seeing malaise once again set in. It is incumbent upon the leader of any division of a university to encourage faculty to pursue new directions and to work with them to develop innovative programs appropriate for the current student body, future student bodies, or populations within the community that could benefit greatly from the university supported effort. Just as an example of one such community interest is the development of a family educational resource center, currently being developed to support parents of school-age children to make their home studies as fruitful as possible. Such a center would be guided by faculty of the School of Education and supported either by private or by public monies. This would give faculty members another dimension for their own specialty and provide much needed support in an urban setting such as that of New York City. The school has already got more than a half million dollars of support from private and public sources to launch this effort. It is merely mentioned here as an example of an extra curricular program that can indirectly further enhance both the reputation and the mission of the School of Education.

Although it is difficult to elaborate fully on the complexities of this effort to effect change, it is the intent of this paper to provide some guiding points to university administrators seeking to affect positive change in their programs, personnel, or their institution as a whole. The extent to which the motives and methods mentioned are applicable to other institutions—especially to those outside the United States—needs to be assessed on an individual basis. In a postscript: Over the past two years and have replicated this procedure (with appropriate modification at Mercy College,New York) with even greater success.

Bibliography

Damrosch D (1995) We scholars: changing the culture of the university. Harvard University Press, Cambridge

Smith T (1994) Changing university culture through promotion policies. In: Frontiers in education conference proceedings

Chapter 13
Curriculum Change at a Japanese Private International University: The Influence of Global and Local Pressures on the 'NEW' Challenge

Malcolm Cooper

13.1 Introduction

> There is nothing more difficult to plan, more doubtful of success, nor more dangerous to manage than the creation of a new system. For the initiator has the enmity of all who would profit by the preservation of the old system and has merely lukewarm defenders in those whowould gain by the new one.
>
> Niccolo Machiavelli, The Prince, 1513.

Discussions started at Ritsumeikan Asia Pacific University in late 2002 on a difficult problem: an urgent necessity for review of the curriculum offered by the University established only 2 years before, in 2000. It had become obvious even in such a short period of time that problems had arisen in the implementation of the APU concept of education and research relevance to the Asia-Pacific Region and its developmental needs between its establishment in the middle 1990s and its implementation on a new campus in Beppu (Oita Prefecture, Kyushu) from 2000. To be able to comment more fully on those problems, it is necessary first to set the scene for APU in this introduction. Under the overall concept of contributing to the peace, democratic institutions and stability of the Asia Pacific Region, APU was set up with the following basic goals:

- Ritsumeikan Asia Pacific University (APU) will aim for excellence in research and education, financial viability in its operations and relevance to the concerns of the Asia-Pacific Region;
- APU recognizes that quality teaching, world-class research, ability to innovate, and the competence to share knowledge will be the pillars of success for the university;

M. Cooper (✉)
Graduate School of Asia Pacific Studies, Ritsumeikan Asia Pacific University,
1-1 Jumonjibaru, 874-8577 Beppu, Japan
e-mail: cooperm@apu.ac.jp

A. Altmann and B. Ebersberger (eds.), *Universities in Change*, Innovation, Technology, and Knowledge Management, DOI: 10.1007/978-1-4614-4590-6_13,

- APU aims to be relevant to the needs of the Region by making these functions problem and practice oriented, holistic, and integrative using multidisciplinary approaches;
- APU recognizes the need to provide policy-oriented advice based on scholarly work to institutions, communities and decision makers in the region, for regional capacity building and as a professional enrichment opportunity for faculty and staff;
- APU recognizes the need to expand its services by providing lifelong learning opportunities in the region;
- APU recognizes that today's modes of knowledge production and application hinge on meaningful partnerships or networks, multidisciplinary approaches, interaction with practical problems, and innovative modalities; and that
- APU is a most relevant initiative to promote the ideals and aspirations of the Ritsumeikan Trust as an international education provider.

In seeking to achieve these goals however, APU has had to take very much into account financial and educational parameters set by the Ritsumeikan Education Trust and the Japanese Ministry in control of higher education, the likely impact of recent and partly identified future changes in Japanese and International higher education, the underlying demographics of its major markets for students (Japan, China, Korea are the largest), and the actual educational needs of the Asia-Pacific region it is trying to develop and/or serve. With regard to the first of these parameters, to date the Trust has been immensely supportive of its new creation, but good financial results must follow for this support to be maintained. In order to help with financial viability it was decided in 2002–2003 that APU's size had to be increased, from 4500 to 6000 students by 2008–2009, rising to 10,000 in say 10 years. The first of the parameters for the 'New Challenge' had therefore been set.

Up to 1998, the Japanese Education Ministry's (Monbushô) view of the tripartite division between national, public (i.e. city or prefecture) and private universities was that National universities should meet the needs of the nation domestically and internationally (e.g. the Universities of Tokyo and Kyoto), City and Prefectural universities should meet the needs of the local community that established them (e.g. Oita University), and Private universities should be mainly responsive to niches that could be identified in the higher education market (e.g. international education as a primary role of a university in Japan; Eades 2001:95; Eades et al. 2005). However, soon after 1998 the pace of reform of the Japanese university system began to accelerate when it was realized that the tri-partite division was not particularly useful for competition in an increasingly international education system in East Asia. The first major new initiative came in 1999 when the Government conditionally approved a plan to turn national and prefectural universities into independent administrative institutions (dokuritsu gyôsei hôjinka) in order to give them more financial and decision-making autonomy (Eades et al. 2005). Despite considerable controversy, both over the intent of the plan and the likely results, this measure was implemented progressively from 2004. While there may still be little consensus about the underlying aims of this reform at time of writing in 2008–2009, or on what will be the precise effects on the national and prefectural universities, these changes meant for the private university market place of some 750 Universities a much greater level of competition in its niche markets than it had hitherto experienced.

Added to this has been the increasing emphasis by the Government on the performance of the University Sector in terms of the quality of their research and development activities. This second initiative dates from 2001 and the result was the Toyama Plan which proposed the establishment of a 'Center of Excellence (COE) Program for the twenty first Century' (Shinohara 2002). This proposal actually built on earlier Ministry thinking about reform that had generated a program of designating 'centers of excellence' which dated back to the mid-1990s, but the new scheme was coupled with the injection of greater resources. The Toyama Plan had three main planks: the reorganization and consolidation of national universities (ominously described as 'scrap and build'); the introduction of private sector management methods to public universities; and the establishment of COE's at institutions that could produce work of international quality. The budget for the program was substantial and in real terms meant that recipient institutions would receive between 100 and 500 million yen per year for 5 years with an interim review of progress after 2 years (in 2004). The money could be used in a number of ways: to fund international exchanges; to fund PhD research and post-doctoral fellowships; to fund research support and training; to support symposia and workshops; and for the provision of new equipment and space for research (Eades et al. 2005). The second major influence on the thinking at APU and in the Ritsumeikan Trust from 2002 was therefore how they could begin to compete with the national and other public universities in this hitherto largely protected government university market for research funds, and how to gain a reasonable proportion of the new research funds to be made available.

In terms of the third major influence, that of changing student demographics, the situation within the Japanese market is indeed grim (see for example, Cooper & Eades 2005), but an institution that could rapidly expand internationally might well offset the accelerating decline in the number of potential Japanese university students (from 2007 less than the number of places available each year) that is leading to an increasing rate of amalgamations and even the closing of universities and campuses in particularly hard hit areas. The establishment of APU as an international university from the outset was therefore seen as the one advantage that might offset all the negative implications of these three factors for the Trust, since it would be a source of new international and domestic research and education strength, attract international students, and thus be of interest to both the diminishing Japanese market and the growing markets in other Asian countries. That this was an advantage that had in truth less substance than originally thought will be discussed below.

The final factor, that of the assumed actual needs of the Asia-Pacific market for undergraduate and postgraduate courses in social science disciplines, including tourism and hospitality, was one that, while being critically important, was heavily dependent on accurate knowledge of these needs, and the availability of effective teaching resources and research facilities at the Beppu Campus of APU. The initially disappointing market reaction to the establishment of the APU Graduate Schools in 2003, and the internal realization that the institution as a whole did not have enough quality resources in its chosen disciplinary areas became another major force in the New Challenge Process that was eventually instituted as a review of curricula, staffing, and research performance in 2005. It is probably true to say that these factors, that in another institution or market might have been the focus of a report on progress toward the implementation of the initial idea for the University, not a complete revamp of its activities, became a dominant force in the new University very early on in the life of the institution.

13.2 Ritsumeikan Asia Pacific University

The falling birth rate in Japan, coupled with the desire of the top Japanese universities to become major international players gave rise to some radical experiments by Japanese institutions in internationalization in the late 1990s. The private Sophia, Waseda, and Ritsumeikan University organizations all recognized that, in order to attract enough students from overseas to offset the expected decline in Japanese students a large part of the curriculum had to be taught in English as well as Japanese (Eades et al. 2005). They also recognized that the bulk of Japan's potential overseas market for higher education lies in East and Southeast Asia. The Faculty of Comparative Culture at Sophia University has taught in English for many years, while in 1998 Waseda University established a bilingual graduate program in Asia-Pacific Studies focusing on international relations and business management, and a separate small International College in 2004. In April 2000, the Ritsumeikan Trust opened the new Ritsumeikan Asia Pacific University in Kyushu focusing on Asia-Pacific development economics, environment, sociology, and management. Although there are some similarities between these projects, APU is perhaps the most radical given its size, location, and the fact that it was established through collaboration between a Prefectural government and a private university. APU, therefore, provides some interesting insights into the motivations behind, and problems involved in, internationalizing and governing higher education in Japan (Eades et al., 2005).

13.3 The Asia-Pacific University Project

The project itself was the result of a meeting of minds between the then Governor of Oita Prefecture, Hiramatsu Morihiko, and the Ritsumeikan Trust. Mr. Hiramatsu is well known for his innovative One Village, One Product program which encourages local towns and villages to concentrate their energies on single products for market. This model has been taken up by governments elsewhere in the Asia-Pacific Region, thus providing Oita and its Governor with an Asia-Pacific network of allied governments, communities, and businesses. Oita's interests therefore meshed with those of the Ritsumeikan Trust, which saw an opportunity to internationalize itself based on penetration of the APU using these networks. The initial curriculum of APU, therefore, focused on the APU, and particularly on management, tourism, information technology, and the environment. Oita Prefecture and Beppu City provided the site and the infrastructure, and the Ritsumeikan Trust provided the buildings, the academic planning, and the brand name.

At the start of this project, the Ritsumeikan Trust had to make a number of strategic decisions in relation to achieving a balance between radical internationalization and appealing to the domestic market. Given that many of the foreign students would be coming from the poorer countries of the region, it was clear that full fee-paying Japanese students would remain extremely important for the financial viability of the venture. APU was set up, using Ritsumeikan models, by a group of senior academics and administrators transferred to Beppu from Ritsumeikan University in Kyoto. Although Monbushô was by the late 1990s worried about the establishment of any new universities given the falling birth and student participation rates, it was willing to consider innovative plans and the APU project clearly showed a way to increase Japan's presence in the international higher education market in the Asia-Pacific Region. In return, Monbushô reserved the right to monitor the new University's degree programs for the first 4 years, which paradoxically made it difficult to change or modify the curriculum and the structure of degree programs at APU until after the 2004–2005 academic year. While the new university embodied the latest ministry thinking, with a streamlined administrative structure presided over by an executive President and Vice Presidents who made most of the decisions, rather than those being made by the 'professors' meetings' as in traditional Japanese universities, it was unable from the start to be flexible enough to cope with some of the problems outlined below because of Ministry control.

The other radical innovation offered by the Trust was that the new university was to be completely bilingual; an unheard of situation prior to 2000 in Japan. The intention was to offer most of the courses in both English and Japanese, sometimes by the same teacher. Intensive English and Japanese language subprograms, during the first 2 years of an undergraduate degree program, were designed to create students who could understand lectures in either language by their third and fourth years. The slightly later graduate school of 2003 was designed to operate entirely in English.

The ways in which all this has worked out during the first 10 years of operation have been both interesting and complex. Bilingualism and cultural diversity has come at a price. A number of the international staff did not understand Japanese, and vice versa, so meetings between them required both simultaneous translation and extensive documentation in both languages. Given the diversity in backgrounds of both staff and students it was likely that there would also be discrepant expectations about teaching standards, on the necessity of language learning taking up 20 % of available credits overall and dominating the critical first years of a degree, about the appropriate nature of classes and examinations, and about the amount of work to be expected from students. But there have also been pleasant surprises as the University has grown to its current size of 6,000 students, such as the outstanding quality of the best students, the relatively low dropout rate and the very high ratio of applicants to places. Many of the international students have become fluent in spoken Japanese and are looking for jobs in Japan, while the standard of English among the Japanese students is much higher than in more traditional universities.

At one level, simply getting a project of these dimensions off the ground is in itself a substantial achievement, but in 2002 new challenges were foreseen with the opening of the graduate school in 2003 and the return of issues of long-term financial sustainability and international competitiveness. One of the financial concerns has been a result of the fact that the recruitment of international students has been heavily subsidized with scholarship money from a variety of sources and, in the longer term, the university will either have to attract more foreign students paying their own way or find more permanent sources of scholarship funding. The problem is also compounded by the likelihood that, if as a result of declining scholarship funds the foreign students disappear, the rationale for many Japanese students coming to APU will also disappear. There is too the problem of attracting, and keeping, good quality international staff. Beppu is comparatively isolated, small, and very domestic in orientation despite its reputation as Japan's hot springs capital, and practical issues, such as the lack of nearby international schools for the children of prospective teaching staff are a problem. Nor was APU ideally placed for the launching of an MBA (Masters in Business Administration) in the new graduate school program due to the lack of locally based large companies to support internship needs.

Finally, the success of the institution will also depend on its research facilities, both in terms of library resources and IT. In relation to the library, APU can draw on the resources of the other Ritsumeikan campuses, offsetting the obvious problems of starting a new library from scratch. Many of the required journals are, of course, available on line in the twenty-first Century. On the other hand, APU is far away from the major libraries of Kansai (Osaka, Kyoto) and Kanto (Tokyo), and the cost implications of a large number of doctoral students for example requiring access to thousands of books and older journals that can only be obtained through interlibrary loan are considerable. Clearly therefore some big decisions were seen to lie ahead in the period 2004–2009, as APU attempted to raise itself to a level where it could compete with the best schools in the Asia-Pacific region, including both North America and Australia, and as Ministry control lessened. However, impetus was given to this attempt by the thought that if it succeeded in this transformation, and if the other leading schools in Japan move in the same direction, the traditional image of Japanese universities in the international market could be totally transformed to the benefit of all.

13.4 The New Challenge

Priority: To increase student numbers at APU (to 7,000–10,000 students) so that it might become fully self-funding within 5–10 years.

Strategies:

- Provide greater diversity of courses with both local and international appeal;
- Strengthen the take-up of language skills, especially among Japanese students;
- Develop an integrated set of research directions/Centers to underpin and expand courses offered;
- Achieve integration between existing Centers and Faculties in APU and with other Ritsumeikan campuses; and
- Fully develop relationships with international academic organizations and private partners.

Actions:

- To achieve these priorities a better integrated set of course offerings is required, based on demand so far revealed by survey and anecdotal evidence.
- This needs to be backed up by fully functioning research centers as both an attractor of higher level students, business relationships, and a source of resources for staff efforts in research; and
- As a strategic direction though, the proposed new curriculum and research centers were to be limited to those that could support a number of different course structures across a number of discipline areas.

APU achieved growth to 4,500 students in its first 5 years and reached 6,000 in 2008. However, this growth is to some extent unbalanced between management and other disciplines, has not yet reached the required critical mass, and is not yet backed up with significant research centers and higher degree opportunities (although there are encouraging signs in tourism & hospitality, in ICT/knowledge management, and in innovation management. Nevertheless, the APU Campus is well situated to attract Asia-Pacific students and is able to offer all the advantages of geographic proximity to an increasingly wide range of services, attractions and lifestyle choices. It is therefore a logical site for increased investment in tertiary education facilities to service the whole APU.

The new challenge process therefore recognized that to take advantage of existing strengths such as the international nature of the campus (80+ countries represented) there needed to be a new course structure NOT based on the amorphous and highly debatable concept of Asia-Pacific Studies, and that students should be able to study at APU and complete identifiable discipline-based degrees in a range of subjects. It goes without saying that innovative methods were also recognized as being necessary in the provision of the required courses (e-learning, short-courses, etc as well as face-to-face lectures), which will change over time, and that existing and new Faculty resources should be integrated with increased research opportunities. Research opportunities and outputs were finally acknowledged as being critical to teaching and scholarship, with the appointment of a Vice President for Research Affairs in 2005, and with the belated recognition that higher degree students need to be an integral part of research, teaching, and scholarship opportunities.

13.5 Multidisciplinary Approaches to Become the Norm

The establishment of research and teaching Institutes, active learning programs and a partial curriculum revamp were the chosen implementation avenues for the New Challenge. The impetus for the creation of institutes arose in response to the need to produce both graduates and postgraduates that are technologically and managerially skilled in areas of growing or evolving economic focus in the Asia-Pacific Region.Our ability to best serve these graduates is to ensure that our own research initiatives keep pace with emerging technology and practices so that these can be channeled back into academic programs through curriculum development and the provision of specialist programs. Recognizing the increasing need for multiskilled graduates, who have first-hand experience of the multidisciplinary approaches that are emerging in both science and the arts, key elements of the institute approach area focus on a multidisciplinary approach to research by Faculty and higher degree students, and active learning by all students. The growing complexity of society has required a shift from the traditional view of academic research as being undertaken primarily by an individual researcher in a particular focused field of study. Research and regional capacity building has become increasingly interdependent upon the knowledge from a number of academic disciplines. Researchers are seeking to join with others within their own, or increasingly, within other disciplines in addressing these new complexities.

While this multidisciplinary approach to research is not a new phenomenon, many research outcomes, even from our young University have required formal or informal collaboration with others, either within or without a particular investigator's discipline. In a growing number of areas, the complexity of research has required more extensive collaboration involving teams of researchers from multiple disciplines working together to expand knowledge. Additionally, it has been important to point out to existing faculty that, in recognition of this growing multidisciplinary need an increasing number of funding bodies have shifted their focus toward the support of multidisciplinary research initiatives (Gwynne 1998).

Changes to the curriculum are also to be organized along Institute lines, although the existing division between Asia-Pacific Studies (Social Science in the main) and Asia-Pacific Management has had to be retained, to the delight of some and the despair of others! It remains to be seen whether the existing silo mentality that this division has generated even in the short life of APU will disappear under the multidisciplinary research and teaching focus mentioned above. More specifically there are now recognizable areas of expertise in the APU academic structure that can be further developed in the future. Some 40 new Faculties have been hired for the 5 Institutes of Language & Culture,Tourism & Hospitality, Health, Environment & Life Sciences, International Strategy, and ICT. The International MBA that APU offers will continue as a separate entity, and additional academic and research clusters in Management of Technology, human resource development, and in Innovation Studies have also been added.

The Institute model is to be supplemented by an active learning program which combines educational continuity with access to specialized courses and 'off-shore' experiences for third and fourth year undergraduates. All students will have to spend at least 1 semester in the later years of their degree away from the campus in specialist courses taken elsewhere, or being involved in particular external research projects. This will be achieved by forging closer links with key industry partners and promoting APU's research expertise through the provision of consultancy services and graduate project work with industry and community partners.

The alternative to building up a reputation through research is to broaden the teaching base and concentrate on vocational rather than academic subjects. From this point of view, the strategy of the Ritsumeikan Trust has been particularly interesting. Although it does not feature in the Shanghai Jiaotong University rankings of excellence for example (Eades et al. 2005), Ritsumeikan University does feature prominently in some Japanese rankings, particularly in rankings of universities by University Presidents in Japan. Its vigorous expansion during the last 10 year has been impressive by any standards, though particularly so given the falloff in the cohorts of high school leavers across the country as a whole. Originally, the Trust operated Ritsumeikan University itself (with 30,000 students, the second largest in Japan), and three high schools. Since the late 1990s, it has opened a second campus of the original university, Biwako-Kusatsu in Shiga Prefecture, the Ritsumeikan Asia Pacific University in Beppu, another high school at Moriyama near Kusatsu (which it purchased from the Shiga prefectural government), a junior school in Kyoto, and a law school and main administration office on a new separate campus in Kyoto. The original target number of students for APU was 3,200, but this was later raised to 6,000 by 2010 (achieved in 2008), and an impressive collection of new buildings have recently been constructed to house these new students.

As for the balance between the academic-research and vocational-teaching models, the situation of APU was at first broadly vocational, but now seems to be much more ambiguous. In the early days, the management side of the program was clearly vocational in nature, with a mixture of management science and economics. The Asia-Pacific studies side of the program was initially divided into environmental, media, and tourism streams, but many of the courses were actually sociology based, and indeed the sociologists and cultural anthropologists were the largest single disciplinary group of academics on the campus. With the revamping of the curriculum for the purposes of expansion, of the five new institutes that have been established those of ICT and tourism are broadly vocational but the other three less so. With the vocational core removed from the Asia-Pacific Studies program as well, it will be interesting to see if it manages to recruit the mass base of students that the vocational-teaching model requires, given that as a private university APU needs to recruit large numbers of students both to keep going and to help subsidize the intake of foreign students, many of whom, particularly in the graduate school, are on some kind of scholarship or fee reduction.

A further complication in the case of APU is the necessity to teach the undergraduate programs in both English and Japanese, given the bilingual and bicultural philosophy with which it was founded. This also creates an administrative burden, as documents have to be translated for meetings, given that many of the senior bureaucrats are from Ritsumeikan originally and are not necessarily fluent in English, while few of the foreigners speak and read Japanese. Meanwhile, the graduate school is taught entirely in English, and so recruits virtually exclusively from overseas. This creates a vibrant and cosmopolitan group of students—but with little or no recruitment of Japanese students paying full fees, the graduate school is by definition subsidized by the rest of the university. The graduate school, therefore, can be seen as an outpost of academic research in what must increasingly be a vocational-teaching environment.

Other indicators show the effect of the basic vocational-teaching structure of the university: the high student to permanent staff ratio, the increasingly large number of teachers on short, fixed term contracts, the comparatively heavy teaching loads, the large class sizes in some lecture courses, and the use of ICT for a considerable proportion of the content delivery. Most crucial of all, many of the teaching staff, not only in the management courses are from business and administrative rather than academic backgrounds. This has developed because there has been until recently an emphasis by university management on teaching at the expense of research, to the point at which the time available during the academic year for actually doing research is increasingly restricted. The management discourse is of course publicly about international excellence in research, including gaining COE status as soon as possible, but the vocational-teaching logic of the institution as a whole means that a coherent program of research has yet to take off in many areas. One problem for APU, therefore, is that to attract quality foreign students for its English language undergraduate program, as well as for the graduate program, it has to be able to compete in the academic-research market at a very high level, but with a vocational-teaching structure aimed primarily at the Japanese market, this is a very difficult goal to achieve.

13.6 Conclusion

A complete re-vamp of an existing educational system is a monumental task, made even more problematical in this case by the youth and relative inexperience of the system it is intended to replace. When lack of experience at the institutional level is coupled with the difficulties of implementing an internationalizing strategy in a Japanese University constrained by the Country's only lukewarm understanding and acceptance of what this actually means, the initial outcome could have been predicted. Conflict over course structures between the various parts of the student body (approximately 50 % are Japanese and 50 % International) occurred. The Japanese students still in the main want the old system of non-specialized education, and the International students remain unhappy that they cannot easily prove that they studied courses of relevance to potential employers. Faculties from the two different basic education traditions of the 'west' and Japan are equally as divided about the merits of a disciplinary-based course system. Given this, it is perhaps remarkable that Ritsumeikan APU has come this far in such a short time. Japanese students have up to now appeared to resist learning English and being fully involved with the international students, but are now expressing much greater confidence in this experience. The New Challenge outcomes have been positive in the main; at the very least they have increased understanding of what it means to be an international university and have created an at times fierce defense of APU in the Japanese system by the very people that had to change most.

It should be noted that, in the case of curriculum change and the Japanese students however, there are supportive dynamics in play as well. As Eades (2001) points out, Japanese students are becoming much more aware of their positions as consumers in what is increasingly a buyer's market. In addition, Japanese companies want graduates with specific internationally realizable skills, and parents see their investment in their children's education as protection for their own futures in an increasingly aged Japan. Moreover, a new generation of high school graduates is appearing who have spent lengthy periods abroad on school exchange programs. These students have fewer inhibitions about speaking English than their counterparts educated only in Japan, and lower resistance to undergraduate course specialization, and therefore constitute a natural market for the kinds of initiatives embodied in Ritsumeikan Asia Pacific University.

Finally, we must not neglect the academics themselves. Here, too, a younger generation is rapidly appearing to take over from the baby-boomers and they are, in many cases, a much more international and cosmopolitan group than their predecessors. Many have been educated abroad, are fluent in English and other foreign languages, and are much more interested in publishing their research internationally. Professional associations and departments with COE money are taking the lead in establishing new journals and publication outlets in English and other languages—online as well as on paper. As universities become increasingly concerned with their research profiles, we may expect the collapse of the age–wage salary structure as the top scholars begin to bargain for salaries commensurate with their value in the global market place. Those that stay in Japan are also likely to put pressure on their institutions to provide a research infrastructure of international standard and this, in turn, will necessitate the professionalising of library and IT support staff. Many observers are sceptical as to whether the transformation of national universities into 'independent administrative institutions' will in general lead to any greater autonomy—but what it will certainly do is allow them flexibility in budgetary allocations to support the kinds of changes the Government has outlined.

In the case of the Asia-Pacific as a whole, the internationalizing experiment that is APU is of considerable interest, and its new curriculum and Institute/research structure is already enabling the University to consolidate in this market. This is helped by the fact that smaller institutions that do not deliver quality product to this market are likely to disappear given the downturn in domestic student numbers. The successful implementation of APU's 'new challenge' will in turn provide a wider financial and student base for the University as it moves closer to celebrating its first 10 years of life and beyond.

The fact that the experiment by the Ritsumeikan Trust has been reasonably successful is however indicated by a completely different benchmark; and this provides an interesting postscript to the pressures and factors that brought the University into being in the first place. APU is now seen as the National Government's preferred source of 'good practice' information and research in the areas of internationalization and new curricula. Considerable funds have been made available to the University (of the order of 3 billion Yen) to study the impact of internationalization on Japanese education and to expand the range of curriculum and pastoral support choices open to international students in this country. It is manifestly obvious that, despite the problems experienced along the way in its first 9 years of life APU was indeed a most relevant initiative to promote the ideals and aspirations of the Ritsumeikan Trust and the Government as an international education provider.

Bibliography

Cooper MJ, Eades JS (2005) Landscape as theme park: demographic change, tourism, urbanizationand the fateof communitiesin 21st Century Japan. Tourism Review International 11(1):9–18

Eades JS (2001) Reforming Japanese higher education: Bureaucrats, the birthrate, and visions of the 21st century. Ritsumeikan J Asia PacificAsia Pacific Stud 8:86–101

Eades JS, Goodman R, Hada Y (2005) The 'big bang' in Japanese higher education. Trans Pacific Press, Sydney

Gwynne P (1998) Programs prepare scientists for business world. The Scientist 4

Shinohara K (2002) Toyama plan: center of excellence program for the 21st century, national science foundation report: memorandum No. 02–05. Tokyo: Tokyo Regional Office, online document. http://www.nsftokyo.org/index.htm Accessed 20 May 2009

Chapter 14
Leading-Edge Technologies and Facility for Competitive Higher Business Education

James R. Haltiner and Gabriel A. Pall

14.1 Introduction

The main purpose of this paper is to present how a new building project with an externally traditional architecture, was developed, through a purposeful design and construction process, into an integrated, innovative environment for competitive higher business education.

The authors briefly review the main characteristics of the Mason School of Business at the College of William and Mary in Williamsburg, Virginia. Then they discuss the information gathering activities and program statement, which served as the basis of the architectural and engineering design. They explain the building project organization and decisions about design features that foster integration of curriculum initiatives and advanced learning technology, along with a much greater and purposeful socialization of faculty, staff, and students.

The paper should offer valuable information to all university leaders and administrators, but especially those who are considering, or are already in the process of acquiring a new facility for their institutions.

J. R. Haltiner (✉) · G. A. Pall
The College of William and Mary—Mason School of Business,
P.O.Box 8795 Williamsburg, VA 23187-8795, USA
e-mail: james.haltiner@mason.wm.edu

G. A. Pall
e-mail: gabe.pall@mason.wm.edu

A. Altmann and B. Ebersberger (eds.), *Universities in Change*, Innovation, Technology, and Knowledge Management, DOI: 10.1007/978-1-4614-4590-6_14,

14.1.1 The College of William and Mary

14.1.1.1 History

Founded in 1693, the College of William and Mary is the second oldest university in North America. The "alma mater" of the United States, William and Mary nurtured the minds of those who inspired the American Revolution and founded the nation, among them Thomas Jefferson and James Monroe. Dedicated to this philosophy and committed to limited enrollment, the College provides high-quality undergraduate, graduate, and professional education that prepares students to make significant contributions to the Commonwealth of Virginia and the nation [See also (Brown and Lord 1999)].

The College of William & Mary is one of the eight schools known as "Public Ivies;" it was named the sixth-best public university by U. S. News and World Report in 2009. William and Mary has an enrollment of 7,500, of which some 5,500 are undergraduates, and 2,000 are graduate and professional students.

14.1.1.2 Administration and Finances

The College of William and Mary is a public university in the Commonwealth of Virginia, governed by a Board of Visitors. The Board, composed of 17 members, is appointed by the Governor of the Commonwealth to serve the College.

Reporting directly to the Board of Visitors, William and Mary is led by President W. Taylor Reveley III., the Provost and six vice presidents who direct the academic and administrative activities and departments at the College.

The vice president for finance oversees the development and administration of the College budget and provides analysis and recommendations to the president. In addition, the finance office coordinates development of operating budget initiatives submitted to the Commonwealth of Virginia and the integration of all budget development activities into the overall planning activities of the College.

William and Mary's operating budgets in support of the College's various programs and activities for July 1, 2008 through June 30, 2009 were $273.0 million.

The College of William and Mary in Virginia is accredited by the Commission on Colleges of the Southern Association of Colleges and Schools (SACS) to award bachelor's, master's, post-master's certificate, doctoral and first professional degrees.

14.1.1.3 Departments and Schools

The College of William and Mary is a college in name only, reflecting the terminology used at the time of its founding. In fact, it is a small liberal arts research university with nationally ranked undergraduate, graduate, and professional programs spread across five separate schools containing dozens of academic departments, interdisciplinary research institutes and state-of-the-art labs.

Arts and Sciences is the largest academic unit on campus, with 12 graduate programs and 35 undergraduate departments and interdisciplinary programs.

The four professional schools include: the School of Education, Law School, Virginia Institute of Marine Science (VIMS), and the Mason School of Business.

14.2 The Mason School of Business

14.2.1 History

The College of William and Mary was one of the first institutions of higher education in the United States with an orientation toward business education, beginning with the use of Adam Smith's Wealth of Nations as a text in political economy in 1798. The formal study of business was initiated in 1919, and a Department of Business Administration was established in 1941. Its first graduate degree program (Master of Business Administration) was established in 1967, and it became the School of Business Administration in 1970 with autonomy over degree requirements and curriculum. In 2006, it became The Mason School of Business, named for benefactor and supporter Raymond A. "Chip" Mason.

14.2.2 Management System

14.2.2.1 Mission and Strategy

In 1999, the Mason School of Business and its faculty adopted a strategic plan to accomplish the School's vision: Become established as a premier, but intimate, business school with a world-class reputation as a source of uniquely qualified future leaders in knowledge-driven business environments.

The following defines the School's educational mission: To nurture creativity, to mentor high-mindedness, to accelerate ambitions of leadership in our students that they might imagine the great business opportunities of the day and seize them. The five prime strategic *goals* currently driving all the planning and operations at the Mason School are:

- Lead business schools in personalized, experience-based education
- Be an agile, innovative enterprise achieving differentiation through programs
- Develop a faculty whose teaching, research, and service influence students, scholars, business leaders, and policy makers
- Engage students through innovative educational experiences that nurture creativity, mentor high ideals, and develop leadership capabilities

- Create graduates who are competitive in their respective job markets

The six key *strategies*—broad courses of actions in the face of uncertainty—have been reaffirmed as relevant for the current economic and highly competitive business education environment. They include:

- Improve MBA rankings to between 30 and 40, and undergraduate and MAcc rankings to top 20 by US News and World Report, Financial Times and Business Week; retain the top five ranking for teaching, published in the Princeton Review.
- Create a culture of innovation
- Engage in continuous curriculum and program improvement
- Lead in having corporations involved in instruction and working side-by-side with faculty
- Increase production of high quality research
- Increase visibility through purposeful marketing and communications

These goals and strategies are under continuing review by the faculty and administration of the School for adjustment to the prevailing economic and business environment. As part of this strategic plan, the need for a new building within the next decade was identified, as a critical success factor in realizing the School's vision.

Responsible for the management of the Mason School is Dean Lawrence B. Pulley. To him report the Associate Dean with responsibility for academic affairs, the Director of Development, the Chief Financial Officer, the Director of Administration and Operations, the Director of Marketing Communications, and the Executive Director for Enterprise Management.

The individual academic degree programs are headed up by Assistant Deans. The oversight responsibility rests with the Mason School of Business Foundation Board.

14.2.2.2 Programs

The Mason School of Business offers three degree programs and a number of business executive education (non-degree) courses. The degree programs and approximate enrollments are:

- Bachelor of Business Administration (BBA) Program (450 juniors and seniors)
- Master of Business Administration (MBA) Program (430 students)
- Master of Accounting (MAcc) Program (90 students)

An MBA degree can be received through the 2-year, 64-credit hour, resident MBA Program (200 students), the Flex (evening) Program (160 students), and the Executive MBA Program conducted over weekends plus in four residency weeks (70 students).

The School has been accredited by the Association to Advance Collegiate Schools of Business (AACSB) since the early 1970s; the Accounting Programs also enjoy AACSB accreditation since a separate accreditation was instituted for Accounting. The various programs have been ranked among the best in the U.S or in some cases worldwide in publications, such as Business Week, the Financial Times, Wall Street Journal, U.S News and World Report, and in The Princeton Review. (The BBA program has been rated in the top 20, the MAcc in the top 30, and Resident MBA in the top 30's through top 50).

14.2.2.3 Curriculum and Learning Environment

The curriculum in each of the degree programs may be considered "traditional" in the sense that:

1. There is a substantial core curriculum covering the main functional areas of business and skill development, supplemented by elective offerings for students to develop focus and depth in a particular discipline.
2. Faculty utilize a variety of teaching methods—lecture/discussion, case method instruction, experiential learning (simulations, competitions, field trips/travel abroad over winter/spring/summer breaks, etc.).
3. Student group study and projects are utilized throughout the curriculum. Study groups are created when students enter the School, in each of the degree programs. These groups are maintained through the conclusion of the core program. Other groups form in electives and special projects.

14.2.2.4 Culture

What does distinguish the School's curricula is the careful management and monitoring of the learning process. The core curriculum is structured and sequenced to expose students to functional area topics and skill development activities across all areas of management. Special topics and speakers are woven into the daily routine. Core faculty groups meet regularly (weekly) to discuss day-by-day implementation of the program and student progress. Since the mid-1980s, each program has had its own faculty leader, termed "assistant dean," to organize the core group meetings, lead the review of curriculum initiatives and coordinate with other area/program activities. Significant curriculum changes, initiated primarily by these program faculty groups, have come about at fairly regular intervals (3–4 years) over the past two decades.

The faculty (approximately 55 tenure track plus a dozen clinical professors) prides itself on maintaining a balance of emphasis on teaching, research, and service. The School has worked hard to attract promising scholars, and research activity and productivity have increased markedly in recent years. At the same time, there continues to be a very strong tradition of excellence in teaching and student mentoring. Smaller class sizes, students' easy access to faculty and student collaboration with faculty on research projects, are hallmarks of the College, and the Business School. In addition, beyond the normal School governance and committee activity, the Mason School and the College encourage faculty to engage in professional service in their academic discipline and in community service. Partly due to its small size and primarily to tradition, the faculty is not grouped in a departmental structure. Interdisciplinary research partnerships and team-teaching flourishes as a result.

14.2.2.5 Curriculum and Program Innovations

In recent years, a number of innovative curriculum initiatives/modifications have been embedded which have significant impact on "personalized, experience-based business education" Four such initiatives are:

1. Career Acceleration Modules or CAMs,
2. Field Consultancy program,
3. Leadership Advantage program or LeAd, and
4. Executive-level business expertise supplied by a group called Executive Partners.

14.2.2.6 Career Acceleration Modules

Co-designed by faculty and industry leaders, CAMs integrate advanced academic training in business with ongoing, direct contact with business experts. Each CAM provides an intensive, 7-week immersion course in academic and experiential activities including hands-on trips to corporate settings, consulting projects, case analyses, business simulation exercises, and an impressive lineup of speakers. Second year MBAs choose two from among a current list of: Entrepreneurship, Corporate Finance, Investments and Financial Services, Real Estate, Business to Customer ("B2C") Marketing, Business to Business ("B2B") Marketing, and Enterprise Engineering. MAcc students also have a separate CAM experience. This immersion in a real business environment allows students to cultivate a wealth of relevant, field-specific experience to discuss during job interviews, and apply immediately to a new career.

14.2.2.7 Field Consultancy Program

The School contracts with major companies across the mid-Atlantic region, deploying teams of 2-year MBA students to work as consultants charged with identifying, researching, and proposing a solution for a real business problem faced by their client organization. Mason School MBAs have confronted challenging assignments in areas, such as corporate and operational finance, marketing, strategy formation, management and organization, logistics and transportation, human resources and information technology. Students with an entrepreneurial interest may choose to work on business start-up projects, under the auspices of the Entrepreneurship Center. Students seeking investment management careers may be part of the Batten Fund experience, managing part of the School's endowment with an equity fund, or researching stocks.

14.2.2.8 Leadership Advantage Program

Strong leadership and well-developed interpersonal skills have been identified as parts of the essential repertoire of successful executives within high-performing organizations. Six leadership competencies were determined through an iterative process of benchmarking and surveying that included input from hiring companies and business school faculty. A unique differentiator of the Mason Leadership Advantage program is that each student is paired with an Executive Partner who provides one-on-one coaching and is dedicated to the student's personal development and growth throughout the 2-year program.

14.2.2.9 Executive Partners

A key resource for each of these initiatives and for the School in general is an organization called "Executive Partners." Williamsburg is fortunate to have a wealth of senior business executives live in the area, and this volunteer group of over 120 active and retired business leaders, from over 20 different industries, share their experiences and guidance with students and faculty of the School. They work collaboratively with career services staff to discuss their own career experiences as a real-world perspective on various paths; they serve as expert advisors on consulting project teams; they are one-on-one mentors for students or personal coaches to help develop skills; and they collaborate with faculty to demonstrate how business theory applies to business reality in elective courses in the MBA curriculum.

14.2.2.10 Current Home of the School and Space Deficiencies

The Mason School had been located in Tyler Hall on the William and Mary campus since 1982 with about 24,000 "net programmable" square feet for classroom and office space. In 1990, the School acquired additional space in an adjacent building, Blow Memorial Hall. Graduate program classes and administrative support offices were relocated to this building in another 10,000 net programmable square feet. Despite modest growth in enrollments since then, the School needed additional office space and occasional classroom space. Some of that office space was scattered across campus and some staff office space was rented in a commercial office park. Neither Tyler nor Blow Hall provided very much common space for student or faculty interaction. Speaker events, with more than 75 attendees, had to be located in a difficult-to-schedule campus facility or at some off-campus hotel or theater. Faculty offices were scattered throughout Tyler Hall over three floors. There were very few team meeting rooms for students or conference rooms for faculty/staff group meetings and very little "gathering space" for student interaction or for socializing. In sum, curriculum initiatives, such as those described above, were severely space constrained..

14.3 Alan B. Miller Hall

14.3.1 Concept Evolution and Design

A decision was made in the late 1990s by the Dean of the School of Business and the Business School Foundation to seek a newly constructed home with all programs and functions *under the same roof*. A conceptual study was undertaken, with input from the leadership of the College and with the help of Robert A. M. Stern Architects, primarily to determine the location of the new building and to establish an initial sizing and cost estimate.

A number of alternative locations were studied, both within and outside the current College campus boundaries. Eventually, the preferred location for the new building was selected at the northwest corner of Jamestown Road and Ukrop Way in Williamsburg, Virginia—at the very western edge of the College campus (see rendering at the front of the paper). For this location, a detailed architectural program, replete with room descriptions, was developed in 2001 with an H-shaped footprint, comprising roughly 174,000 sq ft (14,550 m^2) of gross floor space. This conceptual plan was then utilized over the next few years for fund raising and budgeting.

A critical feature of the building project was the structuring of the relationship between the Business School Foundation and the College (and indirectly, the Commonwealth of Virginia). A Memorandum of Understanding (MOU) was finalized in spring 2005 with the Business School Foundation as the developer of the project and a College Building Committee having oversight. Both the public-private financing package, with the College issuing bonds to partially finance an academic building, and also the building oversight structure, with roughly equal representation from the School and College, were different from anything the College had done previously. Many hours of discussion among the Dean of the School, Foundation Board members, and top College officials (the President and Provost in particular), took place over 2001–2005 to make this a reality.

14.3.1.1 Project Organization

When fundraising efforts proceeded to a point where firm, financial commitments could be made for the project, the Building Committee was formed.

14.3.1.2 Building Committee

TheBuilding Committee included College, School, and Foundation Board members and was co-chaired by the Dean of the Business School and the College Vice President for Administration. It functioned as the top decision-making management body during the design and construction phases. In addition to decision-making, the Building Committee was the coordinator of stakeholder relations management—both for internal and external stakeholders, from the various official local and state permitting agencies all the way to neighbors living adjacent to the new building. The Building Committee's key decisions and actions were at the outset:

- Hiring the project manager;
- Hiring the construction management firm and finally,
- Hiring the architect/engineering firm.

14.3.1.3 Mason School Building Task Force

In spring 2005, planning activities began for the detailed programming needs of the School, and a 19-person task force was formed consisting of Mason School of Business faculty, staff, students, and alumni. Their objective was to engage the many and varied constituents in the planning process, to assess space requirements and the character of the space, and to have input and oversight of the development of an architectural Program Statement. Once the architects were hired, the Task Force would serve as a sounding board and source of feedback for design concepts generated by the architects (e.g., building shapes, and program space adjacencies, and the like).

14.3.1.4 Project Core Team

As design drawings were developed and even well before construction began, a three-person "core team" (a subset of the Task Force) served to work with the project manager, the Dean of the School and the Building Committee, to ensure continuing and effective participation in the design and construction process by the user (the School of Business). This team served as a communication channel, integrating agent and often a decision-making group for design issues or construction changes over the 3 year design and build process. As an example, early in the process when cost estimates suggested that programmed space in the plan (1,86,000 gross sq ft) would not be feasible within budget and quality guidelines, the project core team was able to effect changes in the recommended plan expeditiously and with the backing of the Building Task Force.

14.3.1.5 Architectural Program Statement

Critical to the success of the project was communicating the needs and aspirations of the Mason School to the design architects and engineering firms. The Mason School Building Task Force described above was asked to determine the process for receiving information and input from all constituencies, to selectively visit existing business school buildings and corporate facilities for bench-marking; to report through the chair of the Building Committee; and to monitor progress through the design and construction process.

14.3.1.6 Activities in Developing the Program Statement

Constituent Interviews: Individuals from each component of the School, including administration, faculty, staff, and students, had the opportunity to articulate their constituents' program needs and planning issues and help to define the overall Program Statement.
Benchmarking Site Visits: In addition to a broad inventory of web-based research, members of the Task Force visited eighteen academic and four corporate educational facilities to observe current best practices, as well as to interview participants in the building projects to compile "lessons learned" that could be helpful to this project.
Focus Groups: While the interviews addressed specific needs of individual programs and departments, the focus groups provided interdepartmental commentary on specific building components. Six sessions were held, moderated by the consultant and members of the Task Force on topics, such as: classroom design, technology, common spaces, beyond the classroom learning, research, "look and feel", and student perspectives.
Surveys: While significant numbers of faculty and staff participated in the focus groups, some specific features or decisions benefitted from more complete participation of the users, and surveys were utilized.
Program Analysis Sessions: The Task Force and other guests participated in two interactive planning sessions to identify and validate the values and objectives of the School.

14.3.1.7 Design Attributes

The planning process focused on understanding expectations of various constituents such as:

1. Objectives the building must satisfy (e.g., functionality, cutting-edge technology, long-term adaptability, environmental harmony);
2. Ideal "look and feel" properties of the building (e.g., spacious, inviting, professional, vibrant, architecturally fresh but timeless quality); and

3. Fostering value-add activity and behavior (e.g., teaching, researching, learning, energizing, innovating, networking, mentoring).

Constituents wanted to protect and nourish the School's strong culture of collaboration and access, both between students and faculty, and among faculty across functional lines. And they wanted to expand that collaboration and access to business community and alumni in ways that were not feasible in our old space. When asked to describe a single characteristic that would affect the success of the building, *openness* was the most common response. Rather than simply spacious, the open building should feel inviting and welcoming and support opportunities for interaction. Well-designed common spaces should be as important as formal classrooms because so much learning and relationship building takes place in these spaces.

Tensions, however, exist in the desire for openness along stated needs for visual and acoustical privacy or separation of group activities. While preserving accessibility and collegiality, faculty need privacy for research and course planning/grading. While certain events may bring the entire School together, MBA students, classrooms, and team meetings desire separation from BBA students, classrooms, and team meetings. The goal was to strike a balance with different kinds of spaces to accommodate a range, from various group activities to individual, private personal spaces. Classrooms, too, are as varied as the ways in which people naturally learn and interact. Tiered-horseshoe, fixed-table classrooms are the mainstay, but flexible table layouts and seminar rooms complement, along with a "cluster tier" design layout to accommodate team interaction with classes (described later).

Flexibility and *adaptability* were also key attributes in the planning process. Mindful that the Mason School had undergone considerable programmatic, curriculum, and staff changes over the preceding 4-year period of 2001–2005, as well as technology advances, there was a strong desire to preserve flexibility as much as possible. Excess capacity in cable trays and computer floors in classrooms were sought, and considerable "shell space" was budgeted to allow at least some modest growth in classroom capacity, and suites for research institutes or curriculum initiatives.

The Task Force was certainly influenced by space constraints of the buildings housing the School over the past 15–20 years. Task Force members fought against being "anchored" to the past—ways in which the School was organized, trying to think of new, and better ways of operating. Competitive benchmarking with visits to various business and other professional schools certainly helped, as well as visits to corporate facilities. It became clear to the School's leadership that competitive business education in the twenty-first century required it to operate in a facility which innovatively integrates advanced course content and teaching methods with leading-edge technology, providing an environment conducive to the most productive interaction between students and faculty as a single academic community.

Finally, another essential design consideration of the building was that while its twenty-first century interior should include leading-edge technology, be *sustainable* and efficient to operate, and flexible with regard to changing demands for its constituent spaces and functions, its eighteenth century Georgian exterior design should be time-less and compatible with its colonial William and Mary setting. College and School leaders early and often referred to its 100-year duration—to signify the quality of construction, maintainability, and flexibility for future changes or expansion.

14.3.1.8 Program Statement Results

The 80-page architectural Program Statement, produced in November 2005, was the prime input used as a starting point by the architects and engineers in their design and cost analysis. It presented a description of activities and space requirements associated with the educational, research, and service missions of the School, its faculty, staff, students, and other partners, comprising roughly 186,000 square feet (17,280 m^2) of gross floor space. Beyond the quantitative tabulations, it was also meant to describe the character of the building and its spaces, its look and feel, a facility befitting of the high aspirations of the School, the learning environment therein, and the creative activities of students, faculty, staff, partners, visiting executives, and scholars.

14.3.2 Delivered Facility and Technology

14.3.2.1 Project Management

The overall building project was executed as a construction manager-at-risk contract, and was managed by the highly integrated team of

- The architect/engineering firm of Robert A. Stern Architects of New York and Moseley Architects of Richmond, Virginia;
- The construction manager Whiting Turner; and
- The Mason School project manager.

14.3.2.2 Building Characteristics in Support of Higher Business Learning

Overall Architectural Perspective

The building style represents the historical language of the eighteenth century; it fits well into the Georgian style of the College campus. Being the second largest academic building on campus, it also serves as the appropriate western anchor of the entire campus—anchored at its eastern end by the historic Sir Christopher Wren Building built in 1695.

The internal organization of the building expresses the educational and social mission of the Mason School of Business—designed to respond to the challenges of modern business education. Spaces like the atrium, the public lounges and the abundance of other social spaces (breakout and team rooms, conference rooms, café, etc.), as well as their purposeful overlap with other administrative and faculty areas further promote faculty-student and student-student interaction and networking. Critical architectural decisions were:

- Single, unified front of the building to improve appearance;
- Development of the courtyard as unifying space;
- Balance between short-term and long-term objectives—e.g., upscale finishes as "wow" factor versus concrete block backup to exterior brick skin for durability;
- Hands-on approach by the affected constituencies in such areas as the program statement, classroom design, technology requirements, etc.;
- Balanced design for sustainability—immediate certification advantages versus long-term savings.

Key Building Design Features

The delivered version of Alan B. Miller Hall, with approximately 165,000 sq ft (15,325 m^2) of gross floor area, is designed to have a welcoming atmosphere and when opened in July 2009, appeared as a warm and inviting place providing as many opportunities as possible for students, faculty, staff, corporate recruiters, and other business partners to meet and interact. It incorporates the use of state-of-the-art audiovisual and computer technology to stimulate and enable innovative business thinking and creative approaches to learning and teamwork.

Common Areas for Interaction

The building design includes lots of circulation and common functional areas, such as lounges, wide corridors, informal, and diverse gathering areas for students, staff, and faculty. The front entrance way leads into a spacious three-story atrium and then to a suite of three lounges. Beyond the lounges is a large courtyard with natural grass and patios. Each classroom wing has wide corridors with separate student gathering areas for undergraduate and graduate students (see Table 14.1). Near the front entrance are located an executive dining room, a 100-seat café, and an outdoor café patio with additional seating.

Two open staircases off the atrium lead to a multi-purpose room on the second floor with seating for 400 theater style, or round tables with seating of 260 for a luncheon, dinner, or other seated program. The room can be subdivided for two separate functions and has stage and projection equipment in each section. Gathering spaces also exist on the second and third floors, mainly for faculty, staff, and visitors, but also for student meetings.

Table 14.1 Administrative suites and offices

Programmed space	Previous			New		
	Sq.ft.	No. of rooms	Percent	Sq.ft.	No. of rooms	Percent
Classrooms	10,721	8	29.8	17,690	12	18.8
Other academic space (labs, learning centers)	1,189	2	3.2	7,789	8	8.3
Student areas (team rooms, gathering areas, and lounges)	2,034	10	5.6	7,090	27	7.6
Business Library	1,964	2	5.4	2,307	3	2.5
Executive education	275	2	0.8	5,467	6	5.8
IT programming and support	773	4	2.1	2,927	9	3.1
School and program administration	8,453	61	23.5	11,909	78	12.7
Faculty space (offices, meeting and support rooms)	9,380	61	26.2	15,217	86	16.1
Common areas (entrance, atrium, common lounge)	1,228	4	3.4	4,013	4	4.3
Multi-purpose room	–	–	0.0	5,794	1	6.2
Café and executive dining	–	–	0.0	2,510	2	2.7
Other (storage and shell space)	–	–	0.0	11,113	11	11.9
Total programmed space	36,017	93	100.0	93,826	247	100.0

The table summarizes a fundamental shift in the allocation of space in Miller Hall. Not only is there considerably more space available to academic program areas, information technology support, conference rooms, and other meeting areas, but the percentage allocation shows an increasing emphasis on spaces for interaction outside the classrooms.

Team Meeting Rooms and Conferencing

Student team meeting rooms, 25 in number, are interspersed in the classroom wings of the building on the first floor and in a lower level facility. Separate team meeting rooms exist for executive education programs, and conference rooms are plentiful, some seating 8–10 and others seating 24, interspersed on the second and third floor. A special video conferencing board room for visiting executives or smaller groups is also located on the second floor.

Administrative Suites and Offices

Staff suites were designed with an open workspace environment wherever possible. This open architecture represents a change from the previous closed, cubicle-like staff offices, and should lead to greater collaboration. Access within suites to large, outside windows, and natural lighting is a planned feature of these spaces. Some staff will have closed offices as befits their mentoring, counseling positions, or handling of confidential information. However, about 35 individuals, more than half of the staff of the School, are located in open work space suites.

Classroom Design and Teaching Wall

Appropriately, the design for the building initially focused on the classrooms. Multiple surveys were conducted and focus groups were convened on a variety of classroom-related issues. Many benchmarking visits of other schools, involving perhaps as many as one-third of the faculty, were taken. Certainly, considerable hours of informal conversations, and several physical mock ups were conducted over a 3-year period. Many issues were raised:

- Assurance that the portfolio of classrooms (number of rooms and capacities) aligned with enrollment forecasts for program offerings over the foreseeable future, and also aligned with the character of the School's programs.
- Location of classrooms. There was a desire for separation of undergraduate from graduate program classrooms (separate floors or building wings) and some separation of executive courses and executive MBA rooms. However, there is a need for flexibility to accommodate future demand shifts.
- Based on surveys, focus groups, and many benchmarking visits to other facilities, most faculty preferred a horseshoe-shaped, tiered room design where line-of-sight was excellent not only for the front of the room but for student-to-student case discussion type interchanges. This included considerable attention to detail such as one center aisle versus two for faculty to move around the room, height of the tiering, shape of the "teaching pit" in the center of the room, and an unobtrusive but convenient location of a podium.
- Designing classrooms and adjacencies to accommodate considerable and growing use of team study and team decision-making. While most faculty preferred a tiered horseshoe for most of their class sessions, they also desired the ability to have group dynamics take place during class sessions. The preferred solution was to design a layout that allowed five-six students to "group up" at their classroom seats for a simulation or other experiential learning exercise. Then they could "ungroup" (or regroup) at the discretion of the faculty member running the exercise. As a result, after considerable debate and drawings, the cluster tiered classroom design was adopted for four classrooms (Table 14.1).
- Given the sizable investment, cutting-edge technology in the classrooms with flexibility for future upgrades was expected. Surveys of faculty, focus groups, and benchmarking visits to recently constructed school buildings helped us to engage our architects and consultants and decide on our requirements. Wireless connectivity with hard wiring backup, raised computer floors in all classrooms, high-resolution projection on multiple screens, video conferencing, audio requirements and lecture capture systems, document cameras, etc. were recommended.
- Classroom podiums were another focus—should they be fixed or mobile? What critical components must they contain to keep them unobtrusive in size and what

components could be positioned in a more remote closet or wall cabinet? Much discussion and physical mock ups helped us come to closure on this issue, balancing technical features with ease of use for faculty.

- The front teaching wall was a topic that benefited from many hours of debate and two physical mock ups. At the heart of the debate was divergence of opinion over writing space (blackboard or whiteboard) versus video projection. Like any faculty, there is a wide range of teaching styles and preferences (and no shortage of egos). Some faculty utilize whiteboards extensively in case discussions or lectures and consider it an art form of how to organize information to maximize student learning. Other faculty use video projection almost exclusively and see little need for whiteboards going forward. Almost all faculty desired multiple projection capability so that spreadsheets and power point (or document camera) displays could be shown simultaneously. Most wanted some whiteboard space visible for the students along with video projections. Most faculty also wanted consistency for all rooms for the teaching wall, while some thought some room specialization was desirable.
- The teaching wall adopted is shown in the illustration below (Table 14.1). Except for two smaller seminar rooms, the standard classroom ceiling height (14 ft) and front wall width (22 ft) allowed projection of two wide aspect images (11 ft wide by 6 ft tall) on a permanently mounted screen, side-by-side above white board panels. Additional wide board panels roll up and down behind the projection screen. Because the projection images are about 6.5 ft above the floor, faculty can freely roam the front teaching pit area without obstructing student views. Two mock ups were conducted to test line-of-sight.

In summary: Leading-edge classroom design to accommodate today's highly interactive teaching and learning environment was the key foundation block to the overall building layout and technology content. Key features of every classroom include:

- Individually addressable, remotely controlled multiple (up to three) projectors;
- Teaching wall containing dual screens and simultaneously visible whiteboards;
- Single podium containing session computers and controls;
- Audio/video lecture capture.

Research Environment

While its magnificent visual appeal of Alan B. Miller Hall is undeniable, the building's design is more than skin deep—it offers several functional benefits for research: collaboration, communication, collection, and inspiration.

First, the new building should foster greater interdisciplinary collaboration and co-authorship. In the previous facilities, faculty offices were not physically situated in such a way as to encourage interaction. In the new building, this is to change, and without departmental limitations, natural cross-pollination should grow. For long distance collaboration, much better technology exists for video conferencing, for one-on-one meetings and small group collaboration/teleconferencing. For sponsored research programs, Miller Hall offers opportunities with executive center classrooms, meeting rooms, and considerable shell space.

Second, the new building offers faculty and staff more opportunity to meet, socialize, and communicate across areas and programs. The building offers its own café and faculty dining area, as well as numerous conference rooms, and many informal meeting spaces. Such spaces make it more likely to share research and engender a greater appreciation for the work that is being conducted in the School. More faculty awareness produces appreciation for individual research progress and fuels greater innovation in the faculty's collective efforts.

Third, Alan B. Miller Hall offers a state-of-the-art behavioral lab, survey data collection facilities, financial laboratory, communications lab, e.g., dedicated facilities that were not available to researchers in the previous space. Not only does this enhance the capacity for faculty to conduct meaningful research but also engages potential faculty and peers at other schools to view us as a significant research institution.

Finally, the splendor of the architecture offers inspiration. One cannot step into that space without feeling the desire to be better, to feel worthy of such a magnificent structure. Alumni and other donors seemingly share that excitement.

Special Facilities for Competitive Business Education:

Financial Markets Center

Students pursuing careers in finance, particularly in the areas of trading and investments, must be prepared to work in an environment where success relies on the ability to quickly make sound decisions informed by synthesizing vast amounts of information from a variety of sources. Replicating this type of environment for students cannot be accomplished in a traditional classroom. It requires a space that has the technology and "feel" of a real-world trading room.

While many business schools house a "trading room," the Mason School's Financial Markets Center (FMC) is unique in design, in that it paid special attention to how students and instructors interact. While each student work station includes a computer and dual flat screen monitors, everyone also has unobstructed sight lines to the instructor and ample work space for note taking and personal laptops. In addition, the FMC incorporates multiple projection options for lecture slides and video presentations as well as superior lighting and acoustics. The main room's tiered seating design is flexible enough to handle a standard class size or special smaller work teams. In particular, the more intimate front tier caters to the needs of a small work group. Thus, this room provides perfect work space for the students running the Mason School's Batten investment fund.

Students and faculty are able to access the resources offered in the room in both "classroom" and "financial laboratory" modes. The FMC features real-time financial data and professional research tools to provide students with hands-on technology training. These include several Bloomberg terminals as well as other specialized financial trading software and databases available at each student's workstation. Market price and news display boards and video walls running around the room create a realistic and lively atmosphere for learning. Visitors and students walking past the FMC get a taste of the action just by looking through the FMC's large glass corridor wall. Finally, the FMC is designed to accommodate changes in technology so that the facility remains state-of-the-art.

Behavioral Laboratory

The Behavioral Laboratory planned for the new business school building is designed to support the behavioral research of faculty members in multiple disciplines: marketing, organizational behavior, operations, accounting, and finance. It enables basic and applied research on a diversity of behavioral questions related to investments, marketing, management, and interpersonal issues.

The new facility allows our business school researchers to study the basic cognitive and affective processes underlying effects (processes that people may not be able to recall or represent accurately).

With two group observation rooms and a large survey administration (data collection) room, the laboratory allows researchers to monitor response times, facial expressions, interaction patterns, and even eventually measure eye gaze (e.g., to determine what parts of a marketing message or a web interface capture the participants' attention). The observation rooms allow for participants to interact without constant reminders that they are being observed. Flexible partitions in the large data collection room ensures that participants' responses can be private and not influenced by what decisions are being made by others in the room.

In addition to supporting faculty research, the new facility also lends itself to focus group observation and recording, providing a space for marketing students and MBA students working on field consultancy projects to test new ideas with select samples of consumers or employees. The research space also allows undergraduate students to get hands-on experience in research and data collection, helping them to become better consumers of empirical research [see also (Kornwolf 1989)].

Communications Center (Laboratory)

The Communications Center in Miller Hall is a new venture for the Mason School. Having dedicated space for students to enhance their speaking, writing, listening, and other communication skills acknowledges the importance of these abilities in the professional business world.

As a laboratory, the Center includes integrated space for completing class assignments, student practice, meetings of writing groups, peer reviews of students, and video and sound recording of students for professor feedback. The Center comprises three rooms: a large conference room, a smaller conference room, and an observation/control room that allows confidential observations of students practicing their presenting, interviewing, or other skills related to communication. In addition, a smaller entrance room provides for a small library or student work area.

Each room in the Center contains state-of-the-art technology. Each conference room is outfitted with 32” flat panel video displays with integral stereo loudspeakers. These monitors serve many purposes. Among these is direct observation of students in the other conference room to simulate video conferencing. These monitors are supplemented by two video cameras with control extenders in each conference room to enable images to be captured and controlled of everyone in each room. Split-screen technology allow students to see the people in the other room and also see the video image of people in their own room. In addition, sessions can be recorded and played back for classes or for individual instruction. These technologies may also be used to communicate with people in other sites distant from the Mason School.

The Center allows students to have simulated real-life experiences. It also enables the school to expand and supplement curricular offerings in ways not possible presently. For example, distant learning or meeting management opportunities may be considered.

Business Library

The spaces in the Alan B. Miller Hall designated for the Business Library are utilized as follows:

- Circulation room/casual seating area is the entry way into the Business Library. It contains the information/reference desk and several groupings of chairs and tables for quiet study/reading. The lower walls are lined with shelving for the print and media reference collection.
- The research area (reading room) contains the work stations (carrels) for student research and studying. This area also includes the power sources and data connections (as well as wireless connectivity) for computer use. There are a number of Library-provided computers at several work stations for patron use. The public access printer/copiers are also stationed in this room.
- A computer laboratory structured both for software-intensive classes/coursework and for group study and discussion. It can be used for training/orientation and database demonstrations by the Business Library and is accessible for group study after hours.

Entrepreneurship Center

One of the fast growing and highly sought after areas of business education in the Mason School is on the subject of entrepreneurship. Not only do students receive lectures and presentations on the founding and managing entrepreneurial enterprises, but they also have a chance to actually invest in their own new businesses, and run them from the School.

Unfinished shell space has been set aside for the Entrepreneurship Center. It is designed to facilitate a number of typical entrepreneurial activities, from investment planning, through market research and firm modeling all the way to board meetings of already operating companies. The physical design of the Center allows quick transformation of its 3,000-plus square foot space into a team planning room, a large conference room for meetings and small conferences, or a boardroom to simulate enterprise executive decision-making sessions.

14.3.2.3 Information Technology

Building Technology Infrastructure

The technology infrastructure is powerful and present throughout the building. The building is integrated into the campus communications network. A system for providing unlimited and flexible telecommunications and computer network access at all instructional, research, service, and office locations is installed. In addition to hard-wired cable connections for data to all workspaces, a wireless signal environment is maintained throughout the building. Technology design to accommodate future change was based on providing for growth in both power and bandwidth requirements, including these features:

- Distribution grid on all levels and all areas
- Easy access to pathways/cable trays both vertically and horizontally, including such design features as cable trays to facilitate horizontal and stacked conduits for vertical expansion. The pathways permit cable to be pulled to any point in the building, thereby facilitating future installation of new equipment or relocation of existing equipment.

Internal communications and public signage within the building is implemented through a network of liquid crystal displays (LCD's) distributed on all three floors. There is also a Wayfinder touch panel installed at the main entrance to help visitors find people, events, or spaces within the building.

Classroom/Meeting Room/Conference Room Technology

Technologically, classrooms have smart audio-visual (AV) and computing interfaces that facilitate both lectures and class discussions. Every classroom is equipped with the same basic technology setup and the same universal control interface. These technologies allow faculty to move seamlessly from didactic (e.g., PowerPoint) presentations to group discussion and capture of key points (e.g., whiteboards, digital camera projectors). All on the fly; it is possible to display both simultaneously.

The fixed classroom tables support laptop power and network connectivity at each seat. In flexible classrooms laptop power outlets are in the floor and network connectivity is primarily wireless.

Classroom technology includes "lecture capture", the ability to digitally record lectures, presentations for instantaneous (synchronized) re-broadcasting or asynchronous distribution by other means. Confidence monitors enable teaching faculty to follow the projected material from their podium, without turning around to view the teaching wall.

Classrooms, meeting rooms, and conference rooms are equipped with exterior scheduling display panels that indicate the reservation status of the room, along with basic information on the event taking place there. These digital panels are also connected to the central scheduling system and event calendar for overall monitoring and control.

There is a video teleconferencing (VTC) conference room on the second floor, near the Dean's suite to provide full VTC capability to faculty, staffs, and even invited outside visitors.

Information Technology Support

The Information Technology support area is staffed by eight professionals and a manager. This centralized office area includes:

- Manager's office
- Workstations for up to eight professionals
- Conference area
- Repair workshop, with storage
- Help desk area at the entrance that supports walk-in service
- Counter space with power/network connections to work on laptops and other equipment brought in for service

This arrangement makes communication and interaction among the IT staff natural and easy. At the same time, direct communication between IT and classrooms is provided for to ensure fast response to service calls during teaching events.

14.3.2.4 Sustainability

The two factors which made the design and construction of a sustainable building possible were:

1. The decision to pursue a Leadership in Energy and Environmental Design (LEED) certification, and

2. The availability of a number of LEED-accredited professionals on both the design and construction teams. Overall, the new building received a LEED "gold" rating.

Constructing the new facility at a high level of sensitivity to "green" practices brought cost dividends from the beginning of construction, such as recycling construction waste throughout the entire construction period, and maximizing the amount of construction materials produced or fabricated in the region. Additional efficiency and productivity gains will be realized during decades of future operations, through many of the following features:

- An underground cistern installed in the courtyard to collect rainwater for ground irrigation purposes;
- Occupancy sensors in classrooms and most office areas to turn lights off when the room is unoccupied;
- Choice of "green" certified furniture and carpeting for the entire building;
- A storm water management plan that minimizes the impervious area that produces storm water runoff and includes bio-retention areas;
- Energy efficient solutions throughout the building (energy-conserving lighting and appliances, high-performance wall insulations, energy efficient heating and cooling).

14.4 Conclusion: Factors leading to Project Success

Alan B. Miller Hall was ready for occupancy in July 2009, and classes started late August 2009. The building has met all expectations. The project has been delivered on-time and under budget, and much more importantly, there is a buzz of excitement about the building from each of the constituents.

We are reminded by our project manager of some factors that proved very useful in the successful planning and implementation:

- Widespread initial involvement of the future users (faculty, staff, students, donors, and Foundation Board members): This was accomplished early in the process with interviews, focus groups, and planning sessions, but it continued throughout the project. While everyone's views cannot be implemented, there is a widespread feeling among faculty and staff that they had their chance to influence the result.
- Benchmarking visits: Many relatively new business school facilities have been constructed in North America in the last several years. Some visits were chosen for their overall appearance and design, while others were chosen for special elements or features. Internet websites are useful for gaining perspective, but nothing substitutes for seeing and touching a facility in person.

- Considerable and constant flow of communication with all the stakeholders about the progress: This began with newsletters to faculty, staff, and students while the Task Force was involved with the Program Statement, but it continued with regular updates at faculty, staff, alumni and donor, Foundation Board meetings; and with numerous blogs on web sites. It involved outreach to the broader College community and to the residents of the town of Williamsburg near the building site.
- Numerous and thorough tours of the building during construction led by the project manager: Perhaps as many as a thousand alumni, donors, faculty, staff, and students—including prospective faculty and students—have had hour-long tours of the building. The project manager suggested and avidly supported this activity, and the tours were expected to be well received. In fact, the enthusiasm and excitement generated from the tours has exceeded all expectations. Again, nothing substitutes for seeing a facility in person and touching it.
- Continual involvement of the benefactors: Many trips were taken by the Dean, accompanied by the design architects, to the offices, and homes of key donors and Foundation Board members from the beginning of the project through completion to explain design and site parameters and to seek input on certain decisions. The importance of keeping these key supporters engaged in the process and enthusiastic about the results was critical.
- Continual involvement of the users: Program needs identified in 2001 and again in 2005, were not necessarily the needs existing at our occupancy date of July 2009, since curriculum initiatives are dynamic and programs, enrollments and staffs did change. The three-person Project Core Team served as a filter for communication and construction/design issues with faculty, staff, and Foundation Board members and eventually, all key decisions came back through this core group.
- Continuity of the project leadership teams: Although there has been change in College leadership and several senior staff/faculty within the School, the Dean of the School, the Project Core Team, key Foundation Board, and Building Committee members remained the same key players. The Dean in particular has been a driving force, relationship-builder, and head cheerleader to keep the project on track over an approximately 10-year long period.
- Mock ups: As noted about the value of seeing/touching, mock ups were used for fine-tuning classroom layouts, front teaching walls, podium design, and many architectural/construction details.
- Flexibility/capacity for the future: To the extent possible within budgetary constraints, the building included excess capacity for inevitable technology upgrades as well as "shell space" for future centers, office needs, or a classroom. To the extent possible, classroom footprints were designed to make seating layouts adaptable for future change; classroom floors raised for technology alterations; and excess capacity included in cable trays and IDF closets.

Bibliography

Brown DJ, Lord RG (1999) The utility of experimental research in the study of transformational/charismatic leadership. Leadersh Quart 10:531–539

Kornwolf JD (1989) So good a design. The College of William and Mary, Williamsburg, Virginia

Chapter 15
Leveraging Universities Through IT Governance

Peter Mirski and Dietmar Kilian

15.1 The Problem

European universities are today confronted by major change, largely as a result of the process of standardization of European education systems. The process, which was initiated at the Sorbonne in 1998 and subsequently expanded in the Bologna Declaration and the Prague and Berlin Communiqués, serves the following primary objectives:

- creation of a two-cycle degree system,
- introduction of a credits system,
- modularization of study programs,
- increased student mobility, as well as
- new quality assurance measures (European Commission 2010, online).

In combination with inadequate government funding and increased reporting requirements, these developments influence today's universities in their positioning strategies. Against this background, universities are facing the fundamental challenge of having to attract excellent students, teachers, and researchers, as well as business partners, and society in general. In this context the deployment of information and communication technologies in support of teaching, research, and administrative processes assumes great significance. In the last few years, institutions of higher education have been transformed into "entrepreneurial universities" (Etzkowitz et al. 2000), with a third pillar added to the traditional focus on

P. Mirski (✉) · D. Kilian
MCI Management Center Innsbruck—The Entrepreneurial School,
Universitätsstrasse 15, Innsbruck 6020, Austria
e-mail: peter.mirski@mci.edu

D. Kilian
e-mail: dietmar.kilian@mci.edu

A. Altmann and B. Ebersberger (eds.), *Universities in Change*, Innovation, Technology, and Knowledge Management, DOI: 10.1007/978-1-4614-4590-6_15,

teaching and research. This third pillar—commercial success—requires universities, like businesses, to employ modern technologies to position themselves on the marketplace.[1]

> The Internet university, I am firmly convinced, is the technical innovation that will do more to change universities than any other invention since the introduction of the printing press by Gutenberg. (Ritter 1999, p. 102)

Since the development of the first calculating machine by Konrad Zuse in the 1930s, the development of computing has been closely linked to universities and their needs. A case in point is the Z22, the first machine to be developed to handle complex calculations. Since those days the world has seen a variety of innovations developed in and around universities in the field of information and communication technologies (ICT)[2] with the primary aim of supporting university research. Such university innovations were also of interest to the corporate world. Since the market launch of the Xerox Alto,[3] for example, they have made a significant contribution to greater efficiency in everyday office work (office management systems) and to electronic support and control for business processes (business automation). Nor should one forget ICT-supported developments in teaching (eLearning), which have greatly changed the effective range of today's universities. The Alma Mater is increasingly becoming an Alma Mater Virtualis, a designation that lends expression to the addition of a new distribution channel for the universities' existing teaching offering and to the increasing digitization of university processes.

> ..., the alma mater will survive by offering a lower education quality but will be confronted with global competition from the academic and corporate sectors. The traditional university can evolve to a kind of "alma mater virtualis/multimedialis" by creating a learning and community platform for their students and developing a library of online courses. (Seufert 2008, p. 117)

15.2 Framework Conditions

In view of the cost and complexity of IT systems, such investments presuppose thorough coordination and harmonization with the goals and strategies of the university concerned, especially in view of the need for innovation and process optimization, and the effective allocation of scarce resources. The main considerations

---

[1] The belief that economic agendas are assuming a fundamental role at universities is not undisputed, as shown by Brooks (2005).

[2] The *Internet* developed out of the ARPANET, which was set up at the end of the 1960s as a project run by the Advanced Research Project Agency (ARPA) of the US Department of Defense. It was designed as a network linking universities and research facilities in order to make efficient use of limited computing capacities, first in the USA and subsequently worldwide.

The authors of the *Google* idea, Larry Page and Sergey Brin met at Stanford University in 1995 and developed the first prototype of what is now a major listed corporation.

[3] The Xerox Alto was the first home computer with a graphic user interface.

are listed on the official webpage for eLearning at the European Union's DG Education and Culture. The site also offers the following summary of one of the most important investigations it has commissioned on the subject of ICT and universities:

> From individual initiative to university culture: For most universities a primary challenge is to translate ICT away from individual initiatives into becoming a component of mainstream education, and this is impeded by a combination of the absence of a coherent and comprehensive management approach to ICT integration with a degree of resistance to change in the university culture. (PLS Ramboll Management 2004, online)

Against this background, the role, image, and self-image of university IT departments are changing; university management must now find the middle ground between criticism of the overzealous and premature deployment of IT as formulated by Carr in his three core rules for IT investments (Carr 2003, p. 48) and visionary forecasts of the digitization of our environment (Floridi 2007, p. 59 ff) in order to successfully integrate their IT departments in their strategic and operative processes.

At the same time the heads of IT departments must play an active role in universities' decision making and implementation processes. These requirements are strongly driven by a number of factors: the growing expectations of clients, i.e., students, with regard to service offerings, increased scope for adjustment to the needs of the market, enhanced flexibility deriving from increased competition between universities, rapid change with regard to the relevant legislation, and a growing need for cooperation with corporate and research partners as a path to third-party funding.

According to the above-mentioned study, there are three main drivers for more IT in universities: the internationalization and globalization of the education market, growing demands on the part of students who take the use of IT systems in private life for granted, and the universities' need to improve in terms of quality and efficiency in both administration and teaching (PLS Ramboll Management 2004, online). Teichler (2007, p. 23), too, sees internationalization and the professionalization of university management as the main trends of the last few decades with the greatest influence on changing university structures.

Figure 15.1 shows the different expectations of students, faculty, administrative and research staffs, and business partners. These expectations derive from the fact that the groups involved all have experience with extra-mural IT solutions and have corresponding expectations of university ITS.

The Vice-Chancellor of the Technical University of Berlin formulated her expectations of campus management systems as follows:

> The changes in the university scene in recent years reflect the trend towards the integration of various sectors of the university that previously worked largely independently. The need for integration derives from the expectations of students and faculty for access to numerous services on a self-service basis, as in everyday life, so as to have more time for study and research. Implementation of an integrated service offering, however, presents the universities with various technical and organizational challenges. (Gutheil 2007)

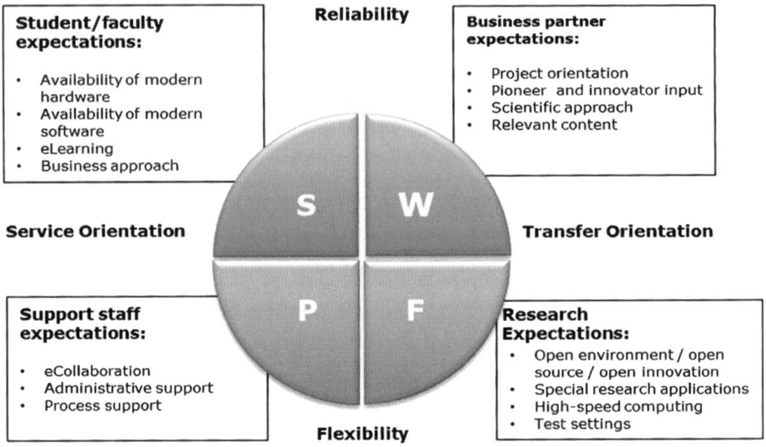

Fig. 15.1 Factors influencing the digitization of universities

Another driving factor is the growing competition between universities and the developing university market. This aspect is a source of major changes and additions to the functions of university IT departments, as active communications and information services play a minor role in a non-competitive market.[4] One of the effects of this factor is the need for structured and standardized data and information management for purposes of data analysis, while data presentation and management in the Internet or Intranet also play a role. In a competitive market, internal university information is also relevant for sourcing and performing structured searches of external information (benchmarks).

A third factor can be found in society's expectations with regard to the further integration of business activities in the university context, as reflected in the growth of integrated projects and joint activities. For university IT departments, this above all involves the need to support collaboration between external and internal actors. Joint data management, authorization rules, investments, and access to infrastructure are challenges that need be addressed in this context.

The last major factor to be considered is internationalization and the need for greater collaboration in the use of research infrastructures. This presupposes the integration of external research and development partners in university and/or research activities. In addition, internationalization is driving user expectations with regard to the multilingual character of IT systems, training for visitors on existing systems, and also the tendency to accept international standards in many

[4] In the following, university IT departments are referred to as "university IT services" (university ITS).

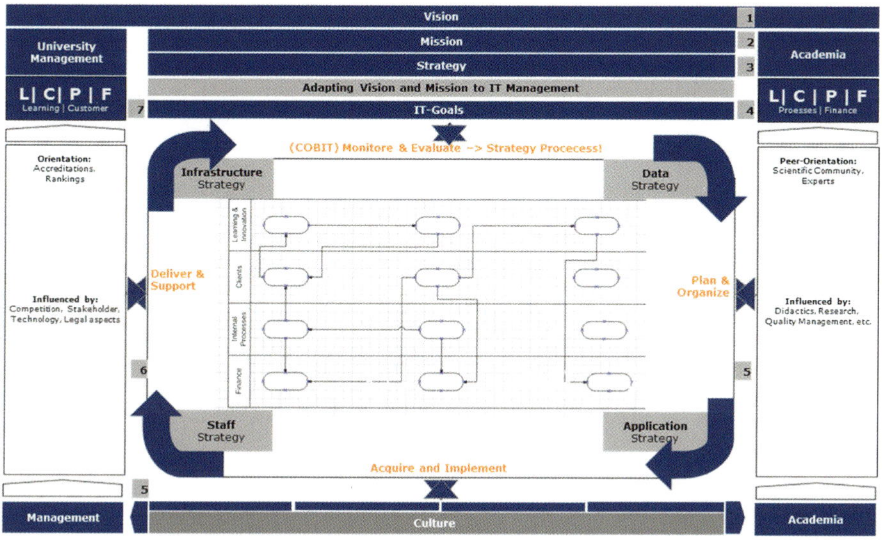

Fig. 15.2 University IT governance model (Mirski 2010, p. 243)

spheres of daily university life. Internationalization also impacts the distributed used of IT infrastructures, as in the case of grid computing.[5]

All these factors are particularly relevant in the university context, although corporate IT departments are facing challenges of an equal magnitude, if not of the same character. The main source of debate on the subject of IT departments is the high level of capital spending on information and communication technologies and hence their effective deployment. In the literature, the term 'IT governance' is now in general use. IT governance describes the integration of IT departments in corporate strategy with the backing of the relevant models and methods. IT governance is derived from the corporate governance philosophy and is targeted at the optimum deployment of IT for the overall success of the company. There are two outstanding institutions working on the theory and practice of IT governance, namely the Sloan School of Management at the Massachusetts Institute of Technology (MIT) with its Center for Information Systems Research (CISR) headed by Professor Peter Weil, and the IT Governance Institute in the UK. Weil's clear definition of the thinking behind IT governance is as follows: "IT governance reflects broader corporate governance principles while focussing on the management and use of IT to achieve corporate performance goals" (Weill 2004, p. 4).

Figure 15.2 shows the aggregated services that are generally to be provided by university ITS plus a further aggregation of four key decision-making factors or

[5] The term 'grid' was coined in the mid 1990s to denote a proposed distributed computing structure for advanced science and engineering. Foster (2001, p. 1).

service groups required for management and integration in university strategies. With external and internal factors influencing the operative and strategic implementation of IT strategy, four items are actively implemented in line with the COBIT® reference model:

- Monitoring & Evaluation
- Planning & Organization
- Acquisition & Implementation
- Delivery & Support.

This reference model, which was developed by Information Systems Audit and Control Association (ISACA), focusses primarily on upgrading the value chain and is targeted at senior management (Hansmann 2009, p. 26).

The purpose of this paper is to show that interaction between university management and university IT departments is essential for optimum results for universities. A model describing this interaction is to be developed and will be proposed. It combines new and familiar items in a joint approach to a university IT governance process.

15.3 The Impact Model

> An IT department that simply waits until somebody else decides something loses respect and recognition and customer satisfaction. That's not the way it works. (Interview, IT manager 2010)

The IT governance model presented here has been developed from Hinterhuber's strategic management model, which provides the frame. It takes account of the need for integration in universities' strategic management processes, as well as international service organization standards, namely ITIL, and IT implementation in projects and controlling COBIT. The impact model incorporates the dual leadership idea in universities (academic and management) with the reference and peer aspects that are relevant for the implementation. It shows the procedures and effects of strategy processes from the vision of the university to the implementation of IT governance within the university ITS department, and its feedback and integration in the strategy process. The model enables universities to organize their individual activities and uses of information and communication technologies to form a complete and logical whole, and to establish meaningful relations between the individual components. This is equally relevant for university management bodies, which often lack the overview to recognize the potential and also the risk factors of IT, and for heads of university IT departments, who may lack insight into the strategic management of universities. The power of the model and its potential applications derives from the use of the terminologies and concepts employed by both parties in an integrated presentation that on the one hand offers a clearer understanding and on the other is a source of specific approaches and procedures designed to facilitate the necessary implementation of IT governance in universities.

15.3.1 The Impact Model for IT Governance in Universities

> Through the potential provided by modern data processing, simulation and digitization, information and communication technologies have also brought fundamental change to many fields of research. (...) A modern IT infrastructure must guarantee management of the research results generated and provide any time/any place access to data and services. (Oberhuemer 2006, p. 33)

The IT governance model for universities provides an integrated picture of the main aspects involved in successful IT governance with the goal of shaping the strategy process and the strategy development and implementation processes needed for an effective IT service department.

Implementation of IT governance starts by formulating the following items: first, the university's vision, second, its more specific policy, and third, the strategies for the university's various fields of action. Since—regardless of the university's formal organization—governing the university must of necessity involve an academic approach on the one hand and a management approach on the other, this dialectic is represented in the model by the pillars on the left and right. For all major decisions, it is necessary to integrate the two sides and their respective arguments, a process that can be handled via various bodies. What is important for the coherence and success of IT governance is an unequivocal formulation—with the backing of as many players as possible—of the university's vision and fundamental values. At this point it should be mentioned once again that basic values like trust or openness can generate very specific IT decisions and implementations, which may either have to be taken in the individual case—and there can be hundreds of such cases—or, and ideally, which can be derived from the university's vision and policies. Trust as a fundamental value, for example, can be reflected in various authorization management decisions (for data access), which would need to be included in the data strategy.

Once the strategies have been formulated by university management, preferably with the involvement of the heads of university ITS, it is essential to develop the university's IT policy and create the corresponding operating framework. The binding definition and review of these objectives is a sine qua non for operative implementation in keeping with a policy of continuous development and improvement.

As a tool for evaluating progress made, use could be made of a strategy map as proposed by Kaplan and Norton, as that combines the four aspects of a balanced performance review with a presentation showing the meaningful links and relationships between the individual strategy elements.

Ultimately the effects of this procedure will have an influence on the university culture as the basis for change management and an expression of the integration of IT governance at the level of university management and Academia.

> Coming from different academic and national traditions, the university appears to be arriving at a common entrepreneurial format in the late 20th century. (Etzkowitz et al. 2000, p. 313)

According to Stratman, universities are distinct organizations that clearly differ from profit-oriented enterprises and also seem to have (too) little in common with purely administrative bodies. If, in the light of increasingly scarce resources, we need to take measures to increase efficiency and effectiveness, and thus improve the university's competitive position, there is still the question of the areas in which this would be most promising and of how the necessary adaptations or changes can be handled, all the more so as, according to Stratman, this does not involve maintenance of a 'trivial machine' but rather is embedded in a complex process of organizational development (Stratmann 2007). His finding is also confirmed in this study, and it sheds light on the reorganization of university IT service departments and their potential. IT reference models have been found to be generally suitable for this purpose and are correspondingly appreciated at the level of IT management. Their application in universities, however, is considered difficult, if not impossible, especially since most European university ITS departments have bureaucratic structures, which must be changed at a higher than departmental level if the measure are to be effective.

The main objective and finding of the underlying investigation relates first of all to the structuring, reflection, and adaptation for implementation in the university environment of the IT management solutions employed in trade and industry in the field of IT governance. This was performed with the help of a questionnaire—with the support of most of the heads of university IT departments in Austria—plus related expert interviews with the department heads. In a triangulation approach, the results were summarized and their relevance presented in the form of a model.

This work was not performed, however, in order to produce another building block for the 'industrialization' of universities. On the contrary: universities are far more than institutions of education and research whose processes can—or must—be 'healed' with the help of modern management methods. As this paper shows, the optimization of existing processes through the introduction of IT governance can help to greatly facilitate daily working and also strengthen the competitive position of the university involved. And competitivity can relate to a combination of many different aspects, such as excellence in teaching, excellence in research, excellence in knowledge transfer to the business community, excellence in management and administration, enhancing the brand value of the university's image, etc.

This paper offers a structured picture of the complexity of the functions of university ITS; it proposes a model based on current standards and also adapted to the specificities of universities, and—in the framework of strategic management—it makes a contribution to the integration of IT departments in university structures. In addition to the theoretical basis, the model has the support of empirical research. It is clear, however, that the findings generated and the model developed need to be adapted to the university concerned and its specific situation, "(...) if we accept that universal best paths for organization are not available to universities" (Wissel 2007, p. 11).

Nevertheless, an evaluation of the empirical findings shows that use of solutions employed in trade and industry—like a service desk for the more effective management of customer enquiries can generate clear improvements in terms of the IT offerings, bearing in mind that a university culture with basic values based on freedom and individuality, tends to prevent the unreflected introduction of such standards.

At all events, the integration of IT departments in the university strategy can be considered a promising solution, as the investigation shows, because it is likely to have positive effects in terms of structural improvements, quality improvements, and innovation.

Increased standardization of university processes is now the order of the day. But, as this investigation shows, the simple transfer of standards and processes that have proved successful in the business world is not necessarily the answer; that solution rarely delivers the desired results.

This paper focusses the challenges confronting university ITS departments and in response proposes a stronger degree of standardization and adaptation of university IT structures to those of the business community. The various processes—some modified, some new—are designed to deliver the motivation, when professionally deployed, to empower the universities to concentrate on those tasks that go beyond the daily round.

However, such structural harmonization—isomorphisms—are no guarantee that structures will actually be improved, and they must always be subjected to careful scrutiny. Lean and sustainable IT support for universities must be based on a coherent overall concept that should never be subjected to experiment or the premature acceptance of external standards.

In view of today's wide range of applications in the field of information and communication technology, and the diversity of solutions available for implementation, the new role of university IT departments additionally proposed in this paper must involve a consultant function, too.

At this point the following criticisms should also be mentioned:

- Duration of the investigation:
- the investigation was conducted over a 4-year period, in which the various steps—from study of the literature to the empirical research and evaluation of the results—were realized.
- Small sample size: as the number of universities in Austria is limited, individual interviews were performed by way of compensation. Extending the investigation to include other countries would certainly round off the picture obtained.

According to Wissel's working hypothesis, the diverse expectations of society in terms of education, research, and science in the modern context are expressed in organizational utopias. In the current discourse, there is first of all the multiversity, second the virtual university, and third the ascetic utopia. The multiversity can be seen as a phenomenon of the growing society with its increasing tendency to scientification. The university is assuming more and more functions as a learning organization. On the other hand, we also have the virtual university, which no longer needs to learn because it is lean and flexible, i.e., it is network-based and virtual. "The tendency is for faculty to no longer be part of the organization but to be located out on the marketplace; scientists constitute a market where knowledge is bought. The organization buys knowledge on that market and sells it on the education market" (Wissel 2007, p. 304).

This classification cannot of course fail to impact the organization and also the self-image of universities and their central service facilities. The core activity of a department at a multiversity may be based on a much less centralized approach and be less economical in terms of resources than that of a virtual university, whose core competence relates to the management function. And there may also be a difference with regard to the need for or the role of IT solutions, whose power in fact lies in networking and the visualization of organizations. The fundamental hypothesis of this investigation was the need to see IT services as a way of increasing the efficiency, effectiveness, and innovative strength of universities. On that basis a model was designed which is targeted at the implementation of a functioning and coherent system that enables the heads of IT on the one hand and university management on the other to work together with the objective of achieving the university's strategic goals with limited resources. The sparing use of resources need not be the main focus of university development, however, even though that was felt to be a central element and source of motivation for the interviewed heads of IT, although it was not explicitly queried, which might possibly have led to other and more profound findings with regard to the factors involved. At all events, the model in itself is shaped by this background situation.

A qualitative study involving heads of university IT departments in Austria, which was performed as part of one of the author's doctoral dissertation, shows that they do not have an unequivocal view of IT governance, but they do associate it with concepts such as added value, reputation, and professionalism. They additionally associate the implementation of IT governance with items like management ratios and their application in the context of the balanced scorecard, and also—and this is particularly interesting—with better communications. With regard to organizational recommendations for improved IT governance, the interviewees speak of the need to develop personal relations with the decision makers in advance of the measures to be taken, to create a help desk, and to establish a steering committee or IT platform for departmental heads to present proposals and give them thorough reflection. It was found that the university's Chief Information Officer has a major role to play and a decisive influence on the anchoring and integration of university IT services in university strategy.

15.4 Summary

This paper, which is based on one of the author's doctoral dissertation, shows that interaction between university management and university IT departments is essential for optimum results for the university deriving from the use of information and communication technologies. A model describing this interaction was developed and proposed in the dissertation. It combines new and familiar items in a joint approach to university IT governance and shows that strategic and operative aspects must be implemented hand in hand in order to generate added value for universities through the deployment of information and communication technologies.

Bibliography

Brooks AC (2005) What do nonprofit organizations seek? (And why should policymakers care?). J Policy Anal Manag 24(3):543–558

Carr N (2003) IT doesn't matter. Harvard Bus Rev 81(5):41–51

Etzkowitz H, Webster A, Gebhardt C, Terra BRC (2000) The future of the university and the university of the future: evolution of ivory tower to entrepreneurial paradigm. Res Policy 29(2):313–330

European Commission (2010) Bologna process: harmonisation of the university systems. URL: http://europa.eu/legislation_summaries/education_training_youth/general_framework/c11088_de.htm (Date of visit: 10-01-2010)

Floridi L (2007) A look into the future impact of ICTICT on our lives. Inf Soc 23(1):59–64

Foster I (2001) The anatomy of the grid: enabling scalable virtual organisations. In: Sakellariou R (ed) Parallel processing: proceedings of the 7th international Euro-Par conference, Manchester, UK, 28–31 August 2001. Springer, Berlin, pp 1–4

Gutheil U (2007) Chancen und Herausforderungen eines modernen. Campus-Managements

Hansmann E (2009) IT messen und steuern. Inf Manag Consult 24(4):25–29

Mirski P (2010) IT-Governance für Hochschulen. Wettbewerbsstärkung von Hochschulen durch Integration interner IT-Abteilungen. Innsbruck, 243

Oberhuemer E (2006) Überlegungen zur Entwicklung einer Contentstrategie für die Universität Wien. In: Mettinger (Hg) 2006 – eLearning an der Universität Wien, Münster, p 33

PLS Ramboll Management (2004) Virtual models of European universities. Draft final report to the EU commission, DG Education & Culture

Ritter UP (1999) Die Internet-Universität, virtuelle Universitäten und die Zukunft der Europäischen Universitäten. Das Hochschulwesen 47(4):102–107

Seufert S (2008) Innovationsorientiertes Bildungsmanagement: Hochschulentwicklung durch Sicherung der Nachhaltigkeit von eLearning. Verlag für Sozialwissenschaften, Wiesbaden

Stratmann F (2007) Vorwort. In: Altvater P (ed) Organisationsentwicklung in Hochschulen, Hannover, p 2

Teichler U (2007) Die Internationalisierung der Hochschulen: Neue Herausforderungen und strategies. Campus, Frankfurt/Main

Weill P (2004) IT governance: how top performers manage IT decision rights for superior results. Harvard Business School, Boston

Wissel C (2007) Hochschule als Organisationsproblem. Neue Modi universitärer Selbstbeschreibung in Deutschland. Transcript, Bielefeld, p 11

Chapter 16
Achieving Success Through Quality: The Role of Accreditation and Continuous Improvement in Management Education

John M. Beehler and Denise J. Luethge

16.1 Introduction

Management educators must all be concerned with the future of business and commerce worldwide. This concern can take various forms. On a macro level, it is important that the economies of the world prosper and grow. This will lead to increased standards of living for all of our citizens and will help us to deal with many of those problems that plague us, including poverty, illiteracy, health, crime, and war. Improved management education is the foundation for continued economic progress. With economic progress comes the ability to fund initiatives that improve life for our world's citizenry. In addition, economic interdependency between countries reduces the probability for war and conflict. Countries that trade together find a common ground in order to cooperate and collaborate across many dimensions. We are all interconnected in the global economy. This is particularly evident today, as illustrated by the events surrounding the current global recession.

On a micro level, management educators are focused on how best to prepare the future graduates of business school programs to meet the needs of the global economy. The world is changing in many ways, and the current generation of students ought to be prepared to face the challenges of a technology-driven and global business environment. This preparation includes skills in innovation and entrepreneurship which are essential to develop the new technologies and businesses of the future. Worldwide talent is critical to successful businesses and future economic development. Other areas where our constituents are demanding

J. M. Beehler (✉) · D. J. Luethge
Haile/US Bank College of Business Northern Kentuky University,
Nunn Drive, BEP Center, Highland Heights, 41099 USA
e-mail: beehlerj1@nku.edu

D. J. Luethge
e-mail: luethged1@nku.edu

A. Altmann and B. Ebersberger (eds.), *Universities in Change*, Innovation, Technology, and Knowledge Management, DOI: 10.1007/978-1-4614-4590-6_16,

more of a focus are sustainability and ethics. In addition to business schools which have developed "sustainable MBAs," many other universities are increasingly attuned to environmental responsibility (Herro 2006). Further, the worldwide financial meltdown in 2008 has caused many to question MBA programs that focus on financial and mathematical modeling to the detriment of a focus on ethics, communication, and the management of people (Mattioli 2009).

In many countries, especially in the United States, there is concern that the students entering our universities are not sufficiently prepared in science and math. This has caused the need for remediation before students can begin their studies at the university level. It also results in fewer students choosing science, engineering, and other technical fields as their major area of study in college. This alone reduces the potential for innovation and entrepreneurship. As management educators, it is important to consider how to promote collaboration between business school students and those in other technical fields as engineering, science, and medicine. It also points to the need to attract those in technical fields to graduate business programs.

As we seek to continually improve management education, we must consider the many factors that affect our ability to meet these challenges. These factors include declining support for higher education at public institutions, the shortage and increasing cost of Ph.D. qualified faculty worldwide, the increasing cost of a technology-driven curriculum, and the need for innovative curriculum delivered in new ways to meet the needs of future students. We also must consider the market in which we compete. The proliferation of alternative sources of management education in our local, regional, national, and international markets confuses potential students and employers. Whether the programs are for-credit or non-credit, the issue becomes how can the consumer differentiate among these programs on the basis of quality? Management educators must identify which niche the business school should occupy in their relevant market and determine how to sell their programs to their constituents.

These and many other challenges face management educators. The purpose of this chapter is to identify the challenges and opportunities for management education in the twenty-first century and to provide a perspective for assuring the quality of business school programs and their graduates in meeting these challenges and opportunities.

16.2 Management Education in the Twentieth Century

In his book, The Future of Management (2007), Hamel notes that business schools have operated on the same basic production model for the past 100 years, using the input → processing plant → output model of educating students (Hawawini 2005; Mair 2002). Indeed, when AACSB International (The Association to Advance Collegiate Schools of Business) first began accrediting schools in 1919, the focus was primarily on the inputs to the education process. In other words, as long as the key inputs of education (i.e., students, faculty, and curriculum) were good, it was assumed that the students would learn the technical material and come out prepared for the working world. Learning was viewed as a by-product of good inputs and assessment methods focused on the quality of these inputs. By the early 1990s, the focus of assessing the quality of business education began to change. The new focus centered on directly assessing student learning via objective measures of performance. Given the mission of the business school and the key learning objectives for each program, the question became whether the students were really learning what they should be learning in the program and if there was direct evidence to that effect. Simply showing that the learning process involved quality inputs was no longer sufficient. Under the new approach, it became the responsibility of the management educator if students' performances were below expectations.

Much of the work on assessing the quality of business schools began with AACSB International. Both American business schools and AACSB International have significantly influenced management education over the last 60 plus years. In the 1960s, business education transitioned from being more of a trade or vocational undertaking to that of an applied social science, thereby gaining in academic respectability, legitimacy, and rigor (Pfeffer and Fong 2002; Cornuel 2007). Later, as the "science of business" grew, so too did the focus on theoretical conceptualizations, statistical analysis, model development, and testing. Research and the creation of knowledge became more important aspects of a business professor's responsibility. However, at the same time as US business schools gained in academic credibility, many questioned whether or not they were losing practical relevancy (Cornuel 2008b; Pfeffer & Fong 2002; Starkey et al. 2004). In fact, in recent years, US business schools have been widely criticized for teaching essentially the same way over the last 20 years, yielding students with limited applicable skills and questionable moral compasses (Pfeffer and Fong 2002, 2004; Starkey et al. 2004; Davis and Botkin 1994; Mintzberg and Gosling 2002).

At the same time, a number of European business schools focused much more on practical experience (such as the fachhochschulen, polytechnics, or hogescholen), where practical training was part of the degree requirement, and contributions to solving problems in companies and/or industries was (and still is) valued. Alternatively, students in Europe could attend economics or commerce programs at traditional universities in a variety of programs, with the nature of those programs varying widely by country. In general, university programs in Europe were somewhat more theoretical in nature but believed to yield more of a practical orientation than their American counterparts. In the early 1980s, the AMBA (then called the Business Graduates Association) began accrediting MBA programs in the United Kingdom (AMBA, n. d.). In 1997, European Quality Improvement System (EQUIS) was established by the European Foundation for Management Development EFMD) for the purpose of accrediting global business schools (EFMD, n. d.). Finally, in 1999, Bologna Declaration was reached with the goal of standardizing degree programs throughout Europe by 2010. As a result of this accord, European education programs should become more comparable and compatible, and the Accord should also increase the competitiveness of individual programs on a continental and global basis (European Commission on Education and Training 2007; Scherer et al. 2005).

16.3 Recent Environmental Changes

Management education worldwide today is a big business. From the 1950s to the turn of the century, the average annual number of business degrees in the US increased dramatically (Pfeffer and Fong 2002, 2004; Zimmerman 2001). According to AACSB International, the number of undergraduate degrees granted in the US increased from 232,636 to 311,574 between 1985 and 2005, while the number of MBA degrees granted during that same period increased from 66,996 to 142,617 (AACSB 2008). Similar increases have been seen across the globe. Worldwide, the number of new graduate management programs increased by 3,710 between 1997 and 2007 (Anderson 2007), with 1,553 in Europe, 708 in North America, and 1449 in Asia, South America, Africa, and Australia. In fact, the AACSB International report notes that the total number of educational institutions offering business degrees at any level in 2006–2007 is estimated at 10,265 (AACSB 2008). Of these over 10,000 programs, less than 10% are accredited by the top three management education accreditation bodies worldwide: AACSB International, EQUIS, and AMBA. Clearly, the proliferation of management programs across the globe will have a significant impact on the way business schools worldwide make strategic and operational decisions in the future.

Although the number of management education programs continues to increase, the shortage of Ph.D. faculty worldwide is critical and getting worse (Hawawini 2005; Pfeffer and Fong 2002; AACSB 2002). In the next decade, there will be a shortage of at least 2,500 Ph.D. business faculty in the US alone (Cornuel 2007). Given the salary differential currently seen between many US schools and European schools, this could result in a large movement of many terminally qualified European faculty to the US seeking higher wages as well as a significant brain drain of Ph.D.s from the developing world (Cornuel 2008a). This is a particular problem for public universities in Europe, Asia, and South America that do not have the tradition of private donations, corporate funding, or large endowments (Dameron and Durand 2009; Hawawini 2005; Thomas 2009). In addition to the movement of faculty abroad, this decrease in the supply of Ph.D.s further increases faculty salaries and the cost of providing classes at a time when government budgets are declining. The ability to attract and retain Ph.D.-qualified faculty in the future will have a significant impact upon an institution's ability to attract quality students, thereby impacting the reputation of programs as well.

In addition to a proliferation of diverse programs, student populations are becoming much more diverse, both in terms of age and experience (AACSB 2002). This is true particularly in developing countries, where programs may be very new and national accreditation or quality standards have yet to be put into place (LeClair 2008). Students seeking business degrees today have a wide range of needs, preferences, and options which influence their choice of degree program and university. This proliferation of business programs has given rise to a variety of distinct customer segments (AACSB 2002). Some master degree programs consist of shorter post-experience degrees and longer pre-experience degrees (Loades 2005), while others focus on specific functional areas (Zammuto 2008). For-profit online programs have undertaken huge promotional campaigns to attract students to their business programs, and they have done so rather successfully. As a result, students have an extensive range of choices when choosing degree programs. However, with over 10,000 business programs worldwide, the quality of these programs varies tremendously.

In addition to a diverse body of students, there are diverse ways of learning. The way knowledge is communicated has not kept pace with the way our students prefer to gain knowledge. We have only begun to tap technology for knowledge dissemination. While students communicate and receive information via Twitter, Facebook, MySpace, Podcasts, and texting, most universities deliver information in lecture halls, not all that different from the lectures of the 1950s and earlier (Shinn 2009). Clearly, one significant change in education over the past decade involves the growth in the number of online management education programs, both in traditional universities with traditional programs and in private and/or public institutions focusing solely on Web-delivered education. In addition, technology has made the world more interconnected and transparent (Smith 2008). Hopefully, this transparency will require corporations to behave much more responsibly and encourage management educators to develop students who think and act ethically. An additional responsibility for management educators is to develop curriculum and educational delivery that involves students with the latest technology, enabling them to participate effectively in the business world. Given the rapid pace of technological change, the challenge for business schools is to keep both hardware and software on hundreds of systems up to date with appropriate training for faculty and staff, both in terms of cost and content (Cornuel 2005). Further, as more for-profit schools expand their online offerings and students demand more flexibility in scheduling (Hawawini 2005), schools must compete by stretching budgets to increase technology expenditures for both for in-class and online class offerings in order to retain students.

As technology has made the world more interconnected, globalization has made the world a much smaller place, especially the business world (Smith 2008). As a result, both employers and students demand an education from business schools with a strong international dimension, one which not only brings the world to the students but also brings the students into the world (Hawawini 2005). This means that those schools with international projects, study abroad programs, and strong international alliances will be able to attract the top students, especially in Europe where the Bologna Accord has increased student mobility via harmonization of programs. (Cornuel 2007; Hawawini 2005; Jain 2008). Thus, Cornuel (2007) feels that it is likely that the wave of the future will be in the strength of the international dimension of a school's faculty, students, curricula, and research production for management education institutions. Cultural differences will become more important as schools focus on global aspects of management and multicultural strategies. European schools, which have long concentrated on the attraction of students across borders, should have a strong advantage in developing this dimension of their programs (Dameron and Durand 2009).

As students demand more global opportunities to meet the needs of employers, businesses also are questioning the relevance of our curricula, particularly for producing graduates who can understand the issues firms face. Business schools worldwide have been criticized for producing MBA graduates who are strong analytically but weak in softer skill areas, such as communication, social responsibility, ethics, and practicality (Cornuel 2008a; Hawawini 2005). In order to ensure that curricula are relevant, schools are increasingly seeking business input and providing students with experiential activities to break down the barriers that exist between theory and practice (Glosten 2009; Jain 2008; Rousseau 2008; Starkey et al. 2004).

Finally, the downturn in the worldwide economy has seen a general loss of wealth globally for individuals, corporations, and governments. This loss of wealth has further impacted countries by decreasing tax revenues, increasing social payments, and stretching government budgets. As a result, government support of public universities throughout the world is decreasing (Hawawini 2005). As budgets are being cut, universities are increasingly looking for alternative sources of funds, either from increasing tuition in traditional program fees, additional revenue from high margin specialization degrees and non-degree programs, corporate giving, and alumni or individual donations. US schools have traditionally been successful in obtaining contributions from corporations, foundations, alumni, and other individuals, in part because state appropriations have covered a decreasing proportion of expenses for a number of years. Most US schools charge tuition to cover the difference, but increasingly schools are looking to outside sources of revenue. However, additional sources of revenue are a huge challenge for non-US institutions that have traditionally received all or nearly all of their operating budgets from the government (Dameron and Durand 2009; Hawawini 2005; Thomas 2009. As government budgets become tighter and funding sources drop, European, Asian, and other global institutions must develop ways to capture additional sources of funds (GFME 2006).

16.4 Meeting the Challenges of the New Environment

As a result of these environmental changes, business schools are trying to change their strategies and methods of operation in order to cope with the new environment. Management education is a very competitive business and failure to assess the challenges and make appropriate changes will have major ramifications for business schools worldwide. Many techniques that business schools teach are critical to use for survival. For example, market research studies and elasticity analyses are necessary to assess the needs of students and employers and the sensitivity of students to changes in tuition structures. Promotion, advertising, and strategic planning are critical to compete. Establishing programs in niche areas where there is a clear need and less competition is one strategy that must be considered.

A key concern is that many of the changes necessary for future success involve substantial costs. The shortage of Ph.D. faculty is a prime example of rising costs. Building networks and alliances with other business schools to increase value and/or share costs of programs is a wave for the future (Scherer et al. 2005), and this can be done both domestically and globally. Given the shortage of Ph.D. faculty worldwide, sharing faculty resources to offer joint programs while meeting quality standards makes sense. AACSB International has established new programs in an effort to help business schools obtain faculty by non-traditional means. One of these, the Bridge Program, focuses on professional qualifications of faculty and is designed to take executives from business and industry and prepare them for teaching in the academic environment. Another program, the Post-Doctoral Bridge to Business Program, is designed to train individuals with non-business doctoral degrees for careers in teaching and researching in the business disciplines. Another option for business schools might be considering the US medical school model of faculty, where clinical faculties focus on teaching classes while research faculties focus on research. This option would allow doctoral students to track into either research or teaching. As it is now, many students enter a doctoral program with the intent of teaching in academe only to find that their program is really a research degree. Companies, students, governments, and the general public are likely more concerned with the educational component of teaching doctoral students to be good teachers, while concern with research tends to be primarily the purview only of fellow academics.

As the number of PhD faculty declines, a number of business schools are using non-PhD faculty from industry. This professionally qualified faculty typically has a number of years of experience, often at quite high levels, and adds great value in the classroom. In fact, many students claim that faculty with real-world experience are often the best teachers. In the future, business schools may want to consider whether or not a PhD is an absolute requirement for teaching, particularly at the undergraduate level.

Using the latest technology in the curriculum and pursuing international opportunities for students and faculty pose resource challenges. A prime way to deal with these fiscal challenges is to apply for government and foundation grants that may be available in some countries, such as grants for technology and internationalization efforts that are available in the US. External fundraising from corporations and foundations is also a possibility for the future. It should be noted, however, that many forms of technology that students and companies currently use have little or no cost to universities. Social media tools such as Facebook and Twitter or communication tools such as Skype allow faculty and students to interact in a variety of ways, and since most students currently use these tools, the learning curve is reduced (except for some less technologically savvy faculty).

Business schools need to become more entrepreneurial in seeking alternative sources of funding for key initiatives. Executive education and training have become commonplace in many business schools for this purpose. In some schools, Executive MBA programs generate substantial funds when business schools are able to maintain autonomy in collecting and retaining tuition and charges for their own use. Lifelong learning programs open another avenue for future funding. This is particularly appropriate in business schools as technology and its applications change very quickly (Hawawini 2005). Business schools have the opportunity to tap their graduates, whether bachelor, MBA, or executive programs, as well as graduates from other programs, and encourage them to keep their skills fresh. Another possibility is to negotiate agreements with the rest of the University for revenue sharing in existing programs once enrollment exceeds certain benchmarks. For example, business schools face significant challenges in the US since they are often "cash cows" providing funding resulting from popular business programs to support other non-business programs across the campus. This funding arrangement typically is not a problem if business schools are provided with a reasonable budget to run their operations in a quality manner with sufficient faculty, staff, administration, and operating budgets. When this is not the case, management educators face even more of a challenge for enhancing their programs.

The challenge in competing for students, faculty, and financial support in light of the many choices available worldwide is more significant today than ever. With the proliferation of programs, business schools need to differentiate themselves to assure success. In this competitive marketplace for management higher education, consumers are seeking clarity while those involved in providing lesser quality programs benefit from a lack of clarity. How can we as management educators who truly care about the quality of our programs and the future of management education help bring this clarity to the marketplace?

16.5 Measures of Quality in Management Education

Today, there are primarily two sources of quality indicators that have taken prominence. The first and most visible source is the many rankings of business schools, MBA programs, and other business programs that have proliferated worldwide. *The Financial Times, Business Week, U. S. News and World Report* and many others publish rankings each year. The major problem with these many rankings is that the criteria and methodologies used vary significantly, resulting in anomalous results. All aspects of the school, regardless of any difference in mission, size, or location, are condensed into one number to provide a ranking. What does the fact that a business school or any of its programs is ranked really mean in the scheme of things? A large number of these rankings are for full-time MBA programs; however, the rankings many times are interpreted as being rankings of the entire business school. There are many other aspects of a quality business school than just its full-time MBA program. AACSB International has issued a report entitled "The Business School Rankings Dilemma" (AACSB 2005) where they outline the many negative repercussions of rankings to the management education community. The report notes that although the measures included in the rankings are often arbitrary, superficial, or unrelated to quality, business schools cannot afford to ignore rankings and often spend scarce time and resources providing information to the media because rankings receive a great deal of attention from alumni, prospective students, and corporate or individual donors.

The second source providing an indicator of quality is business school accreditation. Again, there are a number of organizations worldwide that provide the opportunity for accreditation with a rather wide variance of rigor. This may also cause confusion on the part of the consumer of management education. In the United States, there are regional accrediting bodies that accredit all the programs for entire universities. These accreditations do not provide accreditation specifically for business school programs, although some business schools use regional accreditation as a marketing tool as if it does. In many countries, the government accredits universities and business schools, such as the Spanish Association of Business Management School (AEEDE) in Spain, the Foundation for International Business Administration Accreditation (FIBAA) in Germany, or the Netherlands Flanders Accreditation Organization (NVAO) in the Netherlands. The standards and methods used to attain accreditation vary widely, thereby providing little comparability with business schools from other countries. The Bologna Accord is designed to help address comparability issues throughout Europe, but the standardization of programs will also open the market for students on a continental and global basis, no longer restricting study to a particular country as a function of the national length or structure of programs (GFME 2008).

Finally, there are a number of global accrediting institutions for management education that certify that programs or schools which have achieved accreditation have processes in place to ensure that stated objectives are met and continuous improvement of performance is ongoing. As a result, accreditation has become known as a quality indicator for programs along a number of dimensions (Urgel 2007). For example, in the United States, the three largest business accreditation organizations are AACSB International, the Association of Collegiate Business Schools and Programs (ACBSP), and the International Assembly for Collegiate Business Education (IACSE). The ACBSP and IACSE typically accredit schools that have more of a teaching focus, while AACSB accredits schools with both teaching and research missions and is considered to be the most prestigious type of accreditation for management education schools (Roller et al 2003; Zammuto 2008).

Globally for business schools, there have emerged three major international accrediting bodies for business school programs: the EQUIS, the Association of MBAs (AMBA), and AACSB International (Urgel 2007; Zammuto 2008). Each has a comprehensive series of rigorous criteria for continuous quality improvement that provides assurance for consumers that the programs and graduates are of high quality, and all focus on the school's ability to meet mission and assessment standards. EQUIS, which accredits entire schools, places more emphasis on a school's interaction with the business community and international reach (Zammuto 2008). AMBA, which accredits MBA and DBA programs rather than schools, focuses more on mission, strategy, curricula, corporate interaction, and student and faculty qualifications (AMBA n. d.; Zammuto 2008). These quality accrediting bodies provide an opportunity for differentiating quality management education programs from other programs. Due to their scope, they also provide comparability world-wide. In this competitive, global environment for management education, it is critical that business schools achieve these accreditations to differentiate themselves and promote the quality of their programs.

16.6 Benefits and Costs of Accreditation

Successful business schools will increase quality improvement, and seek accreditation in particular, in order to show their commitment to excellence, quality, and innovation (Cornuel 2007; Greensted 2008). The process of gaining accreditation forces schools to examine their operations, processes, and systems, focusing on activities to increase effectiveness, efficiency, stakeholder involvement, and student achievement (Perrin-Halot and Thomas 2008; Shinn 2008). Once a school achieves accreditation, it becomes a measure of the quality and reputation of the school (Urgel 2007). The benchmarking and standards of quality against which schools are measured for a particular accreditation mean that the schools become part of a group to be considered as the best educational institutions around the world (Zammuto 2008). As a result, schools that have attained the prestigious "triple accreditation," or accreditation by AACSB International, AMBA and EQUIS, market that fact prominently in their brochures and websites. The benefits of accreditation that schools perceive are numerous. In a survey of accredited US business schools, Roller et al. (2003) found that the deans' perceptions of the most common benefits were program improvement, learning from other schools, advantages in marketing, faculty recruitment, reputation, and increased bargaining leverage for university resources for operations and faculty compensation. Urgel (2007) also noted that the brand recognition schools receive as a result of accreditation also helps in the development of global alliances with other top institutions, further facilitating the recruitment of students and faculty (Cornuel 2008b).

In addition to the many benefits of accreditation, there are a number of costs. First, many schools find it difficult to recruit Ph.D. qualified faculty that are often required to meet specific accreditation standards. As noted above, starting salaries have increased dramatically, and with decreasing budgets, many schools, especially smaller schools, have difficulty matching the salaries required to attract these faculty. Smaller budgets also put a strain on resources to fund programs and technology, requiring some schools to scale down operations or focus on smaller, more manageable niches. Also, the time and human resource commitment to attain and maintain accreditation is substantial. Convincing faculty within a school that the benefits of accreditation outweigh the time, effort, and changes required is not an easy task (Roller et al. 2003; Shinn 2008). However, even given the costs, a number of deans and educators believe that not seeking accreditation may have very serious long-term financial and reputational consequences, particularly in those schools with large international student populations (Shinn 2008; Zammuto 2008).

Developing mission-driven standards, revising curricula, assessing student learning outcomes, recruiting top faculty and students and establishing processes that ensure an enriching student experience are standards for most top accreditation programs. Schools and programs that are accredited benefit greatly from accreditation expertise and benchmarking with other top schools and programs. Although benchmarking is a valued activity, simply doing what every other accredited school does will not lead schools to exceptional results (Pfeffer and Fong 2004). In order to be truly successful, schools must carve out their own territory, develop their own value propositions, and deliver their education in better and more innovative ways than their competitors.

16.7 Future of Management Education

The challenges faced by management education include future worldwide growth in demand, availability of funding sources, shortage of Ph.D. faculty, sustaining scholarship, quality assurance, product differentiation, meeting the future workforce needs both locally and globally, relevance of curriculum, use of technology, and globalization. These issues have been identified here and in many venues (GFME 2008; Pfeffer and Fong 2004; Starkey et al. 2004 etc.). For management education to reach its potential and provide for future worldwide economic and social progress, these challenges must be addressed.

There are divergent opinions on how management education should address these challenges. In some cases, it appears that the challenges are competing. For example, Pfeffer and Fong (2004) argue that the career-enhancing, salary-increasing aspects of business education should be discounted with an enhancement of the role of business schools in fulfilling a societal need for a profession of management with its own intrinsic value. Implicit in this notion is the idea that business schools need to become more academic with a focus on research. This is an argument that appears to go against those who believe that business schools have become too academic and have lost touch with practice thereby not meeting the needs of companies who hire their graduates. What is lost in this debate is that both opinions could be right at the same time. There is a need for research that will reveal new knowledge about the practice of management. At the same time, management educators should seek partnerships with the professional community to align business school curriculum, skill development goals, and student experiences with their needs. The results of applied and pedagogical research would likely help both management educators and practitioners accomplish this alignment.

The Global Foundation for Management Education (GFME) is a partnership between AACSB International and EFMD dedicated to addressing key issues facing business schools worldwide. In its report entitled "The Global Management Education Landscape" (GFME 2008), it provides five recommendations to address the major challenges facing business schools:

1. Advocate for quality assurance globally and locally;
2. Invest in mechanisms to engage business and government leaders in envisioning future organizational and societal needs;
3. Facilitate and encourage investments in doctoral degree education and other infrastructure development;
4. Create an international clearinghouse for data and information relating to business schools and management education structures, trends, and practices; and
5. Facilitate multilateral collaboration among business schools.

A premise of these recommendations is that the management education community needs to involve key stakeholders and constituents in the solutions. Business, government, economic development agencies, and others influential in society must be engaged in the process of seeking solutions. While AACSB International and EFMD and their members have the most vested interests in success, they do not believe that they can take on this great endeavor alone (GFME 2008). Another way to approach the challenges is to ask what management educators as professionals can do at the micro level to help meet the challenge. Here are a few suggestions:

- Encourage your best undergraduate and graduate students to consider entering a Ph.D. program in business. Help them understand the benefits of a career in teaching and research as a business professor.
- Become more engaged with professionals in your area of expertise. Listen to their needs and bring these needs to the forefront as curriculum is reviewed. Take on research projects that involve key issues faced in the professional community. Look for relevance and impact as the key reasons for doing your research.
- Seek excellence in all you do whether in research, teaching, service, or administration. Practice what you preach in your courses.
- Set high standards for yourself, your colleagues, and your students. Business practice will not improve unless everyone seeks excellence from the start.
- Promote the importance of accreditation for management education. Awareness is a key factor in helping students, employers, and others value accreditation as a quality assurance mechanism.
- Seek to internationalize your courses and the programs your university offers. Encourage your colleagues to do the same.
- Teach with a passion for your discipline emphasizing relevance, professionalism, ethics, and global citizenry. Help your students understand the impact that can be made in this world.

16.8 Role of the University in Management Education

Most business schools function as an integral part of the larger university. In some cases, the business school is the sole unit in the academic institution; however, this is the exception rather than the rule. What role does the business school play in the university? What role does the university play in defining the role of the business school? The answers to these questions provide perspective to the task of delivering and administering management education.

As a professional school, the business school represents a key tie to business, government, economic development agencies, and other organizations. It is a window through which these constituents view the university. With significant reliance on the business school for employees, expertise, executive training, and academic programs, these constituents come to depend on the business school and to value the university based on its performance. These same constituents bring much potential financial support to the university due to their wealth level and capacity as benefactors. As a result, it is important for the university to have a strong business school with close ties to the community.

Another role for business schools in the context of the university is to bring best business practices to the management of the university. The business school can be looked upon to provide improvements in the university's technology, budgeting practices, marketing and promotion, pricing, strategic planning, communication, and general management. Teams of students can help to solve university issues as course projects. Faculty can serve as consultants (whether paid or not) to provide expertise for specific issues and projects.

One role for the business school is to provide relevance and cross-disciplinary integration in the areas of research and scholarly activity. Business professors can work with those in many other disciplines to tackle real-world problems as part of their research. Some examples include management and marketing professors working with social science professors, finance professors working with math/statistics professors, accounting professors working with law professors, and entrepreneurship professors working on commercialization projects with engineering, medical, and science professors. The synergies resulting from these projects result in greater respect among colleagues campus-wide and better unity across the entire university.

The university can provide many benefits to the business school through its communications, governmental, and public relations, library resources, databases, grant support, enhanced technology, recruitment of quality students, and provision of facilities and infrastructure. In some cases, universities of academic and athletic stature can provide name recognition for the business school. This could also work in reverse if the business school has greater name recognition than the university. The business school operates in the context of the university in which it resides. Both the university and the business school provide many benefits to this symbiotic relationship.

16.9 Conclusion

In this chapter, the challenges and opportunities for management education in the twenty-first century are explored. Management education is critical to future global economic prosperity and the ability to solve many societal problems. Business, government, economic development agencies, other organizations, and the world's citizens have a vested interest in its success. While the challenges identified are many, they can be overcome through collaboration with the key constituents of management education and a commitment to excellence. Quality assurance through accreditation is a key aspect of the future success of management education. Management education associations such as EFMD, AMBA, and AACSB International will continue to play a prominent role assuring continuous quality improvement in management education through accreditation, data collection and analysis, thought leadership, and professional development opportunities.

Bibliography

AACSB international (2002) Management educationat risk. Report of the management education task force to the AACSB International Board of Directors, retrieved 3 April 2008 from. http://www.gfme.org/issues/pdfs/Management%20Education%20at%20 Risk.pdf

AACSB International (2005) The Business school rankings dilemma. Tampa, Florida. Task force of AACSB international's committee on issues in management education

AACSB International (2008) The AACSB guide to business education: 2008 data direct from the source. Tampa, Florida. AACSB International Knowledge Services

Anderson BL (2007). From data to strategy: understanding worldwide trends in graduate management education. GMAC Annual industry conference: reach beyond the horizon, Graduate management admission Council, 1–7

AMBA (Association of MBAs) (n. d.) retrieved 3 April 2009 from. http://www.mbaworld.com MBAWorld/jsp/images/accreditation/pdf/MBAMBA_criteria_0807.pdf

Cornuel E (2005) The role of business schools in society. J Manag Dev 24(9):819–829

Cornuel E (2007) University challenge. Global Focus 1(1):10–14

Cornuel E (2008a) Quo vadis? Global Focus 2(2):24–27

Cornuel E (2008b) The road ahead for European management education. Global Focus 2(3): 20–22

Dameron S, Durand T (2009) 20–20 vision: a dual strategy for European business schools. Global Focus 3(1):22–25

Davis S, Botkin J (1994) The monster under the bed: how business is mastering the opportunity of knowledge for profit. Simon and Schuster, New York

European commission on education and training (2007) The bologna process: towards the European higher education process, 13 Aug 2007, retrieved 27 Mar 2009 from http://ec.europa.eu/education/policies/educ/bologna/bologna_en.html

EFMD (n. d.) retrieved 9 April 2009 from. www.efmd.org

Global foundation for management education (GFME) (2008) The global management education landscape: shaping the future of business schools, retrieved 9 April 2009 from http://www.gfme.org/landscape/reportonlineversion.pdf

Global foundation for management education (GFME) (2006) A global guide to management education, retrieved 9 April 2009 from http://www.gfme.org/global_guide/index.htm

Glosten LR (2009) Recalibrating the core. BizEd, 48–49
Greensted C (2008) Do business schools need formal quality assurance systems? Global Focus 2(1):18–21
Hamel G (2007) The future of management. Harvard Business School Press, Boston
Hawawini G (2005) The future of business schools. J Manag Dev 24(9):770–782
Herro A (2006) Sustainability is growing theme of business schools. World watch Institute, Oct 23, retrieved Aug 27, 2009 from http://www.worldwatch.org/node/4687
Jain DC (2008) Anticipating the future. BizEd, 38–43
LeClair D (2008) Reflections on the GFME report. Global Focus 2(2):30–33
Loades R (2005) Exploring the consequences of Bologna. Forum, Summer, 10–13
Mair D (2002) Think global, act global Australian Financial Review, April 4
Mattioli D (2009) Professor says business schools and students can take away lessons from financial crisis. Wall Street Journal Online, Aug 20, 2009, retrieved Aug 27, 2009 from http://online.wsj.com/article/SB125072494060444569.html
Mintzberg H, Gosling J (2002) Educating managers beyond borders. Acad Manag Learn Educ 1(1):64–76
Perrin-Halot J, Thomas M (2008). Vive l'accréditation. BizEd, Sep/Oct, 32–36
Pfeffer J, Fong CT (2002) The end of business schools? Less success than meets the eye. Acad Manag Learn Educ 1(1):78–95
Pfeffer J, Fong CT (2004) The business school 'business': some lessons from the US experience. J Manage Stud 41(8):1501–1519
Roller RH, Andrews BK, Bovee SL (2003) Specialized accreditation of business schools: a comparison of alternative costs, benefits and motivations. J Educ Bus 78(4):197–2004
Rousseau DM (2008) On organizational behavior. BizEd, 30–31
Scherer RF, Javalgi RG, Bryant M, Tukel O (2005). Challenges of AACSB International accreditation for business schools in the United States and Europe. Thunderbird Inter-national Business Review, 47(6):651–669
Shinn S (2008) Earning excellence. BizEd, 26–31
Shinn S (2009) Dial M for mobile. BizEd, 32–39
Smith N C (2008) Ethics and social responsibility. BizEd, 28–29
Starkey K, Hatchuel A, Tempest S (2004) Rethinking the business school. J Manag Stud 41(8):1521–1531
Thomas H (2009) Business school strategy and the metrics for success. Global Focus 3(1):36–39
Urgel J (2007) EQUIS accreditation: value and benefits for international business schools. Global Focus 1(1):32–36
Zammuto RF (2008) Accreditation and the globalization of business. Acad Manag Learn Educ 7(2):256–268
Zimmerman JL (2001) Can American business schools survive? Rochester Unpublished manuscript, Simon graduate school of business administration

Chapter 17
Uniformity is No Virtue

Ekkehard Kappler

On ambivalence in university evaluation and accreditation.

Revealing the main point of an essay in the title itself is as ill-advised as naming the culprit on the first page of a detective story. But perhaps this is a case where the exception proves the rule. In a competitive society, uniformity is not a virtue. And it is especially dangerous when an exceptional product becomes the subject of inflationary exploitation. Just think of the more than 2,500 MBA programs that now exist. Regardless of their quality, they all take advantage of the highly positive image of the first MBA programs. The column of lemmings heads for the abyss. The problem that has developed in the last few decades from the spread of evaluation and accreditation for universities is in fact the danger of uniformity prescribed and implemented for quality assurance reasons in the higher educational sector in Europe. That would be the exact opposite of competition between universities as a key to improved performance and the opposite of a reform that—so we are told—is designed to replace input control for universities by output control with the aim of increasing the production of ideas and enhancing the quality of the university.

17.1 Retrospect and Point of Departure

It is not so long ago that grades—with the necessary reservations—were seen as a certain measure of student performance. A record of good grades over a longer period of time for the subjects tested has always had a certain currency, and a history of negative grades is definitely not an advantage. The fact that Thomas

E. Kappler (✉)
Department of Organization and Learning, Innsbruck University,
Elisabethstraße 12, 6020, Innsbruck, Austria
e-mail: ekkehard.kappler@uibk.ac.at

A. Altmann and B. Ebersberger (eds.), *Universities in Change*, Innovation, Technology, and Knowledge Management, DOI: 10.1007/978-1-4614-4590-6_17,

Mann was awarded a 'fail' in German and the eminent German surgeon Ferdinand Sauerbruch took home a disastrous school record for the fourth year does not disprove this point. But when people started to realize or at least suspect that grades and school examinations were a key factor in determining the students' futures, the picture began to change. While opportunities in life and the process of selection are based on grades, there is increased pressure, not only on the students in the schools and universities, but also on the teaching staff and faculty. As a father put it to a teacher he was on friendly terms with, 'It's got to be at least a 'B' for my girl in your subject!'—as if grades were something to be negotiated like a pay rise.

The new perception of educational opportunities and the general promotion of education ushered in the heyday of middle-class society. But the greater the awareness became the significance of education, the more the conventional grading system was eroded, with good grades becoming an inflationary product in many cases. Parents became 'trade unionists', representing their children's interests in the schools. And at times of big student populations, the same can be said of the universities. The hardliners continued to defend traditional standards, but not all faculty members are hardliners. And in the long term, a rearguard action is neither a sensible nor a creative strategy. That makes it increasingly difficult to interpret the grades awarded at university.

The rapid increase in student numbers naturally led to an increase in the number of examinations. That triggered several phenomena. Although many personnel managers claim that examination results are not decisive in the case of a first-time application, they are not irrelevant, either—a fact that has led not only to a race for good grades but also to certain bargaining scenarios and practices. Many an overworked university teacher would have found it difficult to maintain their standards over time. 'If students fail, I have even more of them begging for grades in my overcrowded office hours and even more candidates at the next session, which is already full to bursting!' As long as university teachers were not evaluated in any way themselves, they could do what they wanted. At least, that was a widespread public belief, and that belief was reinforced by the not infrequent cases of malpractice unduly generalized.

It is naturally good that university teachers should also be assessed. Normally, they have demonstrated their competence in their respective fields through their various works and publications and in the course of a long appointment process. But even today, the situation is different with regard to their didactic abilities; often enough they do not rise beyond amateur status. And most university examiners do not know the meaning of the term 'examination didactics', as the examinations they set show. In fact, many oral examinations are not far from mental assault. But examiner behavior is not evaluated. It is now general practice to try to assess the quality of the teaching with the help of anonymous questionnaires filled in by the students. That admittedly covers only one standpoint and one perspective, but is an important one. However, it rarely guarantees that the teachers will make sustainable changes in response to the results of the evaluation.

However, clear the need for teacher assessment may be, the methods applied come nowhere near to solving the problems inherent in them. In the big degree programs, the great majority of the teachers are suffering from acute overload in the teaching situation and are trying to make the best of it. Their professional ethos prevents them from kicking over the traces, but appeals to professional ethos are simply a veiled form of exploitation.

There is one negative observation that can be made, however, where inappropriate incentives cause individual examiners to adopt an approach that does not lead to enhanced levels of performance. Offering examiners a certain sum of money per candidate, for example, may cause them to take advantage of examinations to increase their total income. Of course, that is intended, and examinations with large number of candidates are handled as a result. On the other hand, some examiners have gone too far in their desire to generate extra income. When one examination suddenly becomes five without increasing the demands made of the examinees, the incentive is misguided.

In countries with a state university system in which a credit obtained at one university is automatically recognized at all the other state universities, a kind of 'exam tourism' sets in. Coaches are chartered to take students to a university where the examination in a certain subject is a 15-minute oral compared with the 4-hour written examination to be sat at the university the coaches come from. Word quickly spreads as to where the examinations in a given subject are easy and where they are difficult. The students returning to their home university from the easier examination with the better grades in their pockets not only contribute to the examiner's income (and to the economy via their travel expenditures); with their better grades they also increase their chances of receiving a grant to study abroad and other forms of financial assistance.

The increase in the number of students studying abroad—however positive that may be—has also created a number of problems. The differences between the various school and university systems in Europe and also in the USA and all the other countries raise questions of credit recognition, for which answers can be found but without solving the problems at the level of content. Students from aboard sometimes have language problems and sometimes are admired because they do not. That can influence the final grade in either case. Here again, there is a latitude that is difficult to quantify.

Evaluation in the field of research is not without its temptations, either, as in the case of the faculty that improved its results by placing those teachers who had not published anything in the assessment period on the payroll for non-academic staff.

One might say that these cases are excesses of the system, abusive interpretations of the rules, carelessness or even punishable offences, and that they do not offer a true picture of the university. In many cases that would be true, although one probably has to be an insider to see it. The public perception, however, is mainly dominated by reports about problems and poor results in the rankings, for example at the international level. It is this perception that leads to calls for uniform evaluation and accreditation systems. And the more populist the arguments, the greater their effectiveness at election time, in particular when combined with calls for more supervision and tighter controls—a fatal equation, which merely shows that, apart from an authoritarian attitude, the critics are ignorant of the true tasks and techniques of organizational control. The general public, for its part, is not normally capable of reflection on and criticism of the dubious nature—in terms of the theory of numbers and measurement theory—of such demands and the proposed standards of comparison. On the contrary, people tend to assume that the comparisons, based as they are on numbers, will be valid. That is why uniformity is desired or assumed in the context of evaluation. But numbers and figures are not objective. They, too, 'only' tell a story with a meaning that is far from being unambiguous and with vested interests that are not communicated.

In the view of many university teachers, state regulatory measures have proved incapable of guaranteeing the uniformity of the measurement standard, and that has led to calls for other control mechanisms. Attempts have been made to transfer the successful results achieved with the rules of the market economy to the public service sector, but the supposed autonomy that could have led to much greater variety among the universities was hijacked and restricted by the predefined evaluation criteria. Ultimately, that is understandable as state universities are still unable to generate the income needed to finance themselves; as in the past, they are dependent on a big budget provided by the state. If the universities were to charge the fees needed to cover their costs, open university admission would no longer be available to most of today's students, and a guaranteed contribution from the national budget would be essential. And university research could not be financed through student fees in any case. Nevertheless, we still hear the myth of the superior performance achieved by private universities that receive no money from the state. If we take a look at the performance of the universities around the world, we quickly see how unfounded this myth is—quite apart from the measurability myth.

A true story from the world of trade and industry and management consulting reveals similar problems of quantification. A German city is the location of the research center of an international corporation. The Executive Board decided to take a look at the performance of the research center and appointed a world-famous company of management consultants to perform an evaluation. According to the CEO, the consultants' oral report began as follows: 'I can only say with any precision what comes out of the research center every day at 5 p.m.—4,000 employees.' Ar a university can much probably be measured more easily than that: the essays and books produced by faculty, the hours of classes held, the graduates produced, the ratio of graduates to beginners, the students who switch programs, the dropouts, the actual and average length of study, the available places for work and reading relative to the number of students, the maximum occupancy of the lecture halls and classrooms, etc. More difficulty would be encountered with the number of patents registered, hours worked in secondary employment, work performed for the university, the quality of the teaching and examination work, etc. And real problems arise when people think they can measure the quality of scientific work and publications by classifying the journals in which they appear. The journals with the biggest circulations are the mainstream journals. But the mainstream is not normally the place for creativity, imagination, and innovation.

The dominant paradigm is first taken on board until there is no room left. Articles are expected to have ‘connectivity’. And a lack of ‘connectivity’ is often cited as the reason for rejecting a ‘deviant’ manuscript, without realizing that criticism is always directed at the object of its passion, whereas the mainstream can largely be satisfied through assimilation and comparatively boring texts. Thus, the peer review is always in danger of degenerating into a self-defense system for the establishment.

The buzzword of university reform in the 1980 and 1990s was output orientation. The aim was to measure what the universities produce and to measure efficiency, i.e., the relationship between input (e.g. budget) and output. And it soon becomes clear that measuring output is not meaningful if it is not related to input. At university, the input traditionally comprised the process of qualification as a scholar (doctorate and post-doctoral qualifications) and the appointment process, on the one hand, and the allocation of government funds on the other. Without reference to both the qualifications and the funding, the outcome is uncertain. As Wilhelm von Humboldt put it in 1810, ‘Among the professors there may be many who are good teachers but do not further science; that is perhaps only achieved by a few. But in order to find them, the others must be accepted, too’. This statement is still valid today. For a university that is mainly responsible for providing teaching it may even be sufficient, although the teachers really belong in school, i.e., where the pupils are (Humboldt 1982, p. 256).

At university we only find adults of various ages who together produce the university. That is not easy, but it would still be worth the attempt today. ‘We can achieve what is called thought when we think ourselves (…)’ (Heidegger 1992, p. 3). But also: ‘Only when we want what is in itself though-worthy do we have the power for thought’ (Heidegger 1992, p. 3).

That is the point of departure. The university as a loosely coupled system is of necessity a system in which its members are free, freer at least than many other salary earners. University teachers are not badly paid and for many years had tenure (and thus economic independence) and were on the whole free to make use of their time as they saw fit. For many observers, however, they produced too little. But that is a verdict that derives from a concept of closely coupled systems and clear causal chains. In a loosely coupled system with causal chains that are not always clear, and with complex, paradoxical, circular, and mutually dependent relationships, the output does not follow automatically from the input. That is the price to the paid for the chance and for the potential to generate innovation. Loosely coupled systems are more flexible, more adaptable than closely coupled ones, less risky, more imaginative, more creative. They permit a wide variety of potential to develop at the same time. As the positive effects of such opportunities for development can be widely dispersed in time and place, efficiency measurement based on closely coupled causal chains may generate false results for loosely coupled systems. Today’s ‘crazy guy’ may become a famous innovator the day after tomorrow and beyond.

According to Kant, the freedom of loose coupling is the key to the required critical discourse between what he called the lower faculties (especially philosophy) and the norm-setting role of the higher faculties (theology, law, medicine) (Kant 1968). In the eyes of Kant, the conflict of the faculties was not war but antagonism, i.e., a "conflict of two parties united in (their striving toward) one and the same final end (Concordia discors, discordia concors)" (Kant 1968, p. 35). This "Conflict of the Faculties" is a conflict on the basis of necessary change and difference. The uniformity of the norm setting must be overcome again and again in the interest of the required diversity of practical developments. And the "one and the same final end" is only uniform in this abstract formulation. What it means in concrete terms is itself a subject of scientific discourse and must always remain so. This requirement in no way clearly determines the modes of action, behavior, and decision making at the university and thus cannot define the input adequately either. In view of the multifaceted character of scientific enquiry and historical developments, the "one and the same final end" calls first of all for a leap of faith. That it can be abused cannot be denied. But if there is no leap of faith for the management of the university as a loosely coupled system, the development of the university's potential will be arrested by the nets of mistrustful evaluation. The fact that there has been exploitation of the freedom granted cannot be denied, either, as more than the above examples show. Such facts are quoted as arguments for extensive evaluation and accreditation processes, and also for other restrictive measures including the abolition of tenure (with a consequent increase in opportunism, because who will be so stubborn as to oppose the evaluation criteria if that could cost them their job?!). The argument is logical, but does that mean it is proven? Does the output (!) of the measures selected for evaluation and accreditation follow from the input involved?

The buzzword of university reform in the 1980s and 1990s was output orientation. The aim was to measure what the universities produce and also to measure efficiency, i.e., the relationship between input (e.g. budget) and output. But the measurands are not predefined and cannot be taken for granted. All forms of measurement are dependent on the calibration involved, i.e., on a system of created and defined quanta. Once the system has been established, it gradually loses the character of an artifact, and the convention that has been agreed becomes a truth. The trick of the rule is that it relegates its own genesis to oblivion.

"Much has to be done to render diverse phenomena countable quanta in the first place, namely an abstract from many specific qualities by establishing categories of similarity. Measurement is based on classification systems that ignore 'messential' differences and reduce complexity. Once accepted, such systems appear natural and incontestable (Bowker and Star 2000)." (Power 2004, p. 767).

In the case of the established measurands and ratios, their historical dimension is long since forgotten. We have no measure for innovation, for example. At best we could fall back on the difference compared with what existed before, but that guarantees neither a practicable process nor a meaningful result. Things new derive not infrequently from what has been overlooked, discarded, ignored, and defamed, from what is considered worthless, from waste and dirt (Groys 1992). Let us consult Michael Power again: "Today we regard qualities such as weight, hardness and temperature as obviously quantifiable because of the existence of trusted technologies for doing this. But there was a time when the ambition to measure heat was regarded as no more different in principle from measurement of virtue: '…if you can manage to think of measuring heat before the invention of the thermometer, then why should we presumptively exclude certitude, virtue and grace?' (Crosby 1997, p. 14).'(Power 2004, p. 768).

The consequences of this thinking are obvious enough. We do not measure things, nor do we represent the 'truth' or the 'facts', but rather we signify. We establish a relationship in a certain way. In doing so, we willy-nilly exclude other modes of presentation, which may naturally relate to other interests. To clarify this point, let us look at what Victor Burgin[1] has to say about the relationship between image and reality.

[The expression 'measurement', outside of a strictly technological application, may need some explanation. What I am proposing as the object of measurement is not restricted to measuring or other ratios, considered as a set of techniques (although, certainly, technique is to be accounted for within the theory); it is, rather, measuring considered as a practice of signification. By 'practice' here is meant work on specific materials, within a specific social and historical context, and for specific purposes. The emphasis on 'signification' derives from the fact that the primary feature of measuring, considered as omnipresence in everyday social life, is its contribution to the production and dissemination of meaning. To argue that the specificity of the object to be constituted in measurement theory is semiotic is not to restrict the theory to the categories of 'classic' semiotics. Although semiotics is necessary to the proposed theory, it is not (nor would it ever claim to be) sufficient to account for the complex articulations of the moments of institution, text, distribution and consumption of ratios, ledgers, calculations, balance sheets, management information systems, systems of knowledge management or balanced scorecards. Confronted as it is with such heterogeneity, it is clear that measurement theory must be 'inter-disciplinary'; there can, however, be no question of simply juxtaposing one pre-existing discipline with another.

For example, at the moment perhaps the least developed aspect of the emerging theory is the sociological component. Measuring is most commonly encountered in sociological texts as 'evidence', the sociologist operating with the common-sense intuition of measuring as a 'window on the university or other organizations'. This type of sociological encounter with measuring is quite simply irrelevant to the project of measurement theory, which must take into account the determinations exerted by the means of representation upon that which is represented. More pertinent is the sociological description of managerial corporations and institutions. Here again, however, the criterion of relevance applies: a description of, say, the hierarchical structures of command governing the accountants in the field

[1] The basic source for the section between [] is the article 'Thinking Photography' (Burgin 1982)—with friendly agreement to any use of his paper by Victor Burgin to whom I have to say many thanks. I transformed his article in a radical interdisciplinary change from the conceptualization of representation by photography to representation by measuring. Of course, I am responsible for any misunderstandings and misinterpretations.

would be less relevant to the theory than a description of the discourses by which the institution inducts its functionaries, irrespective of rank, into a common belief system, constituting them as 'measuring people'. Certainly, we may expect structures of decision-making to be imbricated within beliefs, but it is the beliefs which are the 'sharp end' of that which informs the social effects of measuring. (Nor is this to suggest that accountants' beliefs are simply 'communicated' to their audiences.)

Measuring theory is not exempt from the call made upon any theory to identify observable systematic regularities in its object which will support general propositions about the object. This is already to establish that theory may be taught, and certainly the elaboration of measuring theory constitutes an intervention, at least in principle, in the field of education. In speaking of education in measuring we should distinguish between two quite different pedagogic practices. In the first, a vocational training is given for some particular staff of industry and/or commerce—as when a school trains people to become accountants or managers. In this type of course academic studies will tend to be pragmatic—their content being determined by its practical bearing on the specific form of measuring being taught. It is teaching and training conventions. In the second type of course no particular vocational training is imposed; the student is asked, rather, to consider measuring in its totality as a general cultural phenomenon, and to develop his or her own ideas as to what direction to pursue. Academic studies in the context of this latter type of course are presented as heuristic—aiming to provide the student with a wide range of facts, and a number of critical tools, in the interests of developing an informed capacity for independent thought. Contrary to their declared intent, the majority of those courses whose concern is with measuring as art belong in the first category rather than the second. They offer a vocational training for that staffs of industry, commerce and educational institutions whose products are plans, ratios, budgets, objectives, calculations. The academic content of such courses tends overwhelmingly to take the form of an uncritical initiation into the dominant beliefs and values prevailing in the economic institution as a whole or in the economy of the institutions as a whole. On such courses 'criticism' and 'history' stand in place of a theory that is reconfirming practice.

Measuring criticism, as it is most commonly practiced, is evaluative and normative. In its most characteristic form it consists of an account of the personal thoughts and feelings of the critic in confronting the work of an accountant or planner or controller or evaluator or accreditator, with the aim of persuading the reader to share these thoughts and feelings. Free reference is made to the biography, psychology and character of the person in question, and even to the critic him/herself. The 'arguments' advanced in criticism are rarely arguments, properly speaking, but rather assertions of opinions and assumptions paraded as if their authority was unquestionable. The dominant discourse of such criticism is an uneasy and contradictory amalgam of Romantic, Realist and Modernist aesthetic theories. The 'history of measuring' predominantly supports such criticism in that it is produced within the same ideological framework. In such 'history' the unargued conventional assumptions to be found in 'criticism' are projected into the past from whence they are reflected inverted in status—no longer mere assumptions, they have become the indisputable 'facts' of history.

I have described the dominant mode of history and criticism of measuring, in which the main concern is for reputations and objects, and in which the objects inherit the reputations to become commodities: a history and criticism to suit the saleroom. Neither history nor criticism is, a priori, committed to this course, and there are indications which follow of alternative approaches to history and criticism. Such alternative approaches reject the tendency to confine discussion of measuring to some narrowly technicist and/or aesthetic realm of ideas; they aim, rather, to understand measuring not only as a practice in its own right but also in its relation to society as a whole. This holistic project has traditionally been that of Marxist cultural theory, which of late has become increasingly engaged with precisely that topic of the production of meaning with which I began.]

In the above quotation [between brackets], the term 'measuring' can easily be replaced by the phrase 'evaluation and accreditation'. To pursue this line of thought further and to see how it can be applied to the question of the extent to which uniformity can be a problem in the context of evaluation and accreditation and how the problem might be addressed, we first need to consider what evaluation and accreditation are.

17.2 Evaluation and Accreditation

There is evaluation and evaluation, and there is accreditation and accreditation. These measures can be seen as both norm-setting in Kant's meaning of the term and also as examples of the antagonism he considers necessary, i.e., the process of setting and criticizing norms together. The recent evaluation debate in particular has shown what that means in concrete terms and that it has practical consequences. The central points of that development are interconnected with the term 'fourth generation evaluation'.[2]

Guba and Lincoln analyze three main problems of the first three generations of evaluation: 'Managerialism', 'Monism of', and 'Cartesianism' (Guba and Lincoln 1989, p. 31–32 and 90). When managers believe to have the right values and are privileged decision makers while other people do not know what to do, we talk about *Managerialism*. Concerning *Monism of Values* 'we would argue that conventional science is as a result a force for disenfranchisement and disempowerment, for maintenance of the status quo (Guba and Lincoln 1989, p. 125).' The attitude of *Cartesianism* believes in a world organized on fundamental principles scientists are able to decode. From a constructivist perspective these positivistic assumptions are far too strong and restrictive. The constructivist approach follows

---

[2] For more details on the following, see also Habersam (1996); and especially Guba and Lincoln (1989).

weaker assumption, a hermeneutic approach, and dialectical dialogs: 'Meaning is constituted in use' (Hedlin 1996)—e.g. in using measures, ratios, indices and standards to create the governable person (Miller and O'Leary 1987). Whenever we talk about evaluating, quality-defining, performance measuring or auditing, we talk about conventions, not truths. In practice, we are confronted with complex problems, competing interests, and the necessity for judgment. We try to resolve problems emerging from practical situations by impersonal, objective, theoretically generalized prescriptions of behavior. But this strategy has consequences. Michael Power's book on the 'The Audit Society' with the subtle subtitle 'Rituals of Verification'[3] shows the ambiguity of this attempt. Translated into German it would mean 'Die geprüfte Gesellschaft'. At first glance, the word 'geprüfte' means 'audited'. But 'geprüfte' is also a word of the Old Testament which means 'the ordeal sent by God.' Is auditing and evaluation one of the seven plagues, sent—not by god but—by enlightenment and its technocratic success during the last three centuries?

Guba and Lincoln take Robert Stake's 'stakeholder approach' to create a *responsive* evaluation procedure conscious of a concrete situation to be handled, its micro- and macro-political circumstances, and the inherently value-laden need for justifications (e.g., why to spent money on higher education).

'Responsive evaluation will be particularly useful (…) when the staff needs help in monitoring the program, when no one is sure what problem will arise (…), when audiences want an understanding of a program's activities, its strengths and shortcomings, and when the evaluator feels that it is his responsibility to provide a vicarious experience (Stake 1983/1973, p. 303).'

The pragmatic argument for *stakeholder involvement* seems to be the following: If stakeholders are not allowed to participate in this process, there is no enough support and acceptance for a solution. Evaluation becomes an interactive process that never ends.

'Responsive evaluation has four phases, which may be reiterated and may overlap. In the first phase stakeholders are identified and are solicited for those claims, concerns, and issues that they may wish to introduce. In the second phase, the claims, concerns, and issues raised by each stakeholder group are introduced to all other groups for comment, refutation, agreement, or whatever reaction may please them. In this phase many of the original claims, concerns, and issues will be resolved. In the third phase, those claims, concerns, and issues that have *not* been resolved become the advance organizers for information collection by the evaluator. … *The information may be quantitative or qualitative.* (…)In the fourth phase, negotiation among stake holding groups, under the guidance of the evaluator and utilizing the evaluative information that has been collected, takes place in an effort to research consensus on each disputed item. Not all such items will be resolved; those that remain become the core for the next evaluation that may be

[3] Cf. Power (1997). In a similar way Hansson (2006), refers to the consequences of an 'evaluation society', e.g. concerning social control at universities.

undertaken when time, resources, and interest permit (Guba and Lincoln 1989, p. 42).‘

Consensus is neither result nor norm, but an *option*. Not all conflicts can be finished. But in most cases they can be handled in a confidential manner if consensus is not a norm but an option. It is also important to understand that this does not imply a container view of information but an emergent view.[4] Information is produced by the selectivity of the individual collection processes and the judgment of users. For this reason, the ‘Fourth Generation Evaluation’ is not only an alternative approach within the field of evaluative practices but also within the field of quality assessment , measuring/controlling, or even performance management practices.[5]

Putting it all together, Guba and Lincoln stress seven characteristics in their ‘Fourth Generation Evaluation’ (Guba and Lincoln 1989, p. 252–256):

1. The socio-political process of, if you want to extend the perspective, ‘assessing quality’, ‘evaluation’, ‘performance measurement and management’ is infiltrated and framed by culture, politics, and self-interest.
2. It is a joint collaborative process, which results sometimes in consensus, and sometimes in an agreement to disagree.
3. Each member of this process serves as both learner and teacher. The role of the evaluator is not to be the boss of the setting. S/He is willing to be taught by all other stakeholders: ‘(...) undoubtedly a new species in the ecosystem’ (Guba and Lincoln 1989, p. 254).
4. The process is unpredictable and emergent. ‘Every step, therefore, is contingent on the previous steps and can be unfolded only serially’ (Guba and Lincoln 1989, p. 255). Design, setting, methods etc., which can be described only retrospectively are not really descriptive but again pieces of a new construction.
5. Not only the process is unpredictable in itself but the outcomes as well. They are not determined by input but by negotiation. ‘It is not less politics in assessing quality that is needed but a finer-grained understanding of the values that underlie the various political and policy positions’ (Guba and Lincoln 1989, p. 255).
6. This process is not producing a picture of the reality, but a new reality; not findings, but literal creations of all participants.

Within this process all the results, conclusions, and recommendations are joint results, conclusions, and recommendations—or nothing. The tragedy is that in everyday life the details of evaluated organizations, their organizational processes are not understood by many politicians and administrators in many universities. That there is a dominant use of cost accounting and control is the attempt to reduce

---

[4] For some impressive cases cf. Jönsson (1996).

[5] There is no fundamental difference between these approaches and their ‘internal debates’ on how to measure and to manage organizations; see Habersam 1997, referring to ‘controlling’ (i.e. the German term for the Anglo-Saxon term measuring and control), Bohni and Ejler (2008), referring to performance management.

the confusion about quality by tools that are a myth, too. Unfortunately, the creative potential of the members of universities is never really developed and put into action. The prevalence of cost accounting and of vulgar interpretations of business administration leads to bureaucratic administration of quantities as the (one and only) indicators for quality (Boyle 2001).[6]

Undoubtedly, there is a necessity of performance measurement and management in and for universities. But a machine model of the university decreases social competence and motivation. It does not lead to insights into the fabric of society. The arguments concerning the conventional and ritual character of counting and calculating, and its built-in danger, are fundamental. Is there a new kind of *Taylorism* coming back called *Evaluationism*? Will mere cost accounting and financial reporting produce very adapted graduates and more or less conventional research? To define quality quantitatively is not enough. It ignores the aspects of quality as a social construction and process of negotiations. For nearly a thousand years the quality of universities has had a polyphonic and recursive character, but this not guaranteed to last.[7]

Consequently, Guba and Lincoln try to avoid the disadvantages of a bureaucratic model. "The world is no longer seen as a closed system operating by immutable laws, which, once discovered, lay an inescapable mandate for behavior on us all" (Guba and Lincoln 1989, p. 256). From my point of view, to overcome the machine model of a university is to be done every day from scratch, because "experts" or "science" are indispensable parts of our society. When we can no longer hide ourselves behind their cloaks, the consequence is that "(...) accountability yields to shared responsibility" (Guba and Lincoln 1989, p. 256). But how are professors, administrators or students held accountable for the state our universities are in? "Much so-called evaluation (quality assessment, performance measurement and management; E.K.) is directed to making this accountability manifest (...)" (Guba and Lincoln 1989, p. 257). Europe-wide testing programs and rankings used to blame teachers, students, or other stakeholders are examples of what happens when evaluative processes in favor of accountability do not obviate the exploitation of the evaluated institutions and their members. "Conventional evaluators do virtually nothing to improve either knowledge or sophistication for any except a few privileged stakeholder groups, mainly clients and sponsors. But fourth generation evaluation shares knowledge and works at improvement of sophistication for all. (...) It is an educative experience for all"

---

[6] It is not by chance that the first cost accounting for universities was implemented by the "Technische Universität München" in Germany. Technicians are really good cost accountants but often lack social competence. And the present economic crisis reveals the illusions strongly connected to cost accounting and balance sheets in terms of bankruptcy and the fraudulences of formerly famous corporations and trusted banks.

[7] Even institutions with a longstanding polyphonic history may introduce evaluation programs "(...) strongly inspired by ISO 9000:2000 standards" (Darchini et al. 2006, p. 15), as the case of the University of Bologna shows.

(Guba and Lincoln 1989, p. 258). Quality and the process of studying means evaluating adults in interaction.

The ideas of Guba and Lincoln, presented more than 20 years ago, lead to a new understanding of the role of evaluators responsible for assessing quality in higher education: Facilitator, story teller and listener, illuminator, mediator are more a political role, although s/he must have technical skills of conventional evaluators. The controller becomes a collaborator, supporting a process of emancipation, not of an investigation. Her/his responsibility is to set the stage for this process, to sharpen the awareness of "reality", to act as change agent and to reconstruct the existing reality constructions. Reflecting the changing nature of "reality", these changes in the role-model of evaluators seem to be even more necessary than before.

"In a changing world, an age of 'liquid modernity' as it has been called (Baumann 2000), the design of a curriculum invokes two kinds of responsibilities. First there are the tacit responsibilities of the students. Should the curriculum be developing among students responsibilities toward (a) a discipline and its standards; (b) the world of work; (c) the wider society; (d) the student her- or himself? It may be said that it is all of those, but then large and possibly intractable problems arise. (…) The second set of responsibilities falls on the curriculum designers themselves. How do lecturers and others in universities who find themselves in positions of responsibility towards curricula understand those responsibilities?" (Barnett and Coate 2005, p. 43).

17.3 Conclusion

In the above discussion, the focus is on evaluation. If no explicit mention is made of accreditation that is primarily because the considerations of the theory of numbers and measurement theory apply in equal measure to accreditation. The motives for the introduction of accreditation processes are also comparable with the case of evaluation. Appointment processes are similar, too. At all events, deconstruction of the conditions and processes involved would be appealing, bordering in some cases on indiscretion perhaps.

"Although all this suggests that we should regard the spirit of performance measurement not as monolithic, but rather as fractured, incomplete and evolving, this spirit is also powerful. Specific measurement systems may be defective and fail, but they also constantly reproduce and reinvent an institutional demand for numbers. Political power can be understood as the ability to make even controversial counting and measurement systems appear natural and unavoidable, preventing the widespread institutionalization of distrust in numbers and supporting a variety of schemes for monitoring and control" (Power 2004, p. 769).

Although controversial and deserving of criticism, evaluation, and accreditation processes are now well established. If we are not willing to abolish them in response to their ambiguity and uncertainty (because it is no longer possible), we have to learn to deal with the complexity and uncertainty of such processes. Then we will find that, when implemented correctly, they deliver useful results. "Performance measurement systems are both contingent and powerful, of varying precision, and are simultaneously democratic and tyrannical as forms of 'normalized transparency'" (Power 2004, p. 780).

Tendencies like uniformity and the excessive reduction of complexity, the signification of certain content orientations, and spoon-feeding programs cannot be ruled out and are indeed to be feared where evaluation and accreditation are handled bureaucratically. Where, in the context of "normalized transparency", norm setting gains the upper hand as normalization, evaluation cannot work. The fact that comparison is of great importance for the further development of the institutions assessed in the framework of evaluation and accreditation programs is almost self-evident. But that must not be permitted to lead to uniformity. The ideas of Guba and Lincoln could counter that with an enlightened process based on discourse.

To apply that process, the autonomy of the evaluated systems must first of all be restored. A system that cannot decide on its own reactions will not change in response to evaluation, either. Since, in a competitive system, diversity—the diversity of ideas—is a prerequisite for the adaptability of the system, and evaluation and related incentive and accreditation systems lead to a reduction of complexity, variety, imagination, creativity, and other strategic potentials, the initial response is likely to be a proposal to abolish evaluation. And that proposal is often voiced. But the response is misguided. Now that they are the fashion, evaluation and rankings will continue to exist and spread. Exact measuring processes deliver punctual trains and flights. The hope of being able to make comparisons and thus find superior yardsticks for our decisions encourages us to use similar processes to evaluate organizations and social relationships. The fact that such an approach can be inadequate will not eradicate the desire to measure and compare. Nor will the question whether the benefits are greater than the costs. And since the decisive factor is always who is doing the measuring, we have to decide how to respond. Who asks about the benefits, benefits for whom, and costs to be borne by whom? What benefits or costs are is not inherent in the measuring process. "It reflects the power and robustness of values other than an unabated need for precision and control" (Power 2004, p. 780).

The increase in evaluation methods and the differences in the results and conclusions are not just cause for criticism; they are there to be exploited. One-off and/or one-sided measurements cannot lead to meaningful conclusions. Conclusions about organizations must be based on a plurality of measurements with different evaluation and accreditation processes. That corresponds—albeit not at the same level of precision—to the techniques of surveying or triangulation. Where evaluation is seen as a complex context-based system while the organizational relationships that constitute the university are treated as multicontextual, the number of evaluations per organization or situation to be assessed must be increased. The differences that then arise make it possible to better recognize the facets and nuances in the overall system evaluated and to possibly process them further in terms of fourth generation evaluation as proposed by Guba and Lincoln. Positioning the research output of a faculty on the basis of just one list of relevant journals and their weightings as proposed by the mainstream representatives of the discipline (Kappler 2009) would not then satisfy the requirements of a serious evaluation process. Abstractly derived comparability and standardization deny the complexity of individual and social relations, which could be handled through a discursive investigation of the wide range of evaluation processes and findings.

It is astonishing to find similar thoughts in the works of Wilhelm von Humboldt. What the founder of the modern university had to say on the subject of the state still applies today, both with regard to the state and with regard to evaluation and accreditation. Of course, the university does not have to be reduced primarily to teaching. It is therefore appropriate to finish with a closer look at Humboldt's ideas.

"What we call (…) higher scientific institutions are, released of all form within the state, nothing other that the spiritual lives of people guided through external leisure or inner striving to science and research. As such, the one ponders alone and collects, another connects with men of the same age, a third gathers a circle of disciples around himself. To this picture the state (or evaluation through diversity—E.K.) must remain true where these undetermined and, as it were, fortuitous activities are to be given more solid form. The state must aim:

1. to preserve this activity in its liveliest and strongest form;
2. to fully and clearly maintain the distinction between the institution of higher education and school.

The state must always be aware of the fact that it does not and cannot really-achieve this aim itself, that in fact it is a hindrance whenever it interferes, that the whole thing works infinitely better without it, and that the facts are really only as follows:

- that, since all disseminated knowledge must be provided with external form and resources in a positive society, the state has a duty to provide them for the works of science;
- that not only the way in which form and resources are provided can be detrimental to the essence of the matter; the very fact that it provide form and resources for something quite alien must of necessity also have negative effects and pull the spirit down from the heights to the plains of material reality;
- and that the state must therefore always keep the inner being in mind to make good what it, albeit unintentionally, has spoilt or hindered.

Under these assumptions it is easy to see that, with regard to the inner organization of the institutions of higher education, it is all-important to respect the principle that science is something that has not yet been entirely found and can never be entirely found and to seek it unremittingly as such" (Humboldt 1982, p. 256–257, (1810) (italics by E. K.)).

The picture of the university that Humboldt had in mind was doubtless not that of today's overcrowded universities. To that extent, we have to make concessions with regard to his ideal picture of university programs and their evaluation. But that does not apply to his view of science as an object of search. In both cases, evaluation can help or it can be too much of a good thing. Its meaning can only unfold in concrete action.

Bibliography

Barnett R, Coate K (2005) Engaging the Curriculum in higher education. SRHE and Open University Press, Maidenhead
Baumann Z (2000) Liquid modernity. Polity, Cambridge
Bohni NS, Ejler N (2008) Improving performance? Exploring the complementarities between evaluation and performance management. Evaluation 14(2):171–192
Bowker G, Star SL (2000) Sorting things out: classification and its consequences. MA, Cambridge
Boyle D (2001) The tyranny of numbers: why counting can't make us happy. HarperCollins Publishers, London
Burgin V (ed) (1982) Thinking photography. Macmillan, London, pp 1–14
Crosby AW (1997) The measure of reality: Quantification and western society. Cambridge University, Cambridge, pp 1250–1600
Darchini D, Giannini S, Gola M (2006) Quality assurance and evaluation of programmes at the University of Bologna. In: Orsingher Ch (ed) Assessing quality in european higher education Institutions. Dissemination, Methods and Procedures. Heidelberg, pp 5–22
Groys B (1992) Über das Neue. Versuch einer Kulturökonomie, München/Wien
Guba EG, Lincoln YS (1989) Fourth generation evaluation. Sage, London
Habersam M (1997) Controlling als evaluation. Potentiale eines Perspektivenwechsels, München/ Mering
Hansson F (2006) Organizational use of evaluations. Evaluation 12(2):159–178
Hedlin P (1996) Accounting investigations. Doc. Thesis, Stockholm
Heidegger M (1992) Was heißt Denken? Stuttgart (originally Tübingen 1984)
Humboldt Wv (1982) Über die innere und äußere Organisation der Höheren wissenschaftlichen Anstalten in Berlin. In: ders.: Werke, Band 4; Schriften zur Politik und zum Bildungswesen. 3. Aufl. Stuttgart, pp 255–266 (originally 1810)
Jönsson S (1996) Accounting for improvement. Elsevier Science, Oxford
Kant I (1968) Der Streit der Fakultäten. In Kants Werke, Akademie-Textausgabe, Band VII, Berlin, pp 1–116 (originally: 1798)
Kappler E (2009) Die List der Listen. Controller Magazin, Heft 1, pp 32–35
Miller P, O'Leary T (1987) Accounting and the construction of the governable person. Acc Organ Soc 12(3):236–265
Power M (2004) Counting, control and calculation: reflections on measuring and management. Human Relat 57(6):765–781
Power M (1997) The audit society: rituals of verification. Oxford University Press, Oxford
Stake RE (1983) Program evaluation, particularly responsive evaluation. In: Madaus GF, Scriven MS, Stufflebeam DL (eds) Evaluation models. View points on education and human services evaluation. Kluwer-Nijhoff, Boston, pp 287–310

Part IV
Contributing to Economic and Social Development

Chapter 18
Higher Education Institutions and Regional Development

Bernd Ebersberger, Sverre J. Herstad and Andreas Altmann

18.1 Introduction

Growth theories generally acknowledge that innovation and knowledge generating activities play a crucial role in determining the growth dynamics and their trajectories in national and regional economies (Solow 1956; Temple 1999; Romer 1990). Innovation—the development of new processes, products, and organizational structures, which are both technologically feasible and commercially successful—is created through the continuous interaction between firms, research institutes, government agencies, financing organizations, and, what is particularly important here, higher education organizations. The exchange of knowledge, human and financial capital, and other resources while enabling innovation embeds the actors in a dense network of interactions at the national, local, and, most of all, at the regional level. This is because regions serve to accumulate and diffuse information and knowledge more intensively through social network formation and labor market mobility, than what is the case at national and international levels (Agrawal et al. 2006; Malmberg and Power 2005; Maurseth and Verspagen 2002). It has been shown that the variety of actors within a region is a strong determinant of innovativeness. This variety is fostered by entrepreneurship.

B. Ebersberger (✉) · A. Altmann
MCI Management Center Innsbruck—The Entrepreneurial School,
Universitätsstrasse 15, 6020 Innsbruck, Austria
e-mail: bernd.ebersberger@mci.edu

A. Altmann
e-mail: andreas.altmann@mci.edu

S. J. Herstad
Norwegian Institute for Studies in Innovation, Research and
Education, Wergelandsveien 7, 0167 Oslo, Norway
e-mail: sverre.herstad@nifu.no

A. Altmann and B. Ebersberger (eds.), *Universities in Change*, Innovation, Technology, and Knowledge Management, DOI: 10.1007/978-1-4614-4590-6_18,

Consequently, the region is increasingly seen as the locus of innovation. Against this background it is remarkable that the discussion and analysis of innovation policy still predominantly focus on national measures (Fritsch and Stephan 2005). This entails the risk of neglecting the need for contextualization of policies according to those specific institutional, technological, and industrial preconditions in a region that are already in place. These conditions often simultaneously represent the main barriers to and opportunities for entrepreneurship, diversification, and growth (Asheim et al. 2007; Karlsen et al. 2011).

The overall target of this contribution is to tie together three rather independent strands of the literature linking regional development, entrepreneurship and higher education. The discussions on regional innovation systems, variety, and specialization, and open innovation will be connected to form a theoretical—and empirically tested—basis, upon which policies for regional entrepreneurship and development can be built. In particular, the discussion highlights the preconditions for entrepreneurship, the role of the entrepreneur, and the role of regional higher education institutions in supporting entrepreneurship.

18.2 Three Points of Departure: Setting the Stage

The discussion here builds on an evolutionary economic tradition, where learning, knowledge, competencies, and their cumulative development are accepted concepts on the micro and firm level as well as on the regional and national level to analyze the interactive innovation activities. Regional innovation systems refer to the interplay between regional industrial structure and a set of knowledge development institutions and mechanisms, which include regional labor markets and higher education institutions. Specialization and variety within this industrial structure plays a crucial role not only in determining the exposure of regions toward cyclical fluctuations and structural disruptions, but also in shaping the opportunity space for future development. If one focuses exclusively on the meta-level argumentation about regions and their characteristics such as specialization and variety, one might overlook that it is individual, micro actors—driven by their individual objectives and strategies—who jointly and interactively determine the emergent properties of a region. Hence, the third point of departure relates to open innovation as a strategic option for interactive knowledge development and exploitation at the firm level.

18.2.1 Regional Innovation Systems

Part and parcel of the contemporary economic landscape is the shift, which has occurred from innovation relying primarily on the internal knowledge bases of firms to innovation becoming embedded in distributed knowledge networks. The concept of innovation systems builds on the idea that linkages, collaboration, and networks composed of a wide variety of actors are crucial for understanding the creation and diffusion of innovations (Edquist 1997). Based on the demarcation between elements that constitute the system and elements that do not, the literature distinguishes between national systems (Lundvall 1992; Nelson 1993; Freeman 1987), sectoral systems (Malerba 2002), technological systems (Carlsson 1995; Carlsson and Stankiewitz 1995; Callon 1992), and regional systems of innovation (Cooke et al. 1997).

Perhaps somewhat paradoxically, the shift toward distributed knowledge networks increases the role of the region as the locus of innovation (Doloreux et al. 2004). This is because regions are characterized by cultural and institutional proximity conducive to trustful—and more flexible forms of—interaction and collaboration. Therefore, regions may serve as a venue for strong intentional and unintentional diffusion of information and knowledge, which does not travel well on far distances. In essence, the region may serve as a containing social structure around the knowledge development processes of individual firms. Regional actors thus accumulate and distribute information and knowledge externalities from these firms. From this follows the formation of territorially embedded knowledge bases, upon which creativity and knowledge creation activities may draw (Rondé and Hussler 2005; Asheim and Isaksen 1997; Maskell and Malmberg 1999).

Also, Porter argues that competitive advantage is generated by localized capabilities, competencies, and interaction structures at the regional level (Porter 1998), and by resources, which are not easy to imitate by distant competitors. The concept of regional innovation systems has been developed to understand how these processes may be better influenced and channeled by means of public policy (Maskell and Malmberg 1999) and the active constructing of knowledge development and diffusion mechanisms which contribute novelty and speed up the process of reconfiguration and exploration.

The concept of regional innovation systems derives its theoretical, empirical, and policy importance from the fact that it stresses the mutual interplay of heterogeneous actors in the innovation process such as funding agencies, policy makers, regulations and standards, financial intermediaries, and last but not least educational institutions.

18.2.2 Technological Specialization and Variety

Direct collaborative linkages and indirect linkages of geographically bounded contexts create localized spillovers, which in turn may reinforce technological development paths and further strengthen collaborative linkages. Combined, this leads to regionally distinct profiles of capabilities and competencies (Storper 1997). Localized externalities and the 'local information ecology' (Gertler 2003) nurtured by proximity create a milieu where the odds are better for individual actors to pick up information, which eventually may turn out to be useful for creating value (Malmberg and Maskell 2002). This includes entrepreneurial opportunities, which can be identified and harnessed at the intersection of existing firms' competencies (Acs et al. 2009). On the other hand, the interdependencies between infrastructure, historical investment, and the cumulativeness of knowledge generation might lead to local lock-ins, resulting in a strong persistence of specialization patterns.

Eventually, the creation of innovation is not a target in itself (Howells 2005). Rather it is the economic growth dynamics associated with the knowledge-based competitiveness of a region, which drives policy interest in regional systems and increases attention toward their characteristics (Fritsch and Stephan 2005). Yet, knowledge has either been interpreted as exogenous to development and economic growth (Solow 1956), or it has been conceptualized as a one-dimensional quantity (Temple 1999; Romer 1990). Only in the Schumpeterian or evolutionary perspective of economic growth variety and heterogeneity of actors, technologies and knowledge have been discussed (Pyka et al. 2000; Cantner et al. 2008; Frenken et al. 2007). Recently, the traditional emphasis on R&D spillovers as sources of growth has merged with approaches focusing on how the composition rather than R&D intensity of regional industries determine growth trajectories, and rejuvenate the interest in place-specific agglomeration economies (Beaudry and Schiffauerova 2009; Frenken et al. 2007; Jacobs 1969).

The composition of the regional economy can be characterized on the basis of whether the industries in the regional economy are related or not. Related variety refers to the variety of knowledge bases, competencies, or technologies, which in combination form the basis for the innovation processes of regions. Related variety is based on the concept of Jacob's externalities (Jacobs 1969). It has to be recognized that variety only provides the basis for novelty to the extent that cognitive distances between competence bases are not excessively large (Nooteboom 2000). Related variety influences the growth trajectories of regions by supplying complementary knowledge bases, which can be combined and re-combined by existing firms, and through new firm formation. It offers a broader search space for solutions to given problems. It also offers a broader and less exhaustible search space for the application of given technologies and knowledge. Frenken et al. (2007) found that related variety indeed exerts a positive effect on employment in a region. Ebersberger and Becke (2010) illustrate how related variety can be conceptualized differently when using publicly available patent data.

On the contrary, unrelated variety is a variety generated by different industrial sectors in a region, which are not related through a common knowledge base. Unrelated variety generates portfolio effects and immunizes the regional economy vis-a-vis exogenous shocks, but comes with the cost that cognitive distance creates friction on the diffusion and reuse of knowledge. Unrelated variety exerts negative effects on unemployment (Frenken et al. 2007). Last, the similiarity of actors associated with Marshallian (Marshall 1920) industrial districts combines the risk of external shocks with the disadvantages of lock-into narrow specialization paths and opportunity spaces.

Specialization and variety within a region are both the cause and effects of certain paths of development, where rejuvenating developments rather originate from related variety than they do from unrelated variety. Yet, the latter ensures more stability in times of fluctuations and instability. The former however, requires a certain degree of heterogeneity within the economy, where—as a condition—the knowledge bases are not too distinct to allow for certain overlap, linkage, and cross-fertilization. However, it is not given in advance which sectors and knowledge bases are potentially related in the sense that they can develop novelty at their intersections eventually do so. The regional innovation system enters this equation as an additional, constructed bridging mechanism, which enables this relatedness to be explored on a more broad basis.

18.2.3 Open Innovation

Turning to the strategic approach of corporate actors it has recently been claimed that corporate innovation is approaching a new era of openness (Chesbrough 2003, 2005). An era of purposeful corporate strategies through which the closed investments in intramural R&D and the hermetically capsulated in-house development are augmented or even substituted (Lazonick 2006, 2007) by extensive use of external knowledge and information sourcing and external pathways to commercialization. Openness of the innovation process increases innovation performance (Herstad et al. 2008) by opening up external interfaces and linking to a universe of new partners and tapping into diverse knowledge and information sources (Ebersberger and Herstad 2011; Laursen and Salter 2006). Corporate entrepreneurship is one of the crucial features characterizing open innovation approaches. Although some claim that these trends are leading to a 'flattened' distribution of productive competencies across actors and space (Friedman 2005; Chesbrough 2003), systematic empirical evidence clearly reveals that they are associated with a process of divergence in growth rates and technological development path. This favors those regions with the most well-functioning accumulation and diffusion mechanisms (Florida 2005; Simmie 2003, 2004) Yet, this in turn means that numerous regional environments are 'out there', outside ones own context of location, full of specialized ideas and knowledge ready to be utilized by those who master the trade of open innovation processes which extend across space as a result of globalization (UNCTAD 2005; Cooke 2005, 2007; Asheim 2005; Bathelt et al. 2004).

Open innovation strategies teach us three lessons. First, open innovation emphasizes the value of heterogeneous information outside the company boundaries. Second, this knowledge should be sought out on an international scale rather than only locally or within national economies. Third, development and the following up of ideas are not necessarily bound to fall into given walls of established organizations. Taking ideas beyond the organizational boundaries is part and parcel of successfully exploring new ideas and insights. This holds both for the corporate world as well as for the science sector. In addition to these structured processes of external commercialization (Lichtenthaler and Ernst 2007), the process also has external effects (Lazaric et al. 2008; Morrison 2008; Owen-Smith and Powell 2004). Entrepreneurship is the key activity within the realm of open innovation to create new ventures based on ideas developed in established organizations, and made available through commercialization efforts or as externalities. It is a key factor in determining the regional absorptive capacity (Carlsson and Eliasson 2002).

18.3 Two Insights: As the Analysis

The three different views on regions, regional systems of innovation, and actors 'strategies arrive at two insights' which stress the importance of heterogeneity and entrepreneurship.

First, the concept of regional systems of innovation puts a strong focus on the contribution of different sets of actors, which—in the light of related variety—ideally should develop different but complementary knowledge assets linked at the regional level by means of collaboration, by labor market mobility, by personal networks, and not least by knowledge development and diffusion institutions. Everything else being equal, higher survival rates of heterogeneous actors increases the diversity in an economy. As argued theoretically and found empirically, increased diversity is linked to an increase in innovativeness (Frenken et al. 2007; van Den Bergh 2008; Woerter 2009). Also, from an individual actor's point of view taping into the diversity of an external pool of knowledge is beneficial for the innovation process (Ebersberger and Herstad 2011; Laursen and Salter 2006). Yet, the region may offer too small a pool and—through historical development—too restricted a set of resources to supply the diversity of knowledge and ideas sought. International sources will have to be utilized in this case (Bathelt et al. 2004). When individual firms engage in such external information or knowledge sourcing, by means of spillover effects they may contribute to enriching the regional competence base further (Graf 2010). As the potential in a regions' competence base is rarely fully explored and exploited by existing firms, entrepreneurship is a key component to the process of identifying and harnessing its social value.

Second, entrepreneurship is also crucial for determining its future social value. Competitive processes inevitably lead to the exit of firms, which is generally regarded as a variety destroying and heterogeneity reducing selection process (Boschma and Sotarauta 2005). Creating new variety or reducing exit is required for maintaining a sufficient level of heterogeneity. Entrepreneurship is one of the pathways to increase heterogeneity or to—at least—maintain its current level. If entrepreneurship is thought of being the activity of starting up a new venture, then entrepreneurship clearly counterbalances the reduction of heterogeneity caused by exit. If entrepreneurship is conceptualized as good and successful leadership and management practice in established organizations contributing to innovation and to the revitalization of the organization, then it reduces exit (Cefis and Marsili 2005; Buddelmeyer et al. 2010). Thereby it keeps the current level of heterogeneity within the economy.

Maintaining heterogeneity and fostering entrepreneurship is therefore a key ingredient for regional development.

18.4 One Bottom Line: As a Lesson for Higher Education Institutions

We have argued so far that the composition of regional innovation systems with their actors is crucial for the innovation led development of regions. We have further argued that the composition of the knowledge base plays a central role in providing opportunities or challenges for the innovation system. Third, we have also argued that the interactive notion of the innovation process induces firms to tap into knowledge sources within and outside of their corporate walls. These three lines of argument put higher education institutions in a central position. First, as active actors in the innovation system connected with literally all types of other actors in the regional innovation system through networks of mutual interaction, through networks of labor mobility flows, and through the educated talent they supply. Second, higher education institutions play a central role in the generation of new knowledge for other actors in the innovation system. Third, higher education institutions serve as a source of inspirations and ideas for companies in their open innovation processes.

The two findings that regional growth and prosperity require heterogeneity and entrepreneurship can provide a structure for strategic development and operational practices for managing higher education institutions in the given context of the region's historical heritage, its specialization, its competences, and its overall strategic aspirations (Asheim and Coenen 2006).

Generally, there are various ways to foster heterogeneity of actors and knowledge, ranging from initiatives securing entrepreneurial opportunity (Acs et al. 2009) to initiatives targeting the exercise of the entrepreneurial function, such as financial incentives to start up a company (Wren and Storey 2002; Girma et al. 2007; Ebersberger 2011).

When it comes to strategically opening the regional economy for regionally beneficial actors attached to a multinational network (Dachs et al. 2008; Ebersberger et al. 2010) higher education organizations can play a leading role in making regions attractive to outside investors by offering an appealing portfolio of study programs at all levels to supply the required labor force. Assuming that these actors remain linked to regional knowledge diffusion infrastructures such as labor markets or higher education institutions, entrepreneurial opportunity is increased.

Breeding new and heterogeneous knowledge in higher education institutions can form part of the basis upon which technological or innovative new ventures can be built (Cooke 2001). This is particularly the case if it occurs in interaction with knowledge-intensive industrial actors, which further increase entrepreneurial opportunity. For managing a higher education institute this requires to strategically aligning the organization with the planned long-range targets of the region. Where these strategic long-range targets do not exist or they have not shared the management of the higher education institution might be found in a position shaping the development. In particular, this may happen in regions with only a few such organizations. In this case, it is crucial to support the region's interactively emerging development path by a heterogeneous set of competencies. Proactive and coordinated development of study programs and of research orientation is crucial in this respect.

It seems particularly important for the higher education institutions to stay abreast the social, technological, and scientific development to be able serve current and future needs of other actors in the innovation system. Generally, the innovation system is as good as its weakest part. But when ever these organizations, that are responsible for the knowledge and competence supply in the region, fall behind, the whole innovation system and the innovation-led development will suffer regardless of the excellence of other parts of the system.

We have argued that higher education organizations maintain a central position in the innovation systems especially when it comes to lay the foundation for the creation of social, economic, or technological opportunities. Once opportunity is created by creation of heterogeneous knowledge bases, the entrepreneurial function must be developed and employed. Without entrepreneurial activity opportunities will just remain being unrealized potential.

The mentioned policy measures such as public funding significantly reduce the risks of and hence improve the incentives for starting up a new company. Successful entrepreneurship requires a whole plethora of skills and capabilities for instance technical, scientific, and management expertise. It requires carrying out a complex set of activities (Lichtenstein et al. 2007) and a considerable amount of entrepreneurial self-efficacy. It has been argued that management education in general and supplementary management education after graduation in particular influence the willingness to start a new venture by supplying required management expertise (Wilson et al. 2007), where target group-specific approaches are required as, for instance, gender plays a significant role the perception of such programs (Ebersberger and Pirhofer 2011).

For the strategic development of higher research organizations this means that the region requires at least one actor to supply education, which facilitates entrepreneurship through providing post-graduate management education for engineering and science graduates. Only then will the region not only generate opportunity but it will also see thriving entrepreneurship with lots of failures but with some successes which eventually support the region in its strive for sustained growth.

At the core of the innovation system in such a region lies the entrepreneurial university that supports growth and entrepreneurship through supplying technological progress and diffusion through intermediaries such as technology transfer offices, incubators, or science parks (Rothaermel et al. 2007).

Bibliography

Acs ZJ, Braunerhjelm P, Audretsch DB, Carlsson B (2009) The knowledge spillover theory of entrepreneurship. Small Bus Econ 32(1):15–30

Agrawal A, Cockburn I, McHale J (2006) Gone but not forgotten: knowledge flows, labor mobility, and enduring social relationships. J Econ Geog 6(5):571–591

Asheim BT (2005) Constructing regional advantage. In: Report, European Commission

Asheim BT, Coenen L (2006) Contextualising regional innovation systems in a globalising learning economy: on knowledge bases and institutional frameworks. J Technol Transfer 31:163–173

Asheim BT, Isaksen A (1997) Location, agglomeration and innovation. Towards regional innovation systems in Norway? Eur Plan Stud 5(3):299–330

Asheim BT, Coenen L, Moodyson J, Vang J (2007) Constructing knowledge-based regional advantage: implications for regional innovation policy. Int J Entrepreneurship Innov Manage 7(2/3/4/5):140–155

Bathelt H, Malmberg A, Maskell P (2004) Clusters and knowledge: local buzz, global pipelines and the process of knowledge creation. Prog Hum Geogr 28(1):31–56

Beaudry C, Schiffauerova A (2009) Who's right, Marshall or Jacobs? The localization versus urbanization debate. Res Policy 38(2):318–337

Boschma RA, Sotarauta M (2005) Economic policy from an evolutionary perspective: the case of Finland. In: Economic geography, papers in evolutionary economic geography, Utrecht

Buddelmeyer H, Jensen PH, Webster E (2010) Innovation and the determinants of company survival. Oxford Econ Pap 62(2):261–285

Callon M (1992) The dynamics of techo-economic networks. In COOMBS R, Saviotti PP, Walsh V (eds) Economic and social analysis of technology. Technological change and company strategies. Economic and sociological perspectives. Academic, London

Cantner U, Gaffard J-L, Nesta L (2008) Schumpeterian perspectives on innovation, competition and growth. J Evol Econ 18(3–4):291–293

Carlsson B (ed) (1995) Technological systems and economic performance: the case of factory automation (vol. 5). Economics of science, technology and innovation, 5. Kluwer Academic Publishers, Dordrecht

Carlsson B, Eliasson G (2002) Industrial dynamics and endogenous growth. Ind Innov 10(4):435–455

Carlsson B, Stankiewitz R (1995) On the nature, function and composition of technological systems. In Carlsson B (ed) Economics of science, technology and innovation, vol 5. Technological systems and economic performance: the case of factory automation. Kluwer Academic Publishers, Dordrecht

Cefis E, Marsili O (2005) A matter of life and death: innovation and firm survival. Ind Corp Change 14(6):1167–1192

Chesbrough H (2003) Open innovation. Harvard University Press, Cambridge

Chesbrough H (2005) Open business models: How to thrive in the new innovation landscape?. Harvard Business School Press, MA Boston

Cooke P (2001) Regional innovation systems, clusters, and the knowledge economy. Ind Corp Change 10(4):945–974. doi:10.1093/icc/10.4.945

Cooke P (2005) Regional asymmetric knowledge capabilities and open innovation. Res Policy 34(8):1128–1149

Cooke P (2007) To construct regional advantage from innovation systems first build policy platforms. Eur Planning Stud 15(2):179–194

Cooke P, Gomez Uranga M, Etxebarria G (1997) Regional innovation system: institutional and organisational dimensions. Res Policy 26(4/5):475–491

Dachs B, Ebersberger B, Lööf H (2008) The innovative performance of foreign-owned enterprises in small open economies. J Technol Transfer 33(4):393–406. doi:10.1007/s10961-007-9058-7

Doloreux D, Parto S (2004) Regional innovation systems: a critical review

Ebersberger B (2011) Public funding for innovation and the exit of firms. J Evol Econ 21(3):519–543

Ebersberger B, Becke FM (2010) Technological specialization and variety in regional innovation systems. In: Ahrweiler P (ed) Innovation in complex social systems. Routledge, London, pp 88–109

Ebersberger B, Herstad S (2011) Product innovation and the complementarities of external interfaces. In: European Management Review (forthcoming)

Ebersberger B, Pirhofer C (2011) Gender, management education and the willingness for academic entrepreneurship. App Econ Lett (forthcoming). doi:10(1080/13504851),2010,503931

Ebersberger B, Herstad S, Lehtoranta O (2010) Bridging the global and the local? MNEs, labor market mobility and localized learning. Mimeo

Edquist C (1997) Systems of innovation: technologies, institutions and organizations. Science, technology and the international political economy series. Pinter, London

Florida R (2005) The world is spiky. The Atlantic Monthly (October 2005)

Freeman C (1987) Technology policy and economic performance: lessons from Japan. Pinter, London

Frenken K, Oort FV, Verburg T (2007) Related variety, unrelated variety and regional economic growth. Reg Stud 41(5):685–697

Friedman M (2005) The world is flat. Farrar, Straus and Giroux

Fritsch M, Stephan A (2005) Regionalization of innovation policy–Introduction to the special issue: Regionalization of Innovation Policy. Res Policy 34(8):1123–1127

Gertler M (2003) Tacit knowledge and the economic geography of context, or the undefinable tacitness of being (there). J Econ Geog 3:75–99

Girma S, Görg H, Strobl E (2007) The effects of government grants on plant survival: a micro-econometric analysis. Int J Ind Organ 25(4):701–720

Graf H (2010) Gatekeepers in regional networks of innovators. Camb J Econ 35(1):173–198. doi:10.1093/cje/beq001

Herstad SJ, Bloch CW, Ebersberger B, Van De Velde E (2008) Open innovation and globalization; theory, evidence and implications. Helsinki. Available from http://www.visioneranet.org/files/391/openING_report_final.pdf

Howells J (2005) Innovation and regional economic development: a matter of perspective? Regionalization of innovation policy. Res Policy 34(8):1220–1234

Jacobs J (1969) The economy of cities. Vintage Books, New York

Karlsen J, Isaksen A, Spilling OR (2011) The challenge of constructing regional advantage in peripheral areas: the case of marine biotechnology in Tromso, Norway. Entrepreneurship & Regional Development (forthcoming)

Koschatzky K (2003) Entrepreneurship stimulation in regional innovation systems—Public promotion of university-based start-ups in Germany. In: Brenner T, Fohrnahl D (eds) Cooperation, networks and institutions in regional innovation systems. Edward Elgar, Cheltenham, pp 277–301

Laursen K, Salter A (2006) Open for innovation: the role of openness in explaining innovation performance among U.K. manufacturing firms. Strateg Manage J 27(March):131–150. doi:10.1002/smj.507

Lazaric N, Longhi C, Thomas C (2008) Gatekeepers of knowledge versus platforms of knowledge: from potential to realized absorptive capacity. Reg Stud 42(6):837–852

Lazonick W (2006) Evolution of the new economy business model. Business and Economic History (Online)

Lazonick W (2007) The US stock market and the governance of innovative enterprise. Ind Corp Change 16(6):983–1035

Lichtenstein BB, Carter NM, Dooley KJ, Gartner WB (2007) Complexity dynamics of nascent entrepreneurship. J Bus Ventur 22:236–261

Lichtenthaler U, Ernst H (2007) External technology commercialisation in large firms. R&D Manage 37(5)

Lundvall BÅ (1992) National systems of innovation: Towards a theory of innovation and interactive learning. Pinter [u.a.], London

Malerba F (2002) Sectoral systems of innovation and production. Res Policy 31(2):247–264

Malmberg A, Maskell P (2002) The elusive concept of localization economies: towards a knowledge-based theory of spatial clustering. Environ Planning A 34:429–449

Malmberg A, Power D (2005) (How) Do (Firms in) clusters create knowledge? Ind Innov 12(4):409–431

Marshall A (1920) Industrial organization, continued. The concentration of specialized industries in particular localities. In: Marshall A (ed) Principles of economics, book IV, chapter X, 9th edn. Macmillan, London

Maskell P, Malmberg A (1999) Localized learning and industrial competitiveness. Camb J Econ 23:167–185

Maurseth PB, Verspagen B (2002) Knowledge spillovers in Europe: a patent citations analysis. Scand J Econ 104(4):531–545

Morrison A (2008) Gatekeepers of knowledge within industrial districts: Who they are, how they interact? Reg Stud 42(6):817–835

Nelson RR (1993) National innovation systems: a comparative analysis. Oxford University Press, New York

Nooteboom B (2000) Learning and innovation in organizations and economies. Oxford University Press, New York

Owen-Smith J, Powell WW (2004) Knowledge networks as channels and conduits: the effects of spillovers in the Bosten biotechnology community. Organ Sci 15(1):5–21

Porter M (1998) Clusters and the new economics of competition. Harvard Business Review, pp 77–90

Pyka A, Cantner U, Hanusch H (2000) Horizontal heterogeneity, technological progress and sectoral development. In: Cantner U, Hanusch H, Klepper S (eds) Economic evolution, learning, and complexity. Physica-Verl, Heidelberg, pp 73–96

Romer PM (1990) Endogenous technological change. J Politi Econ 98:71–102

Rondé P, Hussler C (2005) Innovation in regions: What does really matter? Regionalization of innovation policy. Res Policy 34(8):1150–1172

Rothaermel FT, Agung SD, Jiang L (2007) University entrepreneurship: a taxonomy of the literature. Ind Corp Change 16(4):691–791. doi:10.1093/icc/dtm023

Simmie J (2003) Innovation and urban regions as national and international nodes for the transfer and sharing of knowledge. Reg Stud 37(6–7):607–620

Simmie J (2004) Innovation and clustering in the globalised international economy. Urban Stud 41(5–6):1095–1112

Solow RM (1956) A contribution to the theory of economic growth. Q J Econ 70:65–94

Storper M (1997) The regional world. The Guilford Press, New York

Temple J (1999) The new growth evidence. J Econ Evidence 37:112–156

UNCTAD (2005) World investment report 2005: the internationalisation of R&D

Van Den Bergh JC (2008) Optimal diversity: increasing returns versus recombinant innovation. J Econ Behav Organ 68(3–4):565–580. doi:10.1016/j.jebo.2008.09.003

Wilson F, Kickul J, Marlino D (2007) Gender, entrepreneurial self-efficacy, and entrepreneurial career intentions: implications for entrepreneurship education. Entrepreneurship: Theory Pract 31:387–406

Woerter M (2009) Industry diversity and its impact on the innovation performance of firms. J Evol Econ 19(5):675–700. doi:10.1007/s00191-008-0118-4

Wren C, Storey DJ (2002) Evaluating the effect of soft business support upon small firm performance. Oxford Econ Pap 54(2):334–365

Chapter 19
What Type of Companies Benefits from University Spillovers?

Bernd Ebersberger, Andreas Altmann and Sverre J. Herstad

19.1 Introduction

Over the last decades firms have broken away from purely internally oriented innovation activities to more interactive and open innovation processes (Chesbrough 2003; Christensen et al. 2005), because they recognize that the development and the production of their products has to rely on a wide range of external ideas, component technologies, and complementary capabilities. In a dynamically changing technological and economic environment it is virtually impossible for any single firm to stay abreast of all relevant advances; each and every single one of these advances can be a valuable opportunity for the firms' development of new goods, services or processes which are so important for the firms' competitiveness, the economy's growth, and the society's well-being.

Consequently, firms' success depends on their ability to create and maintain interfaces, which transcend the corporate walls (Nicholls-Nixon and Woo 2003), and it is strongly affected by the firms ability to interconnect these interfaces with their internal processes—especially with those processes that accumulate knowledge and develop capabilities (Van den Bosch et al. 1999; Kogut and Zander 1996).

B. Ebersberger (✉) · A. Altmann
MCI Management Center Innsbruck—The Entrepreneurial School,
Universitätsstrasse 15, 6020 Innsbruck, Austria
e-mail: bernd.ebersberger@mci.edu

A. Altmann
e-mail: andreas.altmann@mci.edu

S. J. Herstad
Norwegian Institute for Studies in Innovation, Research and Education,
Wergelandsveien 7, 0167 Oslo, Norway
e-mail: sverre.herstad@nifu.no

A. Altmann and B. Ebersberger (eds.), *Universities in Change*, Innovation, Technology, and Knowledge Management, DOI: 10.1007/978-1-4614-4590-6_19,

In the mid and late 1980s the introduction of the innovation system concept (Freeman 1987, 1988; Lundvall[1] 1988, 1992; Nelson 1988, 1993) made these increasingly interactive innovation activities accessible to academics and policy makers alike. Among other contributions such as the evolutionary theory of the firm (Nelson and Winter 1982) or the chain linked model of the innovation process (Kline and Rosenberg 1986) the concept of the innovation systems provided the foundation for a more systemic view on the innovation process since it emphasizes that innovation is an uncertain, disorderly, and complex process (Sharif 2006).

In general a system comprises a set of components which serve a common end. Thus, an innovation system is composed of a multitude of interconnected heterogeneous actors, such as firms, research institutes, funding organizations, policy-making bodies, and—most importantly for the context of this research—universities, which jointly and interactively create, accumulate and disseminate knowledge, skills, and artifacts. They thereby contribute to the development, the diffusion and the utilization of innovations and new technologies (e.g. Freeman 1987; Lundvall 1992; Nelson 1993; Metcalfe 1994; Kuhlmann 2001) on a national level (Lundvall 1992; Nelson 1993; Freeman 1987), on a sectoral level (Malerba 2002), on a technological level (Carlsson 1995; Callon 1992), and on a regional level (Cooke et al. 1997).

This research investigates the role of universities in the innovation system in their function as an informal source of inspiration for corporate innovation activities. It, hence, mirrors the evolving context and mission of universities as knowledge hubs and sources of inspiration (Shapira and Youtie 2008). Not unlike Laursen and Salter (2004) or Mohnen and Hoareau (2003) this analysis investigates what factors affect the firms' utilization of universities as inspiration for their innovation processes.

19.2 Theory

Innovations tend to originate from firms that continuously recognize and connect codified and scientific knowledge with their particular market insight and their specialized, often tacit, problem-solving capabilities within and outside their value chain (Jensen et al. 2007; Danneels 2002; Hargadon and Sutton 1997; Katila 2002; Katila and Ahuja 2002). The external networks of firms and the learning processes therein represent the microfoundations for interactive knowledge development and learning embedded in a larger innovation system (Giuliani and Bell 2005; Graf 2010).

In the innovation system, knowledge development and learning are the main activities lying at the core of the innovation system concept (e.g. Hekkert et al. 2007; Lundvall 1992). Herstad et al. (2011) classify the knowledge development

[1] Both Lundvall and Freeman attribute the first usage of the term 'national innovation system' to the other.

and learning activities crossing the corporate boundaries along four dimensions: labor market interactions, sourcing, collaboration, and inspiration through search. These are particularly important for the overall performance of the innovation system, its capability to support corporate innovation success as they strongly determine the innovation performance of firms (e.g. Laursen and Salter 2006; Ebersberger et al. 2012; Ebersberger and Herstad 2012). In addition, universities play a crucial role in each one of these dimensions.

First, labor market transactions lead to an inflow of workers from other firms or of newly graduates and extend the firms' stock of specialized knowledge and expertise with complementary competences (Boschma et al. 2009; Maliranta et al. 2009; Mason et al. 2004). This inflow also extends the firms' access to networks (Agrawal et al. 2006).

Second, firms may source component knowledge or technologies or fully fledged solutions from other corporate actors in the system (van de Vrande et al. 2006). Knowledge may also be sourced as embodied in various forms of software and hardware (Hauknes and Knell 2009) or as contract R&D services (Fey and Birkinshaw 2005; Grimpe and Kaiser 2010; Schmiedeberg 2008) from universities or higher education organizations (Perkmann and Walsh 2008).

Third, due to knowledge being tacit and sticky and due to the complexity and the uncertainty of the innovation process, firms often cannot access knowledge resources of universities by means of the two above-mentioned mechanisms (Hoopes and Postrel 1999). Collaboration for innovation or alliances with scientific partners may be an option in this case. However, this involves specific organizational requirements and challenges. In order to make sure the knowledge is comprehended, assimilated and integrated, firms require internal competences that are complementary to those of the scientific collaboration partners (Nooteboom et al. 2007). For beneficial knowledge exchange with science partners, firms have to allocate sufficient resources (Lam 2000) and management attention (Ocasio 1997) to the effort. Consequently, collaborative linkages are selective and dependent on firm level and context conditions such as the firms' corporate innovation strategy (e.g. Dachs et al. 2008), the firms' structure of the network of affiliates and ownership (e.g. Asheim et al. 2011), and the firms' location and access to labor market flows (e.g. Herstad et al. 2011).

Forth, new market and technology opportunities available externally have to be identified by the firm itself. In contrast to the above-discussed collaboration for innovation this process of inspiration through innovation search (Ahuja and Katila 2004; Katila and Ahuja 2002; Fleming 2001) does not require formal interaction between the firm and the university. The effect of innovation search is contingent on targeting knowledge fields without joint experiences (Hargadon and Sutton 1997; Majchrzak et al. 2004), which puts universities and its knowledge domains in a central role here. Search processes with universities may include the intentional use of information sources such as scientific publications, databases, and science collaboration partners. Yet, search activities often draw heavily on information about research efforts or findings (Cohen et al. 2002) which spills over through layers of personal ties (Agrawal et al. 2006) within networks or communities (Maskell et al. 2006), or in the local environment surrounding the firm (Almeida and Kogut 1999). These knowledge spillovers are crucial for the regional impact of universities.

The knowledge spilling over from universities to firms using this as a source of inspiration for innovation projects is vital for the regional and national impact of universities. For university management, it is crucial to understand the characteristics of the firms utilizing this spillover to be able to identify where this important impact of the university occurs. For governments and funding organizations it is important to identify this as one of the incidences of public spending for universities. Hence, the overall research question is about the firm-specific and context-specific characteristics that influence the firms' use of universities as sources of inspiration.

19.3 Data and Methodology

The data used in this analysis originate from the Community Innovation Survey (CIS). The CIS is a periodic survey of firms' innovation activities to measure innovation. It is carried out by the national statistical offices of (current) EU member states including those of Norway and Iceland. The survey is based on a common set of guidelines for the collection and use of data on innovation activities; in particular, it is based on the Oslo Manual (OECD 1992) and its recent revisions (OECD 1997, 2005).

The strength of the survey is that it is conducted across countries according to a harmonized approach. The CIS includes information about the firm (including ownership), product and process innovation, innovation activity and expenditure, effects of innovation, innovation co-operation, public finding of innovation, sources of search and inspiration, and IP protection.

CIS data is used primarily for three different purposes. First and foremost, CIS data is used as a basis for official innovation statistics of the EU and its member states. Second it is used for policy-driven research and analysis, and is used extensively for analysis in economics (e.g. Veugelers and Cassiman 2006; Cassiman and Veuglers 2002; Cefis and Marsili 2005; Czarnitzki et al. 2007) in management studies (e.g. Laursen and Salter 2004, 2006), and in economic geography (e.g. Simmie 2003; Ebersberger and Herstad 2012).

The overall data set available for the analysis consists of 129,357 observations taken from the innovation surveys of the years 2004 (CIS4) and 2006 (CIS2006). The data are provided by Eurostat and available only at the premises of Eurostat in Luxembourg. It contains the national data set of 20 European countries. It is important to mention here that the available weights are used to extrapolate the results to the level of the economy. A detailed distribution of the national coverage is reported in Table 19.1.

Table 19.1 Composition of the sample

Country	Sample Size
BG	5,046
CY	194
CZ	6,830
DK	3,389
EE	983
ES	30,451
FI	2,472
FR	18,175
GR	3,428
HU	5,201
IT	25,950
LT	1,979
LV	1,683
MT	109
NO	2,768
PT	8,099
RO	3,907
SE	5,795
SI	1,282
SK	1,617
Total	129,357

19.3.1 Dependent Variable

The key variable here is a dichotomous indicator that firms use and appreciate universities as sources of information and inspiration for their innovation activities. The dichotomous variable is constructed from the ordinal survey question about the assessment of universities as sources of information for innovation activities. Companies assessing the importance of universities with the level 'medium' or 'high' on the four-level scale are regarded as appreciating universities as sources of inspiration. In the whole data set only slightly more than 13 % of the innovation active firms appreciate universities in this way. Additionally, we use a dichotomous indicator to identify companies, which are innovation active (N = 50,270).

19.3.2 Independent Variables

A number of country-specific, sector-specific, and firm-specific variables are included in the regression model to investigate the determinants for firms' utilization of universities as sources and inspiration for innovation. *First and foremost*, following the empirical tradition we capture the *firm size* by the natural logarithm of the number of employees.

19.3.2.1 Country and Sector Characteristics

Even the informal industry-science interaction may be influenced by the national framework conditions and the economic and scientific development of the economy. We use *the country groups* developed in Reinstaller et al. (2010) which classifies each of the countries in the data set into one of four groups: The group of Technology Leader Countries (SE, FI, DK, NO, FR, LU), the group of Technology User Countries (HU, EE, CZ, SK, SI), the group of High Income Low R&D Countries (IT, ES, PT, GR, CY, MT), and the group of Low Income, Low R&D Countries (BG, LT, LV, RO).

In addition to the development of the country captured by the country group the use of universities might depend on the size of the science system, which can be approximated by the *country size*. The size distribution of European countries (EU27 + NO + IS) yields a mean of 16 million inhabitants. All countries below this threshold are classified as small countries and all countries above it are classified as large countries.

Appropriability conditions can be operationalized on the sector level. It relates to how well intellectual property can protect new knowledge generated in a given sector to spill over into its environment. In certain industries the conditions are more favorable to protecting intellectual property, whereas in other sectors the conditions are such that spilling over of information, ideas, and knowledge is rather valuable to competitors and cannot be prevented. As in Ebersberger and Herstad (2012) we measure the appropriability regime indirectly employing the spillover approach utilized in Belderbos et al. (2004). There horizontal spillovers are measured directly as the importance firms assign to the information spilling over from competitors. As an indicator for the weakness of the appropriability regime in a sector we measure the fraction of innovating companies assessing information from competitors as important for their innovation activities. We will assume that the appropriability conditions do not only apply to corporate firms but also to universities.

19.3.2.2 Innovation and Knowledge

The innovation intensity is captured by the fraction of turnover spent on innovation activities; that is, the innovation expenditure divided by the turnover. We use the information on search channels to build in indicator of the *cumulativeness* of the knowledge base. We assume that the relative importance of external and the internal search captures the degree to which firm specific knowledge is accumulated and serves as a crucial ingredient to the current innovation process. Consequently, if a firm assigns higher importance to internal sources than to all other external sources, cumulativeness of the knowledge base is assumed (see Peneder 2007).

19.3.2.3 Internationality

Multinationality of a corporate network a firm is affiliated with may have an impact on the access to resources, directly impacting on the immediate need for informal external interfacing with the science system. On the other hand, multinationality of the network might be a precondition to lower the cost for external interfacing with international partners. A firm can be affiliated with a multinational network in basically two different ways—through foreign ownership or through being a *domestic multinational* (Ebersberger and Herstad 2012). The indicator for foreign ownership can be directly derived from the innovation survey as it inquires whether the firm is affiliated with a corporate group. If so, the survey inquires about the country, where the headquarters of the group is located. A dichotomous variable indicating affiliation to a corporate group, which is not headquartered domestically serves as all indicator for *foreign ownership*. The data set contains about 11 % of foreign-owned companies.

We follow Ebersberger and Herstad (2012) in determining the multinationality of a domestically headquartered corporate group and derive it from the information about innovation collaboration. About 1.5 % of the companies in the data set are affiliated to a domestic multinational network.

The effect of internationalization of firms on their innovation activities and their sources of inspiration have been discussed in the literature: Incentives to innovate are related to the size of the market on which the firm can commercialize the innovation. The decision to innovate also seems intensely intertwined with the companies' international orientation. We capture the *international orientation* by a dichotomous variable, which takes the value one if the firm reports that the most important markets are international. The most prominent indicator for international orientation, i.e. share of exports cannot be used as the export is not consistently surveyed as a firm demographic characteristic in the Community Innovation Surveys available.

19.3.2.4 Openness

As Laursen and Salter (2004) show the overall openness of the innovation process is a strong determinant of firms' utilization of knowledge spillovers from universities. We include three measures of openness in the regressions: the *diversity of search* with other corporate actors in the innovation system, the *diversity of collaboration*, and the diversity of the *protection strategy* of the firms. An extensive discussion of these indicators can be found in Ebersberger et al. (2011).

19.3.3 Method

Since the dependent variable is dichotomous we use a probit regression model to determine the effect of the characteristics on the use and appreciation of universities as sources of inspiration. Yet, the dependent variable can only be observed with firms that carry out innovation activities. Hence, we have to control for this selection bias and model the firms' decision to carry out innovation activities by a probit regression model. Including the Mills' ratio of the latter as an independent variable in the first regression model we control for the selection bias in a two-step estimation process.

19.4 Results

The results of the second step of the regression model, that is, the regression of the use and appreciation of universities as sources of inspiration for innovation, are reported in Table 19.2. To investigate the robustness of the models the same regression models are applied to all observations (Model I), to small and medium-sized firms (Model II), to firms in high technology (Hatzichronoglou 1997; OECD 2001) sectors (Model III), to firms in knowledge-based service (Hatzichronoglou 1997; OECD 2001) industries, and to firms from small countries (Model V). Table 19.2 reports the marginal effects rather than the coefficient estimates.

First we find that regardless of the subsample analyzed firm size determines the firms' usage and appreciation of universities as sources of inspiration. The size effect is smallest with knowledge-based services. A particularly strong effect can be found both among firms in high technology sectors and among firms in small countries. The larger the firms the more they seem to use and appreciate universities as sources of inspiration. As discussed above to be able to make good use of the inspiration firms have to comprehend, assimilate, and integrate the inspiration into their business. This absorptive capacity can be assumed to be more fully developed the larger the firm is.

For the total set of firms and for the subsample of SMEs and for the subsample of firms from small countries the openness of the innovation process is a strong determinant of the use and appreciation of external inspiration by universities. It can be assumed that in companies that already pursue an open innovation strategy, the receptiveness for external ideas, and inspiration is higher. Commonly, it is argued that the largest challenge in implementing open innovation strategies is to overcome the not-invented-here-syndrome. Given that, companies already use open innovation strategies it is plausible to assume that the syndrome is no strong obstacle for external ideas. The appreciation of inspiration is of course higher in these firms. Both in high technology industries and in knowledge-based services only the openness towards other—more industry related—inspiration is no determinant for the appreciation of science inspiration.

Table 19.2 Results of the outcome regression (model I–V)

	I	II	III	IV	V
me/se	ALL	SME	High tech	KIBS	Small country
Firm size	0.041***	0.045***	0.073***	0.025***	0.075***
	0.003	*0.004*	*0.018*	*0.006*	*0.006*
Openness of the innovation strategy					
Collaboration diversity	0.031***	0.029***	0.051***	0.044***	0.038***
	0.002	*0.003*	*0.010*	*0.005*	*0.004*
Industrial search	0.023***	0.024***	−0.007	0.007	0.032***
	0.003	*0.003*	*0.020*	*0.007*	*0.006*
Protection strategy	0.014***	0.014***	0.000	0.031***	0.016*
	0.003	*0.003*	*0.014*	*0.009*	*0.007*
Internationality					
Internat. orientation	0.042***	0.041***	0.135***	0.016	0.078***
	0.007	*0.007*	*0.039*	*0.017*	*0.013*
Dom. multinational	0.012	0.004	−0.047	0.027	0.019
	0.013	*0.016*	*0.044*	*0.033*	*0.024*
Foreign owned	−0.028***	−0.029***	−0.050	−0.051***	−0.013
	0.005	*0.006*	*0.027*	*0.012*	*0.011*
Knowledge and innovation					
Innov. intensity	0.089***	0.087***	0.087	0.128***	0.068*
	0.013	*0.013*	*0.080*	*0.021*	*0.030*
Cumulativeness	−0.058***	−0.054***	−0.109***	−0.089***	−0.086***
	0.005	*0.005*	*0.033*	*0.011*	*0.010*
Country and sector characteristics					
Appropriability (weak)	0.238*	0.313**	0.935	0.258	0.315
	0.100	*0.105*	*0.714*	*0.201*	*0.196*

(continued)

Table 19.2 (continued)

	I	II	III	IV	V
Techn. user country	−0.048***	−0.048***	−0.115**	0.008	−0.069***
	0.007	*0.007*	*0.039*	*0.024*	*0.015*
High R&D, low income cntry	0.036***	0.033***	0.06	0.062***	0.098***
	0.007	*0.007*	*0.039*	*0.016*	*0.017*
Low R&D, low income cntry	−0.024*	−0.020*	−0.118**	0.069	−0.073***
	0.010	*0.010*	*0.039*	*0.038*	*0.017*
Small cntry	0.083***	0.080***	0.108*	0.087***	–
	0.007	*0.007*	*0.042*	*0.017*	–
N	50,270	40,769	2,743	10,585	21,220
ll	-1.70E + 04	-1.32E + 04	−1302.561	−3962.581	−9308.18
R2	0.133	0.123	0.084	0.176	0.093
Chi2	2198.0***	1555.0***	121.7***	763.4***	860.3***

Note: Table reports marginal effects. Standard errors in italics. ***, (**, *) indicates significance at the 1 %, (5, 10 %) level. Regression include 17 sector dummies, one time dummy, indicators for opportunity conditions, and for model I–V the inverted Mills' ratio derived from the selection equation not reported here. The results of the selection equation can be obtained from the authors upon request

Internationality of the firm does have in effect on the use and appreciation of the university spillovers. We observe that domestically headquartered firms with an international network do not use university spillovers more intensively. Yet, firms with an international network of affiliates, which are headquartered abroad, report less use, and appreciation of the university spillovers. This can be caused by two phenomena. First, a branch plant syndrome causes reduced embeddedness of the firm in its immediate environment as the mandate of the firm does not extend into knowledge generation and innovation. Hence, these firms will be less likely to use and appreciate university knowledge spillovers. Second, the international network and the international headquarters also serve as sources of inspiration and knowledge spillovers. Although the absorption of these spillovers requires less attention than the management of a collaborative project, attention is a scarce resource, which might be allocated to accessing intra-MNC spillovers and easily transferable knowledge assets where appropriability is less of an issue (Markusen 1995).

The regression results also show that innovation intensity heavily affects the use and appreciation of the university spillovers. Yet, firms that face a high cumulativeness of their knowledge base are less likely to use and appreciate external information; this is also the case for university spillovers.

In sectors with weak appropriability regimes the inspiration by universities is generally more used and appreciated. As the appropriability is generally speaking not strictly determined by the sector it self but rather by the predominant knowledge and technology used in the sector the weak appropriability also refers to the knowledge developed by universities. Where appropriability is weak universities will generally create more spillovers.

Our regression results also show that the technological frontier of the science system and the development of the economy, measured by the level of income, have a strong effect on the use and appreciation of university spillovers. In countries that are not classified at the technological and scientific frontier, that is, the technology-using countries and the low R&D countries, we find a significantly lower likelihood to use and appreciate university spillovers. Yet, in the high R&D and low-income countries the use and appreciation of the university spillovers is between 3 and 10 % points higher than in the technologically leading countries. A strongly developed science system coincides with the need for further economic development. University spillovers seem to be a valuable but rather economical source of inspiration. We also observe that firms in small countries have an 8 % points higher likelihood to use and appreciate university spillovers than firms in large countries.

19.5 Discussion

In this analysis, we have generally confirmed for a data set of European firms what Laursen and Salter (2004) have found for a data set of firms from the UK. The structural dimensions of firms such as size and innovation intensity strongly influence the use and appreciation of the university spillovers. To firmly establish the university in its new role as a knowledge hub university management should not only be interested in strengthening the science-industry collaboration and strategic alliances of the universities and corporate partners, university management should also be interested in the informal interaction generating spillovers and inspiration. In broadening the corporate audience, which benefits from the university spillovers, activities to reduce the dependence on size and absorptive capacity seem required. This can be achieved through provision of low-level access to research results and findings, for instance, by establishing a science fair particularly tailored to the needs and requirements of local and regional SMEs. Also the provision of technical advisory infrastructure such as a technology help desk which is open for external consultation can help companies to get in touch and to get inspired more easily. Supporting the universities publication effort in applied science, business practioneer, or applied science journals can increase the visibility of university research to corporate actors in the innovation system. Generally, the exchange of knowledge and inspiration across institutional boundaries requires the implementation of new methods of communication and tools focusing on mutual participation (Guston 2001).

Additionally, not unlike the findings in Laursen and Salter (2004), we find that managerial decisions as reflected in the overall search behavior and the openness of the innovation strategy heavily affect the use of universities as sources of inspiration for innovation. This indicates that primarily companies with distinct innovation strategy are interested in and receptive for the university spillovers. These are the companies, which have the strongest capacity to use the inspiration beneficially for the regional economy. This entails that this self-selection of firms reduces the university management's need for efforts to select the recipients of the spillovers or to channel these spillovers. As discussed above, providing broad access and broadcasting the research through a number of different channels will be sufficient to attract interested and capable companies to get inspired.

In addition to the findings in Laursen and Salter (2004), we established that the use and appreciation of the university spillovers depend on the regional and national context of the science system and the economic system. Overall our findings do not challenge the results obtained earlier. Yet, they highlight the particular role the university spillovers play in regional and national economies with a low innovation performance and the low growth prospects.

We find that a substantial fraction of 13 % of the innovation-active companies appreciate university spillovers, which is well above the 10 % reported in Laursen and Salter (2004). This, in combination with the findings in the analysis and with our own experience, tempts us to agree with Cohen et al.(2002): Although in the wake of the Bayh-Dole Act and in the wake of the reform of some of the employee invention regulations (e.g. in Germany and Austria) and with substantial investment in the management of university IP in most of the European countries, transfer of IP, nevertheless, seems to be a minor channel of how the innovation system and the corporate actors therein benefit from the findings of university research. Knowledge spillovers informing and inspiring corporate innovation activities tend to be a more relevant channel and require at least as much university management attention than IP issues do.

Bibliography

Agrawal A, Cockburn I, McHale J (2006) Gone but not forgotten: knowledge flows, labor mobility, and enduring social relationships. J Econ Geogr 6(5):571–591

Ahuja G, Katila R (2004) Where do resources come from? The role of idiosyncratic situations. Strateg Manag J 25(89):887–907

Almeida P, Kogut B (1999) Localization of knowledge and the mobility of engineers in regional networks. Manage Sci 45(7):905–917

Asheim BT, Ebersberger B, Herstad SJ (2011) MNCs between the local and the global: knowledge bases, proximity and distributed knowledge networks. In: Heidenreich M (ed) Innovation and institutional embeddedness of multinational companies. Cheltenham

Belderbos R, Carree MA, Lokshin B (2004) Cooperative R&D and firm performance. Res Policy 33(10):1477–1492

Boschma RA, Eriksson R, Lindgren U (2009) How does labour mobility affect the performance of plants? the importance of relatedness and geographical proximity. J Econ Geogr 9:169–190

Callon M (1992) The dynamics of techo-economic networks. In: Coombs R, Saviotti PP, Walsh V (eds) Economic and social analysis of technology., Technological change and company strategies. Economic and sociological perspectives. Academic, London

Carlsson B (ed) (1995) Technological systems and economic performance: the case of factory automation. Kluwer, Dordrecht

Cassiman B, Veugelers R (2002) R&D co-operation and spillovers: some empirical evidence from Belgium. Am Econ Rev 92:1169–1184

Cefis E, Marsili O (2005) A matter of life and death: innovation and firm survival. Ind Corp Change 14(6):1167–1192

Chesbrough H (2003) Open innovation—the new imperative for creating and profiting from technology. Harvard Business School Press, Cambridge

Christensen JF, Olesen MH, Kjaer JS (2005) The industrial dynamics of open innovation–evidence from the transformation of consumer electronics. Res Policy 34(10):1533–1549

Cohen WM, Nelson RR, Walsh JP (2002) Links and impacts: the influence of public research on industrial R&D. Manage Sci 48(1):1–23

Cooke P, Gomez Uranga M, Etxebarria G (1997) Regional innovation systems: institutional and organisational dimensions. Res Policy 26(4/5):475–491

Czarnitzki D, Ebersberger B, Fier A (2007) The relationship between R&D collaboration, subsidies and R&D performance: empirical evidence from Finland and Germany. J Appl Econometrics 22(7):1347–1366

Dachs B, Ebersberger B, Pyka A (2008) Why do firms cooperate for innovation? A comparison of austrian and finnish cis3 results. Int J Foresight Innov Policy 4(3/4):200–229

Danneels E (2002) The dynamics of product innovation and firm competences. Strateg Manage J 23(12):1095–1121. doi:10.1002/smj.275

Ebersberger B, Herstad SJ (2012) Go abroad or have strangers visit? On organizational search spaces and local linkages. J Econ Geogr 12(1):273–295

Ebersberger B, Bloch CW, Herstad SJ and Van De Velde E (2012) Open innovation practices and their effect on innovation performance. Int J Innov Technol Manage (forthcoming) pp 1–22

Ebersberger B, Herstad SJ, Iversen EJ, Som O, Kirner E (2011) Open innovation in Europe. In: Report to the European commisison

Fey CF, Birkinshaw J (2005) External sources of knowledge, governance mode and R&D performance. J Manage 31(4):597–621

Fleming L (2001) Recombinant uncertainty in technological search. Manage Sci 47(1):117–132

Freeman C (1987) Technology policy and economic performance: lessons from Japan. Pinter, London

Freeman C (1988) Japan: a new national system of innovation. In: Dosi G, Freeman C, Nelson RR, Silverberg G, Soete L (eds) Technical change and economic theory. Pinter, London, pp 331–348

Giuliani E, Bell M (2005) The micro-determinants of meso-level learning and innovation: evidence from a chilean wine cluster. Res Policy 34(1):47–68

Graf H (2010) Gatekeepers in regional networks of innovators. Camb J Econ 35(1):173–198. doi:10.1093/cje/beq001

Grimpe C, Kaiser U (2010) Balancing internal and external knowledge acquisition: the gains and pains from R&D outsourcing. J Manage Stud 47(8):1483–1509

Guston DH (2001) Boundary organizations in environmental policy and science: an introduction. Sci Technol Human Values 26(4):399–408

Hargadon A, Sutton RI (1997) Technology brokering and innovation in a product development firm. Adm Sci Q 42(4):716–749

Hatzichronoglou T (1997) Revision of the high-technology sector and product classification, STI working papers 2. OECD Publishing, Paris

Hauknes J, Knell M (2009) Embodied knowledge and sectoral linkages: an input-output approach to the interaction of high- and low-tech industries. Res Policy 38(3):459–469

Hekkert M, Suurs R, Negro S, Kuhlmann S, Smits R (2007) Functions of innovation systems: a new approach for analysing technological change. Technol Forecast Soc Chang 74(4):413–432

Herstad SJ, Pålshaugen Ø, Ebersberger B (2011) Industrial innovation collaboration in a capital region context J Knowl Econ (forthcoming)

Hoopes DG, Postrel S (1999) Shared knowledge, "glitches", and product development performance. Strateg Manage J 20(9):837–865

Jensen MB, Johnson B, Lorenz E, Lundvall BA (2007) Forms of knowledge and modes of innovation. Res Policy 36(5):680–693

Katila R (2002) New product search over time: past ideas in their prime. Acad Manage J 55(5):995–1010

Katila R, Ahuja G (2002) Something old, something new: a longitudinal study of search behaviour and new product introduction. Acad Manage J 45(6):1183–1194

Kline SJ, Rosenberg N (1986) An overview of innovation. In: Landau R, Rosenberg N (eds) The positive sum strategy: harnessing technology for economic growth. National Academic Press, Washington, pp 275–305

Kogut B, Zander U (1996) What firms do? Coordination, identity, and learning. Organiz sci 7(5): 502–518. Retrieved from http://www.jstor.org/stable/2635287

Kuhlmann S (2001) Future governance of innovation policy in Europe—three scenarios. Res Policy 30(6):953–976

Lam A (2000) Tacit knowledge, organizational learning and societal institutions: an integrated framework. Organiz Stud 21(3):487–513

Laursen K, Salter A (2004) Searching high and low: What types of firms use universities as a source of innovation? Res Policy 33(8):1201–1215. doi:10.1016/j.respol.2004.07.004

Laursen K, Salter A (2006) Open for innovation: the role of openness in explaining innovation performance among U.K. manufacturing firms. Strateg Manag J 27:131–150. doi:10.1002/smj.507

Lundvall B (1992) National systems of innovation: towards a theory of innovation and interactive learning. Pinter, London New York

Lundvall BA (1988) Innovation as an interactive process: from user-supplier interaction to the national system of innovation. In: Dosi G, Freeman C, Nelson RR, Silverberg G, Soete L (eds) Technical change and economic theory. Pinter, London, pp 349–369

Majchrzak A, Cooper LP, Neece OE (2004) Knowledge reuse for innovation. Manage Sci 50(2):174–188

Malerba F (2002) Sectoral systems of innovation and production 1. Res Policy 31(2): 247–264. Elsevier. Retrieved from http://www.sciencedirect.com/science/article/pii/s0048733301001391

Maliranta M, Mohnen P, Rouvinen P (2009) Is inter-firm labor mobility a channel of knowledge spillovers? Evidence from a linked employer-employee panel. Ind Corporate Change 18(6):1161–1191

Markusen JR (1995) The boundaries of multinational enterprises and the theory of international trade. J Econ Perspect 9(2):169–189
Maskell P, Bathelt H, Malmberg A (2006) Building global knowledge pipelines: the role of temporary clusters. Eur Planning Stud 14(8):997–1013
Mason G, Beltramo JP, Paul JJ (2004) External knowledge sourcing in different national settings: a comparison of electronics establishments in Britain and France. Res Policy 33:53–72
Metcalfe JS (1994) Evolutionary economics and technology policy. Econ J 104(425):931–944
Mohnen P, Hoareau C (2003) What type of enterprise forges close links with universities and government labs? Evidence from CIS 2. Manag Decis Econ 24(2–3):133–145
Nelson RR (1988) National systems of innovation: preface and institutions supporting technical change in the United States. In: Dosi G, Freeman C, Nelson RR, Silverberg G, Soete L (eds) Technical change and economic theory. Pinter, London, pp 309–239
Nelson RR (1993) National innovation systems: a comparative analysis. Oxford University Press, Oxford
Nelson RR, Winter SG (1982) An evolutionary theory of economic change. Belknap Press of, Cambridge
Nicholls-Nixon CL, Woo CY (2003) Technology sourcing and output of established firms in a regime of encompassing technological change. Strateg Manag J 24(7):651–666
Nooteboom B, Van Haverbeke W, Duysters G, Gilsing V, Van den Oord A (2007) Optimal cognitive distance and absorptive capacity. Res Policy 36(7):1016–1034
Ocasio W (1997) Towards an attention-based view of the firm. Strateg Manage J 18(S1):187–206
OECD (2001) Science, technology and industry scoreboard. OECD Publishing, Paris
OECD (1992) Oslo manual guidelines for collecting and interpreting innovation data, 1st edn. OECD Publishing, Paris
OECD (1997) Oslo manual guidelines for collecting and interpreting innovation data, 2nd edn. OECD Publishing, Paris
OECD (2005) Oslo manual guidelines for collecting and interpreting innovation data, 3rd edn. OECD Publishing, Paris
Peneder M (2007) A sectoral taxonomy of educational intensity. Empirica 34:189–212
Perkmann M, Walsh K (2008) How firms source knowledge from universities: partnering versus contracting. Creating wealth from knowledge: meeting the innovation challenge. Edward Elgar Publishing, p 273
Reinstaller A, Unterlass F (2010) Sectoral innovation modes and the state of economic development : implications for innovation policy in the new member states. In: Radosevic S, Kaderabkova A (eds) The challenge for innovation policy in the new member states. Edward Elgar Publishing, Aldershot, pp 1–27
Schmiedeberg C (2008) Complementarities of innovation activities: an empirical analysis of the German manufacturing sector. Res Policy 37(9):1492–1503
Sharif N (2006) Emergence and development of the national innovation systems concept. Res Policy 35(5):745–766
Simmie J (2003) Innovation and urban regions as national and international kodes for the transfer and sharing of knowledge. Regional Stud 37(6):607–620
Van de Vrande V, Lemmens C, Vanhaverbeke W (2006) Choosing governance modes for external technology sourcing. R&D Manage 36(3):347–363
Van den Bosch FAJ, Volberda HW, De Boer M (1999) Coevolution of firm absorptive capacity and and forms environment: organizational combinative capabilities. Organ Sci 10(5):551–568
Veugelers R, Cassiman B (2006) In search of complementarity in innovation strategy: internal R&D and external knowledge acquisition. Manage Sci 52(1):68–82
Youtie J, Shapira P (2008) Building an innovation hub: a case study of the transformation of university roles in regional technological and economic development. Res Policy 37:1188–1204

Chapter 20
Globalization, Regional Development, and the Evolving Local University Role: The Case of Vestfold, Norway

Sverre J. Herstad and Thomas Brekke

20.1 Introduction

The competitiveness of firms and regions in a globalizing economy rests on their ability to continuously develop and exploit specialized knowledge assets. The development of such assets is contingent on the activities and networks maintained by individual firms (Giuliani 2005); on the composition of the industrial structure (Boschma and Iammarino 2009; Frenken et al. 2007); and on mechanisms that enable knowledge to flow and recombine between activities. As products and processes are becoming increasingly complex and the global division of labor deepens, firms are forced to draw on a wide range of component technologies and complementary capabilities (Rothaermel et al. 2006), and combine leading scientific insights with specialized, experience-based knowledge. Thus, innovation at the firm level is becoming embedded in global innovation networks. These processes link long-term regional development more tightly to the ability to develop and institutionalize an infrastructure for knowledge development and diffusion, which functions independently of whether or not industry maintains local supply chain collaboration.

This chapter investigates the regional development role of a Norwegian university college against the background of actual industry knowledge development and networking characteristics. After a general discussion of conceptual issues, it does so in three steps. First, it investigates how industrial actors in the two

S. J. Herstad (✉)
Nordic Institute for Studies in Innovation, Research and Education,
Wergelandsveien 7, 0167 Oslo, Norway
e-mail: sverre.herstad@nifu.no

T. Brekke
Vestfold University College, Raveien 197, 3184 Borre, Norway
e-mail: thomas.brekke@hive.no

A. Altmann and B. Ebersberger (eds.), *Universities in Change*, Innovation, Technology, and Knowledge Management, DOI: 10.1007/978-1-4614-4590-6_20,

dominating subclusters of the region develop and use different forms of knowledge, by means of linking heterogeneous internal processes to various external actors groups located in the region, outside it and abroad. Second, it describes processes of transformation and adaption to this context at the university college side, explicitly aimed at reinforcing its role in regional development. Third, it shifts focus back toward how this impact present industrial dynamics, and discusses, how this impact could be reinforced by building on the transformation that has already occurred. Particular emphasis is put on the electronics industry, as this has received the strongest education and research attention from the university college. Several references will, however, be made to the engineering cluster, for purposes of comparison.

The township of Horten and the surrounding county of Vestfold is located on the Western shores of the Oslo fjord, approximately one hour by car from the capital city of Oslo. It is hosting a set of specialized electronics and engineering firms (Asheim and Isaksen 2002; Onsager et al. 2007). The evolution of the electronics cluster illustrates the interplay between external inputs, and the cumulative development of knowledge assets at the regional level. During the 1970s, Vingtor Radio transformed itself into a leading developer of ultrasound technology, in close cooperation with Norwegian Technical University in Trondheim (basic technology provider) and the medical science community at University of Oslo (lead user). This formed the basis for what is now GE Vingmed, ultrasound center of excellence for the US multinational General Electric. Another local company, Simrad, used sonar technology developed by Norwegian Defense Research Establishment (NDRE) outside Oslo as the basis for diversifying into fish finding technology. Norcontrol was set up as a joint venture between three companies based outside the region, for the purpose of developing maritime automation and system surveillance equipment. Spin-offs have included now US-owned Park Air Systems (aviation traffic control systems) and Seagull AS (software for on-board training of ship crew). Aktieselskapet Microelectronic (AME) was founded on sensor technology developed at leading Norwegian universities and research institutes, all located outside the Vestfold region. Out of AME grew companies now known as Norspace (communication satellite switching systems), OSI Optoelectronics, and Sensonor (micro-mechanical sensors). Sensonor managed to early position itself as a collaborative partner of the European auto manufacturing industry, partly because it was among the first to develop process technology enabling production of low-cost airbag release and tire pressure sensors. It has later given birth to what is now Memscap AS (high-end sensors for e.g. aviation use) and Ignis Photonyx (optical components for telecommunication equipment). The Electronic Coast collaboration network (EC-Network) now consists of a stable population of 36 member firms, which operate in diverse international markets. Some of these operate on similar or related technological platforms, i.e. 'microelectromechanical systems' (MEMS), and are supported by research and education programs in this field at the regional university college. A larger group of companies have traditionally operated based on bordering component manufacturing and advanced production technology; but this common denominator is weakened due to downscaling and outsourcing. Few companies are now in direct competition with each other.

20.2 Methodology

The empirical analysis is based on interviews with managing directors and R&D executives in eight firms, conducted in two rounds. The first round covered three of the largest and most mature actors within electronics, and focused on issues spanning from overall competence upgrading to the organization of specific innovation projects. A survey questionnaire was then developed, and sent to the 42 member firms of the Electronic Coast and Engineering Coast networks. The survey obtained a total of 31 responses, equal to a response rate of 74 %. Information obtained on mechanisms for competence upgrading were used to group firms according to their "mode" of learning and innovation (Jensen et al. 2007). Five follow-up case-studies were then conducted to ensure a sample, which covered both clusters and each of the different modes identified. Interviews have also been conducted with key personnel at Vestfold University College, in addition to numerous informal conversations and the use of material documenting relevant internal strategy processes from late 1990s until present.

20.3 Conceptual Framework

20.3.1 Industrial Knowledge Development and Innovation

Economists from Adam Smith and onwards have conceptualized development as a process which generate an ever-expanding range of differentiated products and technologies (Knell 2008). As the stock of knowledge available for recombination diversify (Grossman and Helpman 1991), the opportunities for new technology development exponentially grow. 'What firms do 'is therefore identification, coordination, and integration of diverse external knowledge inputs (Kogut and Zander 1996). These are identified through ongoing processes of innovation search. Intentional and unintentional exposure to information defines the search spaces of corporate enterprises (Katila and Ahuja 2002). Evolutionary theorists (Nelson and Winter 1982) have argued that the more diverse the search space is the better are the effects of the alternatives selected. Empirical studies have found the impact of innovation search on subsequent technological evolution to be contingent on spanning organizational boundaries and product domains (Rosenkopf and Nerkar 2001) and to be improving with the diversity information sources used (Laursen and Salter 2006). It is pointed out that the use of mature technologies from outside own sector boundaries can provide as strong an impetuous to innovation as new technologies developed by own sector (Katila 2002). Successful search may trigger the need for subsequent collaboration. Collaborating firms gain access to the tacit components of their partners' knowledge bases, and new knowledge is created which add to the stock of knowledge held by the firms involved. The different actor groups with which collaborative relationships may form differ in what knowledge and problem-solving capabilities they may contribute, at what stage of the innovation process. The successful identification of alternatives through search and transfer of knowledge through collaboration is dependent on absorptive capacity. This capacity is defined partly by the existence of prior related knowledge, which forms the basis for interpretation and transformation. It is also partly defined by the knowledge systems established and operated by firms, which form the basis for attention allocation, communication, and subsequent internal individual or collective learning.

The knowledge systems maintained by firms reflect their dominant 'mode of innovation' (Jensen et al. 2007). The core of the 'science-technology-innovation' (STI) mode is R&D departments of firms, linked externally to recruitment of highly skilled individual researchers, the use of epistemic communities as search space and collaboration with science system actors. The outcome is explicit knowledge, which—importantly—travel well but require adaption to contexts of application before it transforms into innovation. The strength of the mode lies in its ability to draw on and push disciplinary frontiers, explore fundamentally new knowledge independent of specific contexts of application and provide the basis for radical innovations. This is also its Achilles heel; as it is less able to mobilize and develop the knowledge necessary for its output to transform into large-scale industrial application. This means that it does not easily, in itself, translate into industrial activity (Karlsen et al. 2011). The core of the contrasting 'doing-using-interacting' mode is learning work organizations linked to external value chain actors in various forms. This model manages to mobilize and link experience-based knowledge originating in different parts of the organization and value chain; thus ensuring that a stock of knowledge which is context-specific and application-oriented continuously evolves. This sustains an ongoing stream of incremental innovations along established technological development paths and drives the development of highly specialized knowledge assets; but for the same reason comes with the danger of lock-in. Thus, at both firm and regional levels it can be argued that science-based and experience-based knowledge are complementary; in that the impact of either one on firm innovation or regional dynamics is reinforced by the co-existence of the other.

The activities of individual firms in a regional setting may contribute spillovers into the regional system, which then, depending on the diffusion and absorption capacity of the system as a whole, are made available to other firms or used as basis for new firm formation. But as the process of specialization and diversification of inputs available occur on an international scale, geographically bounded search, collaboration and knowledge transfers create a potential for lock-in (Narula 2002) to diminishing return paths. The high cost of establishing extra-regional linkages may combine with the low marginal cost of continuing to use existing ones (ibid); causing actors to over-search local environments (Katila and Ahuja 2002) which do not contain the technological novelties or complementary capabilities needed to sustain innovation-based industrial dynamics (Bathelt et al. 2004; Graf 2010). The successful establishment of regional firms as knowledge and information gravitation points in global networks (Coe et al. 2008; Herstad et al. 2010) increases their individual exposure to information and knowledge diversity, hence increasing both innovativeness and economic performance at the firm level and creating a potential for richer regional spillovers. But it comes with less attention toward local collaborative linkages.

This raises the question of what regional knowledge diffusion mechanisms which remain in play, and thus explain observed clustering tendencies. As experience-based, tacit knowledge predominantly moves through face-to-face interaction with people (Lam 2000), and the majority of job moves occur within regions (Boschma et al. 2008), recent work emphasizes the role of labor market mobility (Eriksson and Lindgren 2009) and personal network formation (Agrawal et al. 2006; Dahl and Pedersen 2004). Research has found clusters of similar or related economic activities to be associated with particularly high degrees of labor mobility (Eriksson et al. 2008; Malmberg and Power 2005); found firms to be able to absorb more diverse competencies if they are recruited locally (Boschma et al. 2009) and pointed to the importance of mobility between research-conducting firms and those which do not (Maliranta et al. 2009). Another important mechanism is spin-offs, i.e. the establishment of new firms to commercialize ideas originating in industry or research communities. These tend to cluster around their parent firms, and can provide strong growth impetuous into the regional system.

Regional knowledge diffusion is intimately interwoven with the composition of the industrial structure, i.e. the set of firms between which knowledge diffuse. Agglomeration economies (Beaudry and Schiffauerova 2009) arise from a high degree of specialization, and the formation of a 'thick' and highly specialized labor market, a common supplier infrastructure and a common research infrastructure upon which technologically similar firms may draw. Cognitive proximity—similarity of activities—combined with co-localization is said to foster trust conducive to information sharing and collaboration, and enable local spillovers to diffuse and be absorbed with little friction. However, homogeneity substantially reduces the likelihood that these spillovers may enter into combinations which are truly novel, and increases the likelihood of negative technological lock-in. It also comes with the risk of competition between firms operating in similar markets; and of exogenous business cycle shocks upon the cluster as a whole rather than individual firms only. Others have therefore argued that diversity rather than specialization in the regional industrial structure is more conducive to knowledge diffusion and innovation. Diversity provides the basis for knowledge diffusion between technologically different activities, and hence for so-called urbanization economies. Diversity is assumed to '(…) facilitate more radical innovation as knowledge and technologies from different sectors are recombined, leading to completely new products or technologies' (Frenken et al. 2007). But diversity comes with the risk of fragmentation (Tödtling and Trippl 2005) caused by cognitive distance

(Nooteboom 2000). Recent work has therefore pointed toward the role of information exchanges and knowledge diffusion between activities which are technologically related, and the mechanisms needed to accelerate processes of reconfiguration in their intersection (Asheim et al. 2007; Cooke 2007; Hargadon and Sutton 1997).

There are several reasons why new firm formation and labor market mobility are insufficient for the purpose of achieving cross-sector knowledge diffusion and exploration of potential new combinations; the primary of which is the tendency of labor markets to form segments around similar activities (i.e. activities identified as related to begin with). Hence, they are more likely to diffuse knowledge between such similar activities that contribute to the exploration of linkages between them. Further, excessive mobility may destroy valuable firm-specific knowledge, hamper the knowledge accumulation of individual firms, and reduce their willingness to invest in competence upgrading (Combes and Duranton 2006). The more specialized knowledge firms are dependent on, the more detrimental can excessive mobility be. Third, in clusters where several firms operate in similar markets, they may share the same business cycle fluctuations and downsize collectively. When this is the case, business cycle fluctuations do not assist in the redistribution of people and knowledge between firms but may rather result in knowledge workers moving from the region. Forth, whereas firms in high velocity sectors may compensate for the outflow of own personnel into the labor market by inflows of competences and ideas from it; firms operating based on more specialized and cumulative knowledge base may see the recruitment of new personnel primarily as a generator of costs related to firm-specific training. Last, new firm formation through spin-offs assumes specific knowledge, technology, and market opportunity conditions which may deviate from those of the industry in question. Although, these occur frequently in sectors such as biotechnology and ICTs, and provide an important basis for the commercialization of world-leading research in such fields when necessary seed and venture capital is present, the rate of new firm formation varies substantially across academic fields, industries, and with different underlying knowledge and opportunity conditions (Breschi and Malerba 1997; Malerba and Orsenigo 1993).

20.3.2 Knowledge Diffusion Infrastructures

This point to the importance of regional knowledge development, accumulation, and diffusion infrastructures which operate independently of local supply chain collaborative linkages, and thus are able to explore new combinations on a more broad basis. Such examples include regional business and technology councils, regional development organizations, and different labor training and mobility schemes. However, these are also examples of mechanisms, which are dependent on the commitment of, leading firm actors, and the successful definition of common interests and objectives among a set of diverse firms; and vulnerable to fluctuations in such commitment. In addition, they may experience problems in adapting to circumstances, which evolve with structural change, even when this structural change can be attributed to the effectiveness of the infrastructure (Asheim and Herstad 2005).

Universities and university colleges may therefore play an important role, by adapting teaching and research to regional potentials and demands (Cummings 1998; Goddard and Chatterton 2003). This is often labeled as the third role or the service role of HEIs (Brulin 1998; Nilsson 2006). These roles are consistent with the triple helix model and its emphasis on a dynamic interplay between industry, research infrastructure, and government (Etzkowitz 2002). It is reflected in recent developments such as those emphasizing research activity and education programs tailored to specific regional industry needs, in turn enabled partly by "(...) a growing acceptance of the need to draw upon knowledge from whatever source may be appropriate to the purpose, rather than from a single disciplinary corpus" (Becher and Parry 2005).

An increasing amount of empirical studies have in the last decades analyzed knowledge transfer processes (Balconi and Laboranti 2006; Bekkers and Bodas-Freitas 2008; Daraio and Bonaccorsi 2007; Kaufmann and Tödtling 2001; Ponds et al.2010; Varga 2009). These studies have shown that collaboration and interaction between university and industry is highly beneficial and cost effective way to transfer knowledge and technology (Etzkowitz et al. 2000), and more so than the 'linear' and often arms-length processes sought stimulated by different technology transfer and licensing schemes. But, these studies have also shown contrasting evidence concerning the importance of the different types of knowledge outputs of university to firms; the spatial extent of knowledge spillovers and to what degree do sectors matters. Ponds et al. (2010) define three main knowledge diffusion mechanisms which are particularly geographically localized;

1. spin-offs,
2. labor mobility, and
3. informal knowledge exchanges through social networks.

Bekkers and Freitas (2008) analyze the importance of a variety of knowledge transfer in The Netherlands, and find that basic characteristics such as knowledge and technological opportunity conditions, as well as the disciplinary background of knowledge, explain the use and importance of different knowledge diffusion channels (2008: 1848).

The diffusion mechanism is reflecting the advantages that firms enjoy in accessing knowledge that spillsover from other firm and research institutes by being located at the same place or near each other. Beside informal social networks, formal networks of research collaboration are also found to be an important diffusion mechanism, which is of particular relevance for science-based industries and advanced engineering (Bekkers and Bodas-Freitas 2008; Ponds et al. 2010), as these companies invest relative heavily in R&D and collaborative close with academia. However, research collaboration (formal network) can lead to not only localized knowledge spillovers but also to knowledge transfer between researchers over long distances (Adams 2002). Yet, according to Lam (2007) such collaboration is part and parcel of a development through which university and industry may create overlapping labor markets, which remain tied to places and enable much richer exchanges of information and knowledge than the collaborative relationship in itself.

It is therefore important to acknowledge how (a) the limitations on local collaborative knowledge development created by globalization applies not least to the relationship between universities and industry; but also (b) how other potential roles for university colleges in the regional innovation system are opened up. By means of education, they enrich the local labor market and contribute to the formation of personal ties across industrial firms; independent of collaboration. By conducting activities perceived as relevant by a broader set of firms, they may also attract the attention of research personnel and contribute to the reinforcement of personal ties and idea exchanges across such firms. Universities may accumulate knowledge from a broad spectra of channels related to scale (regional, national, and international) and industrial sectors, thereby acting as a knowledge bank enabling diffusion independent of specific industrial actors. This illustrate that although the ability of the university college to accumulate and diffuse relevant knowledge into the regional innovation system may be contingent on its collaborative relationships with industrial actors; this role cannot be understood merely by considering the outcome of such collaboration for the individual firms engaging in it.

20.4 University-Industry Dynamics in Context

20.4.1 Industrial Knowledge Development and Networking

We first consider the industrial context into which Vestfold University College (VUC) has attempted to insert itself. With this follows a focus on the knowledge bases developed by industrial firms (Asheim and Coenen 2005); how this reflects in distinctive modes of innovation as well as the geographical configuration and dynamics of external innovation networks. In order to approach this systematically, we draw on the survey information indicating, which mechanisms for competence upgrading that firms perceive are most important. This information is used to construct a set of indicators, which describe the importance of competence upgrading by means of ‘doing, using interacting’ (DUI) and ‘science, technology, innovation’ (STI), respectively. Indicator construction, reliability, and descriptive statistics are given in Table 20.1 below.

These indicators formed the basis for the grouping of firms according to their dominant knowledge development logic, using hierarchical cluster analysis. In accordance with Jensen et al. (2007), we find the two distinct STI and DUI groups, in addition to a large intermediate group of companies, which combine the two modes. Basic descriptive statistics on these clusters are given in Table 20.2 below.

Table 20.1 Modes operationalized

DUI mode composite indicator (1 = high importance - 4 = non existent)	Items entered: Stated importance (1 high—4 not used) of: Competence upgrading through daily work Competence upgrading through teamwork Competence upgrading through customer interaction Competence upgrading through supplier interaction
Reliability (Cronbachs alpha)	0.79
Range	1 (high importance)—2.8 (lowest importance)
Mean	1.62
STI mode composite indicator (1 = high importance—4 = not existent)	Items entered: Stated importance (1 high—4 not used) of: Competence upgrading through R&D Competence upgrading through HEI/ university interaction Competence upgrading through research institute interaction
Reliability (cronbachs alpha)	0.68
Range	1 (high importance)—3 (lowest importance)
Mean	2.01

Source data from the survey

Table 20.2 Basic descriptive statistics

	Combined mode	STI mode	DUI mode	Total
Number				
Electronics	14	2	5	21
Engineering	3	2	2	7
Mean indicator scores				
DUI mode	1.53	2.45	1.37	2.01
STI mode	1.69	1.83	2.91	1.62
N	17	4	7	28

Source: Survey data

Thus, we find a group of seven companies stating that competence upgrading occur primarily through daily, team-oriented work processes, and interaction with customers and suppliers. R&D investments are limited, and those conducted predominantly target-specific customer needs and the refinement of existing technologies (see Table 20.3). Four of these are electronics manufacturers; producing either specialized components or delivering manufacturing, test system and logistics services to system integrators. Two are large maritime engineering and service providers; and all are affiliated with multinational corporate groups. Innovation search patterns are highly oriented toward the mobilization of ideas and

Table 20.3 R&D orientation and R&D investments

	Average R&D intensity	Orientation of R&D (average share of R&D conducted by orientation)			
	Share of turnover	Customer needs	Refinement of existing technologies	New product development	Long-term research
Combined mode	24.71	28.75	37.81	24.38	9.06
STI mode	46.75	5.00	28.75	45.00	21.25
DUI mode	6.29	53.60	35.01	24.40	0.00
Total	23.25	29.92	35.77	27.68	9.20

Source: Survey data

information already existing within own organization and parent group network; and external search and collaboration patterns reveal the overwhelming importance of client firms—located elsewhere in Norway or abroad. In addition, they maintain international search spaces with a distinct focus on their sector communities in general and supplier networks in particular.

These organizations learn on an incremental basis by continuously interpreting streams of external customer and supplier information against the background of existing, experience-based knowledge; and innovation entail a wide range of issues such as improvement of logistics and supply chains, adaption of production tools to specific process needs; design changes on behalf of customer firms to lower production costs and the development of dedicated test equipment. Continuous, complex, and context-specific problem solving thus best describe innovation activities. Inputs from more systematic knowledge development processes enter, but they do so indirectly, through customer and supplier firms located elsewhere. For instance, engineering firms in the region are heavily dependent on interaction with leading subsea system designers, who collaborate with specialized Norwegian research communities. They are also dependent on collaboration with certification agencies such as DNV, which provide quality and compliance control on behalf of authorizes and customers. Competence upgrading by means of external recruitment is considered of relatively low importance, for three main reasons: First, because such competences are not necessarily readily available in external labor markets. Engineering firms experience overall supply deficits, combined with an increasing shortage of engineers with hands-on experience from large vessel or offshore construction. Electronics firms in this group, on the other hand, show a very low rate of employee turnover, which in itself limit renewal through recruitment. Third, because most remaining activities within electronics have strong firm specific components to them; which translate into requirements of firm-specific training and reinforces the reluctance of the companies with respect to hiring new staff.

The mirror image of this is found in another small group of companies which state that core competencies are developed primarily by means of systematic internal R&D, linked to external science system actors; and that learning through daily, team-oriented work processes contribute very little if anything to building these competencies. The four firms constituting this group is found within advanced subsea engineering (recent spin-offs from another engineering incumbent), in the interface between electronics and life sciences, and in the development and production of optics and display technologies. Although, both customers and suppliers are present as information sources and collaboration partners; no single company state that customers are of high importance and external search and collaboration is distinctively oriented toward the science system. Reflecting this orientation is a very high R&D intensity, and a large proportion of this R&D target long-term basic research and the development of new technologies. The external orientation toward science is reflected in an internal competence base, which is stated as easily maintained by external recruitment of personnel with education at PhD and master levels.

However, these DUI and STI mode companies are opposite extremes surrounding a population of companies which state that core competence evolve by means of daily, team-oriented work linked to external customer, and supplier interaction; combined with systematic R&D linked to science system interfacing. These firms thus integrate science-based and experience-based knowledge internal to their organizations, and constitute the core of the regional knowledge base. They are either system integrators who deliver complete product systems to demanding final end uses at e.g., hospitals, airports, or vessels; or component manufacturers which operate in markets, such as aerospace, medical, and subsea. They share the DUI focus on customer search and collaboration externally, and actively search their internal stocks of accumulated daily work and R&D-based experiences. The existence of an R&D-based knowledge stock is indicated by a much higher R&D intensity than what is found among DUI firms (on average 25 % among electronics firms); and by a much more even distribution of this R&D in the range from long-term basic research to specific customer needs. Yet, they are distinctively less oriented toward science system than customer search, and both long-term research and more short-term product development is to a very large degree shaped by existing or expected customer needs.

We now turn to consider how knowledge base characteristics and network configurations contribute to defining regional system characteristics. A main common denominator is the importance of innovation search and collaboration networks which to a large extent target actors and communities outside the region. Another is the importance of experience-based, tacit knowledge; either by itself within the DUI group or as a basis for harnessing the value of science-based knowledge. Related to this is the long-term sensitivity of these activities to the trend of outsourcing production (electronics) and assembly (engineering), processes lubricated by firsthand experience with production among remaining staff in Norway while contributing to hollowing this necessary absorptive capacity out. Last, the attention of firms is distinctively oriented toward the challenges and requirements of their established technological development paths; which either diverge strongly (electronics) or place firms in positions where they are competitors (engineering). Taken together, this portrays a picture of fragmentation between entities, which each on their own are strained by intense competitive pressures, and hollowing-out from globalization. Firms are either technologically too far from each other perceive that there are gains from direct collaboration; or they are two close to each other and point to the risk of diffusing proprietary knowledge to competitors; and they have little leeway to engage in activities on the side of what is at present their operational core. And they are either too oriented toward the DUI mode of specialized knowledge development to perceive that there are any real gains from collaboration with the local university college; or they source their main science-based knowledge inputs elsewhere.

Yet, a striking feature is that the region remains an important venue for those processes which resist formalization, planning, and codification. Just above half of the survey sample state that information flows within the regional 'milieu' is somewhat or very important for own competence upgrading purposes. Interviews confirm that this reflect the reliance of these firms on the local—informal—information ecology, and its overlapping ties of personal networks and arenas for face-to-face contact. The picture comes even more distinct when we consider innovation search; almost all companies outside the STI group state that regional information flows are somewhat or highly important either for competence upgrading or for search. Contribution to this information ecology is formal networks such as Electronic Coast and Avanse, and the activities at VUC and the affiliated NCE. Contrasting this is firm in the STI group, in which no single state that regional information flows support their search activity and only one single firm perceive it as important for own competence development purposes.

The importance of extra-regional linkages clearly emerges at the level of targeted innovation activities, For instance, whereas nine intermediate mode firms state that localized information flows are important for overall competence upgrading, only 2 such firms state that the same transmit information which is used directly as inputs to innovation. At the same time, most firms in this group state that international information flows specific to their sectors as moderately or very important. Only the DUI group remains heavily oriented toward localized information flows; while combining this with orientation toward global sector-specific communities similar to that of the intermediate group.

The university college is clearly present as information source and collaboration partners to the intermediate mode group. Half of this group state that the regional science system is used somewhat or extensively as source of information input to innovation; and all of these collaborate actively with it. This is combined with a strong orientation toward external science system search: More than half states that external science system search provides important inputs to innovation; all but two of which collaborate actively with the regional science system. This means that they serve as 'gatekeepers' (Ebersberger and Herstad 2011; Graf 2010). However, it is largely the mature firms with strong internal capabilities and broad external networks within and outside the region who state collaborative relationships with the regional science system. Our interviews reveal that STI group companies stating collaboration with the regional science system either orient themselves toward specialist consultancy or certification agencies, or, in one case, in essence have outsourced most of their technological development to the UC.

20.4.2 The Repositioning of Vestfold University College

The analysis above point to the predominance of firm or sector specific knowledge development processes by which inputs from outside the region are merged with inputs from actors and environments within it; and by which experience-based knowledge is merged with scientific knowledge. The region in question had developed and institutionalized several diffusion mechanisms outside the realm of the regional university, prior to its more active entry into regional development. The Avanse network operates as a collaborative arrangement between electronic- and microelectronic firms, and enables exchanges of high-skill production personnel. However, its role is diminishing with overall downsizing of production and thus with decreasing reliance on those specialized production skills which it diffuses. No similar mechanism exists within the engineering cluster. In 1998, VUC led the formalization of the Electronic Coast (http://www.electronic-coast.no) project, supported by the public Regional Innovation Program. This had started as an informal network of local business managers working at electronic- and microelectronic companies. The redefined role of the EC-network was to stimulate innovation and entrepreneurship within the industrial cluster of electronic- and microelectronic companies (Finsrud 2007). The re-vitalization process of the EC-network was anchored and organized as a broad participative process involving participants from the University College, Vestfold County Council, Horten Municipality, and electronic- and microelectronic companies.

Yet, by the late 1990s several companies expressed dissatisfaction with the lack of more substantial commitment from VUC. In particular, teaching and research was criticized for been outdated and the educational profile for not being adapted to the specialized needs of the regional industry. At the turn of the century the message from these companies was pretty clear. If VUC had any ambition of engaging with regional industry, VUC needed to make significant changes in their educational programs and research activity. These in turn entailed the breakdown of well-established disciplinary and departmental barriers. Externally, the electronics industry was at this point beginning to feel the combined effects of increased international competition at the component supply and production sides. Leading system developers pointed out that their need for long-term, high-risk investments in complex internal R&D to fight off this competitive pressure was financially difficult to combine with the need for firm-specific investments in the competences of new researchers. Something had to be taken out of this equation, and the latter was the most obvious candidate.

VUC responded from the beginning of 2000, following the election of new principal and new faculty deans. The new principal, an engineer from department of engineering and science, brought with him credibility among the firms as he has worked as project manager for the newly founded EC-network. The new dean from faculty of Science and Engineering similarly gained respect for his proactive attitude toward the needs and demands from the industry as he focused heavily on establishing a constructive dialogue with leading companies.

Based on the experience from the EC-network, the Faculty of Social Sciences developed a tailor made management education program, aiming at improving both management practices and co-operation within the industrial environment. The program was designed for the specific purpose of allowing participants to share their work experience (Gausdal 2007), and thus drew its content from these experiences. In 2003, VUC decided to establish a new master program in microsystem technology, which entailed large financial and professional challenges. As a medium-sized university college, VUC had almost no experience of managing such advanced and expensive master program. In order to get a master program officially certified and considered relevant by industry, VUC needed to obtain the necessary specialized competences; and invest in expensive supportive infrastructure such as clean room laboratory and production equipment. VUC therefore made an agreement with large, leading electronics companies. These were willing to share their technical expertise as tenant professors, and to donate necessary research equipment to the university college (Nilsson 2006). VUC also recruited several key personnel from local companies (professors, phd candidates, and technical assistants). These initiatives and processes combined enabled VUC to establish the foundation necessary for more self-sufficient activity within the MEMS field.

But these processes were not without friction, neither within the university college nor in the relationship toward industry. At the university college side, this involved internal tensions because it entailed the channeling of attention and financial resources toward one specific area, at the expense of other well-established areas. In practice, this meant a substantial reorganization of the engineering department, and downsizing of former academic strongholds. At the industry side, the content of the program was considered critical because it would directly contribute to defining the future "platform" technology for the cluster as a whole. MEMS technology was chosen partly as a result of pressure from leading firms; and legitimized with reference to this being a general purpose technology applicable—and increasingly relevant—across most segments of advanced electronics. It is also a technological field with potential for drawing heavily on other high velocity fields, such as biotech. Others still claim that a stronger emphasis on the "packaging" of advanced electronic components would have better reflected the breadth of activity in the region; contributed more to maintain production capacity and thus competences in the region and added more immediate value to the cluster as a whole. Some firms also saw the build-up of competences at the UC by means of recruitment from industry as a direct threat to their own internal competence base.

Yet, with new staff-members the Faculty of Science and Engineering became more attractive as a partner in several large-scale joint research programs, such as NEWPACK[1] and MULTIMEMS,[2] run by staff member from the University

[1] NEW knowledge and technology for PACKaging of Microsystems (NEWPACK) was a collaborative research program founded by the Norwegian Research Councilin 2003–2006.

[2] MultiMEMS N: Manufacturing Cluster Providing Multi-functional MEMS Services to the Industry is a collaborative research program founded by the Norwegian Research Councilfrom 2003 to 2004.

College in partnership with local industry such as SensoNor and the national research institute SINTEF. Partly based on external founding related to such collaboration with industry, and partly because of the knowledge transfer into the UC which came with them, the Faculty of Science and Engineering manage to finance and build a new institute with a bachelor and master degree program in MEMS technology by 2005. This institute today has 30 employees, hosts 25 phds and is in the process of applying for certification of its own PhD program. The subsequent establishment of a National Center of Expertise in Nano- and Micro-systems engineering marked a shift toward a more active role for the UC as platform technology developer—based on the competence based it had built through its intimate relationship with regional industry.

Summarized, the situation for the University College at the end of the decade was quite different from the situation when entering in the millennium. However, this potential does not at present materialize as growth. The role of VUC as contract research partner for the electronics industry is limited; partly because firms operating outside the MEMS perceive its activities as irrelevant, and partly because firms in this area consider such contract research technologically difficult and strategically problematic. It involves large resources spent on communicating tacit, contextual knowledge to the contract partner, and thus entails exposing proprietary technological knowledge to VUC researchers and—more problematically—students. Its role as a collaboration partner is limited by the deepening embeddedness of firms in their respective global innovation networks, and impacts through the local electronics industry labor market are constrained heavily by the lack of growth among existing firms and the lack of new firm formation.

20.4.3 Discussion

Specialized competences initially contained within a limited number of advanced industrial firms has now in essence been "externalized", subjected to further scientific scrutiny and development, and made available as a platform technology for firms in the region. Against this background it is not surprising to find a strong emphasis in regional development plans on nurturing new firm formation within electronics, based on these competences. In 2008, the NCE partnership developed a new business model for Microtech Innovation, established in 2003 by local government and three leading industrial firms to serve as a commercialization vehicle, but idle while awaiting the build-up of research activity at VUC. This defined MTI not only as the main commercialization engine for NCE and VUC technology, but also as a national innovation and commercialization player in the micro- and nanotechnology area. The MTI board and shareholders approved the new business plan and—model in 2010, and the company established new headquarters in Horten Industrial Park. As of 2010, MTI has project management responsibility for the Norwegian Center of Expertise, and now also incorporates the networking organization Electronic Coast. Yet, after Sensonor established

MEMSCAP in 2000, there have been few signs of new firm formation within electronics based on competences on electronics. Part of this is directly attributed to the complexity of technologies involved; and the negative demonstration effects of earlier entrepreneurship. Although, long recognized both by industry and researchers at VUC, fundamental funding and human capital constraints on new firm formation based on the technologies in question have not been eliminated.

But the real potential for the university college may lie not so much in directly supporting the current—specialized—activities of existing firms, as in the exploration of how these electronics competences can feed into and be fed by activities outside its current domain. It lies in its ability to transcend the cognitive distances which exist across different technologies and sectors; and which is reinforced by the segmentation of labor market mobility and the lack of cross-sector, industry-driven technology exploration. Although the evidence is yet anecdotal, examples of such cross-sector knowledge diffusion point to an important enabling role for VUC and link well up with other research findings pointing to the importance of cross-sector linkages at both firm (Katila 2002, Katila and Ahuja 2002) and regional economy (Cooke 2008) levels. Signals from inside VUC do suggest an increasing recognition of the potential in this role; however, this may be counteracted by internal forces seeking to establish more mainstream technology commercialization schemes.

20.5 Conclusion

This chapter discusses how the contemporary industrial landscape entail that regional innovation systems are deconstructed as sets of value chain collaborative linkages. Firms are embedding themselves in global innovation networks as they are forced to seek out knowledge inputs from diverse sources and places. Our argumentation stresses, in accordance with other research, the predominance of industrial knowledge development processes in which the science system only contribute one—and often minor—piece of the larger puzzle (Isaksen and Karlsen 2009; Karlsen et al. forthcoming; Laursen and Salter 2004). Yet, it simultaneously point to the enduring, even increasing, importance of the local information diffusion ecology; and the potential for innovation to emerge at the intersection between regional knowledge assets, which are already there. In order for the information ecology to survive, and the exploration of cross-sector linkages to occur, a third-party knowledge accumulation and diffusion infrastructure is needed.

Based on this recognition, the chapter has argued that regional universities and university colleges may play a much more vital future role in regional development than traditionally imagined. This is elaborated in three steps. First, the chapter shows how the transformation of Vestfold University College necessitated the build-up of new competences by means of dense industry linkages. From this follows, the importance of recognizing how initial knowledge transfers from industry and into local universities may be necessary. Following from this, it suggests, second, that regional science system actors should avoid thinking of their main role as one of delivering technology to a set of given firms or sectors. While a limited number of large universities which are internationally leading within their technological fields may boost regional development by means of such linear commercialization and spillover processes; the Vestfold case show clearly how industrial firms link up with science system actors elsewhere for the purpose of sourcing advanced, modular science system outputs while remaining dependent on those specialized knowledge assets which enable their commercialization. Hence, it is the accumulation, further refinement and diffusion of these specialized assets which should be the main concern of those universities and university colleges which cannot compete at disciplinary scientific frontiers.

This role is exercised through numerous interlinked mechanisms. The development of specialized education programs is critical, because it enables the build-up of new internal university competences and other "third mission" activities to be linked directly to the primary defined roles of universities and university colleges. This raises the legitimacy of the effort internally in the organization, and strengthens the embeddedness of the new competences within it. Furthermore, it links directly up to the main mechanisms for regional knowledge accumulation and diffusion under conditions of value chain fragmentation and globalization; namely the regional labor market, mobility within it and the resulting formation of personal ties across independent companies. Such ties can be expected to be of increasing importance when the locus of innovation shift away from cumulative activities along established paths and into recombinant innovation across sectors and clusters. Once an education program "core" has been established, the VUC case illustrate how this may simultaneously provide the basis for more advanced research activities and increase the overall attention received by the university college from actors spanning the range from local industry to research communities abroad. With this may follow the development and institutionalization of labor markets which in essence overlap between the spheres of industry and university (Lam 2007). Combined, this vastly increases the ability of the organization to attract students and researchers from abroad, thus further strengthening its ability to support regional labor market dynamics and to serve as a locus for information sharing, idea exchanges, and personal network formation.

The mobilization and commitment of industrial actors required perceptions of future relevance; and choices concerning strategic orientation and content necessitated that divergent views on this from industry could be overcome. The process of transformation at the university college side similarly involved establishing legitimacy within a broad range of professional communities; and institutionalizing the third-mission role of contribution to regional development in a context where individual researcher disciplinary excellence and inter-department competition for scarce resources remain key components of the academic model of work organization and motivation (Becher and Parry 2005; Gibbons 1994). Furthermore; it involved—and still involve—accepting that the visible returns from these activities in the form of firm growth and profit will come outside the realm of the VUC organization in itself; as social returns at the level of the regional economy rather than private returns from licensing income and patent sales. This is part and parcel of successfully exercising a knowledge diffusion role which rest on interactive learning in relationship with industry, and points to how this role differs from one of research commercialization. We therefore warn against the potentially detrimental effects which could stem from a stronger focus from the VUC side on securing its own returns by means of technology transfer schemes. The next steps, which are critical to realizing the potential role of VUC as a driver of regional development; entail a stronger focus on the exploration new linkages between competences already existing—within industrial firms and within the VUC organization in itself. However, this will also serve as a demanding test on the ability of VUC and its surrounding infrastructure to mobilize—internally in own organization and externally among industrial firms—for such radical recombinant activities, and resolve the issues of intellectual property rights and individual private returns which inevitably will arise.

Acknowledgments This chapter is based on research funded by the Norwegian Research Council, under the Regional Development Program, and conducted as part of the "Regional modes of innovation" project lead by University of Agder and Dr. James Karlsen. In addition, the authors wish to thank researcher Siri Aanstad of NIFU STEP for her contribution of background material gathered in relation to ongoing work on changes in the higher education sector. This work is funded by the Norwegian Ministry of Research and Education and coordinated by Agnete Vabø of NIFU.

Bibliography

Adams JD (2002) Comparative localization of academic and industrial spillovers. J Econ Geogr 2:253–278

Agrawal A, Cockburn I, McHale J (2006) Gone but not forgotten: knowledge flows, labor mobility, and enduring social relationships. J Econ Geogr 6(5):571–591

Asheim B, Isaksen A (2002) Regional innovation systems: the integration of local 'sticky' and global 'ubiquitous' knowledge. J Technol Transfer 27:77–86

Asheim BT, Coenen L (2005) Knowledge bases and regional innovation systems: comparing nordic clusters. Res Policy 34(8):1173–1190

Asheim BT, Herstad SJ (2005) Regional innovation system, varieties of capitalisms and non-local relations: challenges from the globalising economy. In: Boschma RA, Kloosterman RC (eds) Learning from clusters: a critical asessment for an economic-geographical perspective. Springer, Dordrecth

Balconi M, Laboranti A (2006) University-industry interactions in applied research: the case of microelectronics. Res Policy 35(10):1616–1630. doi:10.1016/j.respol.2006.09.018

Bathelt H, Malmberg A, Maskell P (2004) Clusters and knowledge: local buzz, global pipelines and the process of knowledge creation. Prog Hum Geogr 28(1):31–56

Beaudry C, Schiffauerova A (2009) Who's right, marshall or jacobs? the localization versus urbanization debate. Res Policy 38(2):318–337

Becher T, Parry S (2005) The endurance of the diciplines. In: Bleiklie I, Henkel M (eds) Governing knowledge: a study of continuity and change in higher education. Springer, Dordrecth

Bekkers R, Bodas-Freitas IM (2008) Analysing knowledge transfer channels between universities and industry: to what degree do sectors also matter? Res Policy 37(10):1837–1853

Bjørn Terje Asheim, Coenen L, Moodyson J, and Vang J (2007) Constructing knowledge-based regional advantage: implications for regional innovation policy. Int J Entrepreneurship and Innov Manage 7(2/3/4/5) pp. 140–155
Boschma R, Eriksson R, and Lindgren U (2008) Labour mobility, related variety and the performance of plants – A Swedish study. Papers in Evolutionary Economic Geography, Utrecht University. Urban and Regional research centre Utrecht
Boschma R, Eriksson R, Lindgren U (2009) How does labour mobility affect the performance of plants? the importance of relatedness and geographical proximity. J Econ Geogr 9:169–190
Boschma R, Iammarino S (2009) Related variety, trade linkages, and regional growth in Italy. Econ Geogr 85(3):289–311
Breschi S, Malerba F (1997) Sectoral innovation systems: technological regimes, schumpeterian dynamics, and spatial boundaries. In: Edquist C (ed) Systems of innovation. Pinter, London
Brulin G (1998) Den tredje uppgiften högskola och omgivning i samverkan. SNS Förlag, Stockholm
Coe NM, Dicken P, Hess M (2008) Global production networks: realizing the potential. J Econ Geogr 8:271–295
Combes PP, Duranton G (2006) Labour pooling, labour poaching, and spatial clustering. Regional Sci Urban Econ 36(1):1–28
Cooke P (2007) To construct regional advantage from innovation systems first build policy platforms. Eur Plan Stud 15(2):179–194
Cooke P (2008) Regional innovation systems, clean technology & jacobian cluster-platform policies. Regional Sci Pract 1(1):23–45
Cummings W K (Writer) (1998) The service university movement in the US: searching for momentum (Article), Higher Education: Springer Science & Business Media B. V
Dahl MS, Pedersen COR (2004) Knowledge flows through informal contacts in industrial clusters: myth or reality? Res Policy 33(10):1673–1686
Daraio C, Bonaccorsi A (2007) Universities and strategic knowledge creation specialization and performance in Europe. Edvard Elgar, Cheltenham
Ebersberger B, Herstad S (2011) Go abroad or have strangers visit? On organizational search spaces and local linkages. J Econ Geogr. doi:10.1093/jeg/lbq057
Eriksson R, Lindgren U (2009) Localized mobility clusters: impacts of labour market externalities on firm performance. J Econ Geogr 9(1):33–53
Eriksson R, Lindgren U, Malmberg G (2008) Agglomeration mobility: effects of localisation, urbanisation, and scale on job changes. Env Plan A 40(10):2419–2434
Etzkowitz H (2002) The triple helix of univesity—industry—government. implication for policy and evaluation (No. 1650–3821). Stockholm: Institutet för studier av utbildning och forskning
Etzkowitz H, Webster A, Gebhardt C, Terra BRC (2000) The future of the university and the university of the future: evolution of ivory tower to entrepreneurial paradigm. Res Policy 29(2):313–330. doi:10.1016/S0048-7333(99)00069-4
Finsrud H D (2007) Electronic coast—fra læring til innovasjonssystem. In: N. I. f. B.-o. Regionforskning (Ed.) Regionale Trender 1 2007 Oslo pp. 41–51
Frenken K, Oort FV, Verburg T (2007) related variety, unrelated variety and regional economic growth. Regional Stud 41(5):685–697
Gausdal A (2007) 'Network Reflection'—a road to regional learning, trust and innovation
Gibbons M (1994) The new production of knowledge: the dynamics of science and research in contemporary societies. Sage Publications, London
Giuliani E, Bell M (2005) The micro-determinants of meso-level learning and innovation: evidence from a Chilean wine cluster. Res Policy 34:47–68
Goddard JB, Chatterton P (2003) The responses of university to regional needs. In: Boekema F, Rutten R (eds) Economic geography of higher education: knowledge, infrastructure and learning regions. Routledge, London, pp 51–532
Graf H (2010) Gatekeepers in regional networks of innovators. Camb J Econ
Grossman GM, Helpman E (1991) Quality ladders in the theory of growth. Rev Econ Stud 58(1):43–61

Hargadon A, Sutton RI (1997) Technology brokering and innovation in a product development firm. Adm Sci Q 42(4):716–749
Herstad S, Bloch C, Ebersberger B, Velde E v d (2010) National innovation policy and global open innovation: exploring trade-offs, balances and complementarities. Sci Publ Policy 37(2):113–124
Isaksen A and Karlsen J (2009) Combined and complex mode of innovation in regional cluster development—analysis of the lightweight material cluster in Raufoss, Norway. Paper presented at the Orkestra workshop, San Sebastian May 13–14
Jensen M, Johnson B, Lorenz E, Lundvall BÅ (2007) Forms of knowledge and modes of innovation. Res Policy 36:680–693
Karlsen J, Isaksen A, Spilling OR (2011) The challenge of constructing regional advantages in peripheral areas: the case of marine biotechnology in Tromso, Norway. Entrepreneurship Reg Dev 23(3–4):235–257
Katila R (2002) New product search over time: pastpast ideas in their prime? Acad Manage J 45(5):995–1010
Katila R, Ahuja G (2002) Something old, something new: a longitudinal study of search behavior and new product introduction. Acad Manage J 45(6):1183–1194
Kaufmann A, Tödtling F (2001) Science-industry interaction in the process of innovation: the importance of boundary-crossing between systems. Res Policy 30(5):791–804. doi:10.1016/S0048-7333(00)00118-9
Knell M (2008) Heterogeneity in economic thought: foundations and modern methods. In: Carayannis E, Kaloudis A, Mariussen Å (eds) Diversity in the knowledge economy and society. Edward Elgar, Cheltenham
Kogut B, Zander U (1996) What firms do? coordination, identiy, and learning. Organ Sci 7(5):502–518
Lam A (2000) Tacit knowledge, organizational learning and innovation: a societal perspective. Organiz Stud 21(3):487–513
Lam A (2007) Knowledge networks and careers: academic scientists in industry–university links. J Manag Stud 44(6):993–1016
Laursen K, Salter A (2004) Searching high and low: what types of firms use universities as a source of innovation? Res Policy 33:1201–1215
Laursen K, Salter A (2006) Open for innovation: the role of openness in explaining innovation performance among UKUK manufacturing firms. Strateg Manag J 24:131–150
Majchrzak A, Cooper LP, Neece OE (2004) Knowledge reuse for innovation. Manage Sci 50(2):174–188
Malerba F, Orsenigo L (1993) Technological regimes and firm behaviour. Ind Corporate Change 2(1):45–71
Maliranta M, Mohnen P, Rouvinen P (2009) Is inter-firm labor mobility a channel of knowledge spillovers ? evidence from a linked employer-employee panel. Ind Corporate Change 18(6):1161–1191
Malmberg A, Power D (2005) (How) Do (Firms in) Clusters Create Knowledge? Ind Innov 12(4):409–431
Narula R (2002) Innovation system and 'intertia' in R&D location: Norwegian firms and the role of systemic lock-in. Res Policy 31(5):795–816
Nelson R, Winter S (1982) An evolutionary theory of economic change. Harvard University Press, Cambridge
Nilsson J-E (2006) The Role of universities in regional innovation systems a nordic perspective. Copenhagen Business School Press, Frederiksberg
Nooteboom B (2000) Learning and innovation in organizations and economies. Oxford University Press, New York
Onsager K, Isaksen A, Fraas M, Johnstad T (2007) Technology cities in Norway: innovating in glocal networks. Eur Plan Stud 15(4):549–566
Ponds R, Oort FV, Frenken K (2010) Innovation, spillovers and university-industry collaboration: an extended knowledge production function approach. J Econ Geogr 10(2):231–255

Rosenkopf L, Nerkar A (2001) Beyond local search: boundary-spanning, exploration, and impact in the optical disk industry. Strateg Manag J 22(4):287–306

Rothaermel FT, Hitt MA, Jobe LA (2006) Balancing vertical integration and strategic outsourcing: effects on product portfolio, product success, and firm performance. Strateg Manag J 27:1033–1056

Tödtling F, Trippl M (2005) One size fits all? toward a differentiated regional innovation policy approach. Research Policy 34:1203–1219

Varga A (Ed.) (2009) Universities, knowledge transfer and regional development: geography, entrepreneurship and policy, Edward Elgar Publishing

Index

A. Altmann and B. Ebersberger (eds.), *Universities in Change*, Innovation, Technology, and Knowledge Management, DOI: 10.1007/978-1-4614-4590-6,

Printed by Printforce, the Netherlands